The European Heritage in Economics and the Social Sciences

Volume 28

The European heritage in economics and the social sciences is largely locked in languages other than English. Witness such classics as Storch's *Cours d'Economie Politique*, Wicksell's *Finanztheoretische Untersuchungen* and *Geld, Zins und Güterpreise* or Pareto's *Trattato di Sociologia Generale*. Since about 1937, partly caused by the forced exodus of many scholars from the German language countries and the international reactions to this event, English has become the undisputed primary language of economics and the social sciences. For about one generation, this language shift did not result in a loss of access to the European non-English sources. However, after foreign language requirements were dropped as entry pre-requisites for receiving the PhD at major research universities, the European heritage in economics and the social sciences has become largely inaccessible to the vast majority of practicing scholars. In this series, we hope to publish works that address this problem in a threefold manner. An aspect of the European heritage in a language other than English should be critically documented and discussed, reconstructed and assessed from a modern scientific point of view, and tested with respect to its relevance for contemporary economic, social, or political discourse. We welcome submissions that fit this bill in order to make the European heritage in economics and the social sciences available to the international research community of scholars in economics and the social sciences.

Jürgen G. Backhaus • Günther Chaloupek
Hans A. Frambach
Editors

Post-war Keynesianism in Germany and Western Europe

Springer

Editors
Jürgen G. Backhaus
Schleiz, Thüringen, Germany

Günther Chaloupek
Austrian Chamber of Labour (retired)
Wien, Austria

Hans A. Frambach
Faculty of Economics
University of Wuppertal
Wuppertal, Nordrhein-Westfalen, Germany

ISSN 1572-1744 ISSN 2197-5892 (electronic)
The European Heritage in Economics and the Social Sciences
ISBN 978-3-032-00497-0 ISBN 978-3-032-00498-7 (eBook)
https://doi.org/10.1007/978-3-032-00498-7

This Springer imprint is published by the registered company Springer Nature Switzerland AG
The registered company address is: Gewerbestrasse 11, 6330 Cham, Switzerland

Contents

1 **Introduction** 1
Günther Chaloupek and Hans A. Frambach

2 **Erich Schneider** 9
Harald Hagemann

3 **Andreas Paulsen and Keynesianism** 35
Heinz Rieter

4 **Karl Schiller: The Triumph and Tragedy of a German Social Democratic Economist** 57
Reinhard Neck

5 **Gottfried Bombach: A Pioneer of Macroeconomics in Post-War Germany and Switzerland** 75
Oliver Landmann

6 **Erich Preiser (1900–1967): Growth and Distribution in a Monetary Economy** 91
Johannes Schmidt

7 **Hajo Riese's "Theory of a Monetary Economy": An Attempt at Reconstruction** 121
Peter Spahn

8 **Kurt W. Rothschild: An Innovative Eclectic Post-Keynesian Economist** 139
Hagen M. Krämer

9 **Post-War Keynesianism in Austria: The Role of Emigrant Economists** 163
Günther Chaloupek

10 John Maynard Keynes' Influence in Norway 183
Arild Sæther

11 Hans Wolfgang Singer: Thoughts on a Keynesian World Economist During the Period of German Post-War Reconstruction 207
Hans A. Frambach

Chapter 1
Introduction

Günther Chaloupek and Hans A. Frambach

Keynesian ideas have been central to the major debates about economic policy and macroeconomic theory for the larger part of the twentieth century. This holds particularly for the age of economic prosperity and sustained growth which followed the period of reconstruction after World War II, before accelerating inflation and the first oil price shock brought an end to what is widely considered as "the age of Keynes". At the same time, differences in economic and political conditions across nations are the reason how and why some countries embraced Keynesianism, while others did not. In the reception and application of Keynesian economics, there are considerable differences between European countries, with respect to economic theory and economic policy, as well as time.

After the end of the war, the economic situation on the continent was different from that of Great Britain and the USA, where a possible recession following the end of the industrial boom in armament production was a major concern of economic policymakers. In most countries on the continent, major parts of infrastructure and industrial production facilities lay in shambles, while there were shortages of food, energy, and raw materials. At the same time, there was the looming threat that rising prices resulting from the release of the high volume of private savings accumulated during war time might develop into hyperinflation, as had been the case after World War I in several countries. Hence, a return to a market economy with free price and wage formation was not seen as a real possibility in the first years after the war, while the system of rationing and control of food, raw materials,

G. Chaloupek (✉)
Austrian Chamber of Labour (retired), Wien, Austria
e-mail: guenther@chaloupek.eu

H. A. Frambach
Faculty of Economics, University of Wuppertal, Wuppertal, Nordrhein-Westfalen, Germany
e-mail: frambach@wiwi.uni-wuppertal.de

J. G. Backhaus et al. (eds.), *Post-war Keynesianism in Germany and Western Europe*, The European Heritage in Economics and the Social Sciences 28,
https://doi.org/10.1007/978-3-032-00498-7_1

and energy inherited from the war economy was retained, as were the administrative controls over imports and exports and foreign exchange.

The only country in Europe where the transition to a market-regulated system was achieved with what would now be called a shock therapy was Germany with the currency reform of 1948 which preceded the foundation of the Federal Republic of Germany in the United American, British, and French occupation zones in 1949. The currency reform marks also the beginning of the social market economy, based on the theoretical foundations of Ordoliberalism and the Freiburg School, as declared concept which came to shape economic and social policies of Western Germany under Christian Democratic Party (CDU) majority governments and their economic minister Ludwig Erhard.

If, with respect to economic policy, Germany took a road different from most other European countries in the "age of Keynes", this contrasts with the strong position which Keynesianism held at major German universities until the 1960s. During that time, the textbooks of Keynesian economists Erich Schneider (*Einführung in die Wirtschaftstheorie,* four parts 1947ff.) and Andreas Paulsen (*Allgemeine Volkswirtschaftslehre*, three parts 1956ff.) were the most widely used for teaching successive generations of economics students. In the political sphere, the Social Democratic Party (SPD) and the trade unions were hesitant to accept Keynesianism, as they continued to favour nationalization and economic planning during most of the 1950s.[1]

In its self-portrayal, the social market economy presented itself as rival concept of Keynesianism. Nonetheless, Keynesian elements were part of Germany's economic policy during the era of Ludwig Erhard, who—in the words of state secretary Alfred Müller-Armack (1966, p. 262)—did not hesitate "to keep the expansion going through anti-cyclical policy programs", and to ensure, if not "full", at least a high level of employment. Besides rhetorics, the crucial difference to Keynesianism was more in the strict commitment of the social market economy to price stability and restraint in monetary policy. The dominance of the concept of social market economy remained unchallenged until the mid-1960s, when, after two decades of sustained economic growth, Germany experienced its first recession (at contemporary standards) in 1966/67.

At this juncture, under a new government formed by a coalition of CDU and SPD, Keynesian anti-cyclical policy was formally introduced as "Stability and Growth Act" under Karl Schiller who had succeeded Ludwig Erhard as economic Minister in December 1966 (until 1972). The Keynesian era continued under the following governments formed by a coalition between SPD and the Freedom Democratic Party (FDP) until the mid-1970s, when "under mounting inflationary pressures and a strong increase of unemployment in 1974-75 following the first oil price shock, Keynesian ideas lost ground against the rising new monetarism launched by Milton Friedman" (Hagemann, 2013, p. 48).

[1] On the relationship between Keynesianism and the SPD, see Held (1982).

As in Germany, in Western Europe, the reconstruction boom of the first post-war years "became self-propelling, nurtured, but not basically propelled by policy" (Maddison, 1976, p. 477). In the period of sustained high growth, there was no need for one of the core elements of Keynesian policy, permanent support of effective demand, nor for the "socialization of investment", which Keynes had envisaged in the famous 24th chapter of the *General Theory.* If there were recessions, they were mild and short, dampened by Keynesian anti-cyclical policies.

A core element of Keynesianism, whose impact is seldom properly appreciated, is the fundamental change in economic thinking through general acceptance of macroeconomic analysis brought about by Keynes *General Theory*, i.e. the comprehensive look at the total economy in terms of big aggregates such as GDP, private and public consumption, investment, total income consisting of wages and profits, and current statistical observation of these magnitudes. This contrasts with the poverty of economic statistics before the war, which "were mainly concerned with prices, interest rates and exchange rates, while there were no government estimates of national income" (Maddison, 1976, p. 466). The introduction of a "Standardized System of National Accounts" (SNA), developed by the OEEC (precursor organization of the OECD) and the UN, provided the basis for empirical application of macroeconomic analysis, which has formed the conceptual structure for economic policy debates since the "return to normal" in the early 1950s. The measures of fiscal and monetary policy were henceforth discussed with respect to their impact on global aggregates.

Macroeconomic thinking became the foundation for a post-war consensus, if not on all essentials of economic policy, so at least on the conceptual framework within which economic policy debates were conducted henceforth. A new economic idea served as "new common ground for positions between which no middle ground had existed before" (Hirschman, 1989, p. 356).

The validity of macroeconomic thinking was denied not only by economists of the Austrian School, but also by Walter Eucken, the principal theoretician of Ordoliberalism, who refused to accept the Keynesian dichotomy between macro- and micro-economic thinking, and thereby rejected the macroeconomic approach to economic policy.[2] Such kind of reservations was not shared by the practitioners of the social market economy, nor by the advocates of Friedman-type monetarism.[3] The latter casts an anti-Keynesian economic policy within a macroeconomic framework of the Keynesian type.

After the war, economic planning originally was advocated as a conceptual rival to Keynesianism by social democratic parties in some countries in their search for an alternative to capitalism, e.g. in Germany and Austria. In other countries of

[2] Eucken refused to accept the Keynesian dichotomy between macro- and micro-economic thinking, and thereby rejected the macroeconomic approach to economic policy. "This kind of global thinking which prevails in the economic policy in most countries does not do justice to economic realities". A full employment policy through expansion of credit "destroys the allocation mechanism of prices, which are either kept fixed or allowed to rise" (Eucken, 1959, p. 101f.).

[3] On this point, see Skousen (2005), p. 240f.

Western and Northern Europe, systems of encompassing economic planning were established which introduced instruments for a more intensive influence on the economic process within a Keynesian framework. In the 1950s and the 1960s, when full employment had been achieved in most European countries, promotion of economic growth emerged as principal goal of economic policy.

The depth of interventionism made possible by the new macroeconomic analysis varied considerably across European countries.[4] In some countries, official national accounts ("National Budget") were used to establish ex ante macroeconomic plans in which specific instruments and measures were assigned to specific targets adopted by the plan (Norway, The Netherlands, less rigorously in Sweden), whose effectiveness was evaluated by a comparison with ex post figures.

The most ambitious post-war planning system was the French *planification* with its 5-year plans which provided forecasts and simulations in disaggregated form. Essentially, these forms of planning were "indicative", using various form of incentives, but not coercive instruments to influence behaviour of economic agents. The intentions of planning "to see the economy as a system of variables and flows to be optimized" (Rosanvallon, 1989, p. 187) turned out to be overambitious.

It appears doubtful that the systems of economic planning established in several Western countries would have found the approval of Keynes, who had recommended to leave decisions about which things should be produced with which inputs and methods to the market. In this spirit, the Beveridge Plan had emphasized that full employment policy implies "socialization of demand", not of supply (Beveridge, 1944, pp. 38, 171, 200, 214). Also, Keynes had expressed his scepticism towards econometric modelling early on. This kind of technocratic self-restraint turned out to be foresighted. All forms of detailed planning in Western market economies declined during the 1970s, being reduced to a routine procedure of economic forecasting. But what appears more important is that in reality, planning regimes were combined with Keynesian economic policies in most cases.

If the Keynesian message was widely accepted in Norway and Sweden (less so in Denmark) in the academic as well as in the political sphere, at the same time the view expressed by Keynes himself that the *General Theory* amounted to nothing less than a revolution in economic thinking provoked disagreement in these countries. For Gunnar Myrdal and other Swedish economists, there was "nothing new" in the *General Theory* (Pekkarinen, 1989, p. 318). Norwegian economists expressed similar doubts (see the contribution by Saether in this volume). Both countries are known for their proto-Keynesian anti-cyclical policies under social democratic governments in the 1930s, as advocated by the Stockholm School, and Ragnar Frisch and the Oslo School, respectively (Pekkarinen, 1989, pp. 318, 334). Both countries developed their own specific economic policy regimes after World War II.

Universities in many countries have met Keynesianism with opposition, while the influence of the new doctrine on economic policies was considerable. This holds for France, where "it was the engineering schools, at ENSAE and ENA, that the

[4]The following is based on Chaloupek and Teufelsbauer (1987), Ward (1976).

discipline (of economics) progressed in post-war years. … Keynesian ideas took roots most rapidly in these milieus, not in the universities" (Rosanvallon, 1989, p. 184). Similarly, in Austria, universities blocked the reception of Keynes' teachings, due to continued influence of the Austrian School and other reasons, while non-academic institutions became strongholds of Keynesian thinking after the war.

The majority of contributions in this volume is devoted to Germany. **Harald Hagemann** deals with Erich Schneider (1900–1970) who played a decisive role in the establishment of Keynesianism in economic theory in Germany after World War II. It was not without a certain irony that an admiring disciple of Schumpeter was primarily responsible for the implementation of Keynesian economics. Major transmission mechanisms were his textbooks which dominated in the 1950s and the 1960s and his function as a chairman of the Theoretical Committee of the Verein für Socialpolitik. Schneider, originally a high school teacher in mathematics, was deeply influenced by Schumpeter with whom he habilitated at the University of Bonn. Schneider became professor in Aarhus, Denmark, for almost a decade, before from 1946 onwards at Kiel he was at the zenith of his academic influence and (inter-) national recognition.

Heinz Rieter writes about Andreas Paulsen (1899–1977), one of the most important pioneers of Keynesianism in the German-speaking world after 1945, who held the chair for economic theory at the Free University Berlin from 1949 to 1967. Practical economic experience and certain maxims of his scientific thinking were decisive for his turn to and approach to *New Economics*: He always analysed economic problems in the context of socio-philosophical and socio-political relationships. In this sense, Keynes' *General Theory* and primarily its economic policy implications seemed to Paulsen a suitable approach to protect market economies from instability of economic activity and thus from losses of prosperity. However, he considered the theoretical explanation to be incomplete if limited to comparative-static analyses of the economic cycle. These should be supplemented or even replaced by dynamic theories that can adequately capture and explain equilibrium and disequilibrium macroeconomic processes over time. As Keynes called for, such theories should draw on psychological factors, which, as "ultimate independent variables", determine economic behaviour guided by expectations.

Reinhard Neck's contribution gives an introduction to the life and academic achievements as well as the political views and successes and failures of the professor of economics and social democratic politician Karl Schiller (1911–1994). It illustrates his endeavours to integrate the market orientation of the Freiburg School with Keynesianism and his conception of economic policymaking built upon these theoretical foundations. Schiller used insights from Keynesianism to successfully combat the recession in Germany in 1966 but failed when it came to use this approach during the inflationary period of the 1970s. He contributed to making the policy stance of the Social Democratic Party of Germany more market-friendly but failed due to the recurrence of Marxist ideology in the party, among other reasons.

When economic growth had become "self-propelling" in the 1950s, the determinants of growth to an increasing degree occupied the centre of macro-economic theory research. Gottfried Bombach (1919–2010) was a macroeconomist at the forefront of a new generation of academics who reconnected Germany to the international research frontier of economics after World War II. **Oliver Landmann's** contribution focuses on Bombach's analyses of the interplay between economic growth, income distribution, inflation, and employment, both during the period of rapid post-war growth and after the productivity slowdown of the 1970s. Bombach wrote widely on the core subjects of macroeconomics, mostly from the vantage point of Keynesian theory. Also, he was influential as advisor to government, first in Germany, later in Switzerland.

Erich Preiser (1900–1967) was one of the most influential economists in Germany after World War II, introducing Keynesian concepts and thereby helping German economics to join the international discussion again. Of Preiser's main areas of research, business cycles, growth, and distribution theories, **Johannes Schmidt's** article discusses his analysis of growth and distribution. Preiser's analysis of growth elaborates on the importance of monetary factors in the process of growth, especially the creation of money and credit by the banking system. Referring to Keynes' insights from the *General Theory* and the *Treatise on Money*, Preiser aims at clarifying the relationships between saving, investment, consumption, and interest. Savings are no longer a precondition for investment, but investment creates the necessary savings. These elements are combined to develop a dynamic analysis which avoids several obscurities of Keynes' system and the static character of the *General Theory*. Furthermore, Preiser shows that money is an endogenous variable in the economic process. In his distribution theory, Preiser combines classical and Keynesian elements: Kaldor's theory of distribution, and social structure as a variable that the mechanism of supply and demand cannot explain. For Preiser, not only economic laws but also power factors determine the functional distribution of income.

Peter Spahn writes about Hajo Riese (1933–2021), the pioneer of a "Berlin School of Monetary Keynesianism", particularly in the 1980s and the 1990s. Riese's research work was based on the roots of monetary theory in the work of Keynes, with a particular focus on the theory of capital and interest rates. While in Keynes, liquidity preference remained an element of money demand, for Riese it formed the central variable of a theory of credit supply. The credit contract is not based on goods or goods equivalents, but on the nominal category of money, because this is the sole medium for the fulfilment of contracts. Besides the interest rate also the rate of return on real capital is determined by the liquidity premium. The central bank has to take into account the almost constitutional significance of monetary stability, which runs counter to the "easy money policy" usually demanded by Keynesians.

The Austrian economist Kurt W. Rothschild (1914–2020) made significant contributions to Keynesian and post-Keynesian economic theory, following a multi-paradigmatic and interdisciplinary approach. His wide-ranging work covers price theory, labour market economics, growth and distribution, power and ethics in economics, and economic policy. **Hagen Krämer's** article focuses on income distribution and growth as central themes in Rothschild's research. Also, it explores Rothschild's theoretical innovations, emphasizing his rejection of mono-causal explanations in favour of an approach that integrates economic, political, and social dynamics. Rothschild's perspective on income distribution as a product of complex interactions between markets, institutions, power structures, and ongoing conflict is a defining feature of his work. His legacy remains a guiding framework for scholars seeking a more holistic and dynamic understanding of income distribution and its policy implications.

Günther Chaloupek's contribution highlights the role of emigrant economists for the spreading of Keynesianism in Austria after World War II. Of some 100 economists of Austrian origin who had left Austria after German occupation in 1938, relatively few returned to Austria after 1945. Barred from teaching at universities, which were mostly unwilling to acknowledge higher academic credentials acquired abroad, returnees turned to other institutions such as the WIFO (Austrian Institute of Economic Research), or the Chamber of Labour. The strong position of Keynesianism in Austria's economic policy after 1945 was to a considerable extent due to the returnees' superior knowledge of modern economics. Against opposition from the conservative party and the Austrian School, and some reservations stemming from the Marxist tradition among Social Democrats, a pragmatic version of Keynesianism gained acceptance in the later 1950s and the 1960s. Due to the central role of the social partnership's wage and price policy, Keynesian policy in Austria was not limited to a mechanistic "hydraulic Keynesianism". At least equally important was the reduction of uncertainty in the expectations of economic agents by stabilizing the framework conditions for business calculation and investment decisions. The policy of Austro-Keynesianism (1970–1995) was able to build on this foundation.

Nomination for the Nobel Peace Prize in 1922 and again in 1923 made Keynes known to a wider public in Norway. **Arild Saether's** contribution on Keynes' influence in Norway informs about the circumstances of this initiative and its eventual failure. Well ahead of the publication of the *General Theory,* Keynes' ideas were integrated into the Norwegian Labour party's economic policy concepts through mediation of the financial journalist O. Colbjørnsen. The reception of the *General Theory* in Norway, as in Sweden, was rather cool. Norway's leading economist R. Frisch thought that, if Keynes' book was "powerful, pointed and convincing", he was not such an inventive scholar as he liked to present himself. It can be questioned to what degree Keynesian economics was a part of the planned economy that characterized Norway in the first 30 years after World War II. In the 1980s, the planned economy was abandoned and a market economy was reintroduced. At the same time, Keynes and Keynesian macroeconomics continued to have a distinctive place in Norwegian textbooks and in the country's economic policies.

Hans Frambach's article outlines key academic milestones of the great economist Hans Wolfgang Singer, who was born in Elberfeld and a student of Joseph A. Schumpeter. Singer emigrated from Germany in 1933 and made a global career as a top official at the United Nations in New York and later as a researcher at the Institute of Development Studies (IDS) at the University of Sussex in Brighton. Singer became best known for his contributions to development economics, which even earned him the reputation of being one of its central precursors. This essay focuses primarily on Singer's fundamental scientific positions on economic theory and policy, which were almost Keynesian in nature, and draw parallels between his thinking and the attempt to establish the Beveridge system during the reconstruction of post-war Germany. Singer's findings and convictions can also be found in the Keynesian economic policy of the great economic expansion phase, as well as in the attempt to introduce the Beveridge system.

Most chapters in this volume are the revised contributions to the 38th Heilbronn Symposium in Economics and the Social Sciences in 2024. On behalf of the entire Heilbronn group, we would like to thank the City Council and the Lord Mayor of the City of Heilbronn for their continued generous support.

References

Beveridge, W. H. (1944). *Full employment in a free society. A report by Lord Beveridge. 2. ed. 1960*. George Allen & Unwin.

Chaloupek, G., & Teufelsbauer, W. (1987). *Gesamtwirtschaftliche Planung in Westeuropa*. Campus Verlag.

Eucken, W. (1959). *Grundsätze der Wirtschaftspolitik*. Rowohlts deutsche Enzyklopädie.

Hagemann, H. (2013). Germany after World War II: Ordoliberalism, the Social Market Economy and Keynesianism. *History of Economic Thought and Policy, 1*, 37–51.

Held, M. (1982). *Sozialdemokratie und Keynesianismus*. Campus Verlag.

Hirschman, A. O. (1989). How Keynesianism was exported from the United States, and other comments. In P. Hall (Ed.), *The political power of economic ideas* (pp. 347–359). Princeton University Press.

Maddison, A. (1976). Economic policy and performance in Europe 1913-1970. In C. M. Cipolla (Ed.), *The Fontana Economic History of Europe* (Vol. 6, pp. 442–508). Collins/Fontana Books.

Müller-Armack, A. (1966). *Wirtschaftsordnung und Wirtschaftspolitik*. Verlag Rombach.

Paulsen, A. (1956). *Allgemeine Volkswirtschaftslehre. 3 parts, Sammlung Göschen, Band 1169/1170/1171*. Walter de Gruyter & Co..

Pekkarinen. (1989). Keynesianism and the Scandinavian models of economic policy. In P. Hall (Ed.), *The political power of economic ideas* (pp. 311–345). Princeton University Press.

Rosanvallon, P. (1989). The development of Keynesianism in France. In P. Hall (Ed.), *The political power of economic ideas* (pp. 171–194). Princeton University Press.

Schneider, E. (1947ff.). *Einführung in die Wirtschaftstheorie. 4 parts*. JCB Mohr Verlag.

Skousen, M. (2005). *Vienna & Chicago friends or foes?* Capital Press.

Ward, T. (1976). National planning and policies in twentieth century Europe 1920-1970. In *The Fontana economic history of Europe* (Vol. 6, pp. 698–736). Collins/Fontana Books.

Chapter 2
Erich Schneider

Harald Hagemann

2.1 Introduction

Schneider was virtually identified with the Keynesian doctrine, and his work can also be seen as a piece of the history of the reception of Keynesianism in Germany.
Karl Häuser (2010, p. 265).

In the reception and application of Keynesianism in the Federal Republic of Germany a great time lag existed between economic theory and economic policy. After World War II economic policy was decisively shaped by Walter Eucken and the Freiburg School as well as by the concept of a "social market economy".[1] It took until the entry of the Social Democrats into government with the Christian Democrats in the first "Grand Coalition" during the recession in December 1966, and Karl Schiller[2] as the new minister of economics, that Keynesianism took a late entry into German economic policy in international comparison.

In contrast, a moderate Keynesianism of the Hicks-Samuelson neoclassical synthesis type had already evolved into the dominant position at most German universities since the early and mid-1950s, with the exception of a few faculties of economics such as Freiburg and Cologne. Erich Schneider (1900–1970) played a decisive role in the establishment of Keynesianism in economic theory in Germany after the Second World War. Schneider had come to Kiel from Aarhus at the beginning of 1946 and published his three-volume *Introduction to Economic Theory*, which

[1] See Hagemann (2017).

[2] On Schiller see the entry by Reinhard Neck in this volume.

H. Hagemann (✉)
University of Hohenheim, Stuttgart, Stuttgart, Germany
e-mail: harald.hagemann@uni-hohenheim.de

J. G. Backhaus et al. (eds.), *Post-war Keynesianism in Germany and Western Europe*, The European Heritage in Economics and the Social Sciences 28,
https://doi.org/10.1007/978-3-032-00498-7_2

quickly became the central textbook in economics for two decades. He was also chairman of the revitalised Theoretical Committee of the Verein für Socialpolitik for many years.

Erich Schneider was born on 14 December 1900 in Siegen, Westphalia, the son of school headmaster Wilhelm Schneider and his wife Marie, née Weber. After graduating from secondary school in Siegen, he had to serve in the army from June to November 1918. From the winter semester of 1918/19, Schneider studied mathematics and physics at the universities of Giessen, Frankfurt am Main and Göttingen before returning to Goethe University in the late summer of 1920. In Frankfurt, Schneider now devoted himself increasingly to the study of economics, having become fascinated by reading an essay by Vilfredo Pareto on the application of mathematics to economics. Schneider received his doctorate there in 1922 with a thesis entitled *Der Kalkül der Schuldverhältnisse angewandt auf solche mit mehreren Geldsorten insbesondere die Geldarbitrage* (The calculation of debt relationships applied to those with several types of money, in particular money arbitrage), under Andreas Voigt (1860–1941). In his farewell lecture in Kiel on 18 December 1968, Schneider (1969: 158) thanked his academic teacher for his first insights into economic theory, in particular for his reference to Gustav Cassel's *Theoretische Sozialökonomie* (1918) which "after decades of sole dominance of the historical school, brought about the renaissance of economic theory in Germany and for us young people the connection to international research".

After completing his state examination in mathematics and physics at the University of Münster, Schneider worked as a secondary school teacher from 1925 to 1936, primarily teaching mathematics: as a trainee teacher in Dortmund, from 1927 as an assessor in Tecklenburg and from 1929 as a master, initially in Koblenz and from 1930 at the Realgymnasium in Dortmund. In the same year, Schneider married Erna Daub. The happy marriage lasted until his death, but remained childless (Hagemann, 2007).

From 1924 onwards, Schneider published mathematical and economic writings.[3] In addition, from 1929 he regularly attended seminars at the University of Bonn with Joseph Alois Schumpeter (1883–1950), with whom he also habilitated shortly before Schumpeter left for Harvard in 1932. Schumpeter's influence was a decisive factor in Schneider leaving the teaching profession in 1936 and from then on concentrating on his economic research and his work as a university professor.

In 1936, Schneider accepted a professorship in business administration at the University of Aarhus and remained there for almost a decade. During this time, Denmark became his second home. In January 1946, Schneider took up the full professorship for economics at the Christian-Albrechts-University in Kiel, where he remained until his retirement after the winter semester of 1968/69 and died on 5 December 1970. Schneider's influence and work reached its peak during his time in Kiel.

[3] For a complete list of his writings, see Bombach and Tacke (1980, pp. 91–192).

In the following Sect. 2.2, I discuss the early phase of Schneider's economic research, which was primarily in the field of microeconomics and was strongly influenced by Schumpeter. In Sect. 2.3, I discuss Schneider's time in Denmark, which largely coincided with the reign of National Socialism in Germany. The academic exchange with his outstanding Scandinavian colleagues in the "years of high theory" shaped Schneider, who also had the advantage that he was far less detached than his colleagues who remained in Germany from the enormously advancing international development of economic research at this time. Schneider capitalised on this and was thus able to publish his opus magnum, the three-volume *Introduction to Economic Theory*, shortly after his return to Germany between 1947 and 1952.[4] Especially with the third volume on macroeconomics, some essays and his influential role as chairman of the Theoretical Committee of the Verein für Socialpolitik in the 1950s and as director of the Kiel Institute for the World Economy in the 1960s, Erich Schneider grew into a central position for the implementation of Keynesianism in economic theory and the catching-up process of German economics after the Second World War (Hagemann, 2019b). In Sect. 2.4 I discuss this important Kiel period in more detail. Section 2.5 deals with some of the honours and distinctions resulting from his academic work. Particularly noteworthy is the strong international recognition at a time when there was not only a politically induced greater reservation towards Germany, but also, exacerbated by the loss of emigrants during the Nazi era, German economics had little outstanding to show for itself. Schneider's textbooks were not only translated into many foreign languages, but the author also received numerous honours from abroad. In Sect. 2.6, I conclude with the question of what kind of Keynesian Schneider was and an assessment of his contemporary and longer-term impact.

2.2 Early Steps

> *Joseph Schumpeter. This brilliant man—characterised by Vienna and Lausanne-, a theorist of the highest calibre, who opened up the realm of theory to me and has had a decisive influence on my life as a researcher and teacher. Through Schumpeter, I came into contact with the relevant research questions and—no less significant—with the scholars working on them."*
> Erich Schneider (1969: 158–9)

> *"He [Dr Schneider] has just been habilitated with brilliancy. (should actually be on the title page!)*
> Schumpeter to Oskar Siebeck, 1 March 1932 (*Letters*, 205)

Schneider first met Schumpeter, who had been appointed to the Chair of Public Finance at the University of Bonn in 1925 as Heinrich Dietzel's successor and thus

[4] A fourth volume on the history of economic theory was published a decade later (Schneider, 1962).

returned to the academic world after a seven-year absence, at the beginning of 1929. It was not far from Koblenz to Bonn, where Schumpeter lived at Koblenzer Straße 39. As Stolper (1994, p. 69) reports, Schneider became both Schumpeter's student and a maths teacher, similar to Richard Goodwin at Harvard later on.

At this time, the question of whether the existence of an economic equilibrium was possible in market forms that were not characterised by the traditional model of free competition, but by oligopolies, duopolies, or monopolistic competition, was a central international research topic. One of the pioneers was Frederik Zeuthen (1888–1959), a professor at the University of Copenhagen, to whose work *Problems of Monopoly and Economic Warfare* (1930) Schumpeter wrote a foreword, in which he spoke of a "bold raid into new and difficult country".[5] Schumpeter was able to encourage his student Schneider to successfully plough this new ground in his habilitation thesis *Reine Theorie monopolistischer Wirtschaftsformen* (Schneider, 1932) and the subsequent work *Theorie der Produktion* (Schneider, 1934a). Alongside Heinrich von Stackelberg (1905–1946) and his *Grundlagen einer reinen Kostentheorie* (1932)[6] and the outstanding Cologne habilitation thesis *Marktform und Gleichgewicht* (Stackelberg, 1934) with the "asymmetric duopoly", Schneider was one of the leading experts in this field, who had to fear no international comparison. Last but not least, however, the disastrous political developments in Germany and the resulting loss of importance of the German language contributed to the fact that the two works by Edward Chamberlin *The Theory of Monopolistic Competition* (1933) and Joan Robinson's *The Theory of Imperfect Competition* (1933), published in the two Cambridges in the year of the National Socialist seizure of power, achieved a greater degree of recognition in the long term. It is significant, however, that Joan Robinson mentions Schneider and Stackelberg's work on the treatment of monopoly problems as important in the preface to her work, but adds critically that in her view "their work is marred by the use of unnecessarily complicated mathematical analysis where simple geometrical methods would serve" (Robinson 1933, p. XV).[7] Conversely, from the perspective of modern

[5] Schumpeter (1927: 255–6) had already criticised in his detailed review of Cassel's *Theoretische Sozialökonomik* that Cassel's treatment of price theory was limited solely to the borderline case of atomistic free competition.

[6] The emphasis on "pure theory" in Schneider (1932) and Stackelberg (1932) reflects both an emphasis on the importance of mathematical analysis with its strict rules of a verifiable, logically incontestable theory and a dissociation from the Historical School. Schneider (1962, p. 295) repeatedly emphasised that Gustav Schmoller, as the leading representative of the younger Historical School, had "fatally torn German economics out of the stream of theoretical thought that was unfolding powerfully all over the world for more than three decades".

[7] Schumpeter (1934b:253) in his review praises Joan Robinson for her "admirable performance", notes "that the book is Marshallian to the core", but also criticises her for her "failing to pay respects to Cournot. … And Walras and Pareto have not written for her. Hence her analysis is strictly an analysis of partial equilibria of single firms or industries." Schumpeter's great interest is also documented by his role as Chairman of the Round Table "Imperfect Competition" of the American Economic Association. See American Economic Review 24 (1), 1934: 21–32.

mathematical economists, it could be argued that Schneider and especially Stackelberg (1934) have gone further in their theoretical analyses and mathematical precision.

The importance of Schneider's *Theory of Production* was immediately recognised by experts. In addition to Zeuthen's favourable review in a Danish journal,[8] there were detailed and predominantly positive reviews by prominent economists such as Nicholas Kaldor,[9] R.G.D. Allen[10] and Herbert Zassenhaus[11] in leading Anglo-Saxon journals. In addition, an Italian translation of the book *Teoria delle Produzione* was published in Milan in 1942.

Even a later doctoral student of Schumpeter at Harvard and renowned economics professor such as Wolfgang F. Stolper recalled Schneider's Bonn inaugural lecture of 6 February 1932 with the innocuous-sounding title "Volkswirtschaftslehre und Betriebswirtschaftslehre" (Economics and Business Administration) decades later: "It dealt with some aspects of production theory. It was mathematical and seemed to the listeners a little like black magic" (Stolper, 1994, p. 69, n.4).

Shortly afterwards, Schneider's protégé Schumpeter moved from Bonn to Harvard University, but in the same year opened important doors for his student's future academic career. Schumpeter arranged for the publication of Schneider's habilitation thesis as Volume 4 of the renowned series "Contributions to Economic Theory" at the Tübingen publishing house Mohr (Siebeck), in which Jacob Marschak's Heidelberg habilitation thesis *Elasticity of Demand* (Marschak, 1931) and, in the same year, Ragnar Frisch's *New Methods of Measuring Marginal Utility* (Frisch, 1932) had previously appeared. With Frisch, Schumpeter lobbied persistently and successfully for Schneider's admission as a Fellow of the Econometric Society.[12] Schumpeter also supported Schneider to obtain a scholarship from the Rockefeller Foundation and, by intervening with Haberler and Morgenstern, helped his student to publish his essay "Kostentheoretisches zum Monopolproblem" (Schneider, 1931) in the leading journal of economics in the German language area at the time.[13]

Schneider's understanding of the role of mathematics in economic theory was shaped from beginning to end by his teacher Schumpeter, as can be seen from his farewell lecture in Kiel "Rückblick auf ein halbes Jahrhundert der Wirtschaftswissenschaft (1918–1968)" (Looking back on half a century of economics 1918–1968; Schneider, 1969) and his last book on Schumpeter's life and work (Schneider, 1970a). Schumpeter had already dealt with this important question in

[8] Nationalökonomisk Tidsskrift 73, 1935: 135–6.

[9] Economica, N.S., 3 (4), 1936: 95–99.

[10] Economic Journal 45, no. 178, 1935: 338–341.

[11] Review of Economic Studies 3 (1), 1935: 35–39.

[12] See, for example, Schumpeter's letter to Frisch, December 3, 1932, in Schumpeter (2000, pp. 227–9). See also Frisch's contribution in the memorial publication for Schumpeter (Frisch, 1951).

Schumpeter became president of the Econometric Society from 1937–1941.

[13] Schumpeter (2000, pp. 196–8).

one of his early essays "On the mathematical method of theoretical economics" (Schumpeter, 1906).

Even before his encounter with Schumpeter, Schneider himself had been inspired by the "theory of general interdependence and economic equilibrium in the form created by Walras and Pareto" through reading Cassel's *Theory of Social Economy* ([1918] 1932) and was stimulated to study mathematics more intensively, as "a real understanding of this theory … is not possible without mathematical knowledge" (Schneider, 1969: 158). Reading Pareto's essay "Mathematical economics" (Pareto [1911], 1955) opened up a new world for him. It was only a few years later that Schneider found a mentor in Schumpeter who explained this terra incognita to him. Only a few months after their first meeting, Schumpeter himself recommended his post-doctoral student Schneider to the publisher Oskar Siebeck as a "competent mathematician" who could review the "scientifically valuable" aspects of Pareto's main work, the *Manuale (1906)*, and at the same time correct "minor errors".[14]

Like Schumpeter, Schneider was convinced that economic theory had only become more and more of a science through increasing mathematisation, thanks to important pioneers such as Thünen, Mangoldt, Cournot, Edgeworth, Walras, Pareto, Fisher, Wicksell and Frisch. Schneider (1969: 163–4) stated somewhat exaggeratedly that the use of the language of mathematics had met with little resistance almost anywhere in the Western world, while the situation in Germany had only changed for the better with Schumpeter's appointment at Bonn. For Schumpeter, every day without reading mathematical books or Greek literature was a lost day, although "he lacked systematic mathematical training" (Schneider, 1970, p. 20).

In his youthful enthusiasm for the newly emerging field of econometrics, Schneider was fully convinced of the unity of economic theory, mathematical methods and statistics propagated by Ragnar Frisch (1895–1973). He published an essay on Thünen in the new journal *Econometrica*, edited by Frisch, as early as the second volume (Schneider, 1934b).[15] He later wrote an essay on Mangoldt's price theory as an important contribution to the history of mathematical economics for the commemorative publication on Frisch's 65th birthday (Schneider, 1960).

In his farewell lecture, Schneider (1969: 164) emphasised that it was "common sense today" that "all economic theory is by nature mathematical theory …". "Theoretical economics" and "mathematical theory" had already become synonyms, Schneider (1962, p. 16) emphasised in Volume 1 of his *History of Economic Theory*. In this sense, Schneider had already stated in the German controversy surrounding Keynes at the beginning of the 1950s that economic statements characterised by mathematical language were "scientific theorems that must be recognised as right or wrong by anyone who can think logically" (Schneider, 1953: 91). No

[14] See Schumpeter's letter to Oskar Siebeck, 3 June 1929, in Schumpeter (2000, pp. 166–7).

The German translation of the work, which was published in Italian in 1906 and in a revised form in French in 1909, was ultimately not realised due to a lack of economic prospects from the publisher's perspective. Schumpeter was aware that Schneider also had a good knowledge of Italian and French.

[15] Schumpeter (1954, p. 466) refers to this essay in his remarks on Thünen.

wonder that "'Schneider school' and 'mathematical school' were then almost synonymous" (Häuser, 2010, p. 254, n. 49).

The publication of the new journal *Archiv für mathematische Wirtschafts- und Sozialforschung* (Archive for Mathematical Economic and Social Research) was an unusual occurrence at a time when mathematical economic research in Germany was eking out a meagre existence in the shadow of the declining Historical School and National Socialism. From its first publication in 1935 until its sudden termination in the war year 1942, eight volumes were published, each with three issues. The editors were the two mathematicians Aloys Timpe and Paul Riebersell. Main driving forces, however, were the three mathematical economists Erich Schneider, Heinrich von Stackelberg and Hans Peter (1898–1959). Peter, who in 1927 had got his habilitation from the University of Tübingen where he was appointed professor only after World War II, reflected on the "Aufgaben und Grenzen der mathematischen Nationalökonomie" (Tasks and limits of mathematical economics) in the very first article of the new journal (Peter, 1935).[16] This triumvirate did not only contribute many excellent articles themselves, but also attracted high-calibre articles from leading foreign scholars, such as Frederik Zeuthen, Jan Tinbergen, Umberto Ricci or Johan Åkerman.

2.3 Denmark

The years in Aarhus were the most fruitful period in my scientific research ever.
Erich Schneider (1966, p. 39)[17]

Schneider first came to Denmark at the beginning of April 1932, when he accompanied his academic teacher on his long-planned lecture tour on the first stop of his Scandinavian journey, which took Schumpeter to Copenhagen, Lund and Stockholm during his last semester in Bonn.[18] In Copenhagen, Schneider also met Zeuthen, who played an important role in his early scientific work, and Jørgen Pedersen (1890–1973), who would shortly afterwards become a close colleague in Aarhus and a lifelong friend. This contributed to Schneider spending his research time as a Rockefeller Fellow in 1933/34 not with Schumpeter at Harvard, but in Copenhagen with Zeuthen and in Oslo with Frisch. Shortly afterwards, when he was invited by Zeuthen to give a lecture on the theory of production in Copenhagen, he impressed his audience with his perfect Danish "without the slightest grammatical error" (Brems, 1987, p. 85).

---

[16] A member of the Econometric Society since 1935, Peter was elected Fellow in 1956. On Peter see Hagemann (2001).

[17] Speeches to celebrate Erich Schneider's 65th birthday on 14 December 1965 at the Institute for the World Economy at the University of Kiel, published by the Society for the Promotion of the Institute for the World Economy, Kiel 1966, p. 39.

[18] See Schneider (1970, pp. 63–4).

In 1936, the University of Aarhus, the second Danish university to be founded in 1928, introduced a new degree programme in economics, which involved a close link between economics and business administration. The two core professorships were filled by Jørgen Pedersen (Economics) and Erich Schneider (Business Administration/Managerial Economics).[19] Schneider was an almost ideal candidate: an outstanding and passionate teacher (see prototypical student Hans-Peter Myrup (1987), later Professor and Vice-Rector in Aarhus for many years) in perfect Danish, who also focussed his research on microeconomics and represented the position of his academic teacher Schumpeter, which he describes as follows: "This interest in microeconomic research as one of the foundations of macroeconomic analysis was alive in Schumpeter from an early stage" (Schneider, 1970, p. 71). Consequently, at Schumpeter's suggestion, Schneider not only gave his inaugural lecture in Bonn under the title "*Volkswirtschaftslehre und Betriebswirtschaftslehre*", but published a collection of important essays under a similar title over three decades later (Schneider, 1964).

In line with his teaching activities, during his time in Aarhus, Schneider published numerous essays on the monopoly and duopoly problem, pricing and cost theory, as well as important monographs on industrial accounting and investment theory, which were later also published in German in revised form (Schneider [1939], 1954 and [1944] 1951b) and translated into Spanish and Japanese.

In the second phase of his time in Aarhus, Schneider increasingly turned to macroeconomic problems and thus, under the strong influence of Wicksell, the Stockholm School, Frisch, but also works on the employment problem by Danish economists such as Jens Warming, Zeuthen and his friend Pedersen, gradually turned to Keynes.[20] The transition was completed with the essay "Zur Frage der Wirkung finanzpolitischer Maßnahmen auf die wirtschaftliche Aktivität" (The effect of fiscal policy measures on economic activity), published shortly before the end of the war, in which Schneider (1944) carried out a comparative-static analysis within a Keynesian macroeconomic model. There he gave an early clear exposition of the multiplier or income-generating effects of a balanced budget independently from Haavelmo (1945). Schneider did not claim originality for his rigorous theoretical analysis of the expansionary effect of an increase of public expenditure completely financed by taxes in a closed economy characterised by Keynesian unemployment. Instead he later himself called it the *Haavelmo theorem*. Both Schneider and Haavelmo join the long list of prominent economists who have made relevant contributions to multiplier theory (Hegeland, 1954).

The discovery of the balanced budget multiplier may be called a special contribution of the "Aarhus school" to which not only Schneider and Haavelmo, a student

[19] In 1938, a second chair of business administration was added, which was filled by Thorkil Kristensen (1899–1989). Kristensen later became Danish Minister of Finance for two years from November 1945 and, after his time at Copenhagen Business School, Secretary-General of the OECD from 1961 to 1969.

[20] On Schneider's slow but then all the more lasting turn to Keynes, see the essay by Schneider's student Harald Scherf (1980).

of Frisch who himself had been Lecturer for Statistics in Aarhus in the academic year 1938/39, and Pedersen belong, but in particular also Jørgen H. Gelting (1912–1994). Gelting, who was a student of Pedersen and later became professor at Aarhus University from 1954–82, had published earlier a pertinent article on the balanced budget multiplier in Danish (Gelting, 1941) that would have justified to talk of the *Gelting Theorem*.[21]

On 31 October 1944, the Royal Air Force carried out a special operation against the Gestapo headquarters in Aarhus. During the German occupation, this was located in the university's central administration building, which was destroyed by the British air raid. As Myrup reports, it was symptomatic of Erich Schneider that even after the university was closed, "he passed on giving lectures in an auditorium at a municipal hospital, and we all came along to listen" (Myrup, 1987, p. 6).

Towards the end of the war and immediately after the end of the war, things became understandably uncomfortable for Germans in Denmark. Schneider, who had been a passive member of the NSDAP since May 1933, a fact that was hardly known in Denmark, where he remained a German citizen the whole time, now found himself in a difficult situation.[22] At the end of the war, the rector of Aarhus University set up a commission to assess Schneider's behaviour during the German occupation since April 1940. As Brems and others report, so-called "good Danes", i.e. those who did not collaborate with the National Socialists during the occupation, above all Pedersen and Zeuthen, did not question Schneider's integrity and "fought bravely for their colleague Schneider and for the legal principle that a man can be indicted for his acts but never solely for his nationality or party membership" (Brems, 1987, p. 87). Hans Julius Brems (1915–2000) had himself completed his doctorate with Zeuthen in Copenhagen in 1941 and moved to the USA in 1951, where he was Professor in Mathematical Economics and History of Economic Thought at the University of Illinois in Urbana-Champaign from 1954 until his retirement in 1986.[23] Even after 1945, Schneider remained a recognised persona grata in Denmark, where he owned a summer house in Skagen and regularly met with Scandinavian friends and colleagues such as Zeuthen, Frisch, Ohlin and others there and at Pedersen's summer house in Silkeborg. Schneider wrote contributions to commemorative publications for Åkerman, Frisch, Iversen, Lindahl, Pedersen and Zeuthen. In retrospect, his departure from Denmark was seen as a great loss for the University of Aarhus and Danish economics. Hylleberg (2001, p. 13) even speaks of a "stain on Aarhus Universitet that can only be explained by the prevailing

[21] On "nascent Keynesianism" in Denmark in the 1930s see also Garside and Topp (2001).

[22] See personal file "Erich Schneider" with the signature R 4901/15160 in the Federal Archives Berlin and Häuser (2010, pp. 241–2) for further details.

[23] From there, after the end of the academic year in the USA at the end of May and before travelling on to Denmark, Brems regularly came to Kiel even a few years after Schneider's death to give special lectures and seminars in the second half of the summer semester. The author of this essay remembers attending a lecture by Brems on von Neumann's growth model as a young doctoral student together with Heinz Kurz and a few other members in the audience.

mood after five years of occupation, together with a lack of stature on the part of some of the colleagues at the time".[24]

2.4 Kiel

In Kiel, Schneider has demonstrated his importance for the post-war history of German economics.
Karl Häuser (2010, p. 243).

My generation owes him the connection to the state of the international debate and the modern attitude towards our subject.
Rudolf Richter (1997, p. 1).

For Schneider, the neoclassical synthesis was so self-understandable that he hardly ever even used the term.
Gottfried Bombach (1987, p. 47).

Schneider had already received a call from Berlin to Kiel University in the summer of 1944 for the start of the 1944/45 winter semester on 1 October, but successfully played for time, since Kiel, as an important port for the navy and production site for submarines, was still suffering from heavy air raids and severe destruction until April 1945. In August 1945, Schneider then accepted the renewed appointment to the Christian-Albrechts University via the British occupation authorities in Schleswig-Holstein. He began his research and teaching activities there in January 1946 and gave his inaugural lecture on 23 January on the subject of "The Face of Economic Theory in Our Time". In the same year he became Vice Dean and in 1947 Dean of the Faculty, later also Rector of the University in the academic year 1959/60.

Within only five years Schneider published his opus magnum, the three-volume *Introduction to Economic Theory*. Volume I, *The Theory of the Circular Flow in the Economy*, appeared as early as 1947 and was one of the first textbooks on modern circular flow analysis and national accounting, comparable to Hicks' *Social Framework* (1942), taking up the ideas of Quesnay, Marx and Keynes.[25] Of its 14 editions published up to 1969, a total of 83,200 copies were sold. In the two decades that followed, it was replaced as the dominant textbook by *Volkswirtschaftliches Rechnungswesen* by Schneider's student Alfred Stobbe (1924–2001), first published in 1966, of whose eight editions published up to 1994 more than 100,000 copies were sold.

Volume 2 *Wirtschaftspläne und wirtschaftliches Gleichgewicht in der Volkswirtschaft*, dealing with the economic plans of households and firms, was first published in 1949.[26] For this textbook on microeconomics, Schneider was essen-

[24] See similarly Brems (1987) and Myrup (1987).

[25] The book was published in 1962 in Japanese and Portuguese, in Persian in 1969 and in Spanish in 1963 already in the fourth edition.

[26] Volume 2 was translated into Japanese, Portuguese and French. Four editions of the Spanish translation were published up to 1963.

tially able to draw on his own earlier analyses of production and cost theory, the theory of market forms, price formation and others. The book was immediately recognised internationally and praised by Schneider's peers in leading journals. For example, Fritz Machlup stated in *The American Economic Review* that "Schneider's exposition of the theory of the firm is superior to anything now available in English" and admired Schneider's "excellent pedagogy" and "outstanding skill in exposition" (Machlup, 1950: 656–7). In particular Machlup pointed out "the cosmopolitan character of the intellectual parentage of the book" and Schneider's skills in elaborating the essential points of the Walrasian system in "one of the best expositions … of the methodological problems of general equilibrium analysis", including "superb explanations of the character of the equations which make up the system - definitional equations, behaviour equations, technological equations, and equations expressing equilibrium conditions" (ibid: 658).

In a longer article on Schneider and Stackelberg, Alan Peacock stated that "Schneider's *Introduction* is a remarkable synthesis of modern economic theory" and noted that his "fusion" of economics and accounting is timely … and fruitful" in applying the *ex post, ex ante* distinction to the adjustment problems of individual firms "arising out of the disparity between its expectations and actual events" (Peacock, 1950: 176 and 179). No wonder that an English translation was published already in 1952 under the title *Pricing and Equilibrium: An Introduction to Static and Dynamic Analysis*.[27] The German original went into thirteen editions until 1972 of which altogether 80,200 copies were sold.[28]

Schneider's trilogy was completed with the publication of Volume III *Geld, Kredit, Volkseinkommen und Beschäftigung* (Money, Credit, National Income and Employment) in 1952. It was this third volume, in which Schneider presented Macroeconomics as Keynesian theory, enriched with some Scandinavian flavour, that played the decisive role for the success of Keynesian economics in Germany. The title, including monetary and real variables, clearly indicates the Keynesian spirit of the book. With the completion of his *Introduction,* Schneider now was often characterised as the "German Samuelson", whose textbook *Economics* interestingly came out in a German translation in the same year 1952 for the first time. Samuelson's book together with Schneider's three volumes dominated the textbook market until the late 1960s.

It was above all the third volume of his Introduction with which Schneider established Keynes' reception in Germany. In many ways, his approach was similar to John Hicks' IS-LM reduction of the Keynesian system, which can be seen as the core of his Keynes interpretation, in which simple and more complex multiplier analyses such as the Haavelmo theorem and Samuelson's accelerator-multiplier model play an important role.

---

[27] London: W. Hodge, third edition London 1962: Allen&Unwin. Later Routledge made several re-prints.

[28] The sales figures of the three volumes are taken from Häuser (2010, p. 260, n.67).

Again, as with the earlier volumes, the book soon was reviewed by well-known peers in leading international journals. Martin Beckmann, in his review in *Econometrica*, noted that "the result is a remarkable success, it pays a tribute both to Dr. Schneider's talents as a writer and to the power of mathematical discipline in presenting economic theory", and attested the author that "the modern theory of employment is developed in loving detail and with a lucidity unachieved in any other textbook known to this reviewer" (Beckmann, 1953: 361–2). The reviewer's final wish of an English translation materialised some years later when *Money, Income and Employment* (Schneider, 1962) was published.[29]

As with the two previous volumes, Schneider endeavoured to keep his finger on the pulse of the times and to incorporate the development of economic theory into the revised editions of his textbooks, which therefore constantly increased in content and scope. The twelfth and final edition of the third volume was published in 1973, which, like the 13th and final edition of Volume II, was revised after his death by his outstanding student Gottfried Bombach. A total of 68,500 copies of Volume III were sold.

With the completion of the third volume, Schneider's *Introduction to Economics* became the new catechism or "bible" of the New Economics. The author of this "canon", Erich Schneider, was now regarded as the "Pope" of his discipline in Germany far beyond the borders of Kiel.[30]

The importance of Schneider's trilogy and his role in the implementation of Keynesianism in Germany and his significance for the process of German economics catching up with international developments after the Second World War was also recognised and addressed in the leading journals at an early stage. Jörg Niehans, for example, used a new edition of "SCHNEIDER's MASTERLY Introduction to Economic Theory" to praise the author as "the leader of its kind in the German language and second to none internationally" and to emphasise that "it is the only comprehensive text I know which connects directly with current research work as reflected in periodicals".[31] A few years later, in an extensive essay "The Old and the New in Some Research Trends in the Literature of German Economics" in the *American Economic Review*, Kurt Rothschild[32] praised Schneider's Introduction to Economic Theory as "one of the best introductions to modern economic analysis available, not alone in the German language but quite generally" (Rothschild, 1964: 4).

The first part of a fourth volume of his "Introduction" with selected chapters from the history of economic theory (with many original texts) was published in

[29] London 1962: George Allen&Unwin, 3rd edition 1966. Volume III was also published in Japanese (1961), Portuguese (1962), Spanish (1963), Sinhala (1968) and Italian (1972).

[30] The metaphors "bible", "canon" or "Pope" are used repeatedly in the excellent article "Erich Schneider und die deutsche Nationalökonomie" by Karl Häuser (2010), correctly reflecting the spirit of the times.

[31] Niehans 1957, *Econometrica*, 25 (3): 491–2.

[32] On Rothschild see the contribution by Hagen Krämer in this volume.

1962.[33] Special space in this volume, which is primarily dedicated to the history of the development of modern microeconomics, is given to those economists who, in Schneider's view, made decisive contributions to the "secure foundation of the theory". In addition to Quesnay, Smith, Ricardo, Mill, Cournot, Dupuit, Menger, Jevons, Walras and Marshall, Schneider includes Marx, Thünen, Herrmann, Mangoldt, Gossen, Stackelberg and himself from Germany. Schneider was unable to complete the planned second volume on the history of macroeconomics during his lifetime.

For a long time, foreign trade issues had not played a major role in his textbooks. Schneider realised this shortcoming at a time of increasing currency turbulence and wrote the textbook *Zahlungsbilanz und Wechselkurs* (Balance of payments and exchange rate; Schneider, 1968) as an introduction to the basic principles of the international monetary system and the monetary problems of foreign trade relations.

Schneider's important and influential essays include in particular his opening lecture "Der gegenwärtige Stand der Theorie der Beschäftigung" (The current state of the theory of employment), with which Schneider (1951a) launched his major Keynesian offensive at the second annual conference of the re-established Verein für Soz(c)ialpolitik in Bad Pyrmont in 1950 that had a particularly attractive effect on younger participants.

Schneider shared with Walter Eucken, who had made Freiburg the stronghold of Ordoliberalism, the sharp criticism of Gustav Schmoller and the Historical School. As his student Bombach (1987) points out, Schneider always advocated the market economy and the principle of monetary stability, which was also emphasised by Eucken. At the same time, however, he emphasised the need for macroeconomic stabilisation policy through an appropriate combination of fiscal and monetary policy on the basis of Keynesian theory. However, the proclamation of Keynesian messages and a fundamentally different understanding of the role of mathematics in economics[34] marked significant differences.[35]

Schneider did not shy away from any controversy, initially in the "dispute over Keynes" against neoliberal economists such as L.A. Hahn (Schneider, 1952) and Wilhelm Röpke,[36] and ultimately in a dispute with the emerging monetarism of Milton Friedman (Schneider, 1970b). While Schneider was no longer able to bring the latter debate to a successful conclusion, he emerged largely victorious from the earlier controversy in the academic debate. The Frankfurt banker L. Albert Hahn, who had been a vehement advocate of credit-financed spending in the early 1920s

[33] Italian 1970, Spanish 1972.

[34] In his main work, *Foundations*, Eucken (1940, p. 56) emphasised that "the increasing mathematisation of economic theory ... is often associated with a decline in actual economic-theoretical thinking".

[35] This did not preclude friendly relations with individual members of the Freiburg School. Bombach (1987, p. 53), for example, refers to the friendly relationship between Schneider and Friedrich Lutz.

[36] On Schneider's three main opponents at the time, Hahn, Röpke and the Vienna-based Hans Mayer, see also Rothschild (1987, pp. 10–11).

and, unlike Schumpeter, had by no means explicitly limited himself to the financing of innovative investments,[37] had long since turned into an anti-Keynesian after the war (Hahn, 1949). At the same time, he repeatedly flirted with the statement that everything that Keynes said was wrong and exaggerated, he himself had said much earlier and more clearly.

Röpke, who as a member of the Brauns Commission in Germany had spoken out in favour of an initial ignition in the fight against secondary deflation during the Great Depression and had thus been very close to Keynes in terms of economic policy, turned into a fervent anti-Keynesian after the publication of *General Theory* (Keynes, 1936). Above all he criticised the inflationary overzealousness of some of Keynes' students (Röpke, 1952). His increasing attacks prompted Schneider (1953) to launch a successful counter-attack, at least in the academic field, in which he criticised Röpke for not being completely up-to-date with the scientific Keynes discussion. In contrast to the latent inflationism of Keynes' theory criticised by Röpke, Schneider emphasised the general character of Keynes' analysis, that allowed economic policy measures to be developed to combat both inflation and deflation.[38] This paved the way for the triumphant advance of Keynesianism of the neoclassical synthesis type in economic theory in Germany, even if it was only to take hold in economic policy for a few years after Karl Schiller took office as Federal Minister of Economics in December 1966, almost a year after Röpke's death in February.

2.5 At the Zenith of Academic Influence and Recognition

The first ten years or so of the Committee were characterised by the strict regiment of Erich Schneider and that was without question Keynesian.
Rudolf Richter (in Schefold, 2004:511)

A powerful instrument for Schneider's implementation of Keynesianism was the Theoretical Committee of the Verein für Socialpolitik that Schneider chaired for more than a decade until 1962.[39] Immediately after the re-founding, he was appointed acting chairman of the Theoretical Committee at the first annual conference, which was to "deal with the moment of time in modern production, the Keynesian 'revolution' in economic theory and the theory and politics of full employment".[40] The driving force behind the founding of the new committee was Schneider, who was also to determine the direction and content of the activities, which only began to intensify with the meeting in Dortmund in January 1953. This led to an extensive abstinence of older professors who were unfamiliar with Keynesianism and/or the

[37] See Hahn ([1920] 2015).

[38] For Keynes' views on inflation, deflation and reflation, see also Barens and Caspari (2015).

[39] For the history and activities of the Theoretical Committee in the first two and a half decades after its re-establishment, see the study by Bertram Schefold (2004).

[40] Albrecht and Arndt (1949, p. 85).

increased use of mathematical methods. On the other hand, under Schneider's leadership, a community of younger aspiring economists emerged who were predominantly committed to a moderate Keynesianism of neoclassical synthesis, increasingly worked with mathematical models and later took up leading professorships, such as Gottfried Bombach (Basel), Carl Föhl (FU Berlin), Heinz Haller (Kiel/Heidelberg/Zurich), Ernst Helmstädter (Münster), Wilhelm Krelle (Bonn), Alfred E. Ott (Tübingen) and Rudolf Richter (Saarbrücken). The first one of the Committee's volumes edited by Erich Schneider in the Verein für Socialpolitik series was published in 1954 and contains contributions on multiplier theory by Rudolf Richter and Herbert Giersch (Schneider, 1954). While Richter deals with Keynes' investment multiplier and also discusses Samuelson's accelerator-multiplier model and the lag problem in particular, Giersch's contribution may come as a surprise from a later perspective. During his time as Schneider's successor as director of the Kiel Institute for the World Economy from 1969 to 1989, Giersch was known for being one of the most prominent voices in the German economic policy debate, in marked contrast to Schneider, and an equally sharp critic of decidedly Keynesian positions and the excessive use of mathematical models in economics.[41] In contrast, Schefold (2004: 589) attests that Giersch in his early contribution "strives towards a neoclassical synthesis without carrying it out, above all by taking into account the interest elasticity of saving".

When Wilhelm Krelle took over the chairmanship in 1962, growth theory, which was booming internationally at the time, had already become a central topic of the Theoretical Committee. Erich Schneider himself became Chairman of the Verein für Socialpolitik from 1963 to 1966.

Schneider was also able to exert a decisive influence in the 1960s by becoming director of the Institute for the World Economy and thus also editor of the internationally renowned journal *Weltwirtschaftliches Archiv* (now *Review of World Economics*). Although Schneider had already been the dominant figure in Kiel economics since the end of the 1940s,[42] he only took over as director of the institute after Fritz Baade's retirement on 1 April 1961. Baade, who had returned from exile in Turkey after the war, had already been appointed full professor and director of the Institute for the World Economy in 1948, but had also been very active politically as a member of the German Bundestag from 1949 to 1965, and in the international agricultural, food and energy policy. With Schneider's leadership and the Institute's greater resources, basic research was strengthened and contacts with leading international representatives of modern economics intensified. On the 50th anniversary of the institute on 18 February 1964, the prize named after the founder Bernhard Harms (1876–1939) was awarded to Gerhard Colm for the first time.[43] Together with Adolph Lowe and Hans Neisser, Colm had been largely responsible for the

[41] The author of this essay still remembers well how, as a student in Kiel, when Herbert Giersch frequently asked the rhetorical question "rigorous or *relevant*?" in his lectures, he briefly irritated the questioner by interjecting "both".

[42] "a patriarch in his faculty" (Rolf Langhammer, quoted from Czycholl, 2014, p. 89).

[43] For the history of the Kiel Institute, see also Zottmann (1964), Czycholl (2014) and Take (2019).

high international reputation of the Kiel Institute for the World Economy in the years 1926 to 1933, which at times also included top-calibre economists such as Wassily Leontief and Jacob Marschak (Hagemann, 2021). Leontief was the fourth recipient of the Bernhard Harms Prize in 1970 after Roy Harrod (1966) and the banker Hermann Josef Abs (1968).

Schneider was now at the zenith of his academic career and received numerous honours, including the Friedrich List Medal in Gold from the Federal Association of German Economists and Business Economists in 1965 and the Grand Cross of the Order of Merit of the Federal Republic of Germany in 1968. He was a member of numerous academies in Germany and abroad.

Of his seven honorary doctorates, Schneider received the first on 23 February 1957 from the Free University of Berlin as a "scholar whose work convincingly expresses the inner connection between microeconomic and macroeconomic research".[44] During this time, Andreas Paulsen[45] was rector of the university, before Carl Föhl (1901–1973) was appointed to a late professorship only a short time later. Föhl, originally an engineer, was the most congenial soul to Schneider. His technically demanding *Geldschöpfung und Wirtschaftskreislauf* (Föhl, 1937) was strongly influenced by Keynes' *Treatise* (1930), but an original work with many parallels to Keynes' *General Theory*, finalised before the latter book was published.[46] Its publication had an early and important influence on Schneider who invited Föhl to give a lecture in Aarhus on "Maintaining Full employment" that was published in a Danish journal (Föhl, 1941).[47] Since then, Schneider and Föhl had a lifelong friendship.

The honorary doctorate from Berlin was to remain the only one from German universities, which were also characterised by the greatest frugality with regard to further appointments to the renowned colleague. As well received as Schneider's excellent pedagogy was by the students, his schoolmasterly and patriarchal manner led to some reservations among his colleagues, despite his personal warmth. The situation was quite different with regard to "foreign honorary doctorates, the number of which none of his German colleagues could match" (Häuser, 2010, p. 247). For example, the Berlin one was followed by further honorary doctorates from the Stockholm School of Economics (1959), the Sorbonne in Paris (1960), the Helsinki School of Economics (1961), the Universities of Louvain (1963) and Rennes (1966) and finally posthumously from the University of Madrid (1971).

Even in the 1950s, when there were still large international reserves against the young, post-national socialist Federal Republic of Germany, and German economics had only a low reputation, Schneider was a major exception. Häuser (2010, p. 267) even goes so far as to claim "that after Eucken's death (1950), Schneider's

---

[44] Homepage FU Berlin.

[45] On Paulsen see the contribution by Heinz Rieter in this volume.

[46] See also Schumpeter (1954, p. 1174) who points out that Föhl's book "sheds what amounts to new light on several Keynesian problems, especially the problem of equilibrium underemployment". Hans Singer, another former student of Schumpeter in Bonn, earlier had described Föhl's book as an "outstanding achievement" in his review in The Economic Journal 48, 1938: 79–80.

[47] The article was reprinted in the second edition of Föhl ([1937] 1955, pp. 409–436).

voice remained the only one that counted abroad". In 1955, Schneider organised the European Congress of the Econometric Society in Kiel, which was attended by the later Nobel Prize winners Ragnar Frisch, Jan Tinbergen and Richard Stone as well as Harold Hotelling from the USA, among others, and Carl Föhl gave a much-noticed lecture.[48] In 1958, Schneider took a prominent position as one of the five international laudators at the major Paris conference to mark the 200th anniversary of Francois Quesnay's *Tableau économique* (1758) As early as 1952, Schneider had been appointed by Robert Marjolin, the Secretary General of the Organisation for European Economic Cooperation OEEC, together with Costantino Bresciani-Turroni, Erik Lindahl, Arthur Marget, Lionel Robbins and Jacques Rueff, to the "high level group of experts", that was to review the internal financial stability of the member states. As Bombach (1971, p. 13) mentions, prominent economists such as Alvin Hansen, John Hicks and Richard Musgrave came to Kiel as visitors, and Jan Tinbergen, who was close to Schneider, became "something of a permanent guest". The international recognition is also reflected in the fact that in the commemorative publication edited by Bombach (1960) on the occasion of Erich Schneider's 60th birthday, *Stable prices in a growing economy. The Inflation problem,* prominent foreign economists, including Frisch, Tinbergen and Pedersen as well as Johan Åkerman, Leon Dupriez, Gottfried Haberler, Alvin Hansen, Ugo Papi, Alan Peacock, Jacques Rueff and others, wrote the vast majority of the contributions.

Among the distinguished economists who were invited by Schneider to give special lectures at the Kiel Institute was also Friedrich August Hayek whose "Competition as a discovery process" (Hayek, 1968) subsequently became one of his best-known ideas representing his evolutionary thinking. However, although both were liberals, they did not click together. Contrary to Hayek, Schneider was a "French liberal" in the sense of an enlightened constructivist rationalism.

His excellent language skills were a great help in Schneider's international contacts. In addition to the Scandinavian languages and English, he also spoke French, Spanish and Italian. As his teacher Schumpeter, Schneider had a particular influence in Italy where numerous of his articles were published. It is noteworthy that Schneider's last greater article "Automation or discretion in monetary policy", that Scherf (1980, p. 58) considers alongside his essay on "The current state of the theory of employment" (Schneider, 1951a) as Schneider's most impressive contribution to the economic debate, was published in Italy in an English and in an Italian version (Schneider, 1970b, c) before it was published in German. In this essay Schneider argues against the misinterpretation of correlations as causality and simplified rules, emphasizes with Wicksell and Keynes the volatility of the velocity of money, and makes a strong plea for the combined application of fiscal and monetary policy that considers the complexities of transmission mechanisms as well as time lags and is appropriate to the economic situation at hand.

Two years after Schneider's death his macroeconomic textbook was published in an Italian translation *Moneta, reddito, occupazione* (Schneider, 1972). Schneider

[48] See Bombach (1987, p. 64).

was best known in Italy for his explanation of Keynesian economics and his participation in the debate on the role of the banking system. Many, but by no means all of his essays were published in the journal *Moneta e Credito*.[49] Augusto Graziani (1933–2014), a leading Italian economist of his time who is internationally known for his emphasis on the credit character of money and as a proponent of a monetary theory of production, elaborated his views under the influence of the monetary theories of Keynes and Schumpeter but also in intensive dialogue with Schneider's position.[50]

2.6 Impact and Appreciation

> *"It's a marvellous thing to be a university lecturer."*
> Erich Schneider[51]
>
> *"He was an emperor of the lecture theatre."*
> Karl Häuser (2010, p. 272).

It is not without a certain irony that it was an admiring disciple of Schumpeter who was primarily responsible for the implementation of Keynesian economics in Germany after World War II. Herbert Giersch (1984), Schneider's successor as the Director of the Kiel Institute for the World Economy, proclaimed the fourth quarter of the twentieth century as "the age of Schumpeter" succeeding the third quarter as "the age of Keynes". He attested his predecessor to be among Schumpeter's students "who later became famous economists" (Giersch 1984: 104), but based his attack against Keynes almost exclusively on Schumpeter's nasty review of the *General Theory*.[52] There Schumpeter (1936) particularly objected against Keynes elevating the unique historical situation of England in the 1930s to general scientific truth, his light-hearted use of economic aggregates, the assumption of a given technology and the message that underconsumption is the main cause of unemployment.

In contrast to Giersch, Schneider surely had two heroes: Schumpeter *and* Keynes. He thus would agree with Wolfgang Stolper, Schumpeter's student at Bonn and

[49] For the long list see the details in Bombach and Tacke (1980, pp. 91–192).

[50] For a most recent analysis see Figuera and Pacella (2025).

[51] Speeches (1966, p. 40).

[52] Schneider (1970a, pp. 56–7) claims that Schumpeter's relationship with Keynes took on hostile traits with the publication of the *Treatise on Money* (Keynes, 1930) and that "the reason for the hostility towards Keynes lies solely in the fact that the publication of the '*Treatise*' shortly before the completion of his own work deprived him of the fruits of years of labour". This statement, however, is problematic. In contrast, Stolper (1994, p. 48) emphasizes that "Schumpeter .. spoke admiringly of the *Treatise* in his Bonn lectures, which may be enhanced by Keynes having nodded his approval to several of Schumpeter's main arguments in the *Theory of Economic Development*, so that "we can rule out jealousy of Keynes's *Treatise on Money*". For a more detailed discussion of the complex relationship between Schumpeter and Keynes see Hagemann (2019a).

Harvard, who, in answer to the question of whether *Schumpeter* or *Keynes* was the greater economist, referred to *Goethe* who, when asked whether he or *Schiller* was the greatest poet, had responded: "That's foolish. People should be glad that there are two such fellows around" (Stolper, 1994, p. XIV).

In their essay on the relationship of Schneider and Schumpeter, Blind and Pyka (2015: 243) point out that despite his admiration for Schumpeter, "Schneider's work shows little if any influence from his Bonn supervisor". This surely does not hold for their common admiration for Walras and Pareto, their views on the role of mathematics in economics, the connection between economics and business administration, and Schneider's early works on microeconomics. However, on the other hand, it is certainly true that Schumpeter's focus on the long-run and cyclical development of capitalist economies and the role of capital accumulation and technical progress had only little impact on Schneider's work.

It is somehow astonishing that Schneider, as an admiring disciple of Schumpeter and an ardent advocate of Keynesianism never made a serious attempt to elaborate an appropriate synthesis. Economic policies in advanced countries may benefit from a complementarity of Keynesian and Schumpeterian ideas, a *Keynes cum Schumpeter* strategy. The double-sided nature of technical progress, leading to an increase of productivity on the supply side but also to product innovations with high potential for an increase in demand, investment and employment, indicates that Schumpeter's vision of the long-run development of capitalist economies could have added value to a modified and enriched Keynesian vision aiming at full employment over time. A combination of a Keynesian-type policy that will raise per capita demand for consumption goods and investment in core public infrastructure with the promotion of research and development of new goods may help to implement the continuous process of structural reallocation of labour between firms and sectors necessary to maintain a high employment level over time.

What kind of Keynesian was Erich Schneider? If we take the widely accepted distinction of Alan Coddington (1983) into a "hydraulic", "fundamentalist" and "reductionist" Keynesianism, there exists agreement that Schneider was essentially a hydraulic Keynesian,[53] strongly influenced by the IS-LM model of the young Hicks and Samuelson's neoclassical synthesis. Schneider thought functionally and often compared the role of the economist with that of an engineer. As his last research assistant Wolf Schäfer (2001, p. 9) points out, it was astonishing that Schneider, in contrast to Keynes, gave hardly any room to the important role of expectations. Uncertainty was a topic even more alien to Schneider who may have feared that an absolutisation of the uncertainty argument would rule out mathematical modelling and ultimately end up in analytical nihilism. "Schneider was thus obviously miles away from fundamentalist Keynesianism" (Rothschild, 1987, p. 25), in whose various approaches (Joan Robinson, Paul Davidson, Sidney Weintraub, Hyman Minsky, George Shackle, Brian Loasby, et al.) expectations and uncertainty play a major role. Schneider's reductionist approach also contrasts with

[53] See, for example, Bombach (1987, p. 46), Rothschild (1987, pp. 23–4), and Schäfer (2001, p. 7).

that of Keynes who had serious doubts that mathematical methods could capture the complexities and interdependencies of the real world in a sufficient way.[54]

It is therefore not surprising that the reinterpretation of Keynes induced by Robert Clower and Axel Leijonhufvud, who extracted the lack of information and resulting failures in intertemporal coordination of economic activities in large complex systems from the economics of Keynes, did not make a greater impact on Schneider. He did not live long enough to see the temporary equilibrium models with quantity rationing emerging that celebrated a breakthrough in macroeconomics with the publication of Edmond Malinvaud's *The Theory of Unemployment Reconsidered* (1977) also in Germany. In this approach transactions can take place at prices that are not market-clearing. Quantity signals in the agents' environments appear as extending rather than rejecting Walras. It is more than speculation that this "reconstructed reductionism", which analyses disequilibrium positions with the same methods and instruments as general equilibrium theory, would have attracted Schneider. A good indicator for this view is the fact that Winfried Vogt, the intellectually outstanding brain in the younger generation of Schneider's students, wrote an article "Walras or Keynes—On the (French) new staging of the neoclassical synthesis" (Vogt 1979) on Malinvaud's theory of rationing that was highly influential in the subsequent debate in Germany.

With regard to Schneider's impact a distinction must be made between the contemporary and the long-run influences. Without doubt he will be remembered for his merits as an academic teacher and a successful textbook author in his lifetime. However, posing the question of Schneider's significance in the history of economic thought, most experts would not challenge the assessment of Karl Häuser (2010, p. 250) stating "that Schneider's own contribution to the progress of theory has not found a significant entry in the book of the history of economics, while his role in the renewal of economics in Germany and in bringing it into line with international developments has been considerable".

"It was Keynes' achievement that turned economic theory into a truly powerful instrument of economic policy", Erich Schneider (1969: 162) emphasized in his Kiel farewell lecture. However, in remarkable contrast to Keynes who was an economist with eminent political interests and activities, Schneider kept a great distance from practical policies, as all observers confirm. Gottfried Bombach (1971, p. 28), who was probably closest to his teacher over decades, clearly states that Schneider "did not think much of the theorist's direct involvement in the political decision-making process. He grandiosely ignored the infinite difficulties of translating theoretical insights into good policy." A consequence of this mindset was that Schneider, in remarkable contrast to his successor at the Kiel Institute Herbert Giersch, was widely absent from economic policy advisory bodies, as the German Council of

[54] See, for example, Keynes (1936, p. 298).

Economic Advisors (founded in 1963) or the scientific advisory boards of the Federal Ministries of Economics and of Finance.[55]

Thus it can be stated that Erich Schneider was entirely a scholar in the sense of Max Weber separating scientific work from value judgements and political activities. However, his last book makes it very clear that his teacher Schumpeter has been the towering influence with regard to this attitude. Emphasizing the high price of the loss of seven years for research and his whole material wealth Schumpeter had to pay for his failure in politics as Austrian finance minister in 1919 and subsequently as a banker, Schneider (1970a, p. 46) states: "Politics and business are world of action. The world of science is the world of meditation and contemplation. The scholar lives in this world of meditation. The world of action is essentially alien to him. It needs people of a completely different intellectual habitus than the world of science; and this is precisely why the *real* scholar, the scholar of *passion*, will usually fail when he enters the political or the business arena."[56]

There exists another significant common ground between Schneider and Schumpeter. Both never wanted to found a "School", but had a great number of excellent students who made an academic career. Schneider (1970, p. 79) refers to Schumpeter's well-known position stating that "nothing was more hateful to him than a pupil who only repeated the teacher", and argues in his own farewell lecture, "I have never wanted to found a school",[57] adding Schumpeter's famous phrase "opening doors" from the latter's Bonn farewell lecture (Schneider, 1969: 165).

The long list of his students who got their habilitation with Schneider at Kiel and later became professors includes Alfred Stobbe (Mannheim), Hans-Joachim Jarchow (Göttingen), Winfried Vogt (Regensburg), Jens Lübbert, Harald Scherf, Uwe Westphal (all Hamburg), Peter Dobias (Göttingen, Paderborn) and Jürgen Rohwedder (Kiel). Particularly proud was Schneider of his early star students Gottfried Bombach (1919–2010), who introduced Keynesianism in Switzerland after being appointed professor at the University of Basel in 1957, and Günther Schleiminger (1921–2008), who made a steep career at international monetary institutions since 1952, including the European Payments Union, the Bundesbank, the International Monetary Fund, and finally at the Bank of International Settlements. Many of the almost hundred economists who got their doctoral degree with Schneider at Kiel later also became university professors. Hajo Riese (1933–2021) and Hansjürgen Ramser (1936–2024) received their PhD degree at Kiel in 1959 respectively 1961, and their habilitation with Bombach at Basel in 1966 respectively 1969. Riese[58] became professor in Linz and at the Free University (FU) Berlin, Ramser in Konstanz.

[55] For greater details see Bombach (1987). On Bombach see the entry by Oliver Landmann in this volume.

[56] See also Schneider (1970a, p. 20) quoting Schumpeter.

[57] See also Vogt (1971, 1980).

[58] On Riese see the entry by Peter Spahn in this volume.

Ramser co-edited with Bombach et al. (1976–1997) six well-researched volumes on Keynesianism (*Der Keynesianismus*), dealing with economic theory, including modern developments in macroeconomics and growth economics, and the debates on monetary and employment policy in Germany in the interwar period (vls. II, III). Bombach's survey article (1965) and Vogt's early advanced textbook (1968) were influential contributions to the German debate on growth theory. Internationally best known is the independent discovery of the "golden rule of accumulation" by Carl Christian von Weizsäcker in his dissertation with Bombach in 1961 (Weizsäcker, 1962) at the University of Basel, where he also got his habilitation in 1965.

Among Schneider's numerous students, who enjoyed a demanding theoretical education, was also Jürgen Kromphardt (born 1933) who got his doctoral degree in Kiel with a thesis on contributions to the theory of growth in 1957, and later his habilitation in Münster in 1967. Kromphardt, who was professor in Gießen since 1968 and from 1980 at the Technical University of Berlin, took the initiative to found the *Keynes Gesellschaft* in December 2003 when he was still a member of the Council of Economic Advisors. With almost 200 members, a publication series and a well-attended annual conference in spring 2025 the Keynes Society is alive and well.[59]

References

Selected Works by Erich Schneider

Schneider, E. (1931). Kostentheoretisches zum Monopolproblem. *Zeitschrift für Nationalökonomie, 3*(2), 185–211.

Schneider, E. (1932). *Reine Theorie monopolistischer Wirtschaftsformen*. Tübingen: Mohr.

Schneider, E. (1934a). *Theorie der Produktion*. Vienna: Julius Springer.

Schneider, E. (1934b). Johann Heinrich von Thünen. *Econometrica, 2*(1), 1–12.

Schneider, E. ([1939] 1954). *Industrielles Rechnungswesen*. Grundlagen und Grundfragen. Tübingen: Mohr.

Schneider, E. (1944). Zur Frage der Wirkung finanzpolitischer Maßnahmen auf die wirtschaftliche Aktivität. *Finanzarchiv*, N.S. 10 (2): 277–287.

Schneider, E. (1947–1962). *Einführung in die Wirtschaftstheorie*. Vols. I_IV.

Schneider, E. Vol. I: *Theorie des Wirtschaftskreislaufs*. Tübingen 1947: Mohr; 14th ed. 1969a.

Schneider, E. Vol. II: *Wirtschaftspläne und wirtschaftliches Gleichgewicht in der Verkehrswirtschaft*. Tübingen 1949: Mohr; 13th ed. 1972.

Schneider, E. Vol. III: *Geld, Kredit, Volkseinkommen und Beschäftigung*. Tübingen 1952: Mohr; 12th ed. 1973.

Schneider, E. Vol. IV: *Ausgewählte Kapitel der Geschichte der Wirtschaftstheorie*. Tübingen 1962: Mohr; 3rd ed. 1970.

Schneider, E. (1951a). Der gegenwärtige Stand der Theorie der Beschäftigung. In G. Albrecht (Ed.), *Die Problematik der Vollbeschäftigung* (pp. 17–32). Duncker&Humblot.

Erich Schneider. ([1944] 1951b). *Wirtschaftlichkeitsrechnung. Theorie der Investition*. Bern and Tübingen: Mohr.

[59] For further details see keynes-gesellschaft.de

Schneider, E. (1952). Hahn contra Keynes. *Schweizerische Zeitschrift für Volkswirtschaft und Statistik.*, *88*(5), 395–404.
Schneider, E. (1953). Der Streit um Keynes. Dichtung und Wahrheit in der neueren deutschen Keynes-Diskussion. *Jahrbücher für Nationalökonomie und Statistik, 165*(1), 89–122.
Schneider, E. (Ed.). (1954). *Beiträge zur Multiplikatoranalyse*. Berlin: Duncker& Humblot.
Schneider, E. (1960). Hans von Mangoldt on price theory: A contribution to the history of mathematical economics. *Econometrica, 28*(2), 380–392.
Schneider, E. (1964). *Volkswirtschaft und Betriebswirtschaft*. Selected Essays. Tübingen: Mohr.
Schneider, E. (1968). *Zahlungsbilanz und Wechselkurs*. Tübingen 1968: Mohr.
Schneider, E. (1969). Rückblick auf ein halbes Jahrhundert der Wirtschaftswissenschaft (1918–1968). *Weltwirtschaftliches Archiv, 102*(1), 157–167.
Schneider, E. (1970a). *Joseph A. Schumpeter – Leben und Werk eines großen Sozialökonomen*. Tübingen: Mohr.
Schneider, E. (1970b). Automation or discretion in monetary policy? *Banca Nazionale del Lavoro Quarterly Review, 23*(93), 111–127.
Schneider, E. (1970c). Automatismo o discrezionalità nella politica monetaria? *Moneta e Credito., 90*, 119–136.
Schneider, E. (1972). *Moneta, reddito, occupazione*. Einaudi.

Other Works

Albrecht, G., & Arndt, H. (Eds.). (1949). *Volkswirtschaftliche Probleme des deutschen Außenhandels*. Duncker&Humblot.
Barens, I., & Caspari, V. (2015). Problem oder Instrument der Wirtschaftspolitik? John Maynard Keynes' Ansichten zu Inflation, Deflation und Reflation. In H. Hagemann & J. Kromphardt (Eds.), *Für eine bessere gesamteuropäische Wirtschaftspolitik* (pp. 249–291). Metropolis.
Blind, G., & Pyka, A. (2015). Erich Schneider: The admiring disciple who did not become a follower. *Journal of Evolutionary Economics, 25*(2), 239–252.
Bombach, G. (ed.) (1960). *Stabile Preise in wachsender Wirtschaft. Das Inflationsproblem*. Erich Schneider zum 60. Geburtstag. Tübingen: Mohr.
Bombach, G. (1965). Wirtschaftswachstum. In: *Handwörterbuch der Sozialwissenschaften* (Vol. 12, pp. 763–800). Göttingen: Vandenhoeck&Ruprecht.
Bombach, G. (1971). Erich Schneider – Mensch und Werk. In *Erich Schneider in memoriam. Ansprachen auf der akademischen Trauerfeier am 18 Juni 1971* (pp. 12–32). im Institut für Weltwirtschaft an der Universität Kiel.
Bombach, G. (1987). Wirtschaftstheorie und Wirtschaftspolitik im Werke Erich Schneiders. In *Festkolloquium in memoriam Erich Schneider* (pp. 43–83). Christian-Albrechts-Universität zu Kiel. Gastvorträge am Institut für Theoretische Volkswirtschaftslehre.
Bombach, G., et al. (1976–1999). *Der Keynesianismus Vols. I-VI*. Berlin, Heidelberg, New York: Springer.
Bombach, G., & Tacke, M. (Eds.). (1980). *Erich Schneider 1900–1970. Gedenkband und Bibliographie*. Kiel: Institut für Weltwirtschaft.
Brems, H. (1987). Schneider and Denmark. In *Festkolloquium in memoriam Erich Schneider* (pp. 84–89). Christian-Albrechts-Universität zu Kiel. Gastvorträge am Institut für Theoretische Volkswirtschaftslehre.
Cassel, G. (1918). *Theoretische Sozialökonomie*. Leipzig: C. F. Winter, 5th ed. 1932; English translation *Theory of Social Economy*. London 1923: T. F. Unwin, revised ed. London 1932: E. Benn.
Chamberlin, E. (1933). *The theory of monopolistic competition*. Cambridge, MA: Harvard University Press.
Coddington, A. (1983). *Keynesian economics. The search for first principles*. London: George Allen&Unwin.

Czycholl, H. (2014). *100 Jahre Institut für Weltwirtschaft*. Hamburg, Neumünster: Wachholtz.
Eucken, W. (1940). *Die Grundlagen der Nationalökonomie*. Jena: Gustav Fischer.
Figuera, S., & Pacella, A. (2025). Banks, intermediation and the endogenous nature of money supply. A note on the contributions of Erich Schneider and Augusto Graziani. *Review of Political Economy*. 37, forthcoming.
Föhl, C. ([1937] 1955). *Geldschöpfung und Wirtschaftskreislauf*. Berlin: Duncker& Humblot.
Föhl, C. (1941). Die Erhaltung der Vollbeschäftigung. *Nordisk Tidsskrift for Teknisk Ökonomi*. 7: 237–264; reprinted in Föhl (1955), pp. 409–436.
Frisch, R. (1932). *New methods of measuring marginal productivity*. Tübingen: Mohr.
Frisch, R. (1951). Some personal reminiscences on a great man. In S. E. Harris (Ed.), *Schumpeter: Social scientist*. Cambridge, MA: Harvard University Press.
Garside, W. R., & Topp, N.-H. (2001). Nascent Keynesianism? Denmark in the 1930s. *History of Political Economy, 33*(4), 717–741.
Gelting, J. (1941). Nogle bemaerkninger om finansieringen af offentlig virksomhed. *Nationaloekonomisk Tidskrift, 79*(5), 293–299.
Giersch, H. (1984). The age of Schumpeter. *The American Economic Review, 74*(2), 103–109.
Haavelmo, T. (1945). Multiplier effects of a balanced budget. *Econometrica, 13*(4), 311–318.
Häuser, K. (2010). Erich Schneider und die deutsche Nationalökonomie. In C. Scheer (Ed.), *Die deutschsprachige Wirtschaftswissenschaft in den ersten Jahrzehnten nach 1945. Studien zur Entwicklung der ökonomischen Theorie XXV* (pp. 235–290). Berlin: Duncker&Humblot.
Hagemann, H. (2001). Hans Peter. In *Neue Deutsche Biographie* (Vol. 20, pp. 233–234). Berlin: Duncker&Humblot.
Hagemann, H. (2007). Erich Schneider. In *Neue Deutsche Biographie* (Vol. 23, pp. 286–287). Berlin: Duncker&Humblot.
Hagemann, H. (2017). Ordoliberalism, the Social Market Economy and Keynesianism in Germany 1945–1974. In R. E. Backhouse, B. W. Bateman, T. Nishizawa, & D. Plehwe (Eds.), *Liberalism and the welfare state: Economists and arguments for the welfare state* (pp. 57–74). Oxford University Press.
Hagemann, H. (2019a). Joseph Alois Schumpeter. In R. W. Dimand & H. Hagemann (Eds.), *The Elgar companion to John Maynard Keynes* (pp. 324–333). Edward Elgar.
Hagemann, H. (2019b). Keynesianism in Germany. In R. W. Dimand & H. Hagemann (Eds.), *The Elgar companion to John Maynard Keynes* (pp. 595–602). Edward Elgar.
Hagemann, H. (2021). The formation of research institutes on business cycles in Europe in the Interwar Period. The 'Kiel school' and (in)voluntary internationalization. In A. Mendes Cunha & C. E. Suprinyak (Eds.), *Political economy and international order in interwar Europe* (pp. 361–382). London: Palgrave Macmillan.
Hahn, L. A. ([1920] 2015). *Economic theory of bank credit*. Oxford University Press.
Hahn, L. A. (1949). Die Grundirrtümer in Lord Keynes' general theory of employment, interest and money. *Ordo, 2*, 170–192.
Hayek, F. A. (1968). *Der Wettbewerb als Entdeckungsverfahren. Kieler Vorträge N.S. 56*. Tübingen: Mohr.
Hegeland, H. (1954). *The multiplier theory*. New York: Sentry Press.
Hicks, J. R. (1942). *The social framework*. Oxford University Press.
Hylleberg, S. (2001). Erich Schneider in Denmark. In *Festveranstaltung zur Erinnerung an Erich Schneider* (pp. 13–14). Christian-Albrechts-Universität zu Kiel. Gastvorträge am Institut für Volkswirtschaftslehre.
Keynes, J. M. (1930). *A treatise on money* (Vol. 2). London: Macmillan.
Keynes, J. M. (1936). *The general theory of employment, interest and money*. London: Macmillan.
Malinvaud, E. (1977). *The theory of unemployment reconsidered*. Oxford: Basil Blackwell.
Marschak, J. (1931). *Elastizität der Nachfrage*. Tübingen: Mohr.
Myrup, H. F. (1987). Grußwort. In *Festkolloquium in memoriam Erich Schneider* (pp. 5–8). Christian-Albrechts-Universität zu Kiel. Gastvorträge am Institut für Theoretische Volkswirtschaftslehre.
Pareto, V. (1906). *Manuale d'economia politica*. Milan: Societa Editrice Libreria. Revised and translated as *Manuel d'économie politique*. Paris 1909: Giard et Brière.

Pareto, V. ([1911] 1955). Mathematical economics. *International Economic Papers. 5*, 58–102.
Peacock, A. T. (1950). Recent German contributions to economics. *Economica, 17*(66), 175–187.
Peter, H. (1935). Aufgaben und Grenzen der mathematischen Nationalökonomie. *Archiv für mathematische Wirtschafts- und Sozialforschung., 1*(1), 1–16.
Quesnay, F. (1758). *Tableau économique*. Versailles.
Richter, R. (1997). Zur Entwicklung der Makroökonomik in den vergangenen 50 Jahren (1947–1997). In *Erich-Schneider-Gedächtnisvorlesung 1997*. Christian-Albrechts-Universität zu Kiel. Gastvorträge am Institut für Theoretische Volkswirtschaftslehre.
Robinson, J. (1933). *The economics of imperfect competition*. London: Macmillan.
Röpke, W. (1952). *Was lehrt Keynes? Frankfurter Allgemeine Zeitung 27*. September.
Rothschild, K. W. (1964). The old and the new – Some recent trends in the literature of German economics. *The American Economic Review, 54*(2.2), 1–33.
Rothschild, K. W. (1987). Schneiders Plädoyer für Keynes. In *Festkolloquium in memoriam Erich Schneider* (pp. 9–27). Christian-Albrechts-Universität zu Kiel. Gastvorträge am Institut für Theoretische Volkswirtschaftslehre.
Samuelson, P. A. (1952). *Volkswirtschaftslehre. Grundlagen der Makro- und Mikroökonomie*. Bund Verlag.
Schäfer, W. (2001). Zur Erinnerung an Erich Schneider. In *Festveranstaltung zur Erinnerung an Erich Schneider* (pp. 3–12). Christian-Albrechts-Universität zu Kiel. Gastvorträge am Institut für Volkswirtschaftslehre, Kiel.
Schefold, B. (2004). Wissenschaft als Gegengabe – Neugründung und Aktivitäten des Theoretischen Ausschusses im Verein für Socialpolitik 1949–1973. *Schmollers Jahrbuch, 124*, 579–608.
Scherf, H. (1980). Erich Schneiders Keynes-Rezeption. In: Bombach/Tacke (1980), pp. 49–61.
Schumpeter, J. A. (1906). Ueber die mathematische Methode der theoretischen Oekonomie. *Zeitschrift für Volkswirtschaft, Sozialpolitik und Verwaltung, 15*(1), 30–49.
Schumpeter, J. A. ([1911] 1934a). *Theory of economic development*. Cambridge, MA: Harvard University Press.
Schumpeter, J. A. (1927). Cassels Theoretische Sozialökonomie. *Schmollers Jahrbuch für Gesetzgebung, Verwaltung und Volkswirtschaft, 51*(2), 241–260.
Schumpeter, J. A. (1934b). Joan Robinson's economics of imperfect competition. *Journal of Political Economy, 42*(2), 249–257.
Schumpeter, J. A. (1936). J. M. Keynes' general theory of employment, interest and money. *Journal of the American Statistical Association, 31*(196), 791–795.
Schumpeter, J. A. (1954). *History of economic analysis*. London: Allen&Unwin.
Schumpeter, J. A. (2000). *Briefe/Letters*. Eds.: U. Hedtke and R. Swedberg. Tübingen: Mohr Siebeck.
Stackelberg, H. von (1932). *Grundlagen einer reinen Kostentheorie*. Julius Springer.
Stackelberg, H. von (1934). *Marktform und Gleichgewicht*. Julius Springer.
Stobbe, A. (1966). *Volkswirtschaftliches Rechnungswesen*. Berlin: Springer; 8th ed. 1994.
Stolper, W. (1994). *Joseph Alois Schumpeter. The public life of a private man*. Princeton University Press.
Take, G. (2019). *Forschen für den Wirtschaftskrieg. Das Kieler Institut für Weltwirtschaft im Nationalsozialismus*. Berlin: de Gruyter.
Vogt, W. (1968). *Theorie des wirtschaftlichen Wachstums*. Berlin, Frankfurt am Main: Vahlen.
Vogt, W. (1971). Erich Schneider and economic theory. *German Economic Review*. 9: 281–304. German translation Erich Schneider und die Wirtschaftstheorie (1972), reprinted in Bombach/Tacke (1980), pp. 13–48.
Vogt, W. (1979). Walras oder Keynes – Zur (französischen) Neuinszenierung der neoklassischen Synthese. In: K. Laski/E. Matzner/E. Nowotny (eds.), Beiträge zur Diskussion und Kritik der neoklassischen Theorie. Festschrift für K. W. Rothschild and J. Steindl. Berlin: : Springer.
Weizsäcker, C. C. von (1962). *Wachstum, Zins und optimale Investitionsquote*. Basel: Kyklos, and Tübingen: Mohr.
Zeuthen, F. (1930). *Problems of monopoly and economic warfare*, with a preface by J. A. Schumpeter. London: Routledge.
Zottmann, A. (1964). *Das Institut für Weltwirtschaft an der Universität Kiel, 1914–1964*. Kiel.

Chapter 3
Andreas Paulsen and Keynesianism

Heinz Rieter

'… knowledge of Keynes' work may not
make you a "Keynesian", but it certainly
makes you a better economist.'
(Andreas Paulsen, 1954: 54)

'Analytical theory has
an *instrumental* character.'
(Andreas Paulsen, 1955: 17)

'In economic theory, there is
no methodological monism…'
(Andreas Paulsen, 1966: 143)

3.1 Background[1] and Personality

Andreas Lorenz Paulsen was born on 4 March 1899 in Flensburg, the son of a ship's captain. After passing the emergency matriculation examination at the local grammar school, he was drafted into the German army in June 1917 and served as a soldier in the First World War until December 1918. He then studied at the universities of Kiel and Leipzig, alternating between courses in economics, law, statistics and journalism. His academic teachers in Leipzig were mainly the economists Karl

[1] For details and references, see Rieter (2010: 53–54, 151–153).

H. Rieter (✉)
University of Hamburg, Barver, Germany

J. G. Backhaus et al. (eds.), *Post-war Keynesianism in Germany and Western Europe*, The European Heritage in Economics and the Social Sciences 28,
https://doi.org/10.1007/978-3-032-00498-7_3

Bücher (who was also the director of the Institute for Newspaper Studies, which he had founded in 1916), Bruno Moll and Max Muss, as well as the statistician Eugen Würzburger, and the economists Ludwig Pohle and Wilhelm Stieda, the jurists Viktor Ehrenberg and Alfred Schulze and the historian Gerhard Seeliger. In 1923, Paulsen was awarded a doctorate with the dissertation *Die Presse der freien Gewerkschaften* (The Press of the Free Trade Unions) which was reviewed by Bücher and Würzburger. He then worked at the Leipzig Chamber of Industry and Commerce, initially as a press officer and editor of its official organ *Mitteldeutsche Handels-Rundschau*, later as a member of its scientific secretariat and finally, from 1942, as its managing director. With the approval of the American military government, Paulsen served as managing director of the Leipzig Chamber of Commerce from May 1945 until its dissolution in early 1946. He also took over the editorial management of the business section of the *Leipziger Zeitung*. At the same time, he accepted a teaching position at the Leipzig Graduate School of Economics (formerly the Graduate School of Commerce) on the topic of *Rebuilding the German Economy* and, with the approval of the Soviet military administration, a teaching position at the Faculty of Economic and Social Sciences at the University of Leipzig. In autumn 1946, Paulsen habilitated at the University of Leipzig in the field of economics with the thesis *Wesen und Ordnungen staatlicher Wirtschaftsplanung* (The Nature and Organisation of State Economic Planning), which was reviewed by the economic historian Friedrich Lütge and the business economist Gerhard Menz. He expanded the work and published it in 1948 under the title *Soziale Gerechtigkeit als Wertnorm der Wirtschaftsordnung* (Social Justice as a Normative Value of the Economic Order). His habilitation was followed by his appointment as a lecturer in economics.

In spring 1947, he was appointed to a professorship in the same subject at the Faculty of Law and Economics at the University of Jena, succeeding Erich Preiser, who had accepted a professorship in Heidelberg. In the summer semester of 1948, the faculty elected him as Pro-Dean. However, at the end of 1948, Paulsen resigned from both posts and fled with his family to West Berlin. On 1 January 1949, he informed the Thuringian Minister of Education and the rector of the University of Jena of the reason in almost identical letters[2]: 'The students in my subject who are members of the SED [Socialist Unity Party of Germany] are obliged by party discipline to see me as a "class enemy" and to regard my teaching as malicious or at least as an insubordinate representation long since refuted reactionary claims. They were obliged to reject papers and exam essays on non-Marxist issues and to submit exam papers to the party before they were handed in. [...] Therefore, every member of the SED is obliged to see in me not a teacher who serves the truth to the best of his

[2]A copy of the letter to the rector was kindly provided by the University Archive of the Friedrich Schiller University Jena (D Nr. 2304, Bl. 555r). It is noteworthy that decades later, in her article about Paulsen in the semi-official GDR *'Ökonomenlexikon'* (Encyclopaedia of Economists), the Jena professor of economics Gisela Kahl (1989: 413) does not say a word about the political motivation behind his move from Jena to West Berlin. She simply states the fact without comment, thus giving the impression that it was a perfectly normal professional change.

conviction, but a political opponent who must be exposed as a charlatan or worse.' On the same day, Paulsen accepted a full professorship in economics at the Free University of Berlin, which had been founded the previous year, and in 1953 the directorship of the Seminar for Economic Theory, which had been established that year. From 1955 to 1957 he served as rector and from 1957 to 1959 as prorector of the FU Berlin. On 31 March 1967, he retired and ended his teaching career. His successor in the chair was the game theorist and later Nobel Prize winner in economics Reinhard Selten, who then moved to the University of Bielefeld in 1973. In retirement, Paulsen devoted himself to philosophical and theological studies until the end of his life (Schilcher, 1974: 203, Wedig, 1999: 36). Andreas Paulsen died on 14 December 1977 in Berlin.

Although Paulsen only returned to the academic environment of a university at an advanced age, he was perceived as an old-school scholar. He combined natural authority with intellectual calibre and was therefore held in high regard both within and outside the university. He was far from seeking to draw attention to himself as a professor or rector. He was reserved and never raised his voice. He spoke slowly and quietly, argued calmly, appeared thoughtful and listened attentively. His handwriting also says something about him—it was delicate and distinctive. In addition, Paulsen had the gift of polishing scientific texts so that the reader was spared dry prose. His public lectures and speeches as rector were equally polished and thought-provoking (see, for example, Paulsen, 1957b, 1957c). Reading them is still inspiring. He took his role as a university teacher very seriously. 'Training students professionally' was one thing, he said in his academic speech at his inauguration as rector (Paulsen, 1955: 27), but 'primarily' it was 'to educate people for whom the integrity of their thinking and intellectual honesty are not for sale'. In this spirit, he treated students as equal citizens of the university with rights and duties, as fellow students in the truest sense of the word, far from any arrogance. Nevertheless, it was not easy for most students to approach him without prejudice. His interdisciplinary education and serious nature created a certain distance. He felt almost collegially connected to his diploma students, doctoral students, habilitation students and research assistants. He saw himself as a lifelong learner, which is why he liked to assign or agree on topics he wanted to know more about. In such cases, he preferred to discuss them undisturbed in the study of his private home. In a letter dated 1 November 1958, he confided to his Leipzig mentor and later friend Friedrich Lütge (1901–1968), who was almost the same age, that he could have imagined a different scholarly life[3]: 'The life of a don or fellow in one of the famous old colleges of Oxford or Cambridge seems to me to be the ideal state for a person who is scientifically and contemplatively minded person!'

[3] Copies of the correspondence between Paulsen and Lütge from that time were kindly provided to me by Knut Borchardt when I was working on my article about the beginnings of economics at the Free University of Berlin (Rieter, 2010).

3.2 Paulsen's Turn to Keynesianism

Paulsen belongs to that generation of German economists who, during their studies, were taught mainly the doctrines of the Historical Schools and their offshoots and tributaries. It is difficult to determine when Paulsen began to occupy himself with more recent economic theories, especially with Keynes' *General Theory of Employment, Interest and Money*. When the book was published in 1936 and translated into German in the same year, he was working as an economic journalist and senior executive at a chamber of commerce and, as in previous years, regularly wrote for business newspapers (see Wedig, 1999: 54 f.). Due to his occupation, he dealt with current business and legal issues in these articles. To my knowledge, Paulsen published only two articles with a distinctly scientific claim before 1945—apart from his dissertation (Rieter, 2010, 155–158): Based on an academic lecture, he wrote an introduction to economics in 1934/36, which was published by an adult education (Volkshochschule) publisher in a corresponding anthology. His text makes no reference to more recent economic theories. The literature that Paulsen cites is limited to National Socialist books and well-known economic works by Bücher, Schmoller, Sombart and Spann. The situation is similar with his monograph *Der volkswirtschaftlich gerechtfertigte Preis* (The economically justified price), written in 1938. The subtitle of which, *Preisbildung und Preisverantwortung in der gewerblichen Wirtschaft* (Price formation and price responsibility in the commercial economy), already reveals that the writing—as stated in the preface—'arose from practice and was conceived for practice'. When Paulsen was able to gain a foothold in the academic field immediately after the end of the war in 1945, the focus of his professional interests inevitably changed. He turned to the topic that was on everyone's mind at the time, namely, creating the economic conditions and economic policy instruments needed to rebuild the destroyed country, alleviate the suffering of the people, and get the economy going and keep it going. As early as December 1945, he took on a teaching position at the Leipzig Graduate School of Economics on the topic *Grundzüge des Neuaufbaues der deutschen Wirtschaft* (fundamentals of rebuilding the German economy). In his aforementioned habilitation thesis, he discusses problems of economic planning and economic order; and in the habilitation colloquium in October 1946, he gave a lecture *Das persönliche Unternehmertum und das sogenannte 'Gesetz der dritten Generation'* (personal entrepreneurship and the so-called 'law of the third generation'). It is likely that he not only studied recent economic literature in these contexts, but also generally informed himself about the state of economic knowledge at the time. After all, it was Friedrich Lütge who took the academic newcomer under his wing. Unlike Paulsen, Lütge had long since made academia his profession (see, among others, North, 2010): not least as a key contributor to the fourth edition of the *Handwörterbuch der Staatswissenschaften* (Handbook of Political Economy) from 1925 and co-editor of the *Zeitschrift für Nationalökonomie und Statistik* (Journal of Political Economy and Statistics) from 1943, he had an excellent overview of developments and trends in the field.

However, Paulsen's turn to (newer) economic theory only became apparent during his brief, abruptly ending stint as a professor in Jena.[4] In the summer semester of 1947, he gave a lecture on trade policy, his traditional field of work, and the basic lecture course in general economics with exercises. In it, he covered microeconomics using the 'theoretical systems' of the English classics as well as those of Marx, Marshall, Wieser and Oppenheimer. In addition, there was a seminar on economics. In the winter semester of 1947/48, the second, macroeconomic part of the basic lecture with exercises followed, alongside an introduction to economics, a lecture on trade policy, and exercises in theoretical economics and the history of economic doctrines. In the summer semester of 1948, Paulsen expanded his range of courses to include lectures on economic policy, the economic and social development of Germany in the nineteenth century and public finance. The plan he had begun in the winter semester of 1948/49 to round off his teaching canon with lectures on theoretical economics, money and credit and again on the history of economic doctrines remained unfinished because, as already mentioned, he was forced to give up his professorship and leave Jena at the end of 1948 due to political reprisals.

Austrian-born Rudolf Schilcher (1919–1975) had decided to study economics in Jena after receiving treatment for his serious war injuries in a hospital in the city, because at that time the duration of study in this subject was—as he later liked to say—the shortest (Rieter, 2010: 167). From his own experience, he therefore knew that Paulsen's courses were attended and particularly appreciated by the majority of students, because they offered a contrasting programme to the obligatory Marxist, or more precisely, Leninist-Stalinist political economy. Paulsen probably only wrote one text from those days that documents his desire to adhere to traditional problems of theoretical economics (Paulsen, 1947). It is a contribution for the magazine *Forum*, a publication of the SED youth organisation *Freie Deutsche Jugend* (Free German Youth), which had invited him to comment on the question of the 'present situation of economic science and the current problems of political economy'. In his statement, Paulsen (ibid.: 286) emphasizes, among other things, that 'the object of knowledge of the previous [!] pure theory has not become obsolete,' and justifies the 'ideal type' of the 'free market economy' as 'one among many possible (that is, logically consistent) orders of the national economy.' His article is an important historical document, showing as it does that in 1947 Paulsen, like other academics in the Soviet occupation zone (Rieter, 2021: 262–282), still believed he could teach and research relatively freely, although the SED regime had long since tightened the ideological thumbscrews. The fact that he also tried to impart Keynesian ideas in his lectures was even less to the liking of the new regime. It was probably to counter this influence on the student body that a lecture on *Keynes vom Standpunkt des Marxismus aus gesehen* (Keynes from a Marxist point of view) was added to the summer semester 1949 study programme. It was given by a loyal SED comrade—Bruno Warnke, who had been appointed to the Chair of Political Economy.

---

[4] I gratefully acknowledge the detailed information about Paulsen's teaching in Jena that I received from Dr. Uwe Dathe of the Thuringian University and State Library in Jena.

In the summer semester of 1949, Paulsen resumed his teaching activities at the Free University of Berlin with full commitment. Apart from a lecture on free and market economy, his earlier field of interest, his course was entirely focused on economic and financial theory. In the following semesters, the teaching announcements reflect his increasing engagement with Keynesianism. Corresponding courses supplemented the multi-part lecture cycle on economic theory: including among others, 'Modern economic theory, in particular the Keynesian system' (winter semester 1949/50), 'Colloquium on selected chapters of modern theory' (summer semester 1950), 'Theory of the business cycle and general theory of employment' (summer semester 1951) and 'Colloquium on capital formation and investment' (winter semester 1952/53). As early as August 1950, Paulsen published a book (1950a) to which he permanently owes the reputation of having been one of the early German-speaking heralds of Keynesianism after 1945: *Neue Wirtschaftslehre. Einführung in die Wirtschaftstheorie von John Maynard Keynes und die Wirtschaftspolitik der Vollbeschäftigung* (New Economics. Introduction to the Economic Theory of John Maynard Keynes and the Economic Policy of Full Employment).[5] Further editions quickly followed: a second, 'revised and expanded' (Paulsen, 1952), a third, 'recast and expanded' (Paulsen, 1954a), a fourth, 'unchanged' (Paulsen, 1958) and finally, in 1969, a reprint of the last edition. In addition, the book was translated into Spanish and published by an Argentinian publishing house (Paulsen, 1957a). He also gives Keynesianism a lot of space in his four-volume textbook *Allgemeine Volkswirtschaftslehre* (General Economics), which has been in print since 1956, has been widely published in the popular *Sammlung Göschen* (Göschen collection) and has also been translated into Spanish (Paulsen, 1959b–1963). From the first to the last edition, this applies not only to the thematically relevant volumes III (production factors) and IV (total employment, business cycles, growth). In the introductory volume I (foundations, economic cycle) and in volume II (households, enterprises, markets), he already clearly points out elements of Keynesian economics to the reader because he considers them to be theoretically and empirically groundbreaking: In volume I, it is the criticism of the so-called classical dogma of harmony of the optimal self-regulation of a (free) market economy (Paulsen, 1956a: 103, 1970a: 126). In volume II, he presents Keynes' theory of consumption and saving by placing it at the beginning of the neoclassical microeconomics presentation (Paulsen, 1956b, 1970b: each ch. II). For teaching and examination purposes, the four volumes were supplemented by exercises and solutions, which, since 1967, were compiled in two volumes by Wilhelm Wedig (1931–2016), Paulsen's long-standing assistant and later professor at the Berlin School of Economics.

[5] Paulsen had probably already written the manuscript for it—at least in large part—during his time in Jena, because his lecture in the winter semester of 1949/50 on 'Modern Economic Theory', in particular the 'System of Keynes', was apparently based on it. This is confirmed by the lecture notes that I received from Jürgen Pahlke, who was then an economics student of the first generation at the Free University Berlin and from 1968 to 1989 Professor of Public Finance at the Ruhr University Bochum (Rieter, 2015: 155).

3.3 Paulsen's Approach to Keynesianism

To understand the perspective from which and the motivation with which Paulsen approached Keynesianism and what prompted him to commit himself to it in a certain way, one must visualise his path into academia, the stages of which I have outlined in the previous section. He came from practice and abruptly switched to academia. Economists, on the other hand, who have already spent their entire professional life or large parts of it as academics and take their profession seriously, are inevitably obliged to take note of developments in the field, to find *nolens volens* an attitude to them and to defend that attitude if necessary. In the case of the so-called Keynesian revolution, such colleagues have been dealing with this since 1936. Paulsen, on the other hand, had to join this scientific discourse and position himself more or less spontaneously after 1945. In doing so, he was apparently supported by a certain understanding of science that was probably also nourished by his practical economic experience, which he never abandoned or modified and always reaffirmed (see, among others, 1950c, 1955): Beyond 'speculative systems' that aim at 'Wesenserkenntnis [recognition of essence] of the economy', an 'exact, i.e. provable' analysis is indispensable (1955: 16), because: 'Without theory, it is not even possible to organise real phenomena, let alone make them comprehensible in their contexts' (1950c: 4). It alone creates the conditions for explaining real phenomena and solving real problems. Therefore, he decrees (1955: 17): 'Analytical theory has an *instrumental* character. Because to the extent that economic interrelationships are revealed through analysis, it is in principle possible to influence them.' It is this conviction that ultimately justifies his interest in economic theory, including that of Keynes, which is directed towards practical application. In fact, he went one step further (ibid.: 13): 'In particular, I want to ask to what extent the organisation of social economic activity can be made controllable by scientific insights.' This is precisely what the subtitle of his *Neue Wirtschaftslehre* (New Economics) implies, in that it explicitly emphasises the economic policy of full employment as the perspective of his book. In the preface to the first edition, he writes (1950a: V): Economic science owes to Keynes' 'New Economics', on the one hand, 'new goals and methods of research', which, however, 'do not depend on the adoption of Keynes' actual system'! That is one thing, but 'it can be said even more decisively that the economic policy of most Western states has undergone a change that can only be explained by the new theoretical approach, and thus by the work of Keynes'. In other words, Paulsen became a Keynesian above all because in Keynes' theory he found a set of instruments that can seemingly solve a dangerous problem of Western economies, both today and tomorrow: namely, to eliminate unemployment and ensure full employment in order to avoid economic stagnation and a loss of prosperity.

This focus is not only expressed in the preface of Paulsen's book. It is also revealed by certain recommended reading selections for 'An Introduction to the Keynesian System' (1950a: 253) and, in addition, to its economic policy significance (ibid.: 253 f.). Apart from the writings of well-known Keynes exegetes

(Dillard, Klein, Joan Robinson, Harrod, Lerner, Pigou, Samuelson, Alvin Hansen et al.), which are still common today and which Paulsen includes in his book, he names six works in the first edition up to the last (1950a: 253 f., 1952: 265 f., 1954a and 1958: 373 f.), that he particularly recommends reading. This is surprising at first, because their authors neither systematically introduce Keynesian theory nor intend to deepen it. The fact that Paulsen nevertheless presents them can be explained by their specific focus: They all revolve around just one economic and/or political issue—that of underemployment and full employment under the auspices of the conditions in the last years of the Second World War or shortly thereafter. In doing so, they primarily refer to Great Britain and the USA. I will briefly characterise these six books.

First, there is John Strachey's *A Program for Progress* (1940). Strachey (1901–1963) was a much-acclaimed writer and English politician in his active days and a colourful personality.[6] Initially, he was close to the later fascist leader Oswald Mosley, but then turned to the Labour Party, sat for them in the House of Commons, took on government posts and loudly propagated Marxist views. He increasingly distanced himself from this in the 1930s and began writing books about how capitalism should be reformed. He was clearly influenced by Roosevelt's New Deal in the US and Keynesianism, whose economic policy agenda seemed to serve his political goals (Strachey, 1940: 43): 'The school of economists of whom Mr. Keynes is the principal spokesman have made a detailed study of what will be the effect in combatting stagnation of the re-employment of men, either directly or indirectly, by the Government. Let us follow their argument [...], for it will enable us to see both the importance and the strict limitations of a programme of public enterprise, as part of the general economic policy which we are seeking'. The second work that Paulsen recommends as a Keynesian *vademecum* points in the same direction, albeit from a different, more liberal perspective, as can be seen from the title: Edward Victor Morgan's book *The Conquest of Unemployment* (1947). It was published by Hugh Molson, a well-known Conservative politician of the time, as part of his *Britain in the Future Series*. Morgan (1915–1996), who taught at various English universities during his lifetime, was actually a specialist in monetary economics, particularly monetary history. However, Morgan's main topic in this book is not the monetary aspects of the *General Theory*, but rather he (ibid.: 6) intends 'to present the most up-to-date results of that work'. In his view, these are 'the reasons for the failure to provide full employment'.

Thirdly, Paulsen sees Kenneth E. Boulding's monograph *The Economics of Peace* (1945a), which was published in German translation in the same year (1945b), as a suitable 'introduction to the Keynes system'. At first glance, this is confusing, since, contrary to Boulding's (1945a: vi, 1945b: 9) explicitly stated 'obligation to the ideas of Lord Keynes', little of it can be found in concrete and systematic terms in his wide-ranging descriptions and analyses. There were probably two reasons

[6] It is therefore not surprising that several biographies have been written about him, the most recent by Noel Thomsen, John Strachey. *An Intellectual Biography,* Palgrave Macmillan, London 1993.

why Paulsen nevertheless recommended the book to his readers and often quoted from it in his own writings. Firstly, he probably liked the fact that Boulding (1992: 49) had come to the conclusion in those years, as he explained in retrospect, 'that if one were going to study any section of the real social world, one could not do this with just economics'. With this view, he became one of the most well-known proponents of the 'integration of social science' (ibid.) and thus accepted being labelled an outsider by the guild of standard economics. On the other hand, one has to bear in mind the circumstances of the time in order to understand the appeal of the book in general and specifically to Paulsen. The terrible war had just ended, and the material and immaterial damage it had caused proved to be so devastating that many people could not even imagine how things could get better. In his book, the avowed pacifist Boulding countered this sense of hopelessness with a vision of an 'economics of peace' that promised golden times (1945a: vi, 1945b: 8 f.): 'For all its darkness, this is a millenial age. For the first time in human history, a world without poverty and without war is technically possible.' He took this view quite literally, because he placed all his hopes in the anticipated technological progress. Paulsen was particularly receptive to this idea, since, as already mentioned, he had already devoted himself intensively to the topic of economic and social renewal during his time in Leipzig and Jena and had great hopes for technological innovations.

Among the works that Paulsen recommends to readers in all editions of his *New Economics* as further important literature on Keynesianism, three publications stand out that are also explicitly dedicated to the employment problem and its significance for the design of the peace economy after 1945: In 1947, the Institute for Economic Research at ETH Zurich, which had been headed by the Zurich economist Eugen Böhler since its foundation in 1938, published a study on employment policy in a democracy in its series of publications on the question of job creation, which had by and large already been completed by the end of the war. The author, Charles La Roche (1923–1973), reports on the goals, principles and methods of Anglo-Saxon and Swedish post-war plans (as the subtitle suggests). He does this in a profound way, with many elements of Keynesian thinking explicitly flowing into his analysis. Paulsen also considers the six studies that were prepared at the Oxford University Institute of Statistics and published in 1944 in a volume entitled *The Economics of Full Employment* to be equally significant. Three of the six authors were German economists (Frank A. Burchardt, who also served as editor, Ernst Fritz Schumacher and Kurt Mandelbaum). They had to emigrate after 1933 because of the Nazi regime and their expertise was now in strong demand (Hagemann, 2024: 32, see also 47). Although Keynesian arguments and hypotheses are rarely quoted directly, according to Burchardt (1944: 19), it is at least 'the gist of this theory'—'systematically developed in the thirties by Lord Keynes and a number of other economists'—that 'forms the background of the studies in this book'. The same spirit pervades the report on *National and International Measures for Full Employment*, which the Economic and Social Council of the United Nations had asked five experts, including John Maurice Clark, Nicholas Kaldor and Arthur Smithies, to produce in 1949. Paulsen (1950a: V f., 1954a and 1958: 5) repeatedly recommends it as a deeper reading.

3.4 Paulsen's Keynesianism

In the very first sentences of his preface to the first edition of *New Economics*, Paulsen (1950a: V) asserts that 'the entire newer economic theory' was only 'revolutionised' by Keynes' *General Theory* to the extent that 'all modern theory has gone through Keynes and is always also an examination of Keynes, even when he is not mentioned'. In this sense, the 'central significance' of the 'question raised by Keynes about the determinants of the level of employment [...] is independent of whether, like Keynes, one assumes the possibility of an equilibrium at underemployment, or, contrary to Keynes, an economically autonomous tendency towards full employment'. Paulsen's adaptation of the *General Theory* is based on four key points, to which, in my opinion, he has consistently adhered (e. g. Paulsen, 1968: 17): (1) 'Due to the prevailing conditions of the time, the problem of underemployment (unemployment) came to the fore for Keynes'. However, his 'theoretical discussions' concern 'the determinants of the level of employment in general'. (2) 'Keynes' system is, in principle, static or comparative-static in construction.' (3) 'The analytical methods developed by Keynes [...] are independent in their application from the adoption of the system as a whole.' (4) 'In the course of general theoretical development, the Keynesian system has not remained dogmatically rigid.' Following these guidelines, Paulsen taught—in keeping with Axel Leijonhufvud's well-known play on words—'Keynesian economics' rather than 'the economics of Keynes', and this, of course, limited to their development and the respective state of literature up to the 1960s, when Paulsen began to turn his attention to other topics.

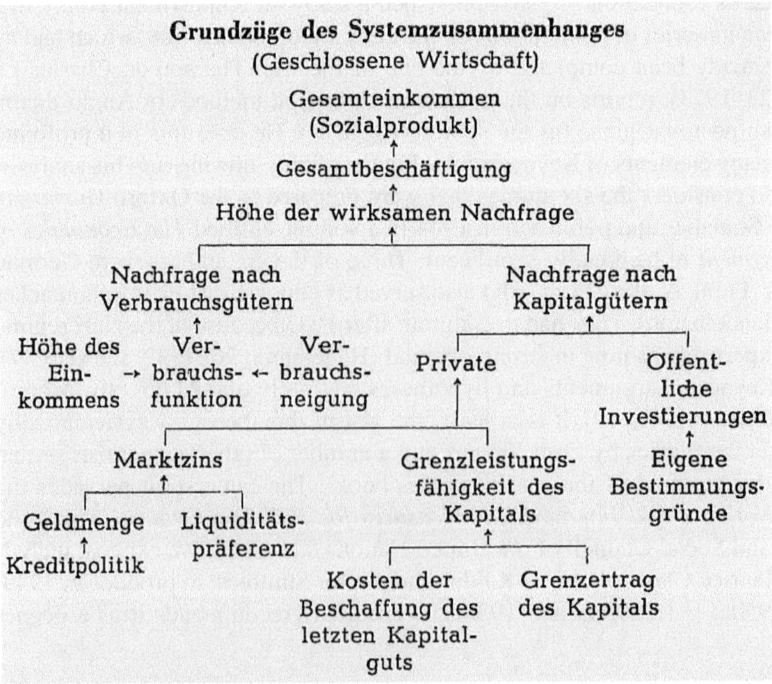

In the diagram shown here for a closed economy (1950a: 66, 1954a and 1958: 46), Paulsen outlines how he recognises the 'basic features of the system context' in Keynes. The presentation 'has only didactic significance' (*ibid.*). This is true insofar as he made frequent use of it in his lectures. However, there is more to it than that. The arrow scheme, which Paulsen deliberately chose, corresponds to his instrumental understanding of economic theory. It traces chains of effects, i.e. functional and perhaps even causal relationships, which allow him to draw economic policy conclusions that are geared towards certain economically and socially desirable goals. In this case, Paulsen's desire to always keep an eye on the applicability of a theory also manifests itself in the fact that he explicitly points out (*ibid.*) that he has not 'registered all the relationships', namely the effects of the multiplier and acceleration principles on the demand for capital and consumer goods. In line with his instrumental approach, his analysis of *New Economics* culminates at the end of the book in chapters with extensive discussions of an anti-cyclical employment policy, especially by means of fiscal policy measures (1950a: VII, 1954a or 1958: XII, XIII).

Paulsen's diagram implies that Keynesianism should be traced mainly in the lines in which it was primarily steered by John R. Hicks and Alvin H. Hansen at the end of the 1930s and in the 1940s and 1950s—as a modelling of the economy that captures the determinants of macroeconomic aggregates and their interdependent relationships, as postulated by Keynes, in functional equations in order to show in comparative analysis under which conditions equilibrium and disequilibrium states of aggregate employment and the national product arise. This approach, often referred to as 'standard Keynesianism', is not, however, regarded by Paulsen (1954a and 1958: 53) as an immovable 'dogma' of economic thought. Rather, he hopes for a fruitful 'merger of what is referred to as the classical tradition with these new approaches'. In this sense, with his *New Economics*, he dares, as it were, the balancing act of reconciling the original, Keynes' *General Theory*, with its transformations and reinterpretations, primarily in the Anglo-Saxon literature, but also with non-Keynesian theories. Rudolf Schilcher (1974: 204) therefore accurately speaks of 'a synthesis of an independent and memorable kind' that distinguishes Paulsen's work 'from other German-language writings on comparable topics, such as the well-known Schneider's "Introduction to Economic Theory"'.

What Paulsen calls the 'Keynesian system' consists of the well-known building blocks: income dependence of consumption and saving, marginal efficiency of capital, liquidity theory of interest with associated demand theory for money, expectation orientation of economic action, concept of effective demand, refutation of Say's theorem, multiplier effects, etc. In the third edition of his *New Economics* (1954a), which was increased by a good 100 pages, and in the fourth volume of his *General Economics* (1960 ff.), he broadened and deepened the analysis on the basis of the rapidly growing Keynes literature, particularly with regard to monetary and interest rate theory, multiplier and accelerator analysis, transmission mechanisms between the real and monetary sectors (Keynes effect, Pigou effect) and, in addition, in many details. In deriving the equilibrium for both sectors and the economy as a whole, Paulsen (e.g. 1959a: 153 f., 1969: 172 f.) follows the well-known 'suggested interpretation' of Hicks, the so-called IS/LM model, which became a school of thought by assuming given expectations for Keynesian macroeconomic behavioural functions and postulating stable equilibrium states. Because the effects of only vaguely quantifiable or even unquantifiable expectations are relegated to the *ceteris paribus* conditions of the model as parameters, they are cancelled and preserved at the same time so that the functional relationships between the independent and dependent variables can be quantitatively examined.

As is well known, Keynes vehemently opposed the interpretation of his theory in a way that limits or neutralises qualitative, hardly or not at all measurable factors.[7] In his reply to the first criticisms of his *General Theory* by prominent economists (Taussig, Leontief, Robertson, Viner), he (1937: 111) insists: 'I am more attached to the comparatively simple ideas which underlie my theory [...]'. That is (1936: 162 f.): 'We are merely reminding ourselves that human decisions affecting the future, whether personal or political or economic, cannot depend on strict mathematical expectations, since the basis for making such calculations does not exist [...]'. The economic conclusions that Keynes draws from this (see Rieter, 1985) are, as is well known, supported by all sorts of psychologisms ('propensities', 'motives', 'instincts', 'illusions', 'animal spirits', 'love of money', 'confidence' et al.), which is why he was and is scolded by economists who work quantitatively and mathematically, as well as by those who trust behavioural science approaches. Paulsen (1954a or 1958: 26 f., see also 1969: 116) sees it differently: 'The importance of this formation of expectations in the Keynesian system cannot be emphasised enough; psychological factors are explicitly taken into account as determining factors of the system in important places', since (Paulsen, 1954a or 1958: 27 f., see also 51) 'behaviour is always guided by psychologically influenced expectations [...] and a theory that abstracts from the influence of psychological factors on economic decisions, is too far removed from reality to be able to interpret it sufficiently'. Paulsen emphasises the problem of successfully endogenising expectations in the 'Keynes system' (Paulsen, 1950a: 131): 'Perhaps it will be shown that the incorporation of this eminently dynamic factor cannot be reconciled with a static basic version of the theoretical system, and that its significance is thus even greater than is expressed by Keynes himself'.

The unease that can be sensed here regarding the (comparatively) static and short-term equilibrium methodology of the 'Keynes system' prompted Paulsen to look more intensively at the possibilities of dynamisation. In doing so, he did not abandon Keynes by any means, because (1954a or 1958: 51; similarly already 1950a: 92, 1950b: 31) 'the *dynamic* content of his theorems [...] is in the whole way of thinking, which consequently leads to the rejection of the mechanical orientation of the system towards a stable equilibrium [...]'. But (1960: 290) 'Keynes still hesitates at the threshold of the transition to the dynamic formulation of his problems'.

[7] Keynes was generally annoyed by interpretations of his work that he considered to be far-fetched. In a letter to A. C. Pigou dated 10 December 1938, he writes: 'What on earth is one to do? One feels rather a fool writing repeated rejoinders on these papers. But if one does not, future commentators, who seldom look up the original, will assume that one accepts the interpretation.' (*The Collected Writings of John Maynard Keynes, XIV,* edited by Donald Moggridge, Macmillan St. Martin's Press, London and Basingstoke 1973: 272).

Paulsen sees the harbingers of such a desirable 'transition' in Dennis Robertson's period analysis to determine the generation and use of income (1950a: 87–89, 1954a or 1958: 82–85) and in the approach of the Stockholm School (1950a: 90–92, 1954a or 1958: 85–87) to not fixate on equilibrium states in theory, but to model equilibrium and disequilibrium macroeconomic processes using an *ex-ante/ex post* methodology in which the formation of ökexpectations is central. Paulsen took part in the discussion, which was partly linked to this, to explore the possibilities and conditions for making macroeconomics more dynamic.

In a lengthy essay (1954b), Paulsen compares how Keynes and Wicksell derive the 'system equilibrium' of the economy using different theoretical requisites. However, Paulsen is not content with mere comparison. He further develops the Keynesian approach in an original way (see Hesse 2010: 300 f.) by determining the macroeconomic equilibrium in a marginal analysis through the interest rate, which balances the marginal costs of money supply with the marginal utility of liquidity. Hesse (ibid.) sees this as a pioneering achievement in that Paulsen 'propagates the existence of a neoclassical balancing mechanism via the marginal utility of the demand for money for the money market, which, given the year of printing, can be considered revolutionary for German monetary theory'. Paulsen builds a bridge to Keynes' approach by showing how the decisions of those who demand money, which they align with price and interest rate expectations, are able to stabilise or destabilise equilibria. With this proof, he sees himself confirmed in the view (1954b: 219 f.) 'that Keynes derives the system equilibrium in the case of underemployment not only from insufficient price and wage mobility, but from the influence of expectations on economic behaviour, and more precisely from the *uncertainty* of the future under the influence of behaviour'.

Paulsen is of the opinion (1950b: 17), however, that such refinements, though ingenious they may be, are pseudo-dynamic, 'since the subsequent integration of dynamics into a static model cannot succeed, but economics must work dynamically from the ground up'. In many of his writings (1949: 32–36, 1950b: 31–42, 1954c: 322, 1966a, 1966b: 308, 1968: 9–12; see also Koblitz & Rieter, 1979), he criticises or qualifies the (comparatively) static methodology with its equilibrium concept, because it cannot adequately depict the economic process to be explained. Instead, he would like to see an economic theory (1950b: 25) 'that is not static in its basic structure, but dynamic, because it incorporates events in time into its heuristic formulations and thus understands ratio as typical economic behaviour in a way that includes anticipation'. In the sense of such 'heuristic settings', he transfers Keynes' hypothesis of a conceivable liquidity preference in the holding of money to 'decisions about production and consumption' (ibid.: 54–70). In addition, he sees psychological factors in risk, chance and gambling that influence the formation of economic expectations and should therefore be included in a dynamic theory that aims to adequately reflect the uncertainty of the future.

Finally, it should be mentioned that Paulsen also received and extensively dealt with Keynesian stagnation theory. As Rudolf Schilcher told me, it was therefore entirely in Paulsen's interest that his student decided to write his doctoral thesis on the concept of long-term unemployment in modern economic theory, particularly in the work of Alvin H. Hansen and J. M. Keynes (Schilcher, 1952). While Paulsen only briefly touched on the so-called stagnation thesis in his textbook (e.g. 1968: 171–174) and in his lectures, he discusses it thoroughly in his *New Economics* (1950a: 143–149 and passim, 1954a or 1958: 302–307 and passim)—and indeed in the way that was widespread at the time (see Kurz, 2021: 32–37) as a structural problem of 'mature' capitalist economies, in which—roughly speaking—the propensity to save is too great and the propensities to consume and invest is too low because, due to the growing capital stock, the marginal efficiency of capital is too low and, due to the liquidity preference, the monetary interest rate is 'caught' in the liquidity trap. In weighing the pros and cons of this reasoning, Paulsen argues with a consideration that is typical of him and goes beyond the purely economic (1950a: 141): In 'human existence' there are 'polar decisions' such as those between progress and security [...]. Secular development seems to push the security factor more to the fore, and this is reflected in the fact that a declining willingness on the part of entrepreneurs to take risks is often observed—a consequence of social change and the greater maturity of the capitalist world'. In this respect, 'psychological and institutional factors have led to the formulation of the *stagnation thesis* [...]' (ibid., similarly 1954a or 1958: 142).

3.5 Paulsen's Contribution to the Spread of Keynesianism in German-Speaking Countries

In the preface to the second edition of his *New Economics*, Paulsen (1952: V) expressly asserts, 'it is not intended to persuade people to adopt "Keynesianism"'. He did not need to do so, however, as he had succeeded in convincingly conveying Keynesian doctrine in a critically appropriated form. Andreas Paulsen, Erich Schneider and Erich Preiser were the first in Germany after 1945 to make Keynesian economics heard and were instrumental in helping it to ultimately achieve a breakthrough in teaching and research as well as in public perception. In doing so, they had to overcome fierce resistance to the new economic thinking well into the 1950s. The 'straw fire of reception'—as Jan-Otmar Hesse (2010: 48) put it—was followed by 'a restoration of old economic thinking, primarily for institutional reasons'. The majority of the professors still working at the time saw themselves as students or descendants of the historical-ethical school and its satellites, or defended classical, liberal or neoclassical positions. One only has to think of the violent, often polemical anti-Keynesian attacks by the eloquent liberal economist and publicist Wilhelm Röpke or the 'new classical' Adolf Weber, the doyen of the German economic guild in the 1940s, or Weber's student Erich Carell, to name just a few (cf. ibid.: 48 f., 292–296, Rieter, 2021: 279 f.). Paulsen also faced such headwinds. The review of his *New Economics* by Karl Muhs (1953) in one of the most renowned German journals is indicative of this. Muhs (1891–1954), who had been a professor of economics in Halle from 1934 to 1945 and received a teaching position for 'economic-social systems of ideas' from the Free University of Berlin in 1950/51, piquantly considers the work of his faculty colleague with a rather poisoned praise (ibid.: 371): Paulsen's 'representation is an expression of the most mature art of interpretation […] of *Keynes's* world of thought […], in order to fully open up *Keynes's* work to German literature, insofar [!] as […] a commendable achievement emerges in it. If we nevertheless object in essential respects, it is because *Paulsen* […] completely identifies with the master's views, without ever seeking the approach of critical probing […]'.

Paulsen contributed to making Keynesianism known in a variety of ways. On the one hand, he succeeded with his publications, and on the other hand with his teaching. He achieved a broad impact with the four volumes of his *Allgemeine Volkswirtschaftslehre* (General Economics), which were published in high numbers in the popular Göschen collection from 1956 to 1970, at times annually.[8] Almost every economics student at German-speaking universities used it as a handy compendium, especially since it presented not only Keynesian macroeconomics, but also the second main stream of modern economic thought, neoclassical microeconomics, both verbally and formally. Paulsen's *New Economics*, which was addressed rather to professionals, also attracted a great deal of attention. It was often cited and sold well.[9] Paulsen was not a university lecturer who excelled rhetorically and kept his audience entertained with anecdotes. Nevertheless, his usually free lecture style was captivating, as he regularly embedded the respective course material in overarching contexts and spontaneously varied it. It was demanding and forced the audience to think and follow the line of reasoning. There were several reasons why his four-hour basic lectures on general economics were so popular. According to the examination and study regulations, they were compulsory for all economics students. It was necessary to attend them regularly because—well into the 1950s—participation had to be certified by the lecturer in the course book. Since the number of economics students rose to around 1000 during the period in question, Paulsen's lectures took place in the university's main auditorium and often had to be transmitted to another lecture hall via loudspeaker. There, an assistant was confronted with the thankless task of blindly tracing the drawings and formulas that the master illustrated and explained in the main lecture hall, with a piece of chalk in hand on a blackboard. There are other reasons that explain the enormous popularity of these lectures. They were accompanied by two-hour exercises, which Rudolf Schilcher (on him, see Rieter, 2010: 167) held for many years, initially as Paulsen's assistant and then as a habilitated lecturer. He did an excellent job of preparing the material covered in the lectures, supplementing and deepening it. In this respect, the lectures and exercises formed a single unit.

---

[8] Werner Schuder, the authorised signatory of the Walter de Gruyter publishing house and at that time the manager of the Göschen collection, told me years ago that the print run of the individual volumes was in the region of 10,000 copies.

[9] The Franz Vahlen publishing house was no longer able to determine the exact number of the various print runs. According to the memory of the publishing director Dieter Sobotka, whom I once asked about it, there were 3000 copies of each edition, which had also been sold.

In addition, an anonymously written[10] mimeographed scriptum *Repetitorium der gesamten Volkswirtschaftstheorie* (repetitorium of the entire economic theory) in five parts was widely distributed among the students, which supposedly presented Paulsen's economic theory in a way that was suitable for exams. Especially in the fourth part, under the title 'The Special Macroeconomic Theory', Paulsen's understanding of Keynesian doctrine was presented. But it was not so much because of such an advantageous learning aid that the majority of students chose Paulsen as their academic teacher and examiner in economic theory. Rather, his range of courses was attractive and considered modern because it was primarily tailored to the newer, neoclassical and Keynesian theory. The decision in favour of Paulsen was further favoured by the fact that the only parallel chair was occupied from 1948 to 1962 by Friedrich Bülow (1890–1962), an old-school economist (Rieter, 2010: 92–106), or rather was represented by him until his death. Bülow was not very familiar with the latest developments in economics and their mathematical and econometric methods and therefore turned more to sociology in his teaching and research (ibid.: 73–80).

Of Paulsen's students who remained committed to economics, Rudolf Schilcher was certainly the one who most closely resembled his teacher in his way of thinking. He taught and researched in this tradition, incorporating newer Keynesian and monetarist approaches, and did so increasingly after he accepted the call to the newly founded Ruhr University Bochum in 1965 to fill the chair of theoretical economics. Many others who had studied under Paulsen also became academics at universities or research institutes, or succeeded in business, administration or politics. They too more or less continued to pursue and develop what they had learned from Paulsen (see Schilcher, 1964, Ollenburg & Wedig, 1979, Rieter, 2015: 153–155).

The reception of Keynesianism in West Germany after the war and its subsequent establishment there in both academic and political circles was observed and commented on with conspicuous intensity in East Germany. Paulsen's positioning played an important role here, as he was considered 'probably the most prominent German-speaking neo-Keynesian' in the GDR (Müller, 1972: 185). In their presentation of Keynesian doctrine or Keynesianism, leading political economists (including Müller, 1967, 1972: 44–185; Behrens, 1981: 213–248) preferred to look through Paulsen's glasses. In that they were guided by his *New Economics* and the corresponding chapters of his *General Economics* and often quoted—mostly correctly—from it. In their assessment of the 'bourgeois economist Paulsen' and his point of view, however, they adhered to the prescribed ideological language. They discredit the Keynesian models, as they called it, 'functional models of state-monopoly regulation' as a 'typical vulgar economic view of state-monopoly capitalism as an

[10] The author was Manfred Melzer (1934–2011?), a student in a later semester when I began studying at the Free University Berlin in 1956. After graduating, Melzer worked from 1962 to 1994 at the *Deutsches Institut für Wirtschaftsforschung* (German Institute for Economic Research) in Berlin, primarily as an expert on the economy of the GDR, on which he published extensively. In 1979, he received his doctorate with a relevant topic at the Free University Berlin.

economic mixed system' (Kahl, 1989: 414) and as the 'dominant conception of the monopoly bourgeoisie' (Behrens, 1981: 216).

3.6 Andreas Paulsen: A Keynesian Economic Theorist?

Paulsen was unquestionably an important interpreter of Keynesianism in the German-speaking world. But he was neither orthodox nor merely Keynesian. He refused to tie himself down as a scholar for two reasons. Firstly, for him (1966a: 143) 'there is no method monism in economic theory'. Therefore, he could not act as a 'normal scientist' (Thomas S. Kuhn), who feels part of a particular scientific community, defined by a firmly delimited paradigm and working with assigned roles to solve all its 'riddles'. On the other hand, he located economics in a structure of thought that includes social science and the humanities (1950c: 3): 'Economics is situated in the midst of the world of people and their social formations, not to be grasped with sharp edges as a limited area, but floating in a tension between the intellectual, the social and the material world'. Therefore, it is not enough just to 'explain the causal and functional relationships' of economic variables, but 'as a child of the mind, the economy wants to be *understood* and demands the empathetic experience of the actions of needy, willing, caring and judging people' (*ibid.*). In this respect, it goes without saying for Paulsen that economics must not avoid the question of how to balance the individual and social principles. He answers it in his writings and lectures to the effect that 'social justice must be guaranteed as a value norm of the economic order' (cf. Paulsen, 1948) so that people can live in dignity and freedom. All this reveals how Paulsen's thinking was rooted in historical-ethical traditions and did not exclude hermeneutic methods of cognition. That is why he also processed the relevant literature, in this case mostly in German, and this in almost all its breadth. To see this, it is enough to glance at the footnotes, bibliographies and indices of his writings.

For Paulsen (1950a: § 2), one of the 'Sinnfragen des Wirtschaftens' (questions of the sense of economic activity) was that (*ibid.*: 11) 'according to the social ideals of Western culture, the free human being [...] should not only see need and coercion in the economy, but also a part of his fulfilment of life [...]; thus, he must not be excluded from the possibility of achieving anything through no fault of his own and thus be placed outside of society [...]'. But 'anyone who believes that social upheaval caused by mass unemployment can be appeased by pointing out unbreakable inevitabilities is mistaken' (1954a or 1958: 5). He saw Keynes' *General Theory* as confirmation of this conviction, as it offered an instrumental approach that avoided such errors and promised an economic solution to the problem. Although Paulsen stuck to the original—as best he could and as often as possible—in his arguments, he was inevitably drawn into the mainstream of Keynesianism of the time, in the form of a comparative-static macroeconomic equilibrium analysis of income and employment, including their implications for business cycle theory. As we know, this concept quickly mutated into the 'neoclassical synthesis' (Samuelson), in which the equilibrium in case of underemployment discussed by Keynes now found its place in the neoclassical standard model as a special case that could only persist in a market and competitive economy as long as frictions, such as rigid prices and wages, an investment trap or an extreme liquidity preference, existed. However, Paulsen only partially implemented this theoretical turnaround. To my knowledge, he neither used the term 'neoclassical synthesis' nor explicitly dealt with this concept. However, it is clear that he did not necessarily trust the so-called self-healing powers of the market and competition (1968: 65): 'In reality, the assumed responsiveness of prices and wages does not exist.' Moreover, it should even be considered (1954c: 322 f.) 'whether or not rigid prices increase the degree of stability of the system'.

In the 1960s, Paulsen was also interested in a whole range of other scientific topics. In a letter dated 28 December 1959, he tells his friend and colleague Friedrich Lütge that he plans to 'try to bring some intellectual order to my plans in the new year. Probably the "main business" of the near future will be the problem of economic growth and inflationary pressure, including the conditions of the so-called developing countries'. And he did not just plan. From then on, Paulsen gave lectures and wrote essays on the subject of developing countries (e.g. 1960a, 1963) and, to an even greater extent, on economic growth (1960b, 1966a, 1966b, see also Schilcher, 1964). Insofar as he refers to Keynes in these works, he once again reminds us of the 'ultimate independent variables' (1966a: 156), namely the 'psychological components for determining economic activity', which Keynes 'inserted in a central place' of his *General Theory* (1960b: 291). He always maintained that he recognised in them an approach that promised to supplement or possibly replace the comparative-static methodology with a more realistic, dynamic analysis of macroeconomic adjustment processes. I believe that helping to fulfil such a theoretical promise was Paulsen's most important concern as an economic theorist.

Rudolf Schilcher, who accompanied and worked with Paulsen the longest on his academic journey as a student, assistant and colleague, speaks of the 'unmistakable "Paulsen style"' (1974: 205) and characterises it as such (*ibid.*): 'This can be seen in a kind of dichotomy. On the one hand, Paulsen strove intensively for formal, often mathematically formulated precision in his statements. [...] On the other hand, however, he was never released from the question of the "Sinn" [meaning, sense] that lies in or behind the formally described phenomena. The socio-philosophical and socio-political background to economic problems was not separated out by Paulsen. [...] He [...] takes a position that assigns theory not to a cloud-cuckoo-land, but to this earth as a field of operation.' I am happy to add a third aspect to this judgement: Not least, Andreas Paulsen (1950c: 4) considered a good knowledge of the history of economics indispensable for solid research, teaching and learning. He demanded of students of economics that they 'have thoroughly read at least one of the great theorists of our science in the original text', because 'what they convey to us permanently is the boldness and discipline, the wide flight and the persistence of scientific thought, the methodology and ethics of scientific work in general'. A legacy that deserves more attention today!

References

Behrens, F. (1981). *Die bürgerliche Ökonomie in der allgemeinen Krise des Kapitalismus.* Akademie-Verlag, Berlin.

Boulding, K. E. (1945a). *The economics of peace*. Prentice-Hall, New York.

Boulding, K. E. (1945b). *Friedenswirtschaft*. Übersetzt von Hans Mast, A. Francke Verlag, Bern.

Boulding, K. E. (1992). Kenneth E. Boulding (born 1910). In: P. Arestis & M. Sawyer (Eds.), *A biographical dictionary of dissenting economists*. Edward Elgar, Aldershot and Brookfield, pp. 45–54.

Burchardt, F. A. (1944). Causes of unemployment. In: *The economics of full employment. Six studies in applied economics, prepared at The Oxford University Institute of Statistics* . Basil Blackwell, Oxford, pp. 1–38.

Hagemann, H. (2024). German-speaking émigré economists in Great Britain and the analysis of the German war economy. In: *History of Political Economy*, 56, annual suppl., pp. 30–52.

Hesse, J.-O. (2010). *Wirtschaft als Wissenschaft. Die Volkswirtschaftslehre in der frühen Bundesrepublik.* Campus Verlag, Frankfurt/New York.

Kahl, G. (1989). Paulsen, Andreas. In: *Ökonomenlexikon*. Hrsg. von Werner Krause, Karl-Heinz Graupner, Rolf Sieber. Dietz Verlag, Berlin, pp. 413–416.

Keynes, J. M. (1936). *The general theory of employment, interest and money*. Macmillan St Martin's Press, London and Basingstoke.

Keynes, J. M. (1937 [1973]). The general theory of employment. In: *The Quarterly Journal of Economics*, 51, pp. 209–223; repr. in: *The Collected Writings of John Maynard Keynes, XIV.* Edited by Donald Moggridge. Macmillan St Martin's Press, London and Basingstoke, pp. 109–123.

Koblitz, H. G., & Rieter, H. (1979). Wirtschaftliches Gleichgewicht – zum "Glanz-Verfall" der zentralen Konzeption der theoretischen Ökonomie. In: Ollenburg & Wedig (1979), pp. 243–273.

Kurz, H. D. (2021). The spectre of secular stagnation then and now. In: *Stagnations- und Deflationstheorien. Studien zur Entwicklung der ökonomischen Theorie XXXVIII.* Hrsg. von Volker Caspari. Duncker & Humblot, Berlin, pp. 9–51.

Morgan, E. V. (1947). *The conquest of unemployment*. Samson Low, Marston & Co., London.

Müller, K. (1967). Der Einfluß des Keynesianismus in Westdeutschland. In: *Bürgerliche Ökonomie im modernen Kapitalismus*. Hrsg. von Herbert Meißner. Dietz Verlag, [Ost-]Berlin, pp. 77–111.

Müller, K. O. W. (1972). *Neo-Keynesianismus. Kritische Untersuchung einer modernen Wirtschaftslehre des staatsmonopolistischen Kapitalismus*. 3. Auflage. verlag das europäische Buch, [West-]Berlin.

Muhs, K. (1953). *Review*: Paulsen, Andreas, Neue Wirtschaftslehre. Einführung in die Wirtschaftstheorie von John Maynard Keynes und die Wirtschaftspolitik der Vollbeschäftigung. Berlin und Frankfurt a. M., In: *Zeitschrift für die gesamte Staatswissenschaft*, 109, pp. 371–376.

North, M. (2010). Friedrich Lütge (1901–1968). In: *Studien zur Entwicklung der ökonomischen Theorie XXV: Die deutschsprachige Wirtschaftswissenschaft in den ersten Jahrzehnten nach 1945*. Hrsg. von Christian Scheer. Duncker & Humblot, Berlin, pp. 383–398.

Ollenburg, G., & Wedig, W. (Hrsg.). (1979). *Gleichgewicht, Entwicklung und soziale Bedingungen der Wirtschaft. Andreas Paulsen zum Gedenken anläßlich seines 80.* Geburtstages mit einer Auswahl von Schriften aus seinem Nachlaß. Duncker & Humblot, Berlin.

Paulsen, A. (1947). Zur Problemstellung der theoretischen Nationalökonomie. In: *Forum. Zeitschrift für das geistige Leben an den deutschen Hochschulen*, 1. Jahr, Heft 8/9, pp. 285–287.

Paulsen, A. (1948). *Soziale Gerechtigkeit als Wertnorm der Wirtschaftsordnung*. Richard Pflaum Verlag, München.

Paulsen, A. (1949). *Die Gestalt des Wirtschaftsmenschen in der theoretischen Nationalökonomie.* Erich Blaschker Verlag, Berlin.

Paulsen, A. (1950a). *Neue Wirtschaftslehre. Einführung in die Wirtschaftstheorie von John Maynard Keynes und die Wirtschaftspolitik der Vollbeschäftigung*. Verlag für Rechtswissenschaft, vormals Franz Vahlen, Berlin und Frankfurt a. M.

Paulsen, A. (1950b). *Liquidität und Risiko in der wirtschaftlichen Entwicklung. Ein Beitrag zur dynamischen Wirtschaftstheorie*. Verlag für Sozialwissenschaften, Frankfurt am Main, Berlin.

Paulsen, A. (1950c). *Wie studiert man Volkswirtschaftslehre?* In: *Mitteilungen der Freien Universität Berlin*, Heft 12, pp. 3–4.

Paulsen, A. (1952). *Neue Wirtschaftslehre. Einführung in die Wirtschaftstheorie von John Maynard Keynes und die Wirtschaftspolitik der Vollbeschäftigung. 2., neubearbeitete und erweiterte Auflage*. Verlag Franz Vahlen, Berlin und Frankfurt a. M.

Paulsen, A. (1954a). *Neue Wirtschaftslehre. Einführung in die Wirtschaftstheorie von John Maynard Keynes und die Wirtschaftspolitik der Vollbeschäftigung. 3., neugefaßte und erweiterte Auflage*. Verlag Franz Vahlen, Berlin und Frankfurt a. M.

Paulsen, A. (1954b). Zins und Systemgleichgewicht. Die Entwicklung des Problems bei Wicksell und Keynes. In: *Weltwirtschaftliches Archiv*, 73, pp. 171–228.

Paulsen, A. (1954c). Zum Theorem des Gleichgewichts einer freien Verkehrswirtschaft. In: *Veritas, Iustitia, Libertas*. Festschrift zur 200-Jahrfeier der Columbia University New York, überreicht von der Freien Universität Berlin und der Deutschen Hochschule für Politik Berlin. Colloquium-Verlag, Berlin, pp. 322–344.

Paulsen, A. (1955). Wirtschaftswissenschaft und die Wirtschaft unserer Zeit. In: *Feier der Rektoratsübergabe der Freien Universität Berlin am 4. November 1955 mit Akademischer Festrede von Professor Dr. Andreas Paulsen*. Berlin, pp. 13–27.

Paulsen, A. (1956a). *Allgemeine Volkswirtschaftslehre I: Grundlegung, Wirtschaftskreislauf*. Sammlung Göschen, Band 1169, Walter de Gruyter & Co., Berlin.

Paulsen, A. (1956b). *Allgemeine Volkswirtschaftslehre II: Haushalte, Unternehmungen, Marktformen*. Sammlung Göschen, Band 1170, Walter de Gruyter & Co., Berlin.

Paulsen, A. (1957a). *La nueva teoría económica. Una introducción a la teoría económica de John Maynard Keynes y a la política de pleno empleo*. Trad. del alemán por Adolfo von Ritter-Zahony. Supervisión por B. Rodríguez Meitín. Prólogo por Oreste Popescu. El Ateneo, Buenos Aires.

Paulsen, A. (1957b). *Universität und Wissenschaft in unserer Zeit. Akademische Ansprachen*. Veröffentlichung der Freien Universität Berlin.

Paulsen, A. (1957c). Vortrag. In: *Berliner Erfahrungen zur geistigen Auseinandersetzung zwischen Ost und West*. Bonner Universitätsreden zu öffentlichen Fragen, Heft 6, Peter Hanstein Verlag, Bonn, pp. 18–36.

Paulsen, A. (1958). *Neue Wirtschaftslehre. Einführung in die Wirtschaftstheorie von John Maynard Keynes und die Wirtschaftspolitik der Vollbeschäftigung. 4., unveränderte Auflage*. Verlag Franz Vahlen, Berlin und Frankfurt a. M.; Reprint 1969.

Paulsen, A. (1959a). *Allgemeine Volkswirtschaftslehre III: Produktionsfaktoren, Geldwesen*. Sammlung Göschen, Band 1171, Walter de Gruyter & Co., Berlin.

Paulsen, A. (1959b–1963). *Teoria general de la economica*. Tome 1–4. Union tipograhica editorial hispano americano, Mexico et al.

Paulsen, A. (1960a). Die Eingliederung armer Länder in den Prozeß der wirtschaftlichen Entwicklung. In: *Universitätstage 1960*. Veröffentlichung der Freien Universität Berlin. Walter de Gruyter & Co., Berlin, pp. 87–97.

Paulsen, A. (1960b). Bemerkungen zur methodischen Behandlung des Wirtschaftswachstums. In: *Festgabe für Friedrich Bülow zum 70*. Geburtstag. Hrsg. von Otto Stammer und Karl C. Thalheim. Duncker & Humblot, Berlin, pp. 287–299.

Paulsen, A. (1963). Unternehmer und Unternehmerleistungen in Entwicklungsländern. In: *Jahrbücher für Nationalökonomie und Statistik*, 175, pp. 385–411.

Paulsen, A. (1966a). *Zur Analytik von Ablaufsprozessen*. In: *Wirtschaftskreislauf und Wirtschaftswachstum. Carl Föhl zum 65. Geburtstag*. Hrsg. von Erich Schneider. Mohr (Paul Siebeck), Tübingen, pp. 143–159.

Paulsen, A. (1966b). Zur theoretischen Bestimmbarkeit der Rostowschen "Stadien". In: *Wirtschaft, Geschichte und Wirtschaftsgeschichte. Festschrift zum 65*. Geburtstag von Friedrich Lütge. Hrsg. von Wilhelm Abel, Knut Borchardt et al., Gustav Fischer Verlag, Stuttgart, pp. 306–324.

Paulsen, A. (1968). *Allgemeine Volkswirtschaftslehre IV: Gesamtbeschäftigung, Konjunkturen, Wachstum.* 5. Auflage, Sammlung Göschen, Band 1172, Walter de Gruyter & Co., Berlin.
Paulsen, A. (1969). *Allgemeine Volkswirtschaftslehre III: Produktionsfaktoren.* 6., ergänzte Auflage, Sammlung Göschen, Band 1171/1171a, Walter de Gruyter & Co., Berlin.
Paulsen, A. (1970a). *Allgemeine Volkswirtschaftslehre I: Grundlegung, Wirtschaftskreislauf. 9.* Auflage, Sammlung Göschen, Band 1169, Walter de Gruyter & Co., Berlin.
Paulsen, A. (1970b). *Allgemeine Volkswirtschaftslehre II: Haushalte, Unternehmungen, Marktformen. 9.* Auflage, Sammlung Göschen, Band 1170, Walter de Gruyter & Co., Berlin.
Rieter, H. (1985 [2014]). Hypothesen zur Erwartungsbildung bei Keynes und Schumpeter. In: *Studien zur Entwicklung der ökonomischen Theorie IV.* Hrsg. von Harald Scherf. Duncker & Humblot, Berlin, pp. 27–72; repr. in: Heinz Rieter, *Ökonomische Theoriegeschichte im zeithistorischen Kontext. Ausgewählte Aufsätze.* Hrsg. von Elisabeth Allgoewer et al., Metropolis-Verlag, Marburg 2014, pp. 155–203.
Rieter, H. (2010). Die Anfänge der Wirtschaftswissenschaft an der Freien Universität Berlin. Personen, Institutionen, Konflikte. In: *Studien zur Entwicklung der ökonomischen Theorie XXV: Die deutschsprachige Wirtschaftswissenschaft in den ersten Jahrzehnten nach 1945.* Hrsg. von Christian Scheer. Duncker & Humblot, Berlin, pp. 25–200.
Rieter, H. (2015). Die Rechts- und Wirtschaftswissenschaftliche bzw. Wirtschafts- und Sozialwissenschaftliche Fakultät im ersten Jahrzehnt der Freien Universität Berlin. In: *Beiträge zur Wissenschaftsgeschichte der Freien Universität Berlin,* Band 7. Hrsg. von Karol Kubicki und Siegward Lönnendonker. V&R unipress, Göttingen, pp. 125–181.
Rieter, H. (2021). Zum Einfluss emigrierter und remigrierter Ökonomen auf die Wirtschaftslehre und Wirtschaftspolitik in Deutschland nach 1945. In: *Belastete Beziehungen. Studien zur Wirkung von Exil und Remigration auf die Wissenschaften in Deutschland nach 1945.* Hrsg. von Kirsten Heinsohn und Rainer Nicolaysen. Wallstein Verlag, Göttingen, pp. 248–284.
Schilcher, R. (1952). *Das Konzept der Dauerarbeitslosigkeit in der neueren Wirtschaftstheorie, insbesondere bei Alvin H. Hansen und J. M. Keynes.* Dissertation, Freie Universität Berlin.
Schilcher, R. (Hrsg.). (1964). *Wirtschaftswachstum. Beiträge zur ökonomischen Theorie und Politik.* Walter de Gruyter & Co., Berlin.
Schilcher, R. (1974). Andreas Paulsen zum 75. Geburtstag. In: *Konjunkturpolitik. Zeitschrift für angewandte Konjunkturforschung,* 20. Jg., 4. Heft, pp. 203–206.
Strachey, J. (1940). *A programme for progress.* Victor Gollancz, London.
Wedig, W. (1999). Andreas Paulsen – Person und wissenschaftliches Werk. In: Der Dekan des Fachbereichs Wirtschaftswissenschaft der Freien Universität Berlin (Hrsg.): *Akademische Gedenkfeier aus Anlaß des 100. Geburtstages von Prof. Dr. Dr. h. c. mult. Erich Kosiol und Prof. Dr. Andreas Paulsen, 18. Februar 1999, Festvorträge.* Berlin, pp. 29–36 und 53–56.

Chapter 4
Karl Schiller: The Triumph and Tragedy of a German Social Democratic Economist

Reinhard Neck

4.1 Introduction

Karl Schiller (1911–1994) is generally regarded as the most important economic policy maker in Germany after Ludwig Erhard (1897–1977). This is astonishing as Schiller was only active as a politician at federal level between 1966 and 1972 and only held office as minister for economic affairs and then minister of finance, in contrast to Erhard, who was also chancellor. From an academic perspective, he did not develop any theorems, so by current standards, Schiller would not count as a productive researcher in economic theory, although he had very good knowledge of the theories of his time. Likewise, he did not develop a system or theory of his own in relation to economic policy. He contributed to the adoption of Keynesianism in Germany after World War II but was by no means the only one to do so. One of his main ideas was the concept of *Globalsteuerung* (overall economic management), which he successfully applied to help overcome the recession in 1966 by using a Keynesian approach to fiscal and monetary policy. Schiller also introduced other concepts such as *Konzertierte Aktion* (concerted action), whereby policy making involved taking interest groups such as organizations of employers and employees on board, and created an institution for this purpose in Germany. Another idea was to plan policies "*aus einem Guss*" (in a coherent way), a holistic concept for planning policies. Despite his apparent liking for planning, Schiller nevertheless rejected the idea of a centrally planned economy, pleading for a social market economy. Creating and implementing these concepts, Schiller aimed at rendering policy making more rational and also contributed to the provision of support for making decisions in macroeconomic policy making, such as a law for stabilization policies, a

R. Neck (✉)
University of Klagenfurt, Klagenfurt, Austria
e-mail: Reinhard.Neck@aau.at

J. G. Backhaus et al. (eds.), *Post-war Keynesianism in Germany and Western Europe*, The European Heritage in Economics and the Social Sciences 28,
https://doi.org/10.1007/978-3-032-00498-7_4

committee of experts to advise policy makers, and quantitative information including national income accounts in Germany.

In this contribution, I outline a brief biography of Karl Schiller (Sect. 4.2) using information provided in the two detailed biographies by Hochstätter (2008) and Lütjen (2008), the former being stronger on Schiller's activities in economics and the latter containing more personal information. Additional biographical material, mostly on his relations to the city of Hamburg, is contained in Bahnsen (2008); the brief, friendly contemporaneous portrait (Lutzeyer, 1969) and the hostile pamphlet (Anonymous, 1969) are less reliable sources. I do not provide detailed documentation of the biographical data, all of which are taken from Hochstätter and Lütjen.

Sections 4.3 and 4.4 describe the main fields for which Schiller is known, his academic work and his activities within the SPD (Social Democratic Party of Germany) respectively. Although they are not completely independent of each other, Schiller supported the postulate of value-free science; hence dealing with the two topics separately should be acceptable despite his sometimes not obeying this postulate. Section 4.5 summarizes and attempts a brief evaluation of the academic economist and politician Karl Schiller. I have to disclose potential bias: when I was young, Karl Schiller seemed to me to be a role model for a politically active economist and he was one reason for choosing economics as my field of study. As my own career was different from his, I hope to be sufficiently objective in evaluating Schiller.

4.2 Karl Schiller

Karl Schiller was born in Breslau (now Wrocław) on April 24, 1911 to a lower middle-class family. His father, an engineer, often had to relocate the family for occupational and, in 1914, military reasons, meaning that young Karl changed his residence and environment six times in the first eleven years of his life. Eventually, in 1922, his parents divorced, and Karl and his mother settled in Schleswig-Holstein, living under miserable conditions, especially after his father became unemployed in 1927. Still, Karl was happy to stay in one town and particularly to attend the same school, the Hebbel School in Kiel. His extraordinary intellectual abilities were reflected in his performance there as he was always the best pupil in his class and only had the best grades in his secondary school leaving examinations (except in physical education). By giving private lessons to other pupils, he could contribute to the meagre income of the small household. Although Karl Schiller showed most interest in the natural sciences and mathematics at high school, he decided to study economics at the Christian Albrecht University of Kiel from 1931.

Economics in Germany at that time had just begun to evolve from a historical discipline into a more analytic one using (a modest amount of) mathematics. Karl Schiller's studies lasted only six semesters, one in Kiel, then two in Frankfurt, one in Berlin, and two in Heidelberg. In 1934, he graduated as *Diplom-Volkswirt* (comparable to a Master's in Economics) and only one year later he received his *Doktor der Volkswirtschaft* (PhD in Economics) at the age of 24. He was influenced by a few professors who were "liberal social democrats," a tradition which gained some influence in the SPD after World War II and which considered liberty to be at least as important as the ideals of social justice and equality. For instance, for Schiller, socialism stood for social mobility thanks to fair opportunities in life rather than privilege, making it possible for intelligent and hard-working people from lower classes to obtain leading positions in society as well (cf. Schiller, 1955b, 33), which he personally tried to realize. Among his university mentors who were committed to this ideal was Adolph Löwe (1893–1995) in Kiel and Frankfurt; indirectly, he was also influenced by the Christian Socialists around Paul Tillich (1886–1965), especially Eduard Heimann (1889–1965). While these people advocated for socialism on moral grounds and for the market principle, Schiller's lecturers Gerhard Colm (1887–1968) and Hans Neisser (1895–1975) in Kiel and Ernst Wagemann (1884–1956) in Berlin argued for active government influence on the business cycle through macroeconomically oriented fiscal policy. Already in his PhD dissertation of 1935 (Schiller, 1936), he recommended job-creating measures with the help of fiscal policy.

During his studies at Heidelberg, Karl Schiller chose Carl Brinkmann (1885–1954), who was a conservative nationalist but not a Nazi proper, although he supported National Socialist (NS) measures for job creation, to supervise his dissertation, attracting the latter's attention in an excellent end-of-course examination. This led to Schiller's employment as Brinkmann's research and teaching assistant and influenced the topic of his dissertation, which his supervisor Brinkmann praised as the "first German economic theory of an economic system of job creation." This dissertation was also sympathetically reviewed in the academic literature but not so by an (anonymous) NS official who criticized it for lacking a "deeper understanding of the specific national-socialist German job creation" (cit. Lütjen, 2008, 58) and for failing to include national-socialist references—a judgment that was very helpful for Schiller after 1945 and yet did not derail his career before the end of NS rule.

In 1935, Karl Schiller took up employment at the Kiel Institut für Weltwirtschaft (Kiel Institute for the World Economy, IWW), which closely cooperated with the Office of Defense Economics and Armament of the German Wehrmacht (armed forces) in the NS era. As early as February 1936, he became director of the research group "Market organization and foreign economics" and mostly worked empirically with six (post-doctoral) assistants on agricultural topics in Germany and abroad. A summary of this work was published as Schiller (1940) and used for his habilitation (the second thesis required in Germany to apply for a position as full professor at a university). Although during his time at the Kiel institute Schiller certainly worked in the service of the NS regime and became a member of the Nazi Party (NSDAP) on May 1, 1937, he cannot be classified as a devoted Nazi because no racist or antisemitic tendencies can be found in his writings, including his private correspondence in so far as it has been preserved. Hence his denazification after the war was relatively unproblematic.

Until its dissolution in spring 1941, the "Research group Schiller," as it had been called since the beginning of World War II, continued to produce contract work for the Wehrmacht, albeit under increasing pressure as its members were successively recruited to the army. Eventually, in May 1941, Schiller himself was called up, but until late summer 1941, he had to attend courses for officers and corporals, which he disliked very much, as he had got married and become father of a daughter in 1940. After Schiller's military service on the Eastern Front started in late summer 1942, he was less troubled by the life-threatening circumstances than by boredom—and by his anxiety about the lack of academic promotion. At least he was promoted very quickly to second lieutenant and lieutenant in the Wehrmacht and could use his skills to organize processes efficiently, which pleased him very much. Later on, he received an offer for a position as associate professor at the University of Rostock, which, however, could not be taken up due to the war. On adventurous routes, he escaped the final battles with the squad under his command and, after a short period in British captivity as a prisoner of war, came back to Kiel in 1945.

Although Schiller was now professor at the University of Rostock, he could not go there as Rostock was in the Soviet occupation zone; therefore, he returned to his former workplace, the IWW. Although this institution had suffered badly in the war, at least its library and its scientific network were still superior to most other places in devastated Germany. Schiller was appointed visiting professor at the University of Kiel and was ordered to go to Hamburg, where the headquarters of the British Occupation Administration for Northern Germany were. His task was to reactivate the publication flagship of the IWW, the journal *Weltwirtschaftliches Archiv*. In January 1946, he published a proposal for the reconstruction of the IWW, which he envisaged as a leading German economic research institute, following the model of US and UK institutes for social research. He argued that the IWW still had international "goodwill" and ignored possible negative effects of the IWW's military connections during the war. For Schiller, the time spent in Hamburg was important as he met and made friends with influential people from political circles, especially those from the SPD, such as Erich Klabunde (1907–1950) and Gustav Dahrendorf (1901–1954); he became a member of the SPD in February 1946.

In June 1946, the military government ordered the mayor of Hamburg to draw up a plan for the economic redevelopment of the city, which was a huge challenge given the chaotic situation and especially the lack of economic data such a plan would require. Schiller was selected as coordinator for this task and proved to be an efficient organizer. From the beginning, he was more optimistic than most of the other members of the committee that the plan could actually be implemented. He was supported in this endeavor by the change in attitude of the Western occupying powers from hostility toward the former wartime enemy to a potential ally against the Soviets in the emerging Cold War. Schiller was so successful at leaving his mark on the committee's work that the results were generally called the "Schiller plan" and his name was indelibly associated with the reconstruction of Hamburg. The plan consisted of three phases: an emergency program to buy time before putting more comprehensive plans into effect; a transition phase, where financial support would be given to maintenance and repair investments only; and the third phase of reconstruction plans proper, with an emphasis on industries to be maintained and expanded. The plan, which was published in April 1947, was characterized by a reliance on measures typical for a planned economy, and also Schiller's few academic publications from that time showed no sympathy for a market economy.

As a side effect of Schiller's work on the development plan, he was appointed full professor of economics and director of the Institute of International Economics at the University of Hamburg in March 1947. He had difficult times rebuilding the teaching and research facilities in view of the shortages and need for improvisation in every area while confronted with 400 students of economics. Schiller was characterized by his students as being well informed about international academic literature, which was partly due to his time at the IWW, but also as being arrogant, vain, and not open to criticism. Altogether, it seems as though Schiller was more suited for an academic career than for a political one, which later caused many problems when he switched to positions in politics where the art of compromising is an essential ability. He did not care much about climbing through the ranks of the party but was most successful when called upon as an external economic expert in challenging situations. As an economic expert, he was a founding member of the scientific advisory board in the Bizone (the joint US and UK occupation zones), which later became the board in the German federal ministry of economic affairs.

This was the case when the position of senator (corresponding to regional minister) for economic affairs and transport in the government of Hamburg was offered to him in fall 1948 by First Mayor Max Brauer (1887–1973), who had won a landslide victory for the SPD in the first elections to the Hamburg parliament in 1946. After some hesitation, Schiller accepted and was sworn in on October 13, 1948, under the condition that he retained his chair at the university. Although limited sovereignty due to the occupation was about to be eased, his position as a regional minister only had limited influence, especially on macroeconomic developments which were Schiller's main interest. The scope for using academic economic insights for regional politics was minor, and Schiller soon became disenchanted and considered terminating his political engagement. Difficulties within the administration contributed to this feeling, including a severe conflict with his personal assistant, Helmut Schmidt (1918–2015); their paths would cross again later in national politics. Hence, Schiller was not unhappy that he had to finish his term of office in 1953 when the SPD lost the regional election and could return full time to his position at the university.

In 1950, Schiller divorced his first wife Lolo and married his former secretary Annemarie, with whom he had two children (as he had with Lolo). He continued his academic activities and his attempts to influence the economic program of the SPD but rejected offers to return to the Hamburg Senate and to run for a secure seat in the *Bundestag* (the German parliament). Neither activity seemed to be rewarding to him, and he redefined his view of the relation between politics and science. The task of science now seemed to Karl Schiller to be to neutralize political irrationalities and introduce scientific rationality into society. This has been interpreted as being Schiller's technocratic utopia for political decisions, centering around the macroeconomic ideas of John Maynard Keynes (1883–1946). Political fighters should give up ideological illusions and use the results of Keynesian macroeconomics (and other scientific theories) to further the goals of improving welfare. To do so, politics should turn to a more objective debate, and economics is a particularly appropriate science to achieve this aim. Especially in his article "*Der Ökonom und die Gesellschaft*" (Schiller, 1955a), Schiller explained his view of the task of the economist to boost rationality in society. However, in the late 1950s, Schiller's activities took place less in the party than in the University of Hamburg, where he was rector between 1956 and 1958.

After the SPD lost the parliamentary election in Germany in 1957, Willy Brandt (1913–1992), the Governing Mayor of Berlin, became the SPD's candidate for federal chancellor (prime minister) of Germany. Brandt was looking for somebody who could contribute economic knowledge to his team both in Berlin and in Germany, which was not Brandt's area of specialization, and asked Schiller to join him. In this case, Schiller agreed without hesitation and thus started a collaboration that would last for more than a decade. In December 1961, Schiller became senator for economic affairs in (West) Berlin. Although this was again a regional political position, it was far more interesting than in Hamburg: it was expected that Brandt would take some of his Berlin team members into his cabinet in case he became chancellor. More important still, the situation in Berlin in 1961 was especially challenging after the erection of the Berlin Wall, which separated West Berlin economically from the rest of Germany, prevented East Germans from commuting into West Berlin, and was expected to have detrimental effects on investment in the city. Such a situation provided many possibilities for an able political organizer to show off his talents.

From the very start in Berlin, Schiller insisted that the city must not rely on subsidies but must demonstrate its ability to survive under its own steam. As a showcase for the Free West toward the totalitarian Eastern Bloc, Berlin had to prove that even under unfortunate circumstances, a democratic market economy can outperform the totalitarian, centrally planned economies of the East. By integrating his economic policy into Brandt's overall policies, Schiller turned West Berlin into a showpiece for the Western model of a free society. His communicative performance was excellent indeed, and although Berlin was still dependent on subsidies from West Germany when Schiller left Berlin for Bonn in 1965, its growth rate was higher than in the Federal Republic. In any case, the impact of Schiller's activities in Berlin was generally regarded by the mass media as creating a sense of excitement about the future hitherto unknown. His technocratic attitude fitted well into the general mood of the time and was congenial to Brandt's image of young, energetic policy makers, following the role model of US President John F. Kennedy and his advisory team of academic "egg-heads."

For the German election of 1965, Brandt nominated Schiller as a member of his shadow cabinet. Schiller, who had become friends with Günter Grass (1927–2015) in Berlin, joined the latter on the campaign trail. Although the SPD did not win the election, despite increasing its share of the vote, Schiller quit his post in Berlin and accepted a seat in the *Bundestag* as a representative of Berlin. He also resumed his academic duties in Hamburg. With a brilliant maiden speech, in which he criticized Chancellor Ludwig Erhard for lacking effective economic policies and demanded a comprehensive and rational policy, Schiller won over his audience and the media, especially those close to the parties in power. Both Schiller's bourgeois style and his competence as a professor of economics were not expected from a Social Democratic politician and later he was frequently regarded as a Christian (CDU) or Free (FDP) Democrat by many voters.

Erhard became increasingly unpopular in his own party, and with the onset of a recession in fall 1966 and defeats of his party at regional elections, his government came under severe pressure. When the FDP left the coalition with the CDU, the government no longer had a majority in parliament. Soon after, a coalition between Christian Democrats and Social Democrats under Chancellor Kurt Georg Kiesinger (1904–1988) was negotiated, and Schiller became federal minister for economic affairs in December 1966. At the beginning of the Grand Coalition between the CDU and SPD, cooperation worked relatively smoothly, especially between Schiller and the minister of finance Franz-Josef Strauß (1915–1988) thanks to the latter's great respect toward Schiller, leading to the pair sometimes being caricatured as "Plisch and Plum," two characters from a children's book by Wilhelm Busch. It took much more effort from Schiller to convince other relevant politicians about the Keynesian expansionary policy he wanted to apply against the recession but eventually he succeeded in realizing his ideas.

A major problem arose when international turbulences shattered the financial markets. Germany was affected by these events because, due to its strong exports, the Deutschmark came under upward pressure. The first reaction of German policy makers was to demand devaluations of seemingly overvalued currencies, especially the French Franc, but also the British Pound and even the US Dollar. Under the influence of the German export industry, the German government rejected demands for revaluing the Deutschmark, although the *Bundesbank* and many German economists considered a revaluation to be necessary. Chancellor Kiesinger was strictly against such a measure and even excluded the possibility of revaluation for the entire period of his chancellorship. Schiller first shared this position but changed his mind when the overheated German economy threatened German price stability and advocated for a revaluation as a countercyclical measure. With Kiesinger and Strauß being strongly opposed, Schiller could not convince the cabinet and argued in the media—against the chancellor—for the revaluation. The SPD, which was not really interested in the topic, backed Schiller and made revaluation a party demand. Schiller turned the issue into a key topic of his campaign for the parliamentary election in September 1969. Although probably only very few voters really understood the economic question, he managed to convince a majority of the virtues of a revaluation—not by his arguments but because they believed in his authority as a professor of economics.

The election resulted in a small majority for a possible coalition between the SPD and the FDP, which was the preferred form of government for most politicians in the two parties. Although other topics were also contested in the election campaign, the revaluation question was deemed by some observers to be so important that they called the 1969 election the "Schiller election." Schiller, whose popularity was, at times, higher than that of Brandt, remained minister for economic affairs and, after the resignation of his favorite enemy, SPD finance minister Alex Möller

(1903–1985), in May 1971, was also given responsibility for this department, becoming "super minister." But in contrast to the extension of his formal power, Schiller's actual importance declined as he had to argue with the other ministers over their budgets, aiming at a more restrictive fiscal policy in view of the inflationary tendencies and rising government budget deficit. To ensure price stability, Schiller preferred a floating exchange rate for the Deutschmark while other members of the cabinet wanted to deal with the speculative inflow of capital by using capital controls. Although first in May 1971, Schiller succeeded to introduce temporary floating of the Deutschmark with the consent of the Council of Ministers of the European Economic Community, later this conflict led to the end of his role in the German cabinet when he fell victim to an intrigue orchestrated by defense minister Helmut Schmidt, the minister in the chancellery Horst Ehmke (1927–2017), and the head of the Bundesbank Karl Klasen (1909–1991), all of them fellow party members and Klasen having been a long-term personal friend.

Schiller resigned, not only from the cabinet but later also his membership of the SPD. Moreover, he joined Ludwig Erhard in a series of advertisements criticizing the government for not being sufficiently faithful to the principles of the market economy, which was widely interpreted as an endorsement of the CDU in the snap Bundestag election of 1972, which was necessary because the coalition government had no majority in parliament after several members of the FDP and the SPD crossed the floor to the opposition over the *Ostverträge*, the Eastern Treaties of the Federal Republic of Germany with the German Democratic Republic, Poland, and the Soviet Union. This was also the main topic in the election campaign, and economic issues were no longer relevant. The popularity of Brandt now surpassed that of Schiller, who was regarded a traitor by many SPD politicians. It should also be mentioned that Schiller's image was also damaged by the behavior of his third wife Etta, whom he had married after divorcing Annemarie and whose relation to him was portrayed as an *amour fou* in some media. After the coalition parties won the election in a landslide victory, Schiller was no longer of interest for the public, except for his private life, which became the target of derogatory news coverage.

Already over 60 years old, Schiller was unable to find employment that he regarded as adequate, and when Etta left him as well, he fell into a deep depression, from which he only recovered slowly with the help of friends and a psychotherapist. He married for the fourth time, and his new wife Sylvia proved to be a stroke of luck for the ex-minister. Gradually, Schiller succeeded in obtaining attractive consultancy jobs for firms and foreign governments, which made him wealthy, and he also restored his relationship with Brandt, the SPD, and even Helmut Schmidt, who had succeeded him as "super minister" and later became chancellor after Brandt resigned due to an espionage affair. Schiller received several academic honors and also returned as a commentator on economic policy topics. In the last year of his life, he wrote a monograph about the difficulties of turning the formerly communist East Germany into a market economy and an open society. On December 26, 1994, Karl Schiller died from an abdominal aortic aneurysm.

4.3 Reconciliation of the Keynesian Message and the Freiburg Imperative

In order to understand Schiller's academic performance, it is necessary to know about the division of the field of economics in the twentieth-century Germany that stems from the nineteenth-century economist Karl Heinrich Rau (1792–1870) and determined curricula and the denomination of economics chairs alike, namely:

- *Volkswirtschaftstheorie* (economic theory),
- *Volkswirtschaftspolitik* (economic policy), and
- *Finanzwissenschaft* (public economics).

Each of these three fields was given approximately equal weight, in contrast to the predominance of economic theory for current academic curricula and chairs. Economic theory was directed toward "pure theory" while economic policy was understood mostly as the application of economic theory to policy problems, which necessarily created overlap between the two. In many cases, professors of economic policy only had superficial knowledge of economic theories and dealt with institutional and historical aspects of the German economy. Even professors of economic theory mostly disliked (and did not know much about) mathematical theories of economics. Moreover, the isolation of the German academic system and the negative selection of professors during the Nazi regime largely restricted the influx of international scientific ideas into the research and teaching of economics at German universities, in economic theory and even more so in economic policy. One of the few genuine new developments in economic policy was the theory and policy of economic orders, which treated similar problems to the Anglo-Saxon theory of economic systems, although often with a more hermeneutic rather than an analytical methodology. Its academic center was the economics department at the University of Freiburg im Breisgau, with Walter Eucken (1891–1950) as its intellectual leader. Their insights into the workings of a market economy were of key importance for the establishment of a social market economy in Germany after World War II. Ludwig Erhard, the father of the German economic miracle, was a member of the Freiburg school.

Karl Schiller had a chair in international economics but certainly belonged primarily to the camp of economic policy. He was a "rare beast" insofar as he had a relatively profound knowledge not only of German work on economic theory but also of key international developments in economic theories due to his work at the IWW before his military service. Furthermore, he liked mathematical theories and quantitative methods and was familiar with the theory of quantitative economic policy and the use of econometric models for economic policy design. Already in his PhD dissertation (Schiller, 1936), he used arguments from the business cycle theory literature of the time, including reference to Keynes's theory of money and Richard F. Kahn's (1905–1989) theory of the multiplier. The main virtue of this monograph is the detailed presentation and statistical evaluation of measures to create employment in the Weimar Republic and in the NS state. Schiller characterizes the former as mostly insufficient and the latter (as cannot be expected otherwise) as more positive, albeit very cautiously in both cases to a large extent. What is remarkable in this book is the general positive view of economic planning by the government; references to possible virtues of market allocation are missing.

The same can be said about Schiller's habilitation thesis (Schiller, 1940), which deals with the regulation of agrarian markets in 33 countries: meticulous presentations of the regulations in those markets, which were generally more susceptible to government regulation, combined with extensive statistical material provide a detailed picture of the topic, albeit with little information on how effective these regulations were. References to theoretical works are rare. Interesting ideas of his own include his classification of forms of market regulation into auxiliary regulations, main regulations (regulations of imports, exports, and internal markets), and, as third and most comprehensive category, a market order as well as his calculation of a measure of the degree of regulation. No critique of market regulation as a matter of principle is present in this text.

An interesting document on Schiller's development of his own position on the question of (centrally) planned versus decentralized market economy is his text about socialism and competition (Schiller, 1955b), which was reprinted several times. Starting with the Socialist Calculation Debate addressed by Wieser, Barone, Mises, Lange, Lerner, and Hayek, among others, Schiller discusses various models of socialism and arrives at the conclusion that a liberal socialism (*freiheitlicher Sozialismus*) is to be regarded as the best variant, characterized by his formula "*so viel Wettbewerb wie möglich, so viel Planung wie nötig*" (As much competition as possible, as much planning as necessary). This formula later found its way into the programmatic documents of the SPD. By critically examining the positions of both democratic socialists and opponents of socialism, he argues for this principle on the basis of scientific theoretical arguments. When writing this essay, Schiller had already gathered experiences as a politician (in Hamburg) and was familiar with the international literature on the possibility or impossibility of rational decision making in a socialist society. What is especially remarkable is his comments on the nature of competition (criticizing the model of perfect competition) as well as that of socialism (rejecting central planning and complete public ownership of means of production).

Both as a professor of economics and a politician in Hamburg, Berlin, and Bonn, Karl Schiller frequently gave speeches about fundamental issues in economic policy. Among the many papers on this topic, I highlight his article in a handbook (Schiller, 1965), which also was reprinted several times and quoted frequently. Although again, at the time, senator in Berlin, here Schiller speaks as a scientist. He first gives an excellent survey of the development of the theory of economic policy, including the current state of the debate, with, among others, the contributions of the Freiburg School and its impact on economic order policy, the theory of quantitative economic policy, the impact of Keynesian macroeconomic theory on economic process policy, the target-means question, and what he called *Globalsteuerung* (overall economic management), its possibilities and limitations. From this, he again derives his formula "As much competition as possible, as much planning as necessary," which he equates to a combination or "reconciliation of the Keynesian message and the Freiburg imperative." This can be interpreted as economic policy along the lines of the "neoclassical synthesis" proposed by Samuelson (1948): policy makers should leave microeconomic decisions to firms and households and let markets coordinate themselves, except for situations where the markets, especially labor markets, do not lead to a general equilibrium, in which case Keynesian theory should guide them to plan measures for realizing overall macroeconomic goals like full employment, growth, price stability, etc.

In this article, and in the others contained in his book about the economist and society (Schiller, 1964), Schiller revealed how he saw his role as an academic economist working as a political decision maker: his knowledge of current economic theories and theories of economic policy should be used to introduce more rationality to politics. Convincing the general public via the media and dealing with other politicians with opposing views by presenting arguments to them, but even more so directly addressing the voters, could eventually pave the way for achieving breakthroughs of a rational viewpoint in economic policy decisions. When he became minister for economic affairs, first in the grand coalition of his SPD with the CDU and then in the small coalition with the FDP, he successfully managed to introduce several decision support systems to advance more rational political decisions, such as national income accounting, medium-term fiscal planning, or the "Concerted Action" (an exchange of information and political goals between the government and interest groups). Schiller created the goal system of *magisches Viereck* (magic square: simultaneous attainment of full employment, price stability, balanced current account, and economic growth). He was also able to implement measures to overcome the recession of 1966–1967 within a very short timeframe by making use of countercyclical Keynesian policies. Although it is still a matter of debate as to how much his policies actually contributed to the economic boom of the late 1960s, Schiller's standing grew enormously, and it certainly helped the SPD in the election of 1969 (the "Schiller election"), when he campaigned in favor of a revaluation of the Deutschmark: as already mentioned, his arguments for this measure were probably understood by only a very small minority of voters, but their belief in the competence of the professor led at least a significant group of middle-class voters to trust him and, thus, to vote for the SPD.

It should be noted that Schiller not only endorsed Keynesianism as a macroeconomic theory and foundation for countercyclical policies but also showed that such policies could be successfully applied to improve employment, growth, and price stability. Without completely abolishing the "Freiburg imperative" of maintaining a free market economy, the addition of countercyclical macroeconomic interventions (in addition to those of social policy, which were already present in the Freiburg conception of the social market economy) allowed policy makers to expand their tool kit with effective instruments for achieving macroeconomic goals. Although it is true to say that Schiller acted on his belief in Keynesian theory and preferred a technocratic application of these instruments, it would be misleading to call him an interventionist, as has sometimes been the case (Bofinger, 2003). His insistence on measures in line with market conditions with which he wanted to secure price stability in the inflation period of the 1970s shows that he was, instead, a true believer in the Freiburg imperative. This eventually led to conflicts with his fellow SPD ministers and his failure as "super minister" in 1972. His temporary endorsement of Keynesianism can also be seen in his academic and political writing after his period as a politician, most notably his final work on the difficulties of and possible policy strategies for German unification (Schiller, 1994). Here he argues not from a Keynesian point of view but rather from supply-side economics, with the matching policy recommendations, such as an emphasis on productivity growth and modest wage increases coupled with warnings about financing the restructuring of the former communist *Bundesländer* (provinces) by increasing debt.

There are at least two other reasons for his eventual failure as a "super minister" than those mentioned already. First, it is always easier politically to implement Keynesian expansionary measures than restrictive ones. Expansions lead to higher income, employment, and growth, which is agreeable for nearly all interest groups. In contrast, restrictive measures may threaten those goals and, therefore, provoke resistance in some or most interest groups. Keynesian policies are asymmetric with respect to their political acceptability. This was not only observed by Schiller in the 1970s, as opposed to the late 1960s but also applies in other countries and contexts. Second, Schiller kept up to date with the theoretical literature in economics only until he became federal minister and—understandably in view of the time constraints for an active top politician—could not do so later on. In the late 1960s and subsequent years, the weakness of Samuelson's "neoclassical synthesis" and of Keynesian economic theory became more visible, and not only Milton Friedman's Monetarism but also other alternatives to Keynesian policies (New Classical Macroeconomics, supply-side economics, etc.) became influential, which implied a turn toward what was (misleadingly) then called "neoliberal policies." This made Schiller's conception of a liberal socialism unfashionable and may have estranged his 1969 voters from him. The turn toward more "neoliberal" policies in other countries (e.g. UK, USA) agrees with this tendency.

Of course, in any case where an originally very popular politician eventually fails, this can also be due to personal circumstances and mistakes. In the case of Schiller, some features of his character contributed to his downfall: his arrogance, his self-centeredness, his lack of loyalty to his cabinet, and his lack of solidarity with his fellow party members can be mentioned here, but also his lack of understanding the more subtle network structures and intrigues of politics, which later on also contributed to the fall of Brandt and Schmidt, who foundered at least as much thanks to their own party as to the political opposition. It is a tragedy not only personally for Karl Schiller but also for the SPD that Schiller, Schmidt, and some others (such as Alex Möller) had political views that were close to each other so that a trustful collaboration between these men would have been of great advantage for them and for the party but was prevented by (often narrow-minded) personality clashes.

4.4 The Rise and Fall of the Social Democratic Politician

Karl Schiller not only helped introduce Keynesianism into the theory and practice of economic policy in the Federal Republic of Germany but he was also important for the reorientation of the ideology of the German social democrats. During the years of the Bismarck Reich, the SPD was originally based on Marxist theoretical foundations. Although the revisionism debate initiated by Eduard Bernstein (1850–1932), who raised doubts about some of Marx's forecasts (especially the immiseration of the proletariat and the collapse of capitalism), led to a more critical attitude toward revolutions and support for a democratic parliamentary approach to socialism, officially, Bernstein was denounced as a heretic. Nevertheless, the party majority followed a more pragmatic policy, which during World War I, led to a split and, after the war, to the final separation of the KPD (German Communist Party) from the SPD. During the Weimar Republic, the two parties only very rarely collaborated with each other, despite their common Marxist roots.

The most important economic theorist of the SPD in the Weimar Republic was Rudolf Hilferding (1877–1941), Austrian by birth and with relations to Austro-Marxism. His book *Das Finanzkapital* (Finance Capital) (Hilferding, 1910) is generally recognized as being one of the most original advancements of Marxist economic theory and influenced Lenin's theory of imperialism. Hilferding argued that cartelization and monopolistic tendencies of capitalism lead to ever higher concentrations of capital, together with the influence of banks and other financial institutions. This could be evaluated positively because it would make the transition to socialism easier, not necessarily requiring the socialization of small and medium enterprises. From these considerations, Hilferding developed his theory of organized capitalism, which was highly influential in the SPD during the Weimar Republic. He was also the German minister of finance twice, for a short period during the great inflation in 1923 and before the Great Depression between 1928 and 1929. Although he was very critical of Lenin and the Soviet Union, which he considered to be totalitarian, his theory of organized capitalism led to conclusions similar to those of the communists. He considered the concentration of capital to be a stabilizing effect for capitalism and opposed proposals for stabilization policies as being unnecessary and counterproductive. The main difference to the communists was, of course, that he argued against revolutions and in favor of a planned economy after a socialist society had been achieved by democratic parliamentary methods.

As Held (1982) shows in much detail, there were already Keynesian thinkers in the SPD before Keynesianism was fully embraced by the party. Already during and after the German revolution of 1918–1919, proposals for creating employment by government measures were raised, mainly based on a business cycle theory of underconsumption; from this source, too, came the rejection of a restrictive wage policy, which is also present in Keynes's economic theory. Authors like Emil Lederer (1882–1939), Fritz Tarnow (1880–1951), and especially Wladimir Woytinsky (1885–1960) argued in favor of measures of employment creation and against Hilferding's position, especially the latter two as economists of the trade unions, with the famous argument that social democrats should work as "physicians at the bedside of capitalism" to support suffering workers already before the arrival of socialism. In contrast, Hilferding supported the procyclical deflationary austerity policy of chancellor Heinrich Brüning (1885–1970, chancellor between 1930 and 1932, after the election in 1930 of a minority government tolerated by the SPD) in order to restore the international position of Germany by attempting to remove the burden of reparations and balance the government budget. Proposals for a countercyclical fiscal and monetary policy by the "pre-Keynesians," especially the WTB (Woytinsky-Tarnow-Baade) plan, did not find the unanimous support of the SPD and the trade unions and even less so of the right-wing parties.

The question as to whether a more Keynesian economic policy could have avoided the economic catastrophe for Germany which eventually resulted in the takeover by the Nazis is undecided. In any case, the measures of the Nazi dictatorship contributed to the recovery of its labor market, and their program for employment creation was essentially based on the ideas of the "pre-Keynesians," although their political orientations were, of course, completely different. When Karl Schiller wrote his dissertation, he was convinced of the expansionary effects of a "Keynesian" fiscal and monetary policy, although he was not yet familiar with Keynes's General Theory, which appeared in the same year as Schiller's work (1936). It is understandable that Schiller was later impressed by Keynesian theory and its policy prescriptions. However, after the war he had also read the main writings of the Freiburg School and other economic works more critical toward Keynesianism, so he was an eclectic with respect to economic theories. It can be disputed whether, as Ott (1978) and Held (1982) claim, the SPD already fully embraced the Keynesian program of macroeconomic policy after World War II, because at least a minority of the functionaries and supporters of the party still subscribed to Marxist ideas. Be that as it may, the development of the party's ideology continually moved toward both Keynesian views and a more positive attitude toward competition and the market economy, especially when the SPD had a lower proportion of the vote than the CDU in the series of elections from 1949 onward.

Karl Schiller was certainly one of the most prominent SPD politicians who favored a market over a planned economy as well as Keynesian macroeconomic theory and policy over Marxism, but he was not the only one. Held (1982) shows that several economic spokesmen for the SPD supported this development before and alongside him. In particular, Heinrich Deist (1902–1964) had similar ideas to Schiller and also argued for downplaying the ideas of a planned economy and the socialization of means of production in the SPD. He was chairman of the economic committees of the SPD and prepared and fought for the *Godesberg* program in 1959; only his premature death prevented him from becoming (shadow) minister for economic affairs. Schiller became his successor as head of the economics committee of the SPD and in 1965 economics spokesman for the SPD in the *Bundestag*; he supported essentially the same ideas as Deist. Against Erhard's concept of the *formierte Gesellschaft* (formed, well-ordered society), Schiller propagated the idea of a *mündige Gesellschaft* (politically mature society). Compared with Deist, he had the asset of being a full professor of economics with the charisma of an expert, which became important for the acceptance of the SPD in the 1960s, especially in the "Schiller election" of 1969.

As I argued in previous sections, there are several reasons for his fall in 1972. An important additional one must be stressed here, and this is the one which Schiller himself probably considered the most important. The late 1960s and early 1970s were the period of the "New Left" student movement. This entailed a renewed interest in Marxist ideas and, together with the "Long March through the institutions," resulted in the intrusion of Marxist ideological positions into established parties, in particular the formerly Marxist SPD. Together with the decline in backing for Schiller by his fellow SPD leaders and cabinet colleagues, the re-ideologization of the party under a Marxist banner also isolated him among the party rank and file and led to his deep fall after he resigned as minister for economic affairs and finance. Attacks from the "left wing" of the party even went so far as to assert that his favorite idea of the "reconciliation of the Keynesian message and the Freiburg imperative" had been alien to the ideology of the SPD from the beginning. His exit from the party may seem understandable under these circumstances, although he regretted this act later and worked hard to become a member again, which he managed to achieve in 1980 with the support of Oskar Lafontaine, the leader of the SPD in Saarland (and later chairman of the party, federal minister of finance, and then leader of a left-wing split from the SPD). The motives of Schiller to re-enter the party were probably more emotional than based on agreement with the economic policy of the SPD, as he continued to be critical of that policy (though less so of the party's representatives).

It is an irony of history that Schiller, who was accused of being a "traitor to the right" of the SPD, endorsed Oskar Lafontaine, who later became a "traitor to the left" of the SPD. Both cases show that the party has become more narrow-minded and mediocre after Schiller's fall. Hochstätter's (2008) conclusion that the SPD has suffered from Schiller's absence as a social democratic economic policy maker is certainly correct. The lack of a consistent program and its orientation toward short-run interventions as well as its low tolerance for unconventional ideas make the party unattractive for voters and can explain unsatisfactory results in elections. Recourse to the ideas and publications of Schiller, such as in Prinz (2007), may be useful, but a more creative attempt at developing a new political program is indispensable. That its competitors among the other democratic parties do not fare much better is only cold comfort, especially in times in which populist and even authoritarian and antidemocratic parties are becoming increasingly successful. Opening up the party to academically founded experts and charismatic personalities would help—ideally persons with both properties such as Karl Schiller.

4.5 Concluding Remarks

This chapter introduces the life and academic and political activities of Karl Schiller, an academic economist who was also active as a politician for the SPD, for English-speaking readers. This should be useful for those who do not read German because virtually everything written about and by him is in that language. The contributions of Schiller can be summarized as follows:

- Schiller was eclectic with respect to economic theories. He was well informed about the different theories of his time and took elements from these theories to develop a conception of economic policy that was based on the Freiburg School of the market order, to which he added the Keynesian prescription of countercyclical fiscal and monetary policies.
- Although Schiller contributed to the introduction of Keynesianism into the German theory and practice of economic policy, he was not in favor of a centrally planned economy but remained devoted to the market economy as appropriate for Germany and to the market order of the social market economy.
- Schiller's approach was technocratic in the sense that he wanted to make policy design more rational and in line with the democratic political system, the open society in the sense of Karl Popper, and the market order.
- Building upon the ideas of other politicians in the SPD, he contributed to orienting this party toward a market-friendly attitude with the slogan "As much competition as possible, as much planning as necessary," which included a replacement of Marxist elements of ideology with Keynesian ones.
- In his work as minister for economic affairs and, for a short period, also of finance, Schiller aimed at managing the German economy according to his idea of reconciling the Freiburg imperative with the Keynesian message. This was successful when dealing with the recession of 1966 but less so when inflation was the main problem.
- Schiller's failure as a politician resulted from the exaggerated demands of his fellow cabinet members but also of the party, especially when the latter came under the influence of Marxist-inspired ideologies. Some personal traits of his also contributed to his failure, as did the lack of an ability to maneuver in the presence of differences of opinion with the changing mainstream of the SPD and with the struggle for power within the party.
- Conversely, Schiller's reluctance to deal with the mainstream of the party shows that he was a politician with a distinct conception of politics, which he also upheld when under pressure from opposing forces. This is a feature of his character that can be said to be laudable and honest. The SPD would have profited in the years after his resignation from the cabinet if it had been more tolerant toward him and had followed his advice and his attitude of using academic insights to solve problems of economic policy.

Altogether, social democratic economic policy making in Germany and elsewhere would be more coherent and effective if it followed the path Schiller proposed. This is also true in the present situation, where different challenges demand a more long-run orientation as well as consistent and rational foundations. Therefore, studying Schiller's approach could contribute to improvements in policy making even today, both in Germany and in other European countries.

References

Anonymous. (1969). *der aufhaltsame aufstieg des karl august schiller*. vpa.

Bahnsen, U. (2008). *Karl Schiller*. Ellert & Richter Verlag.

Bofinger, P. (2003). *Grundzüge der Volkswirtschaftslehre: eine Einführung in die Wissenschaft von Märkten*. Pearson Education.

Held, M. (1982). *Sozialdemokratie und Keynesianismus: von der Weltwirtschaftskrise bis zum Godesberger Programm*. Campus Verlag.

Hilferding, R. (1910). *Das Finanzkapital: eine Studie zur jüngsten Entwicklung des Kapitalismus*. Verlag der Wiener Volksbuchhandlung Ignaz Brand.

Hochstätter, M. (2008). *Karl Schiller: eine wirtschaftspolitische Biografie*. VDM Verlag Dr. Müller.

Lütjen, T. (2008). *Karl Schiller (1911–1994) "Superminister" Willy Brandts* (2nd ed.). Dietz.

Lutzeyer, A. (Ed.). (1969). *Karl Schiller: ein Porträt*. Eurobuch-Verlag August Lutzeyer, Freudenstadt.

Ott, E. (1978). *Die Wirtschaftskonzeption der SPD nach 1945*. Verlag Arbeiterbewegung und Gesellschaftswissenschaft.

Prinz, D. W. (Ed.). (2007). *Karl Schiller: Wachstum, Stabilität, Gleichgewicht*. Keyser Verlag, Berlin.

Samuelson, P. A. (1948). *Economics: An introductory analysis*. McGraw Hill.

Schiller, K. (1936). *Arbeitsbeschaffung und Finanzordnung in Deutschland*. Junker und Dünnhaupt Verlag.

Schiller, K. (1940). *Marktregulierung und Marktordnung in der Weltagrarwirtschaft*. Gustav Fischer.

Schiller, K. (1955a). *Der Ökonom und die Gesellschaft*. Selbstverlag der Universität Hamburg. Reprinted in Schiller (1964).

Schiller, K. (1955b). *Sozialismus und Wettbewerb*. Verlagsgesellschaft deutscher Konsumgenossenschaften, Hamburg. Reprinted in Schiller (1964).

Schiller, K. (1964). *Der Ökonom und die Gesellschaft: das freiheitliche und das soziale Element in der modernen Wirtschaftspolitik*. Gustav Fischer.

Schiller, K. (1965). Wirtschaftspolitik. In: v Beckerath, E. et al. (Eds.), *Handwörterbuch der Sozialwissenschaften*, vol. 12, Gustav Fischer, Stuttgart, J. C. B. Mohr (Paul Siebeck), Tübingen, Vandenhoeck & Ruprecht, Göttingen (pp. 210–231). Reprinted in Schiller (1964).

Schiller, K. (1994). *Der schwierige Weg in die offene Gesellschaft: kritische Anmerkungen zur deutschen Vereinigung*. Siedler Verlag.

Chapter 5
Gottfried Bombach: A Pioneer of Macroeconomics in Post-War Germany and Switzerland

Oliver Landmann

5.1 Introduction

At the end of World War II, Germany was devastated, physically and intellectually. Much of the elite in the arts and sciences was either dead or exiled. A global centre of gravity in many sciences until 1933, Germany had become hopelessly isolated internationally and detached from the advances of the research frontier during the twelve years of the Nazi regime. It was up to a young new generation of academics to repair the damage and to start the long road of catching up with the global state of the art. Gottfried Bombach was a leading representative of that new generation of economists who reconnected German economics with the world in the 1950s and 1960s. In fact, he was among those who introduced Germany to macroeconomics, a subdiscipline of economics which had not even properly existed in 1933.

Gottfried Bombach was born in Kamenz in 1919, the city in Saxony which prides itself for being the place of birth of one of Germany's most influential eighteenth-century writers, Gotthold Ephraim Lessing. In 2016, Kamenz commemorated Bombach by naming one of its streets the "Prof.-Gottfried-Bombach-Strasse". Having been conscripted to serve in the German military in the early days of the war, Bombach took up economics at the University of Kiel in the very first semester after the end of the war. He was a student and later assistant of Erich Schneider who ignited his enthusiasm for macroeconomics. In 1949, Bombach got the chance to

The author thanks Gerold Blümle and Bertram Schefold for valuable comments.

O. Landmann (✉)
Department of Economics, University of Freiburg, Freiburg, Germany
e-mail: oliver.landmann@vwl.uni-freiburg.de; https://www.macro.uni-freiburg.de/team/emeritus

J. G. Backhaus et al. (eds.), *Post-war Keynesianism in Germany and Western Europe*, The European Heritage in Economics and the Social Sciences 28,
https://doi.org/10.1007/978-3-032-00498-7_5

visit Cambridge where he met Joan Robinson, Richard Stone and other eminent economists.

After completing his PhD thesis on the topic of economic growth, he joined the OEEC—later renamed OECD—where he took part in the development of international standards for national income accounting and international real income comparisons.[1] This foundational work was not only essential for the emerging field of empirical macroeconomics, it also shaped his own subsequent research, leaving him keenly aware of the limitations of all official statistics.

Bombach's academic career was launched by an offer to join the University of Saarbrücken in 1956 from where he moved on to the University of Basel, Switzerland, only one year later. He quickly became one of the most influential voices in macroeconomics throughout the German speaking world, teaching and publishing on economic growth, income distribution and the short-run macroeconomics of output, employment and inflation. Eleven of his students went on to become professors of economics themselves.

As an advocate of quantitative, model-based economics, Bombach in a way became a counterpart to his senior Basel colleague Edgar Salin (1892–1974) whose style of economic reasoning was firmly rooted in history and the humanities. Well-versed mathematically as he was, Bombach never had much tolerance for mathematics as an end in itself in economics—"*l'art pour l'art*", as he liked to put it—but insisted that economics be strictly applicable to the pressing topics of society and in line with intuitively sound analysis. Not accidentally, he named his Basel research institute the "Institute for Applied Economic Research". Bombach rejected attractive outside offers, such as one to become director of the renowned Ifo Institute in Munich, to remain faithful to Basel for the rest of his life. He appreciated the academic atmosphere of a department which united economics with the humanities, enjoying the company of the likes of Karl Jaspers, Walter Muschg, Edgar Bonjour, Werner Kaegi and, of course, Edgar Salin.

Jointly with Bernhard Gahlen of the University of Augsburg and with Alfred Ott of the University of Tübingen, Bombach founded the "Economic Seminar of Ottobeuren" in the 1960s, an annual conference which was to become an important event in the calendar of many influential German, Austrian and Swiss economists. Among his publications, a survey of growth theory (Bombach, 1965) and a series of six volumes on Keynesianism, from its origins in the 1930s to the current political and academic debates of the 1990s (Bombach et al., 1976–1997), became standard references. Among his many distinctions, six honorary doctorates, invitations to give the De Vries Lecture in 1985 (Bombach, 1986a) and the Thünen Lecture at the Annual Meeting of the German Economic Association in 1990 (Bombach, 1991a) stand out. As an economic advisor, he was much in demand, both in his native Germany for the economics ministry of Ludwig Erhard, and in Switzerland in several advisory roles for the Swiss government.

Gottfried Bombach died in Basel at the age of 91 in 2010.

[1] For some recollections of this early statistical work, see Bombach (2001).

5.2 Economic Growth: Bombach's Life-Long Preoccupation

Bombach devoted his first research to the theory of economic growth in his PhD thesis, completed in 1952, a 55-page abridged version of which appeared in *Weltwirtschaftliches Archiv* one year later (Bombach, 1953). This work mostly dealt with post-Keynesian growth theory which had independently been developed by Domar (1946) and Harrod (1939). Remarkably, Harrod's (1948) book, which summarized and extended the argument of his 1939 article, was available in a German translation as early as 1949. As Bombach (1991b, p. XIII) told it in retrospect, the publication of this book caused a sensation in Kiel. Whereas Keynes was well known in Germany, his 1936 *General Theory* being available in a German translation in the same year, Harrod's (1939) article in the *Economic Journal*, which had spelled out the main messages of his growth model, appears to have gone largely unnoticed in the isolated Germany of the Nazi era.

At the time, Bombach praised Harrod's work for reframing economic thinking in terms of equilibrium growth, thereby overcoming the limitations of the stationary world of neoclassical theory as well as the curious inconsistency in the Keynesian model which had positive net investment—implying growing production capacity—side by side with a static concept of equilibrium output. Bombach was particularly interested in the assumed technology underlying the Harrod-Domar model. He rejected the widely held view that Harrod's rather pessimistic assessment of the stability of a market economy depended on the assumption of fixed factor proportions in production. A rigidly limitational Leontief-type of production function in capital and labour would have rationalized the conclusion that one of the factors was bound to be chronically underemployed, but it was neither a necessary premise nor was it consistent with observable facts.

As Bombach pointed out, Harrod's assumption of a constant capital coefficient was in line with the findings of Kuznets et al. (1946) who had published the relevant time series for the United States dating back to 1869. Against this empirical backdrop, building a model on the premise of a constant capital-output ratio was prima facie not unreasonable. Bombach (1953, p. 41), too, regarded the capital-output ratio as a "useful tool for the analysis of the trend".[2] However, he was quick to point out that the empirical stability of that ratio did not justify the conclusion that growth theory could safely proceed on the assumption of a fixed proportion of capital and labour in production, let alone that Harrod had made such an assumption. After all, Kuznets et al. (1946) had firmly established that output per worker exhibited a robust upward trend throughout their sample period. Output per worker can be expressed as the ratio of the capital-labour ratio and the capital-output ratio:

$$\frac{Y}{L} \equiv \frac{K/L}{\beta} \qquad Y: \text{output}; L: \text{labor}; K: \text{capital}; \beta \equiv K/Y \tag{5.1}$$

[2]All quotes are translated by the author. When a source is reprinted in Borner and Riese (1991), pages refer to the reprint.

If *Y/L* followed a secular upward trend and the capital-output ratio β was roughly constant, Bombach argued, it was inevitable to conclude that *K/L* followed a secular upward trend, too, thereby contradicting any notion of fixed factor proportions. Ongoing capital-labor substitution, he stated, "is always an essential feature of long-term growth" (Bombach, 1953, p. 51). He thus rejected any representation of technology with fixed capital and labour coefficients as a foundation for the theory of economic growth. Instead, he advocated the use of a Cobb-Douglas production function with a time trend to allow for technical progress over time, as previously proposed by Tinbergen (1942):

$$Y = e^t \cdot L^M \cdot K^n \ (m + n = 1) \tag{5.2}$$

Harrod suspected that market economies had no built-in mechanism to align their "warranted" equilibrium growth rate, as defined by the ratio of their savings rate and their marginal capital coefficient, with their natural growth rate, as determined by population growth and technical progress. With a production function as in Eq. (5.2), this failure could no longer be attributed to technological limitations to factor substitution. Rather, Bombach interpreted Harrod as rejecting the notion that the capital-labor ratio responded to the price signals of the market with sufficient strength for the economy to remain in a steady-state growth equilibrium. In fact, this interpretation was later supported by Harrod (1973) himself in a restatement of his theory. Bombach's reading of Harrod in his 1952 PhD thesis thus set him apart from Robert Solow who, a few years later, was to present his path-breaking neoclassical model as a critique of the Harrod model whose knife-edge property he ascribed to "the crucial assumption that production takes place under conditions of *fixed proportions*" (Solow, 1956, italics in the original). Apart from being at odds with Harrod's thinking on factor substitution, Solow's critique also confused the dynamic knife-edge instability of Harrod's model with the longer-term issue of how equilibrium ("warranted") growth could be aligned with the natural growth rate—a point which Solow acknowledged years later in his Nobel Lecture (Solow, 1988).

At the time, Bombach (1953) concluded that future research should combine the tool of a substitutional production function with the equilibrium conditions of Harrod and Domar. This is precisely what Solow (1956) did soon after when, in a stroke of genius, he connected the dots and started the neoclassical revolution in growth theory. Looking back to his own agenda many years later, it was not without regret that Bombach (1991b, p. XV) noted how close he had actually been to the core of neoclassical growth theory. Specifically, he regretted that the decade his generation had lost due to the war had prevented it from acquiring the necessary technical expertise in handling differential equations to capture the dynamics of economic growth.

About a decade after Solow's initial paper, Bombach (1965) took stock of growth theory in a handbook article which became his most widely read paper and a standard reference for students and researchers in the field of growth theory throughout the German-speaking area—in its ambition and reach akin to what Hahn and Matthews (1964) had accomplished for the English-speaking world. Unlike later synopses and textbooks of growth theory, Bombach did not treat the neoclassical theory as a superior approach that had relegated the post-Keynesian theory to the dustbin of doctrinal history. Quite to the contrary, he portrayed the two strands of thought as competing on an equal footing, spelling out their common roots, their areas of disagreement and their limitations.

He forcefully made the point that growth theory, while describing the laws of motion of a capitalist economy, did not yet offer a genuine explanation of economic growth as long as both technical progress and population growth remained unexplained and labour was treated as homogeneous. He suspected that an important transmission channel of technical progress was the upgrading of labour through education and learning by doing. These gaps in the existing growth models directed his attention towards the economics of innovation, human capital, education and population. The 1960s were a time when Germany invested heavily in the expansion of higher education to meet the rising demand for highly skilled labour. Bombach shared the concern that the education systems of both Germany and Switzerland were badly inadequate in the face of the rapid economic growth of the post-war years. Together with a team of younger researchers at his *Institute for Applied Economic Research* he developed a forecasting model to estimate the demand for skilled labour. He received funding from the OECD and from pertinent authorities in Germany which were all keenly interested in this work. Some of the resulting research is collected in Borner and Riese (1991, Part II).

Bombach remained devoted to the study of economic growth throughout his long academic career. Expanding on his early work for the OEEC, he repeatedly returned to the issues surrounding the measurement of productivity (Bombach, 1959a, 1991a). Having thought hard about the logic of factor substitution and technological progress, he was quick to pinpoint the gaps and errors in the influential analysis of the 'Limits to Growth' put forward by the Club of Rome in the early 1970s (Bombach, 1976a). The invitations to deliver the De Vries Lecture in 1985 and the Thünen Lecture in 1990 provided him with two opportunities to sum up his thoughts on the many facets of post-war growth and on the successes and failures of growth theory in explaining this experience.

Much of his discussion in those lectures centred on the sources of the exceptionally rapid growth enjoyed by industrial countries in the post-war years and on the reasons why this 'Golden Age'—the "trente glorieuses" as the French dubbed it—came to an end in the 1970s. On this question, Bombach refused to join the mainstream of growth economists who, in their attempt to explain the productivity slowdown through the lens of the neoclassical model, directed their entire attention to the supply side:

> I do not share the neoclassical view that there is some sort of natural rate of growth independent of the development of demand. (Bombach, 1986a, p. 70)

While acknowledging the end of technological catch-up and other supply-side factors, Bombach was enough of a Keynesian to attach a significant weight to the monetary and demand-side turbulences of the 1970s as a major cause of the disappointing growth experience of the 1970s and 1980s. He was careful to emphasize, however, that he was not a simple-minded "unreconstructed Keynesian" who believed that "a return to the old growth patterns" could be brought about simply by boosting demand (Bombach, 1986a, p. 71). Rather, he argued that the reliable stabilization of economic activity through appropriate demand management was essential for giving entrepreneurs the confidence and the optimism to keep growth going by expanding and improving the productive capacity of the economy.

In the same vein, he remained open-minded about the potential for the management of the money supply to affect long-term growth. Explicitly referring to the classic study by Friedman and Schwartz (1963), he was convinced that the severe crises of the nineteenth century, not to mention the Great Depression of the 1930s, had left their traces in the long-run trend path of economic growth. This point of view was not too different from Milton Friedman's (1968) famous statement on the role of monetary policy. Whereas Friedman was adamant that the monetary authority could not use its control over the money supply to target a desired rate of real growth, he conceded that if "money gets out of order, it throws a monkey wrench" into that marvellous machinery which has propelled "the astounding growth in output and level of living we have experienced in the past two centuries" (Friedman, 1968, p. 12).

5.3 Economic Growth, Inflation and Income Distribution

Germany's *Wirtschaftswunder* of the 1950s was accompanied by a steady upward creep of the price level which, at below 2%, was moderate by later standards, but high enough for the Federal Financial Court to demand a report from the Bundesbank on the extent of inflation and its future prospect (Bundesbank, 1965). Gottfried Bombach (1959b) raised the question of whether inflation was the price Germany had to pay for the rapid increase in its real GDP. His working hypothesis was that voluntary saving fell short of the high rate of investment required to maintain the ongoing growth of the economy. This argument rested on a firm link between growth and investment as expressed by the Harrod-Domar growth equation:

$$g_Y = \frac{I/Y}{\beta} \qquad g_Y : \text{output growth}; I/Y : \text{net investment rate} \tag{5.3}$$

Bombach never left any doubt about the importance of investment for growth even when Solow's model suggested that changes in the investment rate could not alter the steady-state growth rate due to the diminishing returns to capital and the implied endogenous adjustment of the capital coefficient β. He did not question the logic of the neoclassical result, but dismissed it as irrelevant for any plausible time horizon of economic policy which he argued fell way short of the length of adjustment to a neoclassical steady state.

Bombach's interpretation of inflation in terms of an *ex-ante* saving-investment gap was plainly in the tradition of Wicksell and the pre-*General-Theory* Keynes.

Starting from this premise, he considered various mechanisms by which the *ex-ante* discrepancy between saving and investment could be resolved. First among them was what he thought was the reality of post-war Germany: ongoing price inflation which redistributed income away from workers towards profits, thereby pushing the *ex-post* saving rate up to the level of the investment rate, while exacerbating the concentration of wealth. The similarity of this mechanism to the one described by Kaldor's (1955) model of income distribution did not escape him.

Alternatively, contractionary fiscal and monetary policy could reduce the investment rate to the point of equality with the saving rate. For Bombach, the implied reduction of the real growth rate was not acceptable, however. He explicitly pointed to the need of competing with the high growth rates recorded in the countries to the East of the Iron Curtain (Bombach, 1959b, p. 254). If a high investment rate and high real growth are to be reconciled with price stability, Bombach concluded, wage policy had to come into play. Renouncing their distributional aspirations, unions could secure price stability by subordinating wage policy to this sole objective. Limiting nominal wage growth to the rate of growth of labour productivity, unit-labour costs would be kept stable. In effect, workers would voluntarily have to accept the profit share that would otherwise be enforced by inflation. The economy would in effect operate on what Hicks (1974) would later call a labour standard. At that point, Bombach had arrived at a trilemma of sorts: The three objectives of high growth, price stability and a fair income distribution, however defined, apparently could not be attained simultaneously—"one of the big problems of our time" (Bombach, 1959b).

An additional policy instrument was required if a way out of this trilemma was to be found. Indeed, a solution was suggested by Nicholas Kaldor's (1955) model. Kaldor explained why wage policy was ineffective as a tool to change the income distribution when wages were spent on consumption, inducing an offsetting increase in goods prices as workers fed their higher nominal incomes back into the circular flow of income and expenditure. Instead, he demonstrated how the spending patterns of workers and capital owners were the key to understanding the determination of the functional income distribution. In a refinement of Keynes's (1930) theorem of the widow's cruse, and assuming a fully employed economy, Kaldor's model allowed to derive the profit share in national income as a function of the investment rate and the saving rates out of profits and wages, respectively:

$$\frac{P}{Y} = \frac{\frac{I}{Y} - s_W}{s_P - s_W} \quad \text{with} s_W < \frac{I}{Y} < s_P < 1 \tag{5.4}$$

P/*Y*: Profit share; s_W: saving rate out of wages; s_P: saving rate out of profits.

The Kaldor formula illuminated how the low saving rate of workers, in conjunction with a high investment rate, led to a high profit rate and hence to a high concentration of wealth in post-war Germany. Bombach, along with a number of like-minded economists, concluded that the way to raise the wage share without reducing investment was an increase in the saving rate of workers s_W. Since workers did not appear to be willing to change their consumption and saving behavior on their own, the policy tool favoured by Bombach was a so-called investment wage, i.e. a wage which was in part retained in a saving vehicle instead of being fully paid out to workers in cash. The scheme would have had to be made mandatory for all workers so as to rule out freeriding (Bombach, 1989).

The investment wage looked particularly attractive to its advocates since it promised to kill several birds with one stone:

- It would lead to a more equitable distribution of income by raising the wage share.
- It would place a larger share of newly created wealth into the hands of workers and thereby spread wealth more broadly over time.
- It would allow to keep investment and growth high without stoking inflation.
- It would defuse the conflict between capital and labour by giving workers a stake in capital.

The idea never made much headway in practice. Looking back, Bombach remembers having fought for the scheme "with missionary zeal" and always regarded the failure of policymakers to implement anything faintly resembling an investment wage as a huge missed opportunity (Bombach, 1981, 1989). Apart from the virtue of reconciling high real growth with stable prices, the early phase of rebuilding the capital stock after the devastations of the war would have been the best moment to promote broad ownership of the nation's capital stock. Bombach was particularly disappointed by the rejection of the investment wage on the part of trade unions which hated the idea of turning the working class into partial capitalists and denigrated the idea as "bourgeois social romanticism", prioritizing instead the expansion of the welfare state.

Critics of the investment wage argued that it was not feasible for workers to cut their consumption out of the low incomes they earned and that forcing them to save more was a non-starter, therefore. From the vantage point of the Kaldor model, this objection was simply mistaken. It overlooked the fact that the increased saving rate would apply to a higher wage share so that the consumption standard of the working class would actually rise. This result relied on indirect systemic repercussions in the circular flow of income and expenditure to offset the direct effect of a higher saving rate on consumption. Counterintuitive at first sight, this was yet again a paradox of thrift of sorts. Formally, from Eq. (5.4), the wage share is:

$$1-\frac{P}{Y}=\frac{s_P-\frac{I}{Y}}{s_P-s_W}, \tag{5.5}$$

which implies for the consumption of workers as a share of total income:

$$\left(1-s_W\right)\cdot\left(1-\frac{P}{Y}\right)=\frac{\left(1-s_W\right)\cdot\left(s_P-\frac{I}{Y}\right)}{s_P-s_W} \tag{5.6}$$

With the restrictions on the parameters given in Eq. (5.4), and for given investment I and full employment income Y, it is apparent from Eq. (5.6) that the absolute consumption level of workers is increasing in s_W. At the time, Bombach extensively discussed the premises on which this result was based and defended them, simplistic as they were, as not too unrealistic for the years of the *Wirtschaftswunder* when investment was high, the saving rate of workers was near zero and the economy was on the edge of inflation. He later conceded that he had never managed to get the point across convincingly to audiences in numerous lectures and debates—and he regretted not to have worked with numerical examples to build intuition as he did in his undergraduate classes. Characteristically, he made the point with a numerical example in his reappraisal of the Kaldor model on the occasion of the 25th anniversary of its publication (Bombach, 1981, p. 412). Once the high growth rates and the full employment of the post-war years were past, he did not pursue the investment wage idea any further as he judged the window of opportunity had closed for good.

Distributional issues remained central to Bombach's research, but the focus shifted away from the distribution of functional shares towards "new dimensions" of the income distribution (Bombach, 1972). Instead of the aggregate level of wages, the more granular issue of the role of the wage structure gained importance as unemployment crept up across Europe and Herbert Giersch (1985) coined the term "*eurosclerosis*" to summarize the many rigidities that prevented European economies and labour markets to adjust to structural change. Bombach emphasized 'real wage resistance' as a key impediment to adjustment. He criticized the push to squeeze wage differentials in defiance of market forces that pulled in the opposite direction. He also shared the prevailing conventional wisdom that the United States, with its high degree of wage flexibility, managed to keep unemployment reasonably low in the face of rapidly changing labour market conditions and a falling demand for unskilled labour. Thus, accepting stagnant or falling real wages for unskilled workers, America favoured "low pay to no pay" whereas Europe, averse to widening wage differentials, endured a relentless rise of unemployment, apparently favouring "no pay to low pay". However, Bombach (1986b) refused to subscribe to the notion, popular among advocates of free-market economics, that "every job is better than no job". He was well aware of the risk that low-wage workers could be caught in a poverty trap by unmitigated market forces if the education system did not adequately equip them with the necessary skills.

Yet another dimension of distribution was the intergenerational redistribution of income through the transfer budgets of governments. As welfare systems expanded rapidly while economic growth slowed at the same time, the sustainability of social security systems, in particular the financial burden placed on the generation of the young, began to become major concerns. Also, Bombach accurately predicted that developments in the personal distribution of income would receive much more attention in the future than the stale old dichotomy of labour versus capital income, adding that slowing growth would significantly exacerbate distributional conflicts.

5.4 Inflation, Unemployment and Stabilization Policy

Once neoclassical growth theory had been extended into several directions—two-sector models, ever more complex production functions—and once the golden rule of accumulation had been independently discovered by a number of researchers, Bombach's PhD student Carl Christian von Weizsäcker (1962) among them, the focus of the international macroeconomic research community gradually turned away from growth in the course of the 1960s. The inexorable rise of inflation in the United States lent momentum to the rise of the Chicago School of monetary economics as the leading theory of inflation and as a serious challenger to the ruling Keynesian mainstream in macroeconomics. Friedman's restated quantity theory of money became widely accepted and his k-percent rule for the money supply was put into practice by a number of central banks after the collapse of the fixed-exchange-rate system of Bretton-Woods had freed them to pursue monetary targeting.

Despite the voluminous empirical evidence adduced in support of the monetarist approach, Gottfried Bombach remained unconvinced. In his view, the exclusive focus on the money supply as a driver of inflation failed to get to the root of the problem. He felt the proposition that inflation resulted from an excess of money supply growth over potential output growth was close to a truism with no deeper explanatory power. To understand inflation, he argued, one has to go beyond narrow economic mechanisms and instead focus on unresolved conflicts in society at large. As Rector of the University of Basel, he devoted his keynote lecture on the occasion of the 1973 "Dies Academicus", the annual official ceremony of the university, to the problem of inflation. He set the tone of his lecture by citing his long-time faculty colleague, the philosopher Karl Jaspers:

> Inflation is a consequence of social and economic conflicts not being actually fought. One avoids them by choosing the path of least resistance. False compromises look beneficial and ensure calm for the moment, but make inflation rise subsequently. (Karl Jaspers, cited by Bombach, 1973, p. 363)

The notion of inflation as a vent for unresolved distributional conflicts in society had already had a long tradition in post-Keynesian economics, of course. There was no consensus, however, on whether inflation was part of the problem or part of the solution. Bronfenbrenner and Holzman (1963, p. 626), in laying out a model of what they termed "income inflation", suggested that inflation could act as a "social mollifier" by reconciling inconsistent real income claims in nominal terms, thereby preventing "open social strife". Perhaps sensing that such a "mollifying" property of inflation depended on the money illusion of the competing claimants, Bombach took the opposite stance, siding with Streissler (1973, p. 39) who regarded inflation as a self-perpetuating symptom of social tensions or, as he put it, a "silent civil war".

Unlike many post-Keynesians of his time, Bombach did not believe in the effectiveness of price and wage controls or an 'incomes policy' which he thought were mere tinkering with the symptoms instead of a true cure for inflation. Having framed price stability as a "precious public good", he was well aware of the need for collective action, deeming properly restrictive demand policy a necessary though not sufficient tool in the absence of "a sense of collective social responsibility" for the common good (Bombach, 1973). In contrast, he thought that relying solely on the monetarist recipe of tight money carried the risk of unknown, but potentially serious side effects. This warning, given to a Swiss audience at a time when Switzerland had just abandoned its exchange-rate peg and adopted a strict monetarist money supply rule, turned out to be prophetic.

As it happened, the ongoing Swiss inflation collided with the near-halt of money supply growth, resulting in a shock appreciation of the Swiss Franc on the foreign exchanges and a plunge of Swiss GDP that was unparalleled by any other industrial country at the time. In these turbulent times, the Swiss government and the Swiss National Bank jointly established a council of experts, resembling the German Council of Economic Advisers, appointing Gottfried Bombach as one of its three members. It was a short-lived experiment, ending after only three years and three substantive reports by the council (Expertengruppe Wirtschaftslage, 1977–1980). Still, the council took the opportunity to highlight a number of crucial factors that had made the crisis worse. The procyclical bias of the highly decentralized Swiss fiscal system was one of them. Another was the habit of tying wages to inflation which exacerbated both inflation and recession when Switzerland was hit by external supply shocks. Indexation, not just of wages, but also of government bonds, the tax code and other long-term nominal contracts, had been favoured by many monetarist economists since the 1960s as a device for minimizing the real distortions of inflation and for keeping the costs of disinflation low (Friedman, 1974). However, what could have worked reasonably well in the presence of an inflation that was entirely caused by excessive monetary expansion, turned out to act as an outright fire accelerator when inflation was mainly ignited by the supply-side shock of a skyrocketing oil price. Italy's famous *scala mobile* stood out as a particularly drastic illustration of the perils of indexation.

Switzerland managed to get through the deep recession of the mid-1970s with a minimal increase of unemployment, which was only possible because unemployment was effectively exported abroad by sending scores of foreign seasonal workers back home. But both in the rest of Europe and in the United States, unemployment became the most pressing public policy problem for the first time since The Great Depression. This revived the interest in Keynes and Keynesian theory which had been somewhat put on the defensive by the rise of global inflation and the concomitant monetarist counter-revolution. It was the perfect time for Bombach to start his next major academic endeavour: the edition of a series of six volumes dedicated to Keynesianism and its current status in economic theory and policy (Bombach et al., 1976–1997). Originally designed to comprise but four volumes, this research also set itself the task of exploring the origins of Keynesian thinking in Germany at the time of the Weimar Republic.

A number of smart economists in Germany had developed ideas along similar lines as Keynes in the years 1930-1932, although none of them came close to an intellectual framework as stringent, coherent and influential as the one laid out by Keynes in the *General Theory* a few years later. But some clear analytical thinking did exist that would have shown Germany a way out of the Great Depression well before the Nazi regime seized power in 1933. Unfortunately, these ideas came to nothing. In part, this was due to political constraints. The burden of war reparations and Germany's commitment to the rules of the Gold Standard severely restricted its scope for expansionary macroeconomic policies. But also, the desirability of monetary and fiscal stimulus in a depression, which subsequently was to become the key policy message of Keynesian economics, was vigorously rejected by the pre-Keynesian mainstream in monetary economics, in particular by the Austrian school as represented by Ludwig von Mises and Friedrich August von Hayek.

Bombach had little patience with the moral overtone of the Austrian school and its assertion that excessive monetary expansion during the prior boom phase created distortions in the structure of production which needed to be purged from the system by enduring an extended period of depressed economic activity:

> There was a curious notion of atonement here as if one had to pay for the sins of the past. The great Friedrich von Hayek has expressed the traditional opinion most succinctly: monetary overexpansion was to blame for the crisis; trying to fight the crisis with pointed monetary expansion would thus amount to curing the evil with its own cause! A striking case of how a brilliant, seemingly logical phrasing by a great man can have a lasting tragic influence on policy. (Bombach, 1976b, p. 4)

Turning to the lessons from the turbulent 1970s, Bombach was careful to define a middle ground between two bitterly opposed camps in macroeconomics: on one side the new neoclassical school which thought that the simultaneous increase in inflation and unemployment had discredited Keynesian macroeconomics once and for all (Lucas & Sargent, 1978) and on the other side the unreconstructed "fundamental Keynesians of present-day Cambridge" (Bombach et al., 1976–1997, Vol. III, p. X). What he thought was discredited by events was that overconfident "hydraulic" Keynesianism of the 1950s and 1960s which had been led to believe that macroeconomic demand management had made the business cycle obsolete and that fine-tuning the economy was about as achievable by economists as engineers were capable of fine-tuning a machine. But that was not the end of Keynesian economics: "Upon reading the *General Theory*, not even a hint of the idea of fine-tuning the business cycle can be found" (Bombach, 1983, p. 422). At the very least, he argued, governments should let automatic stabilizers run their course without interfering in a pro-cyclical manner.

In his analysis of why the age of full employment had come to an end in Germany, Bombach emphasized the role of the mechanism of wage determination. He pointed out the obvious conflict between the particular German concept of "Tarifautonomie", i.e. the autonomous wage determination through negotiations between employers and unions, and the full-employment promise of a naïve Keynesian policy framework. There was simply no point for unions to exercise wage restraint if they could rely on the government to take care of the fallout of excessive wage claims. Under these circumstances, a full-employment promise was untenable as it would entail potentially limitless inflation. Perhaps unintentionally, Bombach was led by his analysis to a conclusion akin to Milton Friedman's proposition that monetary policy, or the government for that matter, could not peg the unemployment rate while the determination of wages was left to the private sector.

Bombach attributed the coexistence of full employment with moderate inflation in the period of the *Wirtschaftswunder* to a cautious wage policy which, incidentally, did not depend on an effective control of the money supply. Wage restraint was sustained, he argued, exactly as long as workers were not fully confident that the extraordinary productivity advances of those years would continue. As one of Bombach's favourite lines went, "for a long time, trade unions did not believe in economic growth, and when they had finally learned to count on it, it was over". This was the core of his theory of stagflation.

The final volume of Bombach's Keynesianism project, published in 1997, returned to issues of long-term development, exploring the influence of Keynesian thinking on the theory of economic growth. By the choice of this topic, Gottfried Bombach reiterated his long-held belief that the fluctuations of economic activity, which were typically considered to be the subject of short-run Keynesian macroeconomics, and the long-term growth of the economy, typically addressed within the framework of neoclassical theory, could in fact not be properly separated—even if the practice of academic research and graduate teaching for the most part suggested otherwise. His extensive literature review went as far as to cover endogenous growth theory which was brand-new at the time. He clearly sympathized with the objective of closing the large gap left by the unexplained Solow residual. But he expressed some doubts about the empirical basis of this new approach although he refrained from giving a definitive judgment. Having begun his long and distinguished academic career by dissecting post-Keynesian growth theory almost half a century earlier, it was *déjà vu* for him to see some variants of the new growth theory bring Harrod-Domar-style linear models back into fashion.

5.5 Conclusion

What are Gottfried Bombach's major achievements that will be remembered? To be sure, there is no Bombach model or Bombach alpha that made it into present-day textbooks. His more lasting, if less visible long-term importance derives from his role in reconnecting Germany with modern economics after the war. He influenced the development of macroeconomics in the German-speaking countries through his widely-read writings on economic growth, income distribution, inflation and business cycles, by his role in the German Economic Association (*Verein für Socialpolitik*), particularly in its standing committee for theoretical economics, as a consultant on economic policy, and as an advisor to numerous junior researchers who would later move on to become university professors themselves. His lectures at the University of Basel captivated scores of students over more than three decades, illuminating current economic theory, relating it to current events and embedding it in the longer history of economic thought.

There was no such thing as a "Bombach School" in Basel. His guidance to researchers at his Institute for Applied Economic Research was stimulating, but he granted his students a long leash to explore their own fields of interest and to find their own ways. They were all strongly influenced by his rejection of any type of dogmatism and by his flair for applying stringent reasoning to the most pressing economic concerns of society. As a devoted macroeconomist, he never lost sight of the big picture and stood above the petty political conflicts of the special interests. With his open mind, he was widely accepted and admired by practitioners across the political spectrum, invited as a speaker by trade unions, employers and industrialists alike.

Together with influential scholars such as Walter Jöhr, Friedrich Lutz, Jürg Niehans and Karl Brunner, he shaped the public discourse on economic policy in Switzerland for more than three decades, at times ensuring that the Keynesian perspective was not lost. In this capacity, he regularly made his voice heard in the media or as an advisor to the Swiss government.

On the occasion of Gottfied Bombach's 70th birthday in 1989, a symposium was held in his honour at the University of Basel. Robert Solow accepted an invitation to give the keynote address at this occasion and took the opportunity to discuss Bombach's wide-ranging essays on economic growth that had just been published as the 1986 De Vries Lectures (Solow, 1989). Sure enough, Solow politely pointed out some areas of disagreement, such as the role of aggregate demand for long-run growth, but mainly emphasized their shared vision of the big questions of economics and of what it meant to serve society as an economist. In his own masterful way, he combined his assessment of the current state of economics with his appreciation for Gottfried Bombach:

> I am led to a general hypothesis about our profession. I have the feeling that economics produces fewer and fewer Bombachs as time goes on. That is not to say that economics produces fewer and fewer able and well-trained economists. The number of those appears to be increasing, and their skills improving. The endangered species is the economist who combines two other qualities with technical skill. The first is the informed judgment about economic events that comes with long informal observation of the world of affairs combined with reflection on how it must look to intelligent participants and to intelligent observers. The second quality is the understanding that almost everything that happens in the sphere of economics has moral overtones, and tells us something, not only about the elasticity of this with respect to that, but about the character of our society itself. Bombach has been such an economist. (Solow, 1989, p. 1)

References

Bombach, G. (1953). Zur Theorie des Wirtschaftlichen Wachstums. *Weltwirtschaftliches Archiv, 70*, 110–165. Reprinted in Borner/Riese (1991), 3–58.

Bombach, G. (1959a). Probleme der Produktivitätsmessung. *Konjunkturpolitik, 6*, 321–343. Reprinted in Borner/Riese (1991), 59–81.

Bombach, G. (1959b). Preisstabilität, wirtschaftliches Wachstum und Einkommensverteilung. *Schweizerische Zeitschrift für Volkswirtschaft und Statistik, 95*, 1–20. Reprinted in Borner/Riese (1991), 253–272.

Bombach, G. (1965). *Wirtschaftswachstum, Handwörterbuch der Sozialwissenschaften* (Vol. XII, pp. 763–801). Springer.

Bombach, G. (1972). *Neue Dimensionen der Lehre von der Einkommensverteilung*. Basler Universitätsreden 66. Reprinted in Borner/Riese (1991), 330–361.
Bombach, G. (1973). *Inflation als wirtschafts- und gesellschaftspolitisches Problem*. Basler Universitätsreden 67. Reprinted in Borner/Riese (1991), 365–395.
Bombach, G. (1976a). Wachstumstheorie und Grenzen des Wachstums. In G. Bombach et al. (Eds.), *Ausgewählte Probleme der Wachstumspolitik, Schriftenreihe des Wirtschaftswissenschaftlichen Seminars Ottobeuren* (Vol. 4, pp. 135–159). Mohr. Reprinted in Borner/Riese (1991), 102-126, Mohr.
Bombach, G. (1976b). Einleitung. In Bombach et al. (1976–1997), Vol. II, pp. 1–8.
Bombach, G. (1981). Ein Modell und sein Echo. *Kyklos, 34*, 517–539. Reprinted in Borner/Riese (1991), 396-418.
Bombach, G. (1983). Strategien im Kampf gegen die Arbeitslosigkeit. In Neue Zürcher Zeitung (Ed.), *Arbeitslosigkeit – Schicksal der achtziger Jahre?* University of Freiburg. Reprinted in Borner/Riese (1991), 421–428.
Bombach, G. (1986a). *Post-war economic growth revisited*. De Vries Lecture.
Bombach, G. (1986b). Lohnniveau, Lohnstrukturen und Beschäftigung. *List Forum, 13*, 287–307. Reprinted in Borner/Riese (1991), 429–449.
Bombach, G. (1989, August 29). *"Erlebtes Eigentum" durch Vermögenspolitik—ein Rückblick auf enttäuschte Erwartungen*. Neue Zürcher Zeitung.
Bombach, G. (1991a). Wohlstandsmessung und Wohlstandsvermehrung: Produktivitätsdebatte einst und heute, Thünen Lecture. *Zeitschrift für Wirtschafts- und Sozialwissenschaften, 111*, 1–26.
Bombach, G. (1991b). Vorbemerkungen. In Borner, & Riese (1991), XI–XXVII.
Bombach, G. (2001). Ein „Brief“ an Hans Jürgen Ramser. In S. Berninghaus, & M. Braulke (Eds.), *Beiträge zur Mikro- und Makroökonomik – Festschrift für Hans Jürgen Ramser* (pp. 63–74). Springer.
Bombach, G., et al. (1976–1997). *Der Keynesianismus* (Vol. I–VI). Springer.
Borner, S., & Riese, H. (Eds.). (1991). *Zwischen Wirtschaftstheorie und Wirtschaftspolitik, Ausgewählte Beiträge von Gottfried Bombach*. Springer.
Bronfenbrenner, M., & Holzman, F. (1963). Survey of inflation theory. *American Economic Review, 53*, 593–661.
Bundesbank. (1965, July 21). *Das Ausmaß der Geldentwertung seit 1950 und die weitere Entwicklung des Geldwerts, Report.*
Domar, E. (1946). Capital expansion, rate of growth, and employment. *Econometrica, 14*, 137–147.
Expertengruppe "Wirtschaftslage". (1977–1980). *Lage und Probleme der Schweizerischen Wirtschaft*, 3 Vols.
Friedman, M. (1968). The role of monetary policy. *American Economic Review, 58*, 1–17.
Friedman, M. (1974). *Monetary correction: A proposal for escalator clauses to reduce the costs of ending inflation*. Institute of Economic Affairs, Occasional Paper No. 41.
Friedman, M., & Schwartz, A. (1963). *A monetary history of the United States 1867-1960*. Princeton University Press.
Giersch, H. (1985). *Eurosclerosis, Kiel discussion papers 112*.
Hahn, F., & Matthews, R. (1964). The theory of economic growth: A survey. *Economic Journal, 74*, 779–902.
Harrod, R. (1939). An essay in dynamic theory. *Economic Journal, 49*, 14–33.
Harrod, R. (1948). *Towards a dynamic economics*. Macmillan.
Harrod, R. (1973). *Economic dynamics*. Macmillan.
Hicks, J. R. (1974). *The crisis in Keynesian economics*. Oxford University Press.
Kaldor, N. (1955). Alternative theories of distribution. *Review of Economic Studies, 23*, 83–100.
Keynes, J. M. (1930). *A treatise on money*.
Keynes, J. M. (1936). *The general theory of employment, interest and money*. Macmillan.
Kuznets, S., Epstein, L., & Jenks, E. (1946). *National product since 1869*. NBER Book.

Lucas, R., & Sargent, T. (1978). After Keynesian macroeconomics. In *After the Phillips curve: Persistence of high inflation and high unemployment* (pp. 49–72). Federal Reserve Bank of Boston.

Solow, R. (1956). A contribution to the theory of economic growth. *Quarterly Journal of Economics, 70*, 65–94.

Solow, R. (1988). Growth theory and after. *American Economic Review, 78*, 307–317.

Solow, R. (1989). *Economic growth in theory and practice*. WWZ-Sonderdruck Nr. 1.

Streissler, E. (1973). *Die schleichende Inflation als Phänomen der politischen Ökonomie*.

Tinbergen, J. (1942). Zur Theorie der langfristigen Wirtschaftsentwicklung. *Weltwirtschaftliches Archiv, 55*, 511–549.

von Weizsäcker, C. C. (1962). *Wachstum, Zins und optimale Investitionsquote*.

Chapter 6
Erich Preiser (1900–1967): Growth and Distribution in a Monetary Economy

Johannes Schmidt

6.1 Introduction

Erich Preiser (1900–1967) was one of the most influential economists in Germany. He was one of "the three great Erichs"[1] whose work was responsible for German economics catching up with the international discussion after the Second World War: Erich Schneider, Erich Gutenberg (in business economics), and Erich Preiser. Preiser used Keynesian concepts to a large degree, but he was not merely a follower of Keynes and his work; he developed Keynesian thoughts further and combined them with other strands of thought.

Preiser[2] was born in 1900 in Gera. He studied economics in Frankfurt/Main and graduated in 1924. His doctoral thesis discussed Marx's crisis theory and its further development (*Die Marx'sche Krisentheorie und ihre Weiterbildung*). Franz Oppenheimer was his thesis supervisor. Oppenheimer, who advocated a so-called 'liberal socialism', was one of Preiser's most important teachers. His influence on Preiser's work can be seen most clearly in distribution theory.

In 1930, Preiser qualified as a university lecturer at Tübingen. His teacher there was Wilhelm Rieger, a business economist. In his thesis, which he wrote for becoming a university lecturer ('Habilitation') and which Rieger appraised, he dealt with the relationship between economics and business administration. Rieger influenced

[1] Neumark (1980, p. 241) [„den drei großen Erichs"]. In the paper, all translations of German quotations are the author's.

[2] An exhaustive biography of Preiser is the work of Blesgen (2000).

J. Schmidt (✉)
Hochschule Karlsruhe, Karlsruhe, Germany
e-mail: johannes.schmidt@h-ka.de

J. G. Backhaus et al. (eds.), *Post-war Keynesianism in Germany and Western Europe*, The European Heritage in Economics and the Social Sciences 28,
https://doi.org/10.1007/978-3-032-00498-7_6

Preiser significantly concerning the theory of capital, the role of money and monetary calculation, and the importance of profit and its changes on the economic process.

After publishing his business cycle theory (Preiser, 1933), Preiser became an associate professor in Rostock in 1937. A year later, he became a full professor at the same university. In 1940, he went to Jena, in 1947 to Heidelberg, and 1956 to Munich, where he died in 1967. From 1950 to his death, he was a member of the scientific advisory board of the German Federal Ministry of Economics (‘*Wissenschaftlicher Beirat beim Bundeswirtschaftsministerium*’).

Most of Preiser’s work concerned economic development and growth. However, the topic that was very close to his heart was the theory and policy of distribution. In this realm, Preiser wanted to go beyond the marginal productivity theory: on the one hand, he tried to analyse how power—translated into economic categories—influences the distribution of income; on the other hand, he combined distribution theory with the theory of business cycles and economic growth.

This paper discusses two aspects of Preiser’s work that are of special importance to his contribution to the development of economic thought in Germany after 1945: his analysis of growth—which is closely connected to his analysis of business cycles—and his distribution theory. The paper is structured as follows: Section 6.2 describes Preiser’s analysis of growth and emphasises the importance Preiser attached to money and credit. Section 6.3 analyses his approach to distribution theory, where he tried to combine classical, neoclassical, and Keynesian elements, and Sect. 6.4 concludes.[3]

6.2 Preiser’s Analysis of Growth

6.2.1 The Fundamental Idea of Preiser’s Analysis of Economic Growth

Preiser analyses economic growth by investigating how investment can increase an economy’s productive capacity and how saving and investment are coordinated.

Preiser develops his analysis by confronting it with the ‘classical’ theory as Preiser sees it. In this classical theory, the analysis was carried out in two steps: first, the relative (real) prices of goods and factors of production are determined; second, the quantity theory delivers the necessary multiplicative factor to determine the absolute prices. Preiser states that this ‘classical dichotomy’ is correct if it is confined to analysing a stationary economy.

[3] Due to space constraints, the paper leaves out Preiser’s analyses concerning economic order—a field in which he was influenced by (and discussed with) Walter Eucken and the Ordoliberal school—and economic policy, especially distribution policy. More on these topics can be found in Schmidt (1998, 271ff).

However, according to Preiser, more is needed if processes of growth and development are to be analysed. To do this, three modifications have to be made, which are the central characteristics of the modern economic theory as Preiser sees it (Preiser, 1950, 66):

- Firstly, the focus on prices and costs, which aims to analyse the coordination of economic units, has to take a back seat. A focus on the whole economic circuit must replace the traditional theory's focus. This leads to a different approach to several problems, especially the coordination of saving and investment. In the 'old' theory, these factors are coordinated (and brought into equality, respectively) by changes in the interest rate; in the 'new' theory, changes in income coordinate these activities.
- A second modification comes onto the stage if one abandons the classical dichotomy. Then there emerges a "completely different perspective that comes from proceeding from the thinking of the classical theory, which is oriented towards real economic relations with a quantity theoretic wrap to the perspective of the newer theory which has given up the hypothesis of the mere money veil, has abandoned the coexistence of 'general' theory and monetary theory, and has inserted money as link and factor in the whole economic process" (Preiser, 1950, 66). For Preiser, money and credit as well as the banking system play an essential role for understanding the process of economic growth. Thereby, money can "also deeply influence the relations of prices and therefore income distribution and prices" (Preiser, 1944, 10).
- Thirdly, static and comparative-static equilibrium analysis has to be supplemented by a dynamic or process analysis.

6.2.2 *Preiser's Analysis of the Growth Process*

6.2.2.1 The Basic Definitions: Investment, Saving, and Hoarding

In his analysis, Preiser distinguishes strictly between entrepreneurs and consumers, two groups of actors. Consumers are, at the same time, factors of production that place their services at the disposal of entrepreneurs and become remunerated for these services. The factor incomes also include a 'normal' employer's salary, as the entrepreneur is also a factor of production who is remunerated for his regular services. Regarding profit, Preiser does not include the average employer's salary in this term, but only the profits emerging during investment and growth.

The three central activities in a growing economy are investment, saving, and hoarding, which Preiser defines in the following way (Preiser, 1944, 17ff.):

- *Investment* means enlarging or upgrading productive capacity. Only the entrepreneur makes investments.
- *Saving* has a negative meaning for Preiser: it is an act of the consumer that requires him to refrain from spending parts of his income on consumption goods.

This does not imply any statement of how these parts that are not consumed are used.

- *Hoarding* means saving in liquid form. If somebody wants to save, they can open a savings account (or not use amounts of his current account), i.e., accumulate liquid savings, or buy securities or other assets, i.e., save in non-liquid form. However, this choice is open only for the single saver, not for the entire group of savers. If additional savers want to buy securities and the supply does not increase, they can only buy securities from other savers who, in turn, have to save in liquid form. So, an increase in saving inevitably leads to an increase in hoarding if there is no additional security flotation, e.g., due to additional investments. That means a stand-alone saving increase only has a depressing effect: the demand for consumption goods goes back without automatically initiating compensations, e.g., through higher investments.

These activities and the strict separation of entrepreneurs and consumers form the basis for Preiser's analysis. The starting point is the equilibrium of a stationary economy in which only consumption goods are produced and sold so that the revenue covers the cost of production. In this economy, investments are made to increase productive capacity. How are saving and investment coordinated?

6.2.2.2 The 'Classical' Case: Saving Induces Investment

Preiser considers the 'classical' case—where saving is the necessary precondition for investment in real as well as in monetary terms—as a starting point, but only to dissociate himself from its results for three reasons: first, this approach overrates the importance of saving. In a monetary economy, the primary effect of saving is purely negative: it causes a fall in demand on the market for consumption goods, associated with reductions in prices and/or production restraints (Preiser, 1944, 43).

Secondly, even if an equal amount of investment accompanies saving, the production structure is changed without expanding it; a mere redirection of production cannot expand supply. Furthermore, the central question arises regarding which sources will have the definitive demand to buy the increased amount of goods (Preiser, 1953b, 114).

The third reason for Preiser dissociating himself from the classical approach is that the investment and growth process still needs to be clarified, and its description needs to measure up to the realities of a monetary economy. For Preiser, the fact is crucial that the growth of production would be impossible if the banking system would not grant investment loans (Preiser, 1953b, 113). However, the allocation of these loans makes it necessary to create new money because Preiser thinks that banks are not only *intermediaries*, that is, pool incoming savings and transfer them to entrepreneurs/investors, but *creators* of new money through granting loans. The banking system is more or less independent from the existence of savings when granting loans; savings are not the (financial) precondition of investment. To understand the processes of saving, investment, and growth, Preiser begins with an analysis of the financial flows connected with these processes; to understand them fully, the banking system has to be considered specially.

6.2.2.3 Saving and Investment: The Financial Flows and the Interest Rate(s)

Preiser develops his analysis of the financial flows of saving and investment (in the closed economy) in two steps (Preiser, 1944, 24ff.): in the first step, he assumes that all money consists of bank money, there is no cash; furthermore, there exists only one bank over which accounts all financial transactions are carried out. The important thing is that this bank has no liquidity problem as there is no money drain in the form of cash or to other banks. The bank is free to choose the credit policy it thinks is suitable. In the second step, he assumes a two-stage banking system with a central bank and several commercial banks. In this system, the individual bank has to care for its liquidity; this modifies the results deducted for a single bank.

Step 1: A Single Bank

What do the financial flows connected with a new investment look like when only one bank exists and all payments are made by book money?

The investor or entrepreneur, respectively, who wants to carry out a new line of production or a new investment does not need goods. However, he needs money to buy the necessary factor services (e.g., labour) and finance the planned investment.

The important point is that different economic actors carry out saving and investment. The entrepreneur carrying out an investment does not receive his means directly from savers, but he needs to take out a loan from the bank. Granting a loan means an extension of the bank's balance sheet: its assets (the loan) grow and its liabilities (the loan becomes a deposit in the borrower's current account). As there is only book money in this economy, the loan means an increase in the money supply. So investment means money creation, and for Preiser, this is the crucial precondition for economic growth; production and employment can only be increased if the money supply is increased and an additional *nominal* income is created; the additional *real* income (in the form of newly produced goods) exists only after the increase of the production has been completed.

The independence of investment from saving becomes quite clear here: when granting an investment loan, the bank is completely independent of the dispositions of savers. Furthermore, the loan granted by the bank is not 'additional' in the sense that it exceeds the existing savings; for Preiser, *every* loan granted to an investor by the bank adds to the existing assets and liabilities, and the amount of money relinquished through the loan has no connection to the amounts savers dispose of (Preiser, 1944, 27).

What are, on the other hand, the effects of saving (in the sense of a voluntary restraint of consumption)? If there are no additional securities or other non-liquid saving media, the saver can only hoard his deposits or open a savings account. The bank's balance sheet has not been changed (at all events, amounts on current accounts are switched to savings accounts), but the decision means a quiescence in the circulation of money. For Preiser, both processes—creating money by investment and suspending money by saving—are different and stand-alone transactions (Preiser, 1944, 27).

Is there any connection between the monetary flows connected with saving and investment? The classical and neoclassical theory regards interest rate movements as the central link between saving and investment: higher saving lowers the interest rate and leads to higher investment, bringing these two factors into equilibrium.

However, Preiser is also sceptical in this respect. Preiser distinguishes between two different kinds of interest rates (Preiser, 1944, 28ff.): the bank rate ('*Bankzins*') and the bond rate ('*Effektenzins*').[4]

The *bank rate* describes the complex of banking-related rates (deposits, loans etc.). It is assumed that it is the short-term lending and borrowing rate, although Preiser does not say that explicitly. As the bank has (by assumption) no liquidity problem to solve, it is free to choose any rate it sees as suitable. The bank can be active or passive when acting on the market: if it is passive, it grants every loan at the chosen interest rate; in this case, investors'/entrepreneurs' demand for loans is the decisive factor. If the bank is active, it tries to practise a certain credit policy and considers macroeconomic factors. However, in the case of a passive policy, neither can increased investment induce an increase of the bank rate, nor can increased saving induce a reduction of the rate. Assuming that the bank has no liquidity problem, changes in interest rates can only be the result of the bank's active policy (Preiser, 1944, 29).

The *bond rate* shows the return on non-liquid assets of every kind: securities in a narrow sense, real estate, and so on. Again, Preiser is not explicit about the term, but it is assumed that the bond rate shows the conditions for longer-term borrowing and lending. These assets are not as liquid as bank accounts, so the bond rate is normally above the bank rate. If the bank did not exist, an investment exceeding saving would increase the bond rate, as the increased amount of securities entrepreneurs supply to finance their investment would reduce their price. On the other hand, increased saving in non-liquid assets would reduce the bond rate because of the increased demand for securities. However, this result becomes irrelevant if one takes the bank into account. If the bond rate tended to increase because of an increase in investment, the entrepreneurs/investors could fall back on bank loans; if the bank is passive, these loans are at their disposal at an unchanged bank rate so that the potential change of the bond rate does not come into effect. If the bond rate decreases because of an increase in saving (and draws near the bank rate), savers could fall back on liquid saving modes so that the ultimate decrease in the bond rate is small or nil.

---

[4] I chose the translations 'bank rate' (Bankzins) and 'bond rate' (Effektenzins) because Keynes used these two terms in his *Treatise* (Keynes, 1971, 179), and their definition is very similar to Preiser's. Preiser may have taken this distinction from Keynes.

These considerations lead to the result that, for Preiser, the bond rate does not have a stand-alone significance in addition to the bank rate: If the bank raises the bank rate, savers sell securities, so the bond rate also rises; if the bank lowers the bank rate, savers' demand for securities increases, and the bond rate also goes down. That is, the bank rate leads, and the bond rate follows.[5]

Is there a connection between investment and interest? Preiser has investigated this question in detail (Preiser, 1958). The result is that a decreasing bond rate can induce investment to a certain degree, especially if the investments are capital intensive; interest payments are a significant part of operating costs and require long-term financing. However, as we saw earlier, the most important factor for a decreasing interest rate is the bank's policy: even if it cannot reduce the bond rate directly, it can finance the investor's outlays by granting him a loan on the bank rate. So, a high bond rate may hamper the propensity to carry out certain investments, but it does not preclude the implementation of investments that were planned without considering the bond rate. So, neither does an increase in saving diminish interest nor does an increase in investment raise interest. The decisive factor is the bank's policy: it can determine the bank rate and so—at least indirectly—also the bond rate (Preiser, 1944, 37).

Step 2: A Two-Stage Banking System

So far, Preiser assumed the existence of a single bank with no cash, so it has no liquidity problem to solve. In the second step, he weakened this assumption and assumed a two-stage banking system with several commercial banks and a central bank; the assumption of a closed economy and the absence of cash were maintained. The most important difference in the case of a single bank is that banks now have to care for their liquidity as they need central bank money for the clearing process.

If the banks expand their loans because of increased investment, they need more central bank money. The central bank can choose whether it wants to grant the respective discount credits at the previous rate, i.e., if it wants to stay passive or whether it wants to restrict the credit expansion and, therefore, increase the bank rate. That means that even if there are several commercial banks and a central bank, an increase in investment is neither a necessary nor a sufficient condition for an increase in the interest rate; rather, it is the result of a deliberate banking policy (Preiser, 1944, 38).

[5] There is one qualification to this result: if one regards savers' dispositions of *existing* savings (instead of additional savings), there can be the case that due to an increased liquidity preference, savers try to exchange their securities for liquid assets (savings accounts, etc.). This reduces the price of securities, increases their return, and increases the distance between the bank rate and the bond rate. Result: An increase (decrease) in the liquidity preference can increase (decrease) the bond rate.

What are the results of increased saving in the case of several commercial banks? The decisive factor is whether the savers strive for liquid assets (savings accounts) or non-liquid ones (securities, etc.). If people save in liquid form, it is important to note that banks do not receive any additional money, which could better their liquidity because the money on the existing accounts is, at all events, merely shifted (e.g., from current accounts to savings accounts). There could be a small liquidity-enhancing effect if the reserve requirements for savings accounts are lower than for current accounts, but this effect is quite modest. On the contrary, the most important effect of a higher liquid saving lies in its impact on demand: higher saving leads to a reduction in demand; the firms suffering from that reduction of demand may have difficulties paying their interest and debts which they have incurred to start their production and to pay the factor services. This, in turn, will make banks more careful when granting new loans. They might even increase their interest rate to limit further credit creation. So, higher saving might lead to the seemingly paradoxical result of a higher interest rate instead of a lower one (Preiser, 1944, 38f.)—and the reverse is true for reducing liquid saving. Here, one finds a result similar to that of Keynes: an increase in liquidity preference, i.e., an increase in saving in liquid form, can lead to an increase in the interest rate. However, for Preiser, this effect—which does not necessarily arise in any case—does not result directly from the higher liquidity preference of the public; the crucial question is again how it affects the banking system and its liquidity.

The result is different if savers strive for non-liquid assets: on the one hand, the bond rate could decrease due to the increased demand of savers, but in this case, the savers could switch to liquid assets so that the rate decrease would not become effective. However, on the other hand, the higher demand for non-liquid assets enables entrepreneurs/investors to consolidate earlier investments that bank loans have financed: they float securities and pay back the bank loans with the proceeds. In this case, the increased demand for securities is matched by an increased supply. In effect, the bond rate does not change, but the banking system's liquidity changes for the better. Moreover, this enables the bank to expand its credit granting and cut interest rates.[6]

6.2.2.4 The Real Processes of Saving and Investment

The Basic Multiplier Process

After considering the financial flows connected with saving and investment, the real side of the processes of saving and investment are analysed. Preiser describes these processes in detail (especially in Preiser, 1955). The most important point in Preiser's analysis is that he considers not only the income streams (consumption,

---

[6] Preiser is not explicit about the fall in demand that also occurs in the case of non-liquid saving. The effect of falling demand on investment should be weighed against the interest-decreasing effect resulting from bank loan consolidation.

investment, saving, and income) as in the traditional Keynesian-oriented analyses but also the formation of profits—which in turn influence the production decisions of firms—and the movement of prices that begins after the creation and use of the new money. Furthermore, Preiser divides the economic process into periods to clarify the events more clearly.

The process described by Preiser is a multiplier process which runs as follows: the entrepreneurs/investors pay the services necessary for carrying out the new investment by using the money created by the loan they take from the bank. So the receivers of this money, e.g., the (new) employees in the investment goods industry, get additional nominal income. This new income leads to an additional demand on the market for consumption goods, but new consumption goods have not been produced. Therefore, the prices of consumption goods increase so that producers can make additional profits. Preiser calls these profits "dynamic profits of market condition" (*dynamische Marktlagengewinne*) and marks them with the letter Q.[7] These profits are the offset entry of investment in the national accounts; they are part of 'corporate saving'. In this process, a real restraint of consumption occurs because of the increased prices of consumption goods; this process is called 'forced saving'—a process already described by Wicksell (1898 [1997]). The Q-profits are larger or smaller depending on the amount the newly employed workers save out of their income. The firms to which these profits accrue are incentivised to increase their production in the next period. This again leads to additional income, increased demand for consumption goods, additional (albeit smaller) Q-profits, etc. The process stops and reaches a new equilibrium when investment and voluntary saving are equal, and the Q-profits are zero. As the production of consumption goods also increases in this multiplier process, the initial price increases are gradually reduced; in the end, the price level is the same as at the beginning. Preiser shows that the price increase is only temporary because an increased production compensates them. So, money creation is only potentially inflationary: if one considers the whole expansion process, the price level remains constant if production is increased.

Preiser shows in his multiplier analysis that investment determines saving, not the other way round as supposed in the 'classical' and neoclassical approaches and that saving in the sense of a voluntary restraint of consumption is not the essential precondition for investment; in fact, money creation through the granting of loans to investors/entrepreneurs is essential for getting development and growth started and for creating the definitive demand necessary for the sale of the newly produced goods.

Underemployed and Fully Employed Economy

However, Preiser also brings a differentiation into the picture. As already said, the core of Preiser's argument is a multiplier analysis: an autonomous investment induces additional income and production, and in the course of this process,

---

[7] The basic idea (as well as the letter) is taken from Keynes's "windfall profits" in his *Treatise on Money* (Keynes, 1971, pp. 112 ff.).

Q-profits are the offset entries of investment; gradually, new (voluntary) savings arise out of the newly created income until they match the higher investment. In analysing the real side of this process, Preiser asks whether this process always works favoured and whether the new investment can always be carried out and lead to a higher income. To analyse that, Preiser makes a distinction between an underemployed economy (*'unterbeschäftigte Wirtschaft'*) and a fully employed economy (*'vollbeschäftigte Wirtschaft'*) (Preiser, 1944, 44ff.).

In the underemployed economy, the process runs as described in the previous section. After autonomous investment, new factors of production, especially labour, are employed that were unemployed before. The expansion of the economy poses no special problems; investment automatically creates the required savings.

The situation is quite different in the fully employed economy. Here, at first, no unemployed production factors are at the investor's disposal. So he has to remove them from other utilisations, e.g., from the consumption goods industry, normally by bidding up wages. If factors move from the consumption goods industry to the investment goods industry, the output of the former decreases. As the demand for consumption goods stays the same (or increases slightly), there are also Q-profits in the consumption goods industry. Therefore, counterforces will emerge in the consumption goods industry to regain lost employees by bidding up wages. So, whether the planned investment can be carried out effectively is unclear. Whether it can be carried out depends on the elasticity of the production, which, according to Preiser, is low in a fully employed economy. In this case, the investment must be accompanied by voluntary saving so that the required production factors are available. For Preiser, this is the justified core of the traditional doctrine that (voluntary) saving is a necessary precondition for investment (Preiser, 1944, 48).

However, this distinction raises an important question: when is an economy fully employed so that voluntary saving is necessary for the success of an investment? Preiser himself says that the elasticity of production is the decisive factor, which cannot be determined only by looking at the unemployment rate. In his paper on saving and investment, published in 1944, Preiser states that after the war, saving will be a necessary factor for carrying out investments—not because of a lack of labour, which will, in fact, be abundant, but because of a lack of real capital labourers need to work with. As the capital stock is partially destroyed and run down, voluntary saving is necessary to carry out investments (Preiser, 1944, 64). However, later, Preiser had to correct himself on this point. He realised that the reconstruction of the German economy had succeeded without voluntary saving. In 1959, he said in a lecture that German industry was rebuilt after the war without voluntary saving (Preiser, 1959, 120). To explain that phenomenon, he sketched the explication described above: the reconstruction was financed by the creation of credit money, which granted entrepreneurs/investors the necessary means. As a conclusion from this analysis of the real side of the growing economy, one can say that the idea of a fully employed economy with a low elasticity of production seems to be a fuzzy concept: neither the rate of unemployment nor the given stock of resources and capital seems sufficient to state with certainty that an economy is fully employed. So, the usefulness of this concept remains undetermined.

6.2.2.5 The Significance of Saving

If one regards voluntary saving by households, its significance seems quite limited—on the contrary, it leads to a drop in demand. At all events, it has a positive effect only in a fully employed economy as it releases production factors for use in the investment goods industry. However, Preiser sees a significance for saving in two other respects, briefly hinted at before: in social policy (especially distribution) and banking policy.

As assumed in the description of the multiplier process, an investment is financed—at least in the first step—by a loan granted to the investor by the bank. Investment and the creation of related money leads to Q-profits. These, in turn, enable entrepreneurs to pay back their debt or to carry out further investment via self-financing. However, instead of high Q-profits, it is conceivable that the additional income will be saved, at least in part. New savers interested in non-liquid assets, e.g., securities issued by corporations, come onto the market. These corporations could repay their bank loans by floating new securities and getting longer-term investment financing. According to Preiser, this consolidation of investments has two effects: firstly, it promotes a more equal distribution of wealth and property in productive assets, one of Preiser's most important political concerns. Secondly, it enhances the banks' possibility to grant credit further, as the consolidation betters their liquidity. The banks must be concerned about consolidating every investment loan they have granted, for without such a consolidation, they would own a large block of long-term assets. So, consolidation secures the flexibility of commercial banks and the central bank's management possibilities. Only in this respect does the parlance of 'legitimising' investment through saving make sense (Preiser, 1950, 78).

To summarise, Preiser's position concerning saving is the following (Preiser, 1953b, 118): saving contributes nothing to the financing of an investment. However, saving in non-liquid form (especially securities) facilitates the financing of further investments by the banks as the consolidation improves the liquidity of commercial banks and the banking system. Furthermore, a greater demand for securities may lead to a reduction in the bond rate. It can ease the implementation of investments that may be hampered by a high bond rate (house building, utilities, etc.). Nevertheless, this is all saving can be credited with. For most investments, the interest rate has a low significance; they are implemented and financed without saving playing much of a role. The macroeconomic significance of saving lies in the same realm as its significance for the individual: acquiring and distributing personal assets.

6.2.3 The Similarities and Differences with Keynes and the Post-Keynesians

As was stated in the first sections, Keynes' work and ideas heavily influenced Preiser's macroeconomic analyses. Nevertheless, there are similarities and differences between Keynes' and Preiser's approaches, as will be shown in this section. Furthermore, Preiser's analysis points to certain aspects of modern post-Keynesian theory.

6.2.3.1 Preiser's Combination of *Treatise* and *General Theory*

Preiser combined two strands of Keynes' theory, namely the analysis in his *Treatise on Money*, with the central idea of effective demand in his *General Theory*.

Preiser's papers tie up to the definitions and analytical schemes in Keynes' *Treatise*. In the *Treatise*, Keynes starts from an economy with two sectors: an investment goods sector and a consumption goods sector. These sectors' (equilibrium) outputs are given, and the product prices are flexible. In an exogenous shock, unexpected profits or losses emerge due to differences between revenues and costs (per unit)—the so-called "windfalls". Keynes marks them with the letter Q. In reaction to the shock output, employment and, at a later stage, factor prices adjust until a new equilibrium is reached. How this long-term equilibrium will be interpreted is ambiguous, especially if it also means a full-employment equilibrium in the labour market. Normally, the *Treatise* is regarded as a work on monetary themes rooted in the classical theory: it accepted the long-term reference point of a given equilibrium output, the determination of which is not analysed, only deviations and disequilibrium processes; unemployment is a matter of cycles and disequilibrium (Klausinger, 1991, 144f.).

Nevertheless, the *Treatise* contains numerous elements Preiser adopted for his analyses: the definition of saving, profits, and investment, as well as the distinction between normal profits or employer's salary on the one hand and windfalls on the other (Keynes, 1971, 112ff.): saving and investment are independent decisions taken by different persons. Saving is a purely negative act of the consumer, namely not to consume parts of his income. Investment, on the other hand, means to implement a new production process (Keynes, 1971, 155). Furthermore, Keynes distinguished between "the normal remuneration of entrepreneurs" (Keynes, 1971, 111)[8] and his windfall profits (or losses), which result from external shocks. Preiser defined these terms similarly: his Q-profits are modelled on Keynes' windfalls. But for Keynes, their significance lies in the business cycle; they are not weaved into the description of growth processes, as in Preiser's work.

In the *Treatise*, Keynes deviated from classical analyses insofar as saving and investment do not adjust smoothly and do not need to be equal, as seen in the 'banana parable' (Keynes, 1971, p. 158 ff.).[9] The *Treatise* does not yet contain an

---

[8] Keynes defined this term as follows: "I propose to define the 'normal' remuneration of entrepreneurs at any time as that rate of remuneration which, if they were open to making new bargains with all the factors of production at the currently prevailing rates of earnings, would leave them under no motive either to increase or decrease their scale of operations." (Keynes, 1971, 112).

[9] The 'banana parable' is as follows: Assume an economy in which there is only one (perishable) consumption good, namely bananas. In the beginning, there is an equilibrium between saving and investment. Then, a thrift campaign is started, which leads to a lower consumption of bananas but without a higher investment. This, in turn, causes losses in production and induces producers to cut output and employment. Another demand shortfall follows this reduction, and so on. For Keynes, this deflationary process has no endogenous point of rest: "Thus there will be no position of equilibrium until either (a) all production ceases and the entire population starves to death, or (b) the thrift campaign is called off or peters out as a result of the growing poverty, or (c) investment is stimulated by some means or another so that its cost no longer lags behind the rate of saving" (Keynes, 1971, 160).

unemployment equilibrium, which is, in turn, a central concept of the *General Theory*. Furthermore, saving in the *Treatise* is an exogenous factor independent of income, and there are no mechanisms for equilibrating saving and investment (through changes in income).

This leads to the *General Theory*'s theoretical novelties. These novelties are foremost that saving and investment are coordinated by quantity adjustments, i.e., movements in output. The movements of the output themselves restore a new equilibrium with no further tendency to change, but this new equilibrium does not need to coincide with full employment.

However, in the *General Theory*, Keynes no longer distinguishes accurately between planned/expected and realised variables. Especially, there is no distinction between expected and realised profit (cf. Klausinger, 1991, 162ff.). The reason is the different question: the equilibrium output is no longer given or exogenous, but its determination is the central problem. Therefore, Keynes works with another definition of income, saving, and investment than in the *Treatise* (Keynes, 1973, 63):

Income = value of output = consumption + investment
Saving = income − consumption
Therefore, saving = investment

Keynes wants to show in the *General Theory* that, from a macroeconomic point of view, income and output are determined by individual decisions on consumption and investment; savings are merely a result of these decisions. Each investment creates the necessary savings through changes in income. The mechanism for that is the multiplier.

Keynes no longer does a process analysis in the *General Theory* but considers only short-term equilibrium states emerging after the multiplier process is finished. This explains why the equality of saving and investment is an identity and an equilibrium condition. "[W]ith given long-period expectations saving must be equal to investment as a condition of equilibrium, otherwise the multiplier would still be in operation and income would still be changing. In equilibrium, saving must by definition be identically equal to investment, as they both bear the same relation to the level of realised income; as $Y = I + C$ and $S \equiv Y - C$ so that $S \equiv I$" (Fletcher, 1987, 88).

Preiser, on the other hand, sticks to the analytical apparatus of the *Treatise* in his work. He considers the *General Theory*'s renunciation from a process analysis—which Keynes still used in the *Treatise*—as a regression. For Preiser, using the equation $I = S$ instead of $I = S + Q$ obscures important aspects of the whole process. Nevertheless, most notably, sticking to the apparatus of the *Treatise* gives Preiser starting points for dynamizing the static system Keynes developed in the *General Theory* (Preiser, 1951, 175).

For Preiser, the central idea of the Keynesian Revolution lies in the theory of effective demand, i.e., in the determination of income and employment through the interaction of consumption and investment function. Preiser links this idea of a demand-determined national income in the *General Theory* to the analytical apparatus of the *Treatise*. Preiser outstrips the idea of a pre-determined equilibrium output around which there are only fluctuations, primarily of the price level; his analysis of growth processes transcends the short-period view of the *General Theory*. This analysis is carried out with the help of process analyses, which are contained in the *Treatise*. So Preiser manages better to map entrepreneurial considerations and to make clear how the changes in income and the movements towards a new equilibrium come about. As he shows in detail in Preiser (1955), the changes in output result from changes in prices and profits.[10]

6.2.3.2 Liquidity Preference, Interest Rates and Endogenous Money

Preiser also combined Keynes' thoughts from the *Treatise* and from the General Theory concerning the significance of interest rates: in the *Treatise*, Keynes distinguished between the bank rate ("the effective rate for lending and borrowing which prevails in the market ... of money for short periods") and the bond rate ("the complex of interest rates effective in the market for borrowing and lending of money for longer periods"; Keynes, 1971, 179). The definition is similar to Preiser's use of 'Bankzins' and 'Effektenzins', and he probably took this distinction from the *Treatise*. But Preiser draws more radical conclusions from this distinction than Keynes: for Preiser, the bank rate is very significant for determining the bond rate; the banking system and the central bank, in particular, can determine the rates to a large degree. Moreover, Preiser does not refer to the Wicksellian distinction between the money rate and the natural rate of interest as Keynes still does in the *Treatise*.

Similar to the abdication of process analyses in the *General Theory*, Keynes does not give a detailed account of the monetary sector in this work as he did in the *Treatise*. So, the significance of the banking system for the interest rate is no longer apparent there. The most important theme for the determination of interest is the liquidity preference. Given the money supply, the interest rate is determined by the liquidity preference of the public. Changes in saving and/or investment can influence the interest rate only if they change the public's liquidity preference. In a paper written one year after the *General Theory*, Keynes introduced another motive of money demand to incorporate the financing of investments: the finance motive. This motive results from the fact "that an investment decision [...] may sometimes involve a temporary demand for money before it is carried out" (Keynes, 1937b, 246). Therefore, investment may influence interest, but this influence is not due to the investment as such but to the fact that planning a big investment leads to a demand for finance—which is nothing else but an increase in the demand for money and is, therefore, on a par with other reasons for money demand (transactions motive, precautionary motive, and speculative motive). "Thus, it is precisely the

[10] By reconstructing Keynes's theory of effective demand, Klausinger (1991, 162ff.) shows that this is basically also the case in the *General Theory*, but it is less apparent due to Keynes's abdication of the analytical apparatus of the *Treatise*.

liquidity-premium on cash ruling in the market which determines the rate of interest at which finance is obtainable" (Keynes, 1937b, 248). On the other hand, it is not possible to offset this influence on the interest rate through higher saving: "If there is a change in the liquidity position, the public can save ex-ante and ex-post and ex-anything else until they are blue in the face, without alleviating the problem in the least—unless, indeed, the result of their efforts is to lower the scale of activity to what it was before. [...] The investment market can become congested through a shortage of cash. It can never become congested through shortage of saving" (Keynes, 1937a, 668f.)

In Preiser's theory, the liquidity preference of the public does not have the same prominent place as in Keynes'. The most direct influence of an increased liquidity preference is on the bond rate. If the liquidity preference of the public rises, people shift their (existing) savings away from securities towards liquid savings accounts. This raises the bond rate and the difference between it and the bank rate. Nevertheless, the bottom line is that this does not necessarily mean an increase in the bank rate and restraint on investment; entrepreneurs can still fall back on bank loans, and whether the bank rate rises depends to a large degree on the central bank's policy.

The other influence of the public's liquidity preference in Preiser's theory is this: if people increase saving and wish to save in a liquid form, this means a fall in demand, which might complicate firms' redemption of their outstanding loans. This could lead to an increase in interest as banks become more careful in granting new loans. So, the result is similar to Keynes': trying to save more in liquid form could lead to a higher interest rate. However, this result does not come directly from a higher liquidity preference: Preiser has an intermediate link in his causal chain, namely the banking system, its operations and liquidity. The banking system and the central bank's policy are at least equally important for determining the interest rate. This can be seen again if people want to increase their savings and wish to buy securities, that is, to save in a non-liquid form. That promotes the consolidation of investments, betters the liquidity of the banking system and reduces the bank rate. Again, the functionality of the banking system is important for Preiser when considering the determination of interest rates.

Preiser takes a middle position between a liquidity preference theory and a theory of endogenous money. The former takes the money supply as given and regards the liquidity preference as the sole or at least most important determinant of interest; Keynes does so in the *General Theory*. The latter regards the money supply as completely demand-determined and sees no role whatever for liquidity preference (e.g. Moore, 1988). As Preiser sees money as an endogenous variable and money creation (in the form of credit money) as an important precondition for investment and growth, he is a forerunner of modern endogenous money theorists. However, he also sees liquidity preference's (albeit limited) role in determining interest. In this respect he points to modern developments in post-Keynesian monetary theory, which tries to combine these two strands of thought (Dow, 1997).

6.3 Preiser's Distribution Theory

Distribution theory was very close to Preiser's heart in his academic work, although the corresponding essays only make up a small part of his writings. The common denominator of Preiser's writings on distribution theory is the endeavour to regard sociological factors—first and foremost: social power positions—as an integral part of distribution theory. However, Preiser does not want power to be understood as a direct influencing factor on distribution; such an explanation is, in reality, the renunciation of an explanation. Since distribution is a pricing and market process, it must, therefore, be shown in what form power manifests itself on the market and influences distribution (Preiser, 1948, 227). Preiser's writings on distribution theory clearly show two things: firstly, the different doctrines and schools that have shaped Preiser, and secondly, his endeavour to unite these different doctrines and influences into a consistent system.

6.3.1 *Static Distribution Theory: Quasi-Monopoly and Marginal Productivity*

6.3.1.1 From Oppenheimer to Quasi-Monopoly

Preiser's theoretical interest in distribution issues is focused on the functional distribution of income. His views are based on a twofold division of the subject matter: at the beginning, there is the question of why certain types of income, primarily all types of property income, exist. The question how large the shares of the various types of income are is answered in a second step.

For the first question, Preiser refers back to his teacher Franz Oppenheimer—who described himself as a liberal socialist—and his *class monopoly theory*. For him, liberal socialism is a social order in which competition still prevails, but only labour income still exists, while profit and rent are no longer received as unemployed income (Oppenheimer, 1964, XX); differences in income are only based on differences in qualifications. However, as he finds it, the economy does not correspond to this ideal; rather, positions of power play a significant role, which arises, for example, through private ownership and unequal distribution of the means of production. For him, however, such a position of power is not created through purely economic transactions between free and equal people. Rather, it is the result of a violent appropriation either through robbery or with the help of the state.

For Oppenheimer, private ownership of land and the associated "land barrier" ("*Bodensperrung*") were at the centre of theoretical and social reformist interest. Appropriating the originally free land by a section of society creates a class state. If free access to the land is blocked, the landowners—even if they do not explicitly unite—face the landless workers as monopolists; they have a *class monopoly*. Since the landless workers, on the other hand, are urgently dependent on the sale of their labour power, they have to put up with a deduction from their labour income, which goes to the landowners. This situation, which Oppenheimer uses to explain the existence of the land rent, gives rise to a second situation: the free labourers whom the large landowners cannot accommodate migrate to the cities to earn a living there. They form the industrial reserve army, which now also gives the owners of other means of production (which, in contrast to land, can, in principle, be multiplied) a monopoly-like position and thus enables them to realise a capital profit.[11]

Preiser did not share Oppenheimer's almost manic adherence to the idea of the land barrier but maintained that the emergence of profit and property income was based on the private ownership of the means of production, which prevented all economic subjects from having unhindered access to these means of production. In addition, real capital can be produced and multiplied, but this multiplication is limited. "Thus, the entire stock of real capital (including land) is a limited stock at any given moment" (Preiser, 1959, 300). To this the unequal distribution must be added that makes utilisation as a source of profit possible. Preiser envisages a society with an equal distribution of wealth that only knows labour income. For him, such an equal distribution would mean that everyone would only use their wealth to support their production—Preiser speaks of labour property in this context (Preiser, 1934, 58). Interest-bearing utilisation would be impossible in the case of equal distribution "because, as a rule, there would be no demand for the use of other people's means of production or because—in the case of own use—a mark-up on the price of the products by *all* would leave the income of each individual the same as without a mark-up" (Preiser, 1959, 300). However, this conclusion is not compelling: instead of using his assets to run his business, the asset owner could prefer to work as an employee in a company and invest any assets he has on the capital market at a profit. In this case, the lending of assets and the associated interest payment may lead to wealth inequality (if the borrower can increase his income through this transaction to a greater extent than the lender's income is reduced) and, thus, again, to the occurrence of profit.

6.3.1.2 The Marginal Productivity Theory in Preiser's Version

Preiser criticises marginal productivity theory on three accounts: first, its attempt to explain distribution using natural economic relationships; second, its inadequate consideration of power and its significance for income distribution; and third, as a consequence of this, the lack of problematisation of the relative scarcity of factors of production. Preiser's concept of merging marginal productivity and quasi-monopoly theory arises from the last criticism.

According to Preiser, marginal productivity theory seeks the answer to the question of which distribution would occur if only purely economic aspects were considered (Preiser, 1953a, 279). This leads to the laws of production and the theory of

---

[11] For an analysis of Oppenheimer's theory, see Kurz (1996).

imputation. When rationalising the factors of production (labour, land, and material means of production), it is essential to correctly impute each factor's productive contribution with the help of marginal productivity considerations (Preiser, 1953a, 280).

In Preiser's view, the short-circuit that marginal productivity theory draws from this is that these considerations are transferred from *imputation* to *distribution*. To each factor of production, the productive contribution to which it is entitled based on imputation is distributed. Distribution is, therefore, subject to the same concept as production.

However, according to Preiser, this is a fallacy. Strictly speaking, this consideration only applies to labour. Here, the person and their productive contribution cannot be separated. The situation is different for the other productive services: land and material means of production. Although their productive contribution must be *imputed* to them for rational use, there would be no a priori reason not to *distribute* the (net) production yield entirely to labour. Preiser says this is different in a market economy due to the aforementioned private property.

Private property, not economic necessity, is the reason why the owners of assets (land, material means of production) receive a share of the production yield. Only the land and real capital are necessary for production, not their owners.

Preiser's second criticism of marginal productivity theory is the lack of, or rather insufficient, consideration of power factors and their influence on distribution. He does not want to stop at monopolistic market situations, which are usually mentioned as the prime example of economic power; much more important for Preiser is the power that arises from the distribution of property, which is also the reason for property income (Preiser, 1953a, 285).

The distribution of ownership finally leads to Preiser's third criticism of the marginal productivity theory, namely the lack of problematisation of the relative scarcity of the factors of production, especially labour. In Preiser's view, the marginal productivity theory was too generous in its calculations with a given, constant supply of factors of production. In contrast, the supply of labour and the (functional) distribution of income depend on the distribution of property. This leads to Preiser's proposal of combining marginal productivity and quasi-monopoly theory.

6.3.1.3 The Combination of Both Theories

Preiser's decisive link for the connection between marginal productivity and quasi-monopoly theory is the elasticity of the labour supply. As mentioned, Preiser accuses marginal productivity theory of assuming a constant supply of production factors, especially labour. For Preiser, however, this assumption is by no means compelling. A constant supply of labour only exists for the worker with no assets: he must take the wage that is offered to him and cannot wait to see whether he may have a better opportunity later (Preiser, 1948, 234).

However, this constant labour supply is not mandatory: an elastic labour supply that responds to the wage rate offered leads to a higher wage rate being paid to workers. Moreover, for Preiser, ownership is the decisive reason for an elastic labour supply (Preiser, 1948, 237).

Therefore, Preiser's combination of marginal productivity theory and quasi-monopoly theory can be summarised as follows: the distribution principle or the principle of factor pricing, on which the marginal productivity theory is based, remains unaffected. However, Preiser primarily problematises the supply of factors, particularly labour. Factors are not available in a certain, exogenously given quantity but must be made available on the market. The extent of this supply depends crucially on the distribution of ownership; because ownership makes it possible for the worker not to have to accept any remuneration; he can wait, and his labour supply becomes elastic.

This means that distribution is also permanently dependent on sociological factors, not only on production's technical or natural-economic conditions. At the same time, the central idea of the quasi-monopoly theory is brought to the fore: property income does not arise because of the positive contribution attributed to a factor of production but because of the ownership of this factor of production.

6.3.1.4 Problems of Preiser's Approach

Apart from the question of whether the disposal of wealth makes the labour supply more elastic, Preiser's approach has one major objection, which relates to his attempt to integrate quasi-monopoly and marginal productivity theory. Despite Preiser's criticism of marginal productivity theory, his approach is not quite as radical as he would like it to be. He does not touch the price formation principle of marginal productivity theory. The prices of the various production factors or productive services are determined simultaneously by supply and demand. This becomes clear in the example Preiser gives (Preiser, 1953a, 276ff.): he creates a simple general equilibrium system with only one consumption good and two production factors. Six equations (two supply functions of the production factors, one demand function of the households, two supply functions of the companies for the output or—alternatively—two demand functions of the companies for the input and one market equilibrium condition) help determine the six unknowns of the system (price and quantity of the consumption good, prices and quantities of the production factors).

Preiser's combination of quasi-monopoly and marginal productivity theory is now reflected in the supply functions of the factors of production that are determined by psychological and sociological data. However, the functions are constants when given quantities of production factors are assumed.

An essential condition for the fact that these functions are not constants is the distribution of ownership. However, this can be easily integrated by the general equilibrium theory, namely in the form of initial endowments. But this does not result in a decisive revision of marginal productivity theory; at most, it rightly rejects some ideological elements that could be found in some variants of marginal productivity theory,[12] which justify the actual income distribution and do not address the initial distribution. However, general equilibrium theory can certainly do the latter. The quasi-monopoly theory becomes just an appendix of it (Kurz & Kalmbach, 1981, 303); it disappears in the system of general equilibrium theory.

However, Preiser has recognised the shortcomings of his static distribution theory. The main problem for Preiser is that the introduction of supply functions instead of given factor quantities is also inadequate. Preiser is concerned with "the actions and reactions of the parties fighting for their share of the social product" (Preiser, 1970a, 48). In order to depict this, Preiser leaves the framework of marginal productivity theory and turns to more Keynesian-orientated theories.

6.3.2 Dynamic Distribution Theory

As already mentioned, one of Preiser's complaints about marginal productivity theory is its static character—static both in the sense that it is unable to "capture the process triggered by the continuous change in macroeconomic data" (Preiser, 1959, 304), and in the sense that economic growth itself is only very imperfectly described and explained. However, this is precisely what, according to Preiser, is necessary: you can only get a grip on income distribution and its changes if you simultaneously deal with the formation and change of national income. Conversely, the theory of income formation also needs to be linked to the distribution theory.

When Preiser's dynamic distribution theory is mentioned, this usually refers to his macroeconomic approach to distribution; its centrepiece is the structural degree of monopoly and is based on the theories of Kalecki (1987)and Kaldor (1955/1956).

6.3.2.1 The Basic Framework of Dynamic Distribution Theory: Structural Degree of Monopoly and Economic Demand

Preiser's starting point for deriving the degree of monopoly is, not surprisingly, the class or quasi-monopoly theory. Suppose the means of production are unequally distributed. In that case, the entrepreneur can achieve a profit by adding a mark-up to the labour costs. The degree of monopoly is simply the ratio of unit profit to price, i.e., the sum of unit wages and unit profit.

In his description, Preiser concentrates on the wage demands of workers and the price setting of entrepreneurs (Preiser, 1970a, 15). These wage and price demands should now be within a framework that makes them appear realistic and enforceable. In particular, this means that the price setting of the entrepreneurs (and thus the profit rate demanded by them) should not be followed by new wage demands on the

[12] For example, John Bates Clark's view, also mentioned by Preiser, that the 'rent getter' is also a 'product creator'.

part of the workers. Both sides should orient themselves to the actual possibilities in the distribution dispute. These possibilities are given by the social structure—which Preiser does not describe in detail, however—and this is expressed in a certain social degree of monopoly, i.e., the ratio of unit profit to price. According to Preiser, this structural degree of monopoly determines distribution in the long term.

In contrast, total economic demand, for example, only has a transitional effect on distribution. Suppose changes in demand lead to changes in distribution (such as through higher investment) that do not correspond to the goals and possibilities of the economic agents. In that case, there are corresponding reactions (such as additional wage demands) that restore a new long-term equilibrium corresponding to the social structure.

Nevertheless, Preiser does not want to underestimate the long-term importance of demand factors, as they also change the relative scarcity of production factors and, therefore, the social structure and distribution (Preiser, 1970a, p. 16).

However, Preiser initially excludes all changes in demand or growth processes that change the social structure and distribution. In addition, he assumes the validity of Say's law in order to eliminate all cyclical problems.

As already mentioned, the starting point is the pricing of entrepreneurs. Due to the distribution of ownership, entrepreneurs can impose a certain profit mark-up on their costs. In macroeconomic terms, i.e., disregarding all intermediate inputs of the companies, this amounts to a surcharge on labour costs. However, this surcharge is not proportional. This is because, in his view, the variable to which the companies orientate themselves is the profit rate π, with

$$\pi = \frac{P}{K}$$

K is the capital invested; according to Preiser's concept of capital, it is simply the amount of money invested. With the desired profit rate π, the amount of the (desired) profit sum, P, is also given. Since Preiser assumes full capacity utilisation of the plants and a limitational production function, the production quantity x and the number of working hours a are also given with a given K.

Preiser now looks for the reference value for the surcharge z, by which the desired profit rate π is to be achieved. For him, a percentage mark-up on labour costs is ruled out. This is because the wage rate has no fixed relationship to the rate of profit and, therefore, represents "an extraneous element" (Preiser, 1970a, 17). It is, therefore, better for Preiser to relate the surcharge to the labour hours, a, which are in a fixed relationship to K. In this case, the result is

$$P = \pi K = az$$

$$z = \pi \frac{K}{a}$$

For Preiser, the surcharge z is a monetary amount, i.e., an absolute surcharge. It results from the pursuit of a certain rate of profit. The mark-up now varies according to the intensity of capital, whereby Preiser also assumes that a uniform rate of profit is sought in all industries. For Preiser, this direct derivation of the (absolute) mark-up from the desired rate of profit has the advantage "that the problem of equalising the rate of profit does not even arise" (Preiser, 1970a, p. 19).

Considering the unit profit or the surcharge per unit, z_c, leads to Preiser's social degree of monopoly. The mark-up per unit is obtained by:

$$xz_c = \pi K = az$$

$$z_c = \frac{a}{x} z$$

With the labour costs per unit, l_c,

$$l_c = \frac{a}{x} l$$

you get the price p:

$$p = l_c + z_c = \frac{a}{x} l + \frac{a}{x} z = \frac{a}{x}(l + z)$$

If the unit profit is now related to the price, the result is

$$\frac{z_c}{p} = \frac{z_c}{l_c + z_c} = \frac{z\frac{a}{x}}{l\frac{a}{x} + z\frac{a}{x}} = \frac{z}{l + z} = \frac{P}{Y} \equiv \overline{\mu}$$

This gives us the social degree of monopoly, which Preiser describes as $\overline{\mu}$ and which is the 'supply-side' determinant of income distribution.

The basic idea in connection with the structural degree of monopoly is as follows: the economic agents have a certain idea of the 'right,' appropriate distribution, which they can enforce depending on their respective power. This social distribution of power is expressed in the structural degree of monopoly, based on a specific ratio of (unit) profit and product price. Preiser does not go into detail about the factors that determine this degree of social monopoly, "ultimately [it is] the relative rarity of the so-called factors of production that determines the degree of monopoly" (Preiser, 1970a, 22). However, this relative rarity is not given. However, it can be influenced—and as Preiser has emphasised, the distribution of property and wealth is a factor that significantly determines relative scarcity.

The structural degree of monopoly also forms the centre of gravity to which the actual distribution tends. Therefore, the degree of monopoly indicates the distribution in the long-term equilibrium.

In addition to this structural factor, economic demand and its distribution between investment and consumer spending also influence distribution. Preiser introduces the demand side with the Kaldor equation (Kaldor, 1955/1956). He thus has two equations for the distribution of income or the profit share: firstly, the equation of the structural degree of monopoly, which indicates the long-term distribution; secondly, Kaldor's demand equation, in which the distribution is "determined by the utilisation structures of the social product" (Oberhauser, 1996, p. 130)—with the investment share $\frac{\overline{I}}{Y}$ as the most important independent variable; furthermore, c_U is the propensity of entrepreneurs to consume, and s_A the workers' propensity to save..

$$\frac{P}{Y} = \frac{z}{l+z} = \overline{\mu}$$

$$\frac{P}{Y} = \frac{\overline{I}}{Y} \cdot \frac{1}{1-c_U - s_A} - \frac{s_A}{1-c_U - s_A}$$

Equating the two equations gives the following equilibrium value for national income:

$$Y = \overline{I} \cdot \frac{1}{\overline{\mu}\left(1-c_U - s_A\right)+s_A} \equiv \overline{I}\frac{1}{\sigma}$$

This gives an expression corresponding to the simple multiplier formula, but a more complex expression has replaced the simple savings rate—σ. The result is: "The level of national income—and thus its growth—depends not only on investment and the propensity to consume but also on the distribution of income as it results from the structural data" (Preiser, 1970a, 24).

Yet, it would be a coincidence that the planning of the economic agents resulted in both equations having the same (equilibrium) value for the national product. Instead, adjustment processes change the (nominal) national income until equilibrium is reached again. If (autonomous) investment expenditure $\overline{I}$ increases, for example, this leads to rising prices and thus—according to the second equation—to a higher profit share. However, as neither wages nor the profit mark-up z have been increased, this distribution no longer corresponds to general expectations and wage demands will be made by employees. If there is full employment, the result is only a nominally higher national income (Preiser, 1970a, 24f.). Preiser does not say this explicitly, but he seems to assume that nothing will change in real terms. However, increasing investment expenditure, rising prices and wages mean that the investment cannot be realised in real terms. The argument is reminiscent of the analysis of the relationship between saving and investment in the fully employed economy. There, however, the problem was that labour had to be diverted from other uses to carry out the investment in real terms. In a market economy, this is only possible by outbidding wages. But the higher wages and the possibly poached labour from the consumer goods industry lead to higher (Q-) profits in the consumer goods industry, which leads to an incentive to bring back the poached labour through higher wages.

The outcome of this process is uncertain—it may end with the investment not being realised and only a generally higher price and wage level. However, in this case, the argument based on the structural degree of monopoly is superfluous; wage increases occur automatically at full employment if the intended restructuring of production towards higher investment expenditure is to be realised.

Preiser's second train of thought, which assumes that the increased investment is feasible and considers its capacity effect, is more plausible. Preiser assumes a growing population and free labour market reserves: there are no difficulties in finding labour at previous wages to carry out the investment and produce goods with the newly constructed facilities. However, investing leads to price increases, thus increasing the profit ratio.[13] The investments lead to increased supply one or more periods later. However, if prices have risen, selling the increased output may be difficult unless either the income effect of additional investment provides a remedy or wages are increased. If neither of these occurs, there is excess capacity, which leads to a decline in investment.

> If sales are already uncertain, this decline in investment will exacerbate the situation. In any case, prices will fall, and thus, profit share for given wages. In this case, equilibrium is not achieved by a planned reaction on the part of the wage earners, but rather automatically, so to speak, not to say behind one's back. (Preiser, 1970a, 25f.)

However, if investment expenditure also rises (and the profit share thus remains higher than the structural monopoly ratio dictates), the most likely outcome will be a reaction from employees in the form of higher wage demands.

Higher investment expenditure leads to a higher profit ratio than corresponds to the structural degree of monopoly. At the same time, wage demands by employees bring the profit ratio back to the level determined by the structural degree of monopoly.

> This interplay characterises the growing economy. It only comes to rest when the national income increases at a rate corresponding to investment and the structural degree of monopoly because the latter also determines growth. So if the national income grows at this rate, the structural degree of monopoly ultimately provides the measure of distribution. (Preiser, 1970a, 27)

6.3.2.2 Problems of Preiser's Approach

Preiser's approach of combining Kaldor's theory with social and structural factors was well received. Preiser's name can be found in the relevant literature and textbooks today. He was also supported in enriching distribution theory by including social factors.[14] Nevertheless, his approach was not without criticism. One example is Erwin Scheele, who also refers to Preiser in a review article on macroeconomic distribution theories (Scheele, 1963, 227ff.). Preiser took up this criticism and

---

[13] It should be remembered that full capacity utilisation is not necessary for price increases to occur; what is necessary and sufficient is that $I > S$ (ex-ante in each case) and that production is not infinitely elastic; in this case, higher investment expenditure leads to higher prices and to Q profits.

[14] See Rothschild (1965) as an example of a related approach.

discussed it with other objections in a follow-up word to the second edition of *Wachstum und Einkommensverteilung*. Scheele's criticism and Preiser's rebuttal are curious because they revolve around an illusory problem.

Scheele reproduces Preiser's approach in seven equations, whereby I follow Preiser's notation and also leave the order of the equations as Preiser lists them (Preiser, 1970a, 51 ff.):

$$P = \pi K \tag{6.1}$$

$$P = az \tag{6.2}$$

$$p = \frac{a}{x}(l + z) \tag{6.3}$$

$$Y = xp \tag{6.4}$$

$$Y = L + P \tag{6.5}$$

$$L = al \tag{6.6}$$

$$Y = c_A L + c_U P + \overline{I} \tag{6.7}$$

Equations (6.2)–(6.4) yield the planned distribution according to the social degree of monopoly $\overline{\mu}$:

$$\frac{P}{Y} = \frac{z}{l + z} = \overline{\mu}$$

The Kaldor equation is obtained from (6.5) and (6.7):

$$\frac{P}{Y} = \frac{\overline{I}}{Y} \cdot \frac{1}{1 - c_U - s_A} - \frac{s_A}{1 - c_U - s_A} = \overline{\mu}'$$

In this system of equations, c_U (resp. s_U), c_A (resp. s_A), $\overline{I}$, K, π, a and x are given variables. The unknowns are p, l, z, Y, P and L. The system is overdetermined as there are only six unknowns but seven equations. Above all, according to Scheele, national income and distribution already result from the first six equations: "The circular flow theory, the condition that planned savings and investments must coincide, has no function at all in Preiser's system." (Scheele, 1963, 229).

Preiser responds to this criticism by saying that Scheele overlooks the fact that in Eqs. (6.1) and (6.2), the planned profit (P_P), but in (6.5)–(6.7), the realised profit (P_r) is meant. If you replace the variables accordingly, you get seven unknowns for seven equations. However, an additional equation must now be introduced to close the system, namely the equilibrium condition

$$\overline{\mu}' = \overline{\mu} \tag{6.8}$$

But now, again, an additional unknown seems to be necessary so that the system is not overdetermined. Preiser does not feel affected by Scheele's criticism, however, because, as he writes,

> autonomous investment is *only provisionally* assumed when considering the factors that act on the demand side and which are then contrasted with those on the supply side, whereby the question of the consistency of the overall system *initially* plays no role; as has just been shown, it only arises when the equilibrium condition is added as the eighth to Scheele's seven equations. Then, however, one of the two variables that express the behaviour of the entrepreneurs must adapt to the other, be it π or $\overline{I}$. (Preiser, 1970a, 53, italics in the original in blocked print)

Furthermore, $\overline{I}$ will adapt since π as an expression of the social structure is difficult to influence.

The snag in this argument is that Scheele's initial accusation—that the system is overdetermined—does not apply. Apparently, neither author considered it necessary to solve the entire system once.

If (6.3) is inserted into (6.4), the result is

$$Y = a(l + z)$$

As $z = \frac{\pi K}{a}$, there is $Y = al + \pi K = L + P$ (according to (6.1) and (6.6)).

However, this is identical to Eq. (6.5), which is therefore superfluous. The system contains only six independent equations, sufficient to determine all the unknowns.

By replacing P with P_P in (6.1) and (6.2) and P_r in (6.5) and (6.7), (6.5) becomes an independent equation again, but Preiser's addition of the equilibrium condition $\overline{\mu}' = \overline{\mu}$ is then superfluous. This is because this condition is equivalent to $P_P = P_r$. However, this already results from the seven initial equations (and otherwise, it would not be a long-term equilibrium).

The modelling can illustrate some of the simple relationships that Preiser has in mind, but only in a very rudimentary way. This modelling almost inevitably ignores the conflict between social groups over their share of the social product, which he emphasises so strongly. Preiser can only model the long-term equilibrium that occurs at the profit rate that is accepted by all. This is concealed by this simple model insofar as it appears that any profit rate could be set because the profit rate is understood as an independent variable and the wage rate as a dependent variable. This is, of course, possible, but one must remember that the actual argument disappears under this formal apparatus. The profit rate π used in the model is the result of the dispute; the formal determination of a certain rate is seen as already completed.

Another critical point lies in the relationship between the degree of monopoly and the rate of profit. The degree of monopoly in society is expressed in a certain ratio of unit profit to price and, thus, in a certain profit share. Preiser specifies this share as the long-term centre of gravity of the distribution around which the actual distribution fluctuates. In Preiser's simple model, this profit share corresponds to a certain uniform profit rate that the entrepreneurs/capitalists (can) achieve.

This unambiguous relationship between the profit share and the rate of profit already poses a problem, as it is due to the special production-theoretical preconditions under which Preiser discusses the problem. Despite the openness to different production techniques (which manifest themselves in different capital intensities) and different products (Preiser, 1970a, 17), Preiser works with a one-product economy. He also does not have an input-output structure of production such that the goods produced in one sector serve as input for another. Only such a one-product economy guarantees that a certain equilibrium profit rate corresponds to a certain profit share and vice versa. In the case of several goods produced with different labour intensities or in the case of different capital intensities, this clear relationship disappears.

6.4 Conclusions

The preceding analysis clearly shows the complexity of Preiser's work. Preiser has understood how to combine different theoretical traditions into interesting new considerations, even if the integration has not been fully successful in every case. If we conclude by asking about the outstanding features of Preiser's work, the following points can be mentioned:

Preiser's analysis of growth processes has revealed the importance of monetary factors in understanding such processes and helps to clarify the relationships between saving, investment, consumption, and interest. With its balanced analysis, his work can also represent a bridge to post-Keynesian approaches.

In developing Keynes' ideas further, Preiser has succeeded in preserving the essential insights of Keynes' *General Theory* and, at the same time, utilising a dynamic set of analytical tools, the neglect of which in the *General Theory* has contributed considerably to the weaknesses attributed to this work. As a result, Preiser often arrives at much clearer explanations than Keynes. He was more careful than many other Keynesians not only to work with macroeconomic aggregates but also to include the considerations of consumers and especially entrepreneurs in his analyses. His theories are, therefore, much less susceptible to the accusation of a lack of microeconomic foundations that has often been levelled against Keynesian approaches. On the other hand, his modelling is more realistic and target-oriented than many modern variants, which only work with a representative individual and need to pay more attention to the problems of market interaction.

His theory of distribution directs attention back to non-economic or power factors, which also significantly influence income distribution in the long term. With his dynamic distribution theory, Preiser has moved quite far away from marginal productivity theory in terms of his intentions. But although he still formally pays homage to it in an overview article on distribution theory (Preiser, 1959, 306), none of this can be found in his theory in *Wachstum und Einkommensverteilung* (1970a). Formally, of course, this is partly because marginal productivity theory is microeconomically orientated, whereas Preiser's approach is macroeconomic although he does not remain without a microeconomic foundation but works with behavioural equations that primarily relate to the price-setting and, thus, distribution decisions of entrepreneurs/capitalists. However, he does not use the instrument of marginal productivity theory but a mark-up theory.

By emphasising social structure as an essential datum of distribution theory, Preiser emphasises a key point that represents an important addition to Kaldor's circular flow distribution theory.

In some respects, Preiser's analysis of distribution combines classical and Keynesian analysis. Keynesian is the work with macroeconomic variables or aggregate demand in the Kaldor equation. Two things are classical about Preiser's approach: firstly, the search for a long-term equilibrium; secondly, the specification of the social structure as a datum and, thus, as a variable that the mechanism of supply and demand cannot explain. Preiser thus further developed his view that it is not exclusively pure economic laws that determine distribution but that power factors also play a role. In doing so, he set himself apart from simple neoclassical ideas such as the marginal productivity theory and naïve Keynesian models, which seek to derive income distribution solely from the composition of macroeconomic demand.

References

Blesgen, D. J. (2000). *Erich Preiser: Wirken und wirtschaftspolitische Wirkungen eines deutschen Nationalökonomen (1900-1967).* Springer.

Dow, S. C. (1997). Endogenous money. In G. C. Harcourt & P. A. Riach (Eds.), *A 'second edition' of the general theory* (Vol. 2, pp. 61–78). Routledge.

Fletcher, G. A. (1987). *The Keynesian revolution and its critics. Issues of theory and policy for the Monetary production economy.* Macmillan.

Kaldor, N. (1955/1956). Alternative theories of distribution. *Review of Economic Studies, 23*(2), 83–100.

Kalecki, M. (1987). *Krise und Prosperität im Kapitalismus: ausgewählte Essays 1933–1971* (Postkeynesianische Ökonomie) (Vol. 2). Metropolis.

Keynes, J. M. (1937a). The "Ex-Ante" theory of the rate of interest. *Economic Journal, 47*, 663–669.

Keynes, J. M. (1937b). Alternative theories of the rate of interest. *Economic Journal, 47*, 241–252.

Keynes, J. M. (1971). *A treatise on money. Vol. 1: The pure theory of money. (The collected writings of John Maynard Keynes, Vol. 5).* Macmillan.

Keynes, J. M. (1973). *The general theory of employment, interest and money. (The collected works of John Maynard Keynes, Vol. 7).* Macmillan.

Klausinger, H. (1991). *Theorien der Geldwirtschaft. Von Hayek und Keynes zu neueren Ansätzen.* Duncker & Humblot.

Kurz, H. D. (1996). Franz Oppenheimer und das Problem der 'Bodensperrung'. In V. Caspari & B. Schefold (Eds.), *Franz Oppenheimer und Adolph Lowe: zwei Wirtschaftswissenschaftler der Frankfurter Universität* (pp. 65–120). Metropolis.

Kurz, H. D., & Kalmbach, P. (1981). Elemente einer neuklassischen Analyse von Verteilung, Wert, Akkumulation und Beschäftigung: eine Skizze. In W. J. Mückl & A. E. Ott (Eds.), *Wirtschaftstheorie und Wirtschaftspolitik. Gedenkschrift für Erich Preiser* (Schriften der Universität Passau. Wirtschaftswissenschaften) (Vol. 2, pp. 283–311). Passavia Universitätsverlag.

Moore, B. J. (1988). *Horizontalists and verticalists. The macroeconomics of credit money*. Cambridge University Press.

Neumark, F. (1980). *Zuflucht am Bosporus: Deutsche Gelehrte, Politiker und Künstler in der Emigration 1933–1953*. Knecht.

Oberhauser, A. (1996). Die Bedeutung der Kreislauftheorie der Verteilung für Wirtschaftstheorie und Wirtschaftspolitik. *Jahrbücher für Nationalökonomie und Statistik, 215*(2), 129–142.

Oppenheimer, F. (1964). *Theorie der reinen und politischen Ökonomie. Part 1: Grundlegung*. Gustav Fischer.

Preiser, E. (1933). *Grundzüge der Konjunkturtheorie*. Mohr.

Preiser, E. (1934). *Gestalt und Gestaltung der Wirtschaft. Eine Einführung in die Wirtschaftswissenschaften*. Mohr. Reprinted in: Preiser (1975), pp 13–148 (quotes according to reprint).

Preiser, E. (1944). Sparen und Investieren. *Jahrbücher für Nationalökonomie und Statistik, 159*, 257–309. Reprinted in: Preiser (1963), pp. 9–64 (quotes according to reprint).

Preiser, E. (1948). Besitz und Macht in der Distributionstheorie. In *Synopsis. Festgabe für Alfred Weber* (pp. 331–358). Schneider. Reprinted in: Preiser (1963), pp 227–246 (quotes according to reprint).

Preiser, E. (1950). Geldschöpfung oder Sparen? Ein Beitrag zur Diskussion um die aktive Konjunkturpolitik. *Jahrbücher für Nationalökonomie und Statistik, 162*, 245–259. Reprinted in: Preiser (1963), pp. 65–81 (quotes according to reprint).

Preiser, E. (1951). Das Doppelgesicht der Keynesschen Theorie. *Kyklos, 5*(1/2), 75–81. Reprinted in: Preiser (1970b), pp. 170–178 (quotes according to reprint).

Preiser, E. (1953a). Erkenntniswert und Grenzen der Grenzproduktivitätstheorie. *Schweizerische Zeitschrift für Volkswirtschaft und Statistik, 89*, 25–45. Reprinted in: Preiser (1963), pp 265–289 (quotes according to reprint).

Preiser, E. (1953b). Der Kapitalbegriff und die neuere Theorie. *Jahrbücher für Nationalökonomie und Statistik, 165*, 241–262. Reprinted in: Preiser (1963), pp 99–123 (quotes according to reprint).

Preiser, E. (1955). Multiplikatorprozeß und dynamischer Unternehmergewinn. *Jahrbücher für Nationalökonomie und Statistik, 167*, 89–126. Reprinted in: Preiser (1963), pp 124–167 (quotes according to reprint).

Preiser, E. (1959). Distribution. *Handwörterbuch der Sozialwissenschaften, II*, 620–635. Reprinted in: Preiser (1963), pp. 290–318 (quotes according to reprint).

Preiser, E. (1963). *Bildung und Verteilung des Volkseinkommens. Gesammelte Aufsätze zu Wirtschaftstheorie und Wirtschaftspolitik*. Vandenhoeck & Ruprecht.

Preiser, E. (1970a). *Wachstum und Einkommensverteilung* (Sitzungsberichte der Heidelberger Akademie der Wissenschaften, Philosophisch-historische Klasse, 5. Abhandlung) (3rd ed.). Carl Winter.

Preiser, E. (1970b). *Politische Ökonomie im 20. Jahrhundert: Probleme und Gestalten*. Beck.

Preiser, E. (1975). *Wirtschaftswissenschaft im Wandel. Gesammelte Schriften zu Wirtschaftstheorie und Wirtschaftspolitik. (Collectanea, Vol. 38)*. Georg Olms.

Rothschild, K. W. (1965). Theme and variations — Remarks on the Kaldorian distribution formula. *Kyklos, 18*, 652–669.

Scheele, E. (1963). Die makroökonomische Theorie der Einkommensverteilung: Fortsetzung. *Jahrbuch für Sozialwissenschaft, 14*(2), 141–235.

Schmidt, J. (1998). *Wachstum und Verteilung in der Geldwirtschaft. Das wissenschaftliche Werk Erich Preisers (1900–1967). (Hochschulschriften, Vol. 41)*. Metropolis.

Wicksell, K. (1898 [1997]). *Geldzins und Güterpreise. Eine Untersuchung über die den Tauschwert des Geldes bestimmenden Ursachen. Facsimile edition of the first edition published in 1898*. Wirtschaft und Finanzen.

Chapter 7
Hajo Riese's "Theory of a Monetary Economy": An Attempt at Reconstruction

Peter Spahn

7.1 Introduction

Hajo Riese (1933–2021) was a scholar of Erich Schneider and later of Gottfried Bombach; from the 1970s onwards, he developed into a critic of the prevailing economic theory and policy, which also included an examination of post-Keynesian doctrines. Over time, he thus took up a position between the established fronts of the academic world; this also applied to most members of the "Berlin School of Monetary Keynesianism" (which existed for one to two decades), of which he was the *spiritus rector*. The following chapter briefly highlights some of the central elements of Riese's academic work and then concentrates on his project of a "Theory of a Monetary Economy". Above all, it aimed at a new version of a monetary theory of interest, which provides a fundamental alternative to the neoclassical theory of interest that is still prevalent today. Finally, a look is taken at the economic policy implications of this new interest rate theory, which, despite its orientation towards Keynesian building blocks such as the category of liquidity preference in particular, differs markedly from the usual policy of Keynesianism.

7.2 Scientific Vita

In private conversation, Riese ironically distanced himself time and again from the fashions of research business, which, following the discovery of unknown Keynes manuscripts, had long been preoccupied with the question of "what Keynes *really* meant". However, looking at his own work, the question of "what Riese *really*

P. Spahn (✉)
University of Hohenheim, Tübingen, Germany, Hennentalweg 16, 72070

J. G. Backhaus et al. (eds.), *Post-war Keynesianism in Germany and Western Europe*, The European Heritage in Economics and the Social Sciences 28,
https://doi.org/10.1007/978-3-032-00498-7_7

meant" inevitably arises. His countless writings on the subject of monetary and capital theory, of macro theory and policy, some of them presumably not reviewed and corrected, including many unpublished manuscripts with hundreds of pages, pose some puzzles even in their original German language; an anthology of some texts translated into English is also likely to have left foreign readers with question marks.[1] In the Festschrift for Riese's 60th birthday, Kurt Rothschild (1993, 473) attested to the jubilarian that he was not a "comfortable contemporary" and took little account of his readers. His texts and lectures offered unusual perspectives, original insights and blunt judgements. Whether he was able to convince the majority of readers and listeners is another question. He himself did not endeavour to win over majorities. He was not interested in compromising on issues of content in order to forge coalitions in academic debates.

The fact that Riese would become the founder of a "Berlin School of Monetary Keynesianism" was not necessarily foreseen in his academic career. His studies and doctorate in Kiel brought him into contact with Erich Schneider, a leading representative of German post-war Keynesianism. This familiarised him with circular-flow relationships and monetary policy issues, but his dissertation dealt with "Structural Problems of Economic Growth". In the 1960s, he published on questions of neoclassical growth theory and habilitated under Gottfried Bombach in Basel with a study on the economics of education. Then, the Cambridge-Cambridge debate on capital theory not only prompted him to draw a line under growth theory, but also to critically revise the theoretical foundations of the various areas of economic policy (Riese, 1970, 1975a).[2]

As a representative of a paradigmatic epistemology, the question of the demarcation criteria between the various "schools" of economics has always preoccupied him. In methodological terms, however, he always remained an uncompromising supporter of what he called "liberal market theory". For him, this meant the postulate that market movements (as in the programme of neoclassical General Equilibrium Theory) should be described from agents' choices through price-quantity relationships. It was also essential for him to adhere to the concept of equilibrium. Although disequilibrium theories try to score points by referring to empirical realism, logically they only deal with deviations from equilibrium. The functioning of a system can only be understood through equilibrium theory, because this describes the core of the causal relationships. Finally, Riese was also extremely sceptical of calls for interdisciplinary extensions to economic theory. Ideas, such as in Keynes, of referring to findings from psychology, for example, when analysing central economic variables such as interest rates, were anathema to him, and heterodoxy was almost a dirty word.

[1] Detailed lists of his publications can be found in Stadermann and Steiger (1993a, 487 ff.) and in Riese (2001, 1447 ff.). The English anthology is edited by Hölscher and Tomann (2003). For an earlier German version of this contribution see Spahn (2024).

[2] For further biographical details and a sketch of the development of Riese's scientific career, see Stadermann and Steiger (1993b).

From the mid-1970s, following an analysis of anti-inflationary policy in the debate between Keynesianism and Monetarism, Riese's work focussed on Keynes. This led to large-scale drafts of a Theory of a Monetary Economy, which however was not finalised in a monograph and thus not completed.[3] In the early works, the intention to present the project as a new interpretation or construction of Keynes's theory was still recognisable; however, "Keynes" soon disappeared from the title. The differences to Keynes—both from a theoretical and an economic policy perspective—ultimately seemed too great to him. Was Riese a Keynesian? What is a Keynesian?

This question lures us into an endless dispute about a definition of Keynesian theory: what are the decisive doctrines or beliefs? The time-bound nature of the debate must also be taken into account. The so-called New Keynesian theory following Woodford (2003), with its building blocks of an endogenous money supply and an indispensable anti-cyclical interest rate policy committed to the Taylor Principle, has taken up core points of Keynesian thinking, above all the threat of macroeconomic instability. Nevertheless, in terms of its methodological and substantive foundations, this New Keynesianism is considered a modern neoclassical approach that enriches optimal growth theory with some market imperfections in order to appear suitable for a short-run business cycle theory.[4]

Riese's "world", on the other hand, was still that of the outgoing dispute between Fiscalism and Monetarism. At this time, the debates on the understanding and further development of Keynes' theory were characterised on the one hand by the rationing approach founded by Clower (1963), on the other by the "fundamental Keynesianism" embodied by Davidson (1978) and also by the discussion of forgotten and previously unpublished texts by Keynes from the 1930s.[5] It is characteristic of Riese that he only takes up this literature in passing. In general, one has the impression that he did not approach Keynes by studying preconceived opinions in the Keynesian literature, but rather with the unbiased view of an economist who—coming from a neighbouring research field of growth theory—opens up a new perspective on the subject.

Riese also did not engage in a textual exegesis of Keynes's writings, but asked the other way round, what Keynes "should have written" in order to develop a critical and constructive alternative to neoclassical theory and policy, from which he had turned away in no uncertain terms in the early 1970s (Riese, 1972a, 1972b, 1975b).

[3] A book publication on the *Theory of Inflation* (1986a) only briefly touches on the theoretical core of the Theory of a Monetary Economy and provides more of a problem-related and economic policy analysis. There were, of course, important, and in some cases more extensive, published essays on the actual topic (Riese, 1983, 1987a, 1988, 1994, 1995a); they are referred to in this chapter without direct references to the respective sources. Most of the texts are reprinted in Riese (2001).

[4] Even neoclassical economists reacted to this with a shake of the head: "No account has been given of how and why a decentralised economy could behave as if guided by a Ramsey maximizer" (Hahn & Solow, 1995, 2, cf. Solow, 2008). On this debate, see Landmann (2015) and Spahn (2016, 157 ff.), among others.

[5] Volumes 13, 14 and 29 of Keynes's *Collected Writings* are particularly important here.

The criteria for such a desired theoretical development were presumably different for Riese than for Keynes. While for the latter the focus was on explaining and overcoming an economic crisis that had persisted since the early 1930s, for the former the sober analysis of the functional mechanisms of the monetary economy was important; if it turned out that unemployment, for example, was one of the unavoidable side effects of the capitalist system, which was otherwise regarded as clearly advantageous, it made little sense for Riese to want to fight against the laws of the market with a social reformist ethos. He took great pleasure in pointing out scientific weaknesses in left-wing Keynesian writings and was probably closer to the Marxists than to social-democratic economists, who repeatedly could not resist the temptation to see Keynes as a scientist committed to the interests of the working class.

On the other hand, Riese without any doubt used Keynesian macro theory to criticize neoclassical ideas on the diagnosis and treatment of economic crises. He countered various accusations that trade unions were pushing through real wages that were too high and governments decided on too high budget deficits—real wages and budget deficits are not choice variables, but market variables whose level is determined endogenously in the macroeconomic process. Likewise he argued against popular neoclassical claims that lower wages and more saving would "free up room for more growth"—saving does not release additional financial resources, and corporate profits are the circular-flow consequence of, not the prerequisite for investment. He also rejected the thesis that the German economy was suffering from inefficient allocation structures and needed to be revitalised with the help of modern supply policy—the Schumpeterian entrepreneur is of no help if the path of demand is not driven by the Keynesian investor.[6]

Riese's reference to Keynesian economics was not limited to the *General Theory*. He also rated the importance of the *Treatise on Money* very highly—in this work Keynes had even achieved important insights in some points, which were unnecessarily revised again in the later book. This applies above all to the relationship between investment and saving: under the *Treatise* assumption of full employment, a positive discrepancy is reflected in price increases and so-called Q-profits (undistributed corporate saving), while Keynes (1936, 378–79), with his remark in the *General Theory* that neoclassical theory would come into its own again at full employment, seems to suggest that saving would then again drive investment. However, the fact that investment expenditure is limited by the availability of money, but not by saving, is generally true. Last but not least, the German "economic miracle" can be explained neither by regulatory policy ("*Ordnungspolitik*") nor by the voluntary renunciation of consumption by households; rather, Q-profits

[6]In other works, Riese dealt with questions of the state of macroeconomics, economic growth, currency competition, international debt, development and transformation problems, etc., which are not taken up in this chapter. The high originality and quality of these texts is largely unaffected by the critical arguments on his Theory of a Monetary Economy presented below. His writings are often characterized by a rare combination of essayistic, non-formal style and a strict emphasis on analytical contents (see, for example, Riese, 1981, 1986b).

provided the financing and the confirmation of the profit expectations in the investment boom (Riese, 1979).

7.3 The Nominal Core of a Monetary Economy

With respect to the topic of unemployment, Riese saw the *General Theory* as an attempt to provide an explanation based on interest rate theory. This Keynesian intention could not be captured by a mere interaction of the goods and labour market, as in Clower (1963); Leijonhufvud's (1968) rediscovery of the monetary Keynes came closer to this goal. Keynes' (1933a) vision of a "Monetary Theory of Production" aimed at a conception of economics that differed from that of the "classical school". Riese agreed with this, but distinguished between a theory of the production of resources (classical), a theory of the exchange of resources (neoclassical)[7] and the Theory of the Monetary Economy. In this latter economic system, the appropriation of resources takes place exclusively via money, which is offered indirectly by the central bank and (as will be shown) directly by owners of monetary assets. While money has at best an auxiliary function in the first two systems, in a monetary economy money is indispensable, not neutral and therefore "essential".

The exclusive appropriation function of money refers to a cash-in-advance restriction, which can be justified either on microeconomic terms by analysing information and transaction costs or on macroeconomic terms by proving the systematic lack of marketability of other resources kept by economic agents. For Riese, who rarely dealt with microeconomic details, the second explanation would be more likely. In an economy characterised by under-utilisation and unemployment, transactions in dominant buyers' markets are primarily restricted by the disposal of money, also because the availability of endowments in the form of resources does not ensure access to the credit market.[8]

Riese (1995a, 47) saw the "specific nature of money" in its capacity as the sole "medium of fulfilment of contracts". Money is not considered as a medium of exchange, but as a means of payment. The former suggests that although money facilitates the exchange of goods, it is essentially dispensable. The latter postulates

[7] Riese only emphasised this first distinction between an economy of production and an economy of exchange at the beginning of his research on Keynesian economics. This distinction is still upheld today in parts of the history of economic thought—the fundamental reference here is the neo-Ricardian Pasinetti (1977)—despite emphatic criticism, for example by Frank Hahn (1982), who insisted on the analytical compatibility of Walras's and Sraffa's theories. Walras himself had unequivocally pointed out the connection between scarcity and production: "Useful things limited in quantity are *things that can be produced and multiplied by industry*. In other words, they are reproducible. I mean by this that it is worth while producing them and increasing their quantity as much as possible by regular and systematic efforts" (1874, 67, cf. Dragendorf, 1988).

[8] Davidson (1981) expressed this in such a way that the "gross substitutability" between all goods and the medium of exchange, money, is not given.

that there is no exchange of goods; an obligation resulting from the appropriation of goods (and transfer of assets) can only be solved with money. This view of money as a means of debt repayment seems immediately obvious—but leaves the question unanswered of why contracts are concluded in monetary units in the first place; however, Riese does not pose this question.[9]

The convention of using an institutionally provided currency as a means of payment requires monetary stability—on this point, Riese (1983, 111) was an uncompromising "hawkish" economist.

> Money exercises [...] its function as a public good. This function determines the role of the central bank. As an institution of the legal system, it must ensure that money can satisfy its function as a stamp of fulfilment of obligations. It thus functions as an institution that has to guarantee the functional conditions of the monetary system, while the production of liquidity, the economy of the production of liquidity, is performed by the asset owners.

Before examining the role of these wealth holders, it is helpful to insert Rothschild's (1993, 475–76) summary of Riese's theory, in which the above point is expressed in similar terms:

> The scarcity of money, which thus becomes the decisive macroeconomic budget constraint of the monetary economy, is ensured by the socially necessary shortage of 'basic money', i.e. central bank money (which Riese alone regards as 'money'), because this is the prerequisite for money being able to fulfil its exchange functions and being held by asset owners as a component of their assets.

Rothschild thus illustrates the central connection between the regulatory importance of price stability and Riese's characterisation of the market system as a nominal economy. The latter idea is in conflict with any standard economic theory, which generally tends to transform all economic variables into real variables before proceeding to analytical work. In General Equilibrium Theory, real initial endowments form the starting point for the production of utilities. For Riese (1988, 381–82), on the other hand, "the core content of the monetary theory of production [...] can be summarised in such a way that money forms the general budget constraint of the market system". However, this is only conceivable at a stable price level. The scarcity of money makes goods and labour tendentially abundant, and the equilibrium condition is not the clearing of goods and labour markets, but the fulfilment of nominal obligations.[10] As an aside, the special real efficiency of the market economy results, as also echoed by Schumpeter, from the compulsion of companies to

[9] Of course, this criticism can also be directed at mainstream monetary macro theory, which commonly emphasises that "agents negotiate nominal contracts, but care only about real values". Goodhart mockingly asked: "Why do they behave in a way that leaves themselves open to presumably undesirable surprises, rather than agree on indexed real contracts?" (1994, 102–03, cf. Heering, 1999). If agents insist on payment for their services in money, they do not necessarily succumb to a money illusion, but demand payment in a medium that protects them from the information, transaction and trust problems that would arise in agreements on direct reciprocal barter of goods and services.

[10] The vision of a nominal economy has been further developed by Stadermann and Steiger (2001) and Stadermann (2006).

reduce their debt by means of an innovative supply of goods. Minsky (1984, 454), who was not particularly appreciated by Riese, expressed a similar view:

> An economy where money is created by banking processes that finance the acquisition of capital assets and the production of investment outputs has [due to nominal redemption commitments] essentially a nominal core.[11]

However, Minsky (1980) also, and this provoked Riese's disapproval, regarded money as a disruptive factor that undermined the coherence of the market system (many Post-Keynesians and "fundamental" Keynesians followed his lead). Unemployment, financial instability and insecurity are seen to be the key elements of the resultant "pathological" market constitution. Implicitly, the moneyless exchange economy is described as a perfect world in which equilibrium and full employment prevail.

Unfortunately, Keynes (1933b) had already created the basis for this strange world view with his much-cited comparison of a "co-operative economy" and an "entrepreneur economy". Here Keynes compares a co-operative, one-good, economy, without money, with a multi-product, monetary, economy. In the first case, real wages are negotiated directly, which are transferred in units of the produced good; in the second, nominal wages are paid, which the companies have to earn through the uncertain sale of their products. In the first case, full employment prevails as a result of the flexible real wage; in the second, there are macro imbalances as a result of variable money holdings, sales crises and uncertain expected returns on investments.

With reference to this scenario, Post-Keynesians continue to "prove" the disruptive potential of money in a market economy to this day. They advocate an unconvincing chain of argumentation which, starting from uncertainty, leads to money demand, and from an excessive interest rate level thus brought about to unemployment, by which a monetary economy is obviously virtually defined.[12] But Keynes' comparison, which did not make it into the *General Theory* for obviously good reasons, is of course skewed. If one were to contrast a one-good economy with a multi-product economy, both without money, it would be immediately apparent that the latter functions much worse without money than with money. Workers do not want to be paid with their own products. The contracts would be burdened with

[11] A fitting passage that emphasises the monetary nature of credit contracts can already be found in Keynes's work (1931, 151): "There is a multitude of real assets in the world which constitute our capital wealth [...]. The nominal owners of these assets, however, have not infrequently borrowed money in order to become possessed of them. To a corresponding extent the actual owners of wealth have claims, not on real assets, but on money. A considerable part of this 'financing' takes place through the banking system, which interposes its guarantee between its depositors who lend it money, and its borrowing customers to whom it loans money wherewith to finance the purchase of real assets. The interposition of this veil of money between the real asset and the wealth owner is a specially marked characteristic of the modern world."

[12] "In a certain world, there would be no reason for holding money, nor would there be any involuntary unemployment" (Davidson, 1978, 12, cf. 213; 2007, 44 ff., 87; Bertocco, 2013). Already Dillard (1955, 12) had stated: "Money as a store of wealth stands as a barrier of full production, that is, unemployment is caused by money."

higher information and transaction costs, and market clearing equilibria would be highly unlikely. Frank Hahn was therefore quite right to judge that money played a disastrous role in this scientific debate from beginning to end: "The idea that unemployment would not occur in a barter economy is grotesque" (1977, 258, cf. Gale, 1982, 182 ff.).

Turning against the Post-Keynesians, Riese (1990, 15) emphasised that money does not disrupt the market economy, but rather defines its constitutional order: money establishes "the coherence of the market system by the fact that, as a uniform category, it forms the universally valid identification of the fulfilment of contracts". The market society demands the recognition of formal rules, given by law and solvency. Transactions are calculated and paid for in nominal units. This is the alternative to a non-monetary economy, in which transfers of goods lead to a network of heterogeneous liabilities in real terms which have to be settled in kind. A market economy, on the other hand, is a payment economy.[13] Obligations are largely repaid on the spot. Since money allows the immediate equalisation of intertemporal liabilities by transferring a definite means of payment, the time aspect can be kept out of economic relations to a certain extent. This is not captured by Keynes' famous statement "*The importance of money essentially flows from its being a link between the present and the future*" (1936, 293).

7.4 A Monetary Theory of Interest

The actual motivation behind Riese's Theory of a Monetary Economy certainly does not lie in his interest in the typically Keynesian topic of full employment. Rather, he was concerned with the old, yet fundamental question of how to explain a positive interest rate, or more generally: a positive rate of return on capital under competitive conditions in equilibrium. Referring to Böhm-Bawerk's three-volume work on the "Capitalzins", Wicksell (1901, 154) said:

> The real theoretical difficulty is [...] to explain how, under stationary conditions, the possession of capital can remain a permanent source of income.

For Riese, the most important part of the *General Theory* was the 16th chapter with the remarks on the theory of capital. Here Keynes (1936, 213) distanced himself from productivity-based explanations of the return on capital:

> It is much preferable to speak of capital as having a yield over the course of its life in excess of its original cost, than as being *productive*. For the only reason why an asset offers a

[13] Here there is a link to Luhmann's sociological approach. "The problem of scarcity is brought by money [...] into the form of money scarcity. The problem of scarcity [...] arises when someone *excludes others from access to resources in the interest of their own future*. The question is: when and how is he allowed to do this? [...] The answer, made possible by the communication medium of money, is: *when he pays*. [...] Money is the triumph of scarcity over violence" (1988, 252–53, cf. Spahn, 2002).

> prospect of yielding during its life services having an aggregate value greater than its initial supply price is because it is *scarce*; and it is kept scarce because of the competition of the rate of interest on money. If capital becomes less scarce, the excess yield will diminish, without its having become less productive—at least in the physical sense. I sympathise, therefore, with the pre-classical doctrine that everything is *produced by labour.*

The last sentence should probably be understood to mean that Keynes agrees with Böhm-Bawerk's and Schumpeter's criticism of the classical surplus theory of capital profit. With free market access, companies compete for scarce production factors until the pure company profit approaches zero due to rising factor prices. This means that the social product is distributed to the providers of labour (and land)—unless a portion flows to the owners of capital via interest.

As Keynes rejected the neoclassical explanation of interest rates, he also claimed to make a new contribution to the theory of distribution with his monetary theory of interest rates. This claim has almost been lost in the reception of his theory.[14] This is probably also due to the fact that he banished the credit market from the *General Theory* as the "natural place" for an explanation of interest rates, due to his rejection of the Loanable Funds Theory, and instead included interest in the function of the demand for money.[15] Later, liquidity preference was generally accepted as an element of imbalance constellations on the money market, but productivity and drift continued to be regarded as "fundamental" factors in the explanation of interest rates and thus profit rates.

Keynes had remained ambiguous in his own explanations of interest rate theory. The "speculative motive" of money demand only addresses the interest rate risk in an ordinary portfolio—a standard topic of every neoclassical financial market theory, which is incomprehensibly treated as a special feature of Keynesian theory in the textbook literature to this day. The liquidity premium of money, presented in the 17th chapter of the *General Theory*, differs only gradually from the liquidity premium attached to other assets: Keynes fails to clearly define the interest rate as the price of solvency. Instead, there are evasions into psychology, uncertainty is presented as the cause of interest rates, and, after all, the interest rate is seen as a conventional phenomenon.

The key idea of Riese (1986a, 53) was to make liquidity preference a determining factor of the money supply, which thus becomes a market-endogenous variable:

> The willingness to give up liquidity represents an offer to give up money for a certain period of time in order to receive a premium, interest, in return. In this way, however, the holding of money becomes a renunciation of a money supply; it appears as a (hidden) category of money supply, but not as a category of money demand. The liquidity premium granted by holding money is a subjectively determined interest rate, the introduction of which into

[14] See, however, Kregel (1976, 7), Nell (1988) and Mongiovi (1990).

[15] The subsequent theoretical discussion, characterised in particular by the contributions of Hicks, justified this approach by arguing that Walras's Law meant that the credit market could easily be replaced by the money market. However, to my knowledge there is no evidence that Keynes, who was trained by Marshall, thought this way at all. In a 1934 letter to Hicks, Keynes wrote: "Walras's theory and all others along those lines are little better than nonsense" (quoted from Bridel, 2021, 756 n.).

> economic analysis represents a methodological trick in order to provide a price-theoretical foundation for the renunciation of supply by asset owners.

The somewhat confusing way of talking about an individual money supply should not obscure the fact that the argument is of course about credit supply, which has tended to be ignored in Keynesian theory to date. This implies, of course, that the non-neutrality of money emphasised by Riese proves to be self-evident, as a neutrality of credit has never been claimed. However, unlike to neoclassical economics, credit is not extended in terms of goods or goods equivalents, but in nominal monetary units. Riese's adherence to the term "money supply" serves the purpose of establishing a connection to the provision of base money by the central bank: The gross credit volume—i.e. the monetary budget constraint—is not determined by monetary policy, but by the portfolio decisions of private asset holders and banks.[16]

> Formally, the central bank as a producer of means of payment constitutes the budget restriction; materially, however, the control function of the economic process is incumbent on the asset owners as disposers of means of payment, because the maintenance of solvency requires an assessment (of the security) of the return flow of means of payment, which limits credit production, regardless of the extent to which base money is available from the central bank. A monetary economy thus receives its basic foundation from the fact that asset owners keep the supply of (central bank) money scarce. (Riese, 1989, 21)

There are two arguments against the possible accusation that Riese's model is based on money illusion:

- We might conceive of an implicit contract between the central bank and asset owners stating that the latter only fulfil the economic task of supplying credit at their own risk if monetary policy guarantees price stability in principle. This means that the monetary budget restriction has a real value. If, however, the central bank fails, the contract is cancelled and the asset owners change currency; at least that is its threat, which works through the dangers of capital flight and currency devaluation.
- Decisions on the structure of asset holdings are about returns, taking inflation into account of course, but not about goods equivalents, i.e. not about the price level. Intertemporal comparison of the utility of goods and time preference only play a role in the case of accumulation and dissolution of assets, in the saving decision. But this is not essential for institutional investors (proponents of consumption-based asset pricing theory naturally see things differently).

---

[16] These are not seen as credit intermediaries, as in neoclassical economics up to the present day, but as credit creators. Deposits, created in this process as a by-product, are to be understood as current central bank money credit from the public to the banks. With regard to the interaction between commercial banks and the central bank, Riese (1991, 1993a) particularly praised Bagehot's early insight into the necessity of the "open discount window", i.e. an endogenous base money supply. Both Keynes and Friedman knew that practical monetary policy does not work in the literal sense by setting a "given" money supply. The scarcity of money is guaranteed by the fact that for every unit of central bank money, whether banknote or bank reserve, there is an economic agent who directly or indirectly pays interest to the central bank for holding this central bank money (Riese, 1995a, 58).

Like the granting of credit by asset owners, their direct investment in the production process is also to be understood structurally as an abandonment of money holding. Riese's vision (1987b, 163) can be described by Money–Goods–Money' as in Marx:

> Capital represents an advance of money which is necessary for the realisation of production. Consequently, the rate of profit is also a price for the surrender of liquidity, is a monetarily determined interest rate or [...] an interest rate that emerges on the goods market.

Wealth owners start the capitalist "exploitation" process with their money advance, whereby capital is not understood as a means of production but as a sum of value. But the explanation of surplus value is different from Marx: production already begins charged with interest.[17] The interest demand in the credit supply is determined by the individual liquidity preference of asset owners, more precisely: by the liquidity premium as a non-pecuniary own interest, which they assign to the holding of money in their portfolio. In the market solution, the uniform rate of return on capital is thus formed (neoclassical interest rate theory, as intertemporal price theory, can only determine a variety of interest rates on the variety of goods). This is summarised once again in Rothschild (1993, 475):

> *It is not the scarcity and productivity of real capital* that determine profit and, through it, the real interest rate, *but the scarcity of money* and the price to be paid for making it available that determine the interest rate and, through it, the scarcity of capital goods and profit.

Interest is the price for solvency in the current period—and insofar not an intertemporal price (Riese, 1995a, 55; 1995b, 82). One can only enter the market hall of the economy with money, so to speak, and interest is the entry price to be paid for the temporary disposal of money. If we now take a closer look at the choice of asset owners, the decision between money, financial assets and real assets is, as usual, controlled by expected returns and risks. Riese (1985, 20) determines the intrinsic interest rate of money mostly indirectly, namely solely through the risk (for Riese: the uncertainty) of capital losses on other assets. Money is held in short supply because of this uncertainty.

> This liquidity premium can only be interpreted in such a way that it is the result of the assessment of the gross return flow of investments, its increase thus indicates a (cyclical and crisis-induced) growing uncertainty of the refunding of money and thus represents the price-theoretical equivalent of a decline in the supply of money.

This is linked to the more far-reaching hypothesis that "as the supply of money increases, the security of the return on assets decreases" (Riese, 1986a, 61 n.). Such an assumption is questionable, however, because under competitive conditions the risk of investment projects should be independent of the individual credit volume.

[17] This corresponds to the closure of the degree of freedom in distribution theory proposed by Sraffa (1960, 39) in his neo-Ricardian production price model: "The rate of profits, as a ratio, has a significance which is independent of any prices, and can well be 'given' before the prices are fixed. It is accordingly susceptible of being determined from outside the system of production, in particular by the level of the money rates of interest."

This indirect determination of the liquidity premium is compatible with the idea of an "intrinsic value" of money based on solvency. This is because this value is reduced by expected losses on invested sums of money: the proportion of safe money in the portfolio becomes smaller. However, by focussing on the default risk of capital investments, Riese surprisingly ignores the specification of the liquidity premium formulated by Keynes' student Hugh Townsend (1938) in a letter to Keynes:

> The reluctance to part with liquid money—the property of liquidity which gives it exchange value and enables people to obtain interest by parting with money under contract—has its origin in the doubts of wealth-owners as to what may happen to values *before the end of any interval, however short*; and I suggest that the basic cause of interest is bound up with this.

According to this view, the liquidity premium is not a reaction to expected payment defaults at the end of the investment period, but reflects the subjective loss of solvency during the investment period. Keynes (1938) explicitly endorsed this view in his reply to the letter:

> An essential distinction is that a risk premium is expected to be rewarded on the average by an increased return at the end of the period. A liquidity premium, on the other hand, is not even expected to be so rewarded. It is a payment, not for the expectation of increased tangible income at the end of the period, but for an increased sense of comfort and confidence during the period.[18]

Roots of Riese's credit-supply calculus can be traced back to a simple portfolio model presented in an early contribution of Hicks (1935) where agents choose between money, financial and real assets. The liquidity premium of money is yet absent, but money is kept due to the uncertainty of duration and return of other investments. A positive rate of interest emerges because agents are risk averse, as in Tobin's (1958) well-known money demand model. More recently, Hahn and Solow (1995, 105 ff., cf. Spahn, 1998) suggested a macro model based on a similar portfolio choice where the liquidity premium on money determines the rate of profit. Unfortunately, Riese has not formally elaborated his own model (nor has he made any other reference to the relevant financial market theory); thus some conceptual ambiguities remain. The relationship between the interest rate determined by Riese's credit market and the central bank's interest rate policy and the issue of the term structure of interest rates also remains open.

[18] The issue is made more puzzling by the fact that Riese in private discourse even described the derivation of the liquidity premium from the default risk as malpractice: the declaration of interest is then reduced to a mere insurance premium. More detailed treatments of this topic can be found, for example, in Jäggi (1986, 158 ff.), Spahn (2016, 52 ff., 80 ff.) and—with specific reference to Riese—in Dragendorf (1988) and Heering (1991).

7.5 Macroeconomic and Economic Policy Consequences

In principle, Riese (1994, 126) accused Keynes of merely providing a "theory of effective demand in the context of neoclassical economics" and of not having overcome the dichotomy between the theory of money and the theory of value. He had not achieved his goal of a monetary theory of production. In the *General Theory* there is "no profit-orientated production that becomes an asset value by means of a profit that arises from a mark-up on factor costs".[19] Keynes and the Keynesians are seen to understand macroeconomic imbalances and unemployment as deviations from a neoclassical equilibrium solution; a call on monetary and fiscal policy ought to repair this market malfunction. According to Riese (1985, 22), this is downright contrary to the order of the market system in a monetary economy. Keynes does not understand,

> that the scarcity of money is not an inherent evil of a monetary economy, but expresses its conditions of existence. Thus he is also unable to grasp that unemployment results from the endeavours of the owners of wealth to maintain the dominance of the scarcity of money over the scarcity of resources in order to preserve their control function in the economic process and their ability to generate profit income. In this way, Keynes's fundamental insight into the necessity of a monetary determination of interest, the explanation of interest from the scarcity of money, comes into contradiction with his policy of easy money.

An interest-rate policy that goes against the interests of asset owners is doomed to fail. The only way for economic policy to conform to market principles is to stimulate the willingness of creditors to invest, so that a reduction in interest rates results as a market outcome. In principle, however, fiscal policy should be limited to accepting cyclical budget deficits and monetary policy should be committed to price stability (Riese, 1992, 1995c).[20]

Unemployment thus appears to Riese as a necessary systemic feature of a monetary economy, the fight against which creates macroeconomic instability: full employment threatens the outbreak of cumulative inflation. This argument raises questions. Firstly, the terms appear to be imprecisely defined: full employment as a labour market equilibrium implies precisely that there is no inflationary pressure. Secondly, there is a substantive proximity here to the post-Keynesian link from money to unemployment (see above), which Riese otherwise vehemently rejected.

But the fundamental question is why unemployment should be necessary at all in order to maintain the interest claim of the owners of financial assets. For Riese (1995a, 57), unemployment is:

[19] This criticism is completed by the odd assertion: "The word *production* does not occur in the *General Theory*"(Riese, 1994, 128).

[20] Riese's (1993b) criticism of German monetary policy in the final phase of the EMS stands in a certain contrast to this: the Bundesbank should have accepted the (local) key currency character of the Deutschmark and pursued an interest rate policy orientated towards a balance of payments equilibrium. However, it remains unclear how inflation could have been combated in other ways in the wake of German monetary union.

> the functional principle of capitalism corresponding to the existence of buyers' markets. It is the necessary condition for profit not to be eroded by competition.

However, this recourse to the criticism of classical profit theory is inappropriate within Riese's approach, because a liquidity premium given by individual preferences keeps the interest rate above zero from the supply side and thus closes the classical degree of freedom in the theory of distribution. This is precisely why Riese (1994) declared Sraffa, posthumously, a Keynesian.

In the same context, Riese (1988, 386; 1986a, 66) writes that with the scarcity of money and capital by the owners of wealth, the use of resources must also be limited "so that prices can rise above costs and a profit is made". However, the Cournot solution outlined here, in which profit follows from a scarcity of production, is only valid in partial-market analysis, but it violates the fundamental relationship between production and income in the economy as a whole: if less is invested, there is also less demand. This is particularly true from a long-term perspective, which Riese wants to set against Keynes' short-term theory. Through their willingness to give up liquidity, asset owners enable "production [...] that pushes towards demand". The Theory of a Monetary Economy postulates cleared goods markets and is based "on the effectiveness of Say's law, when a produced supply creates its demand" (Riese, 1986a, 44, 1–2). And of course, this last statement is in open contradiction to the core of Keynes' theory.

7.6 Concluding Remarks

Taking stock, it seems obvious that Riese's approach ultimately appears to move away from Keynesian thinking. This is regrettable simply because the macroeconomic conclusions he draws are implausible and actually unnecessary to support the monetary interest rate theory presented. A monetarily determined interest rate does not require unemployment in equilibrium, at least not for reasons of distribution theory. However, there is no question that a central bank committed to monetary stability must prevent wage inflation resulting from overemployment. The fact that Riese has made few friends among traditional Keynesians with his increasingly clear advocacy of a stability-orientated monetary and fiscal policy does not necessarily speak against his approach.

As early as in Keynes (1936, 157 n.), there is a hint hidden in a footnote saying that interest is ultimately "a payment for borrowing *money*". In the history of economic thought, this has always been a controversial point. In pre-classical economics, the statement was taken for granted. Thereafter however, the view prevailed that credit is essentially a loan of goods and—which is by no means logically compelling—is granted out of current real income; consequently, time preference is the factor determining interest rates. The influence of money on the interest rate was only given via a fluctuating velocity of circulation. The fact that money is actually transferred in the credit contract—and that this is to be seen in the light of a stock-theoretical analysis—henceforth only played a role in applied portfolio theory, but not in the "pure" theory of capital and interest.

Riese's vision of a monetary credit and portfolio theory picks up this trail again; it clarifies why credit in capitalism should be analysed in terms of money lending and not as goods lending, and why, besides default risk, liquidity preference is more important than time preference. This approach requires a new look at the level of nominal-monetary relations in the market economy and may also provoke a conflict with the prevailing economic theory, which describes the economy primarily in terms of the disposition of real factors. For this dispute, Riese (1995a, 61) has left us economists a final consolation:

> Capitalism is highly indifferent to what people, including scientists, think of it. That is why it is able to function even if the scientists' insights are inadequate or even wrong.

References[21]

Bertocco, G. (2013). On Keynes's criticism of the loanable funds theory. *Review of Political Economy, 25*(2), 309–326.

Bridel, P. (2021). The part played by general equilibrium in the liquidity preference vs loanable funds episode (1936–1956). *European Journal of the History of Economic Thought, 28*(5), 753–786.

Clower, R. W. (1963). Die keynesianische Gegenrevolution—Eine theoretische Kritik. *Schweizerische Zeitschrift für Volkswirtschaft und Statistik, 99*(1), 8–31.

Davidson, P. (1978). *Money and the real world* (2nd ed.). Macmillan.

Davidson, P. (1981). Post Keynesian economics—Solving the crisis in economic theory. In D. Bell & I. Kristol (Eds.), *The crisis in economic theory* (pp. 151–173). Basic Books.

Davidson, P. (2007). *John Maynard Keynes*. Palgrave Macmillan.

Dillard, D. (1955). The theory of a monetary economy. In K. K. Kurihara (Ed.), *Post-Keynesian economics* (pp. 3–30). Allen and Unwin.

Dragendorf, R. (1988). Zinssatz und Profitrate in der (neu-) klassischen und keynesianischen Theorie. In *Ökonomie und Gesellschaft, Vol. 6, Die Aktualität keynesianischer Analysen* (pp. 121–147). Campus Frankfurt.

Gale, D. (1982). *Money—In equilibrium*. Cambridge University Press.

Goodhart, C. A. E. (1994). Game theory for central bankers—A report to the governor of the Bank of England. *Journal of Economic Literature, 32*(1), 101–114.

Hahn, F. H. (1977). Keynessche Theorie und Allgemeine Gleichgewichtstheorie—Überlegungen zu einigen aktuellen Debatten. In H. Hagemann et al. (Eds.), *Die neue Makroökonomik—Marktungleichgewicht, Rationierung und Beschäftigung* (pp. 240–259). Campus Frankfurt. 1981.

Hahn, F. H. (1982). The neo-Ricardians. *Cambridge Journal of Economics, 6*(4), 353–374.

Hahn, F. H., & Solow, R. M. (1995). *A critical essay on modern macroeconomic theory*. Blackwell.

Heering, W. (1991). *Geld, Liquiditätsprämie und Kapitalgüternachfrage—Studien zur entscheidungstheoretischen Fundierung einer Monetären Theorie der Produktion*. Transfer.

Heering, W. (1999). Privateigentum, Vertrauen und Geld—Überlegungen zur Genese von Zahlungsmitteln in Marktökonomien. In K. Betz & T. Roy (Eds.), *Privateigentum und Geld—Kontroversen um den Ansatz von Heinsohn und Steiger* (pp. 99–143). Metropolis.

[21] (Quotations from German texts have been translated by using the DeepL software.)

Hicks, J. R. (1935). A suggestion for simplifying the theory of money. In J. R. Hicks (Ed.), *Critical essays in monetary theory* (pp. 61–82). Clarendon Press. 1979.

Hölscher, J., & Tomann, H. (Eds.). (2003). *Money, development and economic transformation—Selected essays by Hajo Riese*. Palgrave Macmillan.

Jäggi, C. M. (1986). *Die Makroökonomik von J. M. Keynes*. Springer.

Keynes, J. M. (1931). The consequences to the banks of the collapse of money values. In *The collected writings of John Maynard Keynes, Vol. IX, essays in persuasion* (pp. 150–158). Macmillan. 1972.

Keynes, J. M. (1933a). A monetary theory of production. In G. Clausing (Ed.), *Der Stand und die nächste Zukunft der Konjunkturforschung* (pp. 125–127). Duncker & Humblot.

Keynes, J. M. (1933b). The distinction between a co-operative economy and an entrepreneur economy. In *The collected writings of John Maynard Keynes, Vol. XXIX, the general theory and after—A supplement* (pp. 76–87). Macmillan. 1979.

Keynes, J. M. (1936). The general theory of employment, interest, and money. In *The collected writings of John Maynard Keynes* (Vol. VII). Macmillan.

Keynes, J. M. (1938). Letter to Hugh Townshend. In *The collected writings of John Maynard Keynes, Vol. XXIX, the general theory and after—A supplement* (Vol. 1979, pp. 293–294). Macmillan.

Kregel, J. A. (1976). *Theory of capital*. Macmillan.

Landmann, O. (2015). Short-run macro—The end of the 'new' neoclassical synthesis? In H. J. Ramser & M. Stadler (Eds.), *Entwicklung und Perspektiven der Wirtschaftswissenschaft. Wirtschaftswissenschaftliches Seminar Ottobeuren* (Vol. 41, pp. 3–18). Mohr Siebeck.

Leijonhufvud, A. (1968). *On Keynesian economics and the economics of Keynes—A study in monetary theory*. Oxford University Press.

Luhmann, N. (1988). *Die Wirtschaft der Gesellschaft* Suhrkamp. 1996.

Minsky, H. P. (1980). Money, financial markets, and the coherence of a market economy. *Journal of Post Keynesian Economics, 3*(1), 21–31.

Minsky, H. P. (1984). Frank Hahn's 'money and inflation'—A review article. *Journal of Post Keynesian Economics, 6*(3), 449–457.

Mongiovi, G. (1990). Keynes, Hayek and Sraffa—On the origins of chapter 17 of 'The General Theory'. *Economie Appliquée, 43*(2), 131–156.

Nell, E. (1988). Does the rate of interest determine the rate of profit? *Political Economy, Studies in the Surplus Approach, Vol. 4*(2), 263–268.

Pasinetti, L. L. (1977). *Lectures on the theory of production*. Macmillan.

Riese, H. (1970). Das Ende einer Wachstumstheorie. *Kyklos, 23*(4), 756–771.

Riese, H. (1972a). Ordnungsidee und Ordnungspolitik—Kritik einer wirtschaftspolitischen Konzeption. *Kyklos, 25*(1), 24–48.

Riese, H. (1972b). Schritte zu einer ökonomischen Theorie der Evolution. In B. Gahlen & A. E. Ott (Eds.), *Probleme der Wachstumstheorie* (pp. 380–434). Mohr Siebeck.

Riese, H. (1975a). *Wohlfahrt und Wirtschaftspolitik*. Rowohlt.

Riese, H. (1975b). Politische Ökonomie oder mathematische Scholastik? Genesis, Bedeutung und Grenzen neoklassischen Denkens. *Zeitschrift für Wirtschafts- und Sozialwissenschaften, 95*(3), 193–222.

Riese, H. (1979). Theoretische Grundlagen stabilitätspolitischer Kontroversen. *Kyklos, 32*, 219–235.

Riese, H. (1981). Wirtschaftspolitik unter dem Regime der Stagnation—Bemerkungen zu einem Symposion des Deutschen Instituts für Wirtschaftsforschung. *Konjunkturpolitik, 27*(4), 227–246.

Riese, H. (1983). Geldökonomie, Keynes und die Anderen—Kritik der monetären Grundlagen der Orthodoxie. In *Ökonomie und Gesellschaft, Vol. 1, Die Neoklassik und ihre Herausforderungen* (pp. 103–160). Campus Frankfurt.

Riese, H. (1985). Keynes' Geldtheorie. In H. Scherf (Ed.), *Studien zur Entwicklung der ökonomischen Theorie* (Vol. IV, pp. 9–26). Duncker & Humblot.

Riese, H. (1986a). *Theorie der Inflation*. Mohr Siebeck.

Riese, H. (1986b). Keynes, Schumpeter und die Krise. *Konjunkturpolitik, 32*(1), 1–26.

Riese, H. (1987a). Aspekte eines monetären Keynesianismus—Kritik der postkeynesianischen Ökonomie und Gegenentwurf. In K. Dietrich et al. (Eds.), *Postkeynesianismus—Ökonomische Theorie in der Tradition von Keynes, Kalecki und Sraffa* (pp. 189–206). Metropolis.

Riese, H. (1987b). Keynes als Kapitaltheoretiker. *Kredit und Kapital, 20*(2), 153–178.

Riese, H. (1988). Keynesianische Kapitaltheorie. In H. Hagemann & O. Steiger (Eds.), *Keynes' General Theory nach fünfzig Jahren* (pp. 377–401). Duncker & Humblot.

Riese, H. (1989). Geld, Kredit, Vermögen—Begriffliche Grundlagen und preistheoretische Implikationen der monetären keynesianischen Ökonomie. In H. Riese & H.-P. Spahn (Eds.), *Internationale Geldwirtschaft* (pp. 1–59). Transfer.

Riese, H. (1990). *Geld im Sozialismus*. Transfer.

Riese, H. (1991). Stand der Geldforschung—Regression und Fortschritt. In H. Riese (Ed.), *Grundlegungen eines monetären Keynesianismus—Ausgewählte Schriften 1964–1999* (Vol. 2, pp. 398–406). Metropolis.

Riese, H. (1992). Edgar Salin und das Ende der liberalen Wirtschaftsverfassung der Weimarer Republik—Überlegungen zu seinem 100. Geburtstag am 10.2.1992. *List Forum für Wirtschafts- und Finanzpolitik, 18*(1), 7–18.

Riese, H. (1993a). Bagehot versus Goodhart—Warum eine Zentralbank Geschäftsbanken braucht. In *Riese H, Grundlegungen eines monetären Keynesianismus—Ausgewählte Schriften 1964–1999* (Vol. 2, pp. 409–468). Metropolis.

Riese, H. (1993b). Schwäche des Pfundes und Versagen der Deutschen Mark—Anmerkungen zur gegenwärtigen Krise des Europäischen Währungssystems. In P. Bofinger et al. (Eds.), *Währungsunion oder Währungschaos? Was kommt nach der D-Mark?* (pp. 161–188). Gabler.

Riese, H. (1994). Keynes, Sraffa und die monetäre Theorie der Produktion. In E. Matzner & E. Nowotny (Eds.), *Was ist relevante Ökonomie heute? Festschrift für Kurt W. Rothschild* (pp. 123–164). Metropolis.

Riese, H. (1995a). Geld—Das letzte Rätsel der Nationalökonomie. In W. Schelkle & M. Nitsch (Eds.), *Rätsel Geld—Annäherungen aus ökonomischer, soziologischer und historischer Sicht* (pp. 45–62). Metropolis.

Riese, H. (1995b). Geld—Zeit—Wert. Grundfragen einer Ökonomik der Zeit. In B. Biervert & M. Held (Eds.), *Zeit in der Ökonomik—Perspektiven für die Theoriebildung* (pp. 69–91). Campus.

Riese, H. (1995c). Das Grundproblem der Wirtschaftspolitik. In K. Betz & H. Riese (Eds.), *Wirtschaftspolitik in einer Geldwirtschaft* (pp. 9–28). Metropolis.

Riese, H. (2001). *Grundlegungen eines monetären Keynesianismus—Ausgewählte Schriften 1964–1999*. Metropolis.

Rothschild, K. W. (1993). Money, money, money... Einige Bemerkungen zu Hajo Rieses Theorie einer Geldwirtschaft. In H.-J. Stadermann & O. Steiger (Eds.), *Der Stand und die nächste Zukunft der Geldforschung* (pp. 473–479). Duncker & Humblot.

Solow, R. M. (2008). The state of macroeconomics. *Journal of Economic Perspectives, 22*(1), 243–246.

Spahn, P. (1998). Moderne Makroökonomie nach Hahn und Solow—Ein Bericht. *Jahrbücher für Nationalökonomie und Statistik, 217*(3), 359–378.

Spahn, P. (2002). Die Ordnung der Gesellschaft als Zahlungswirtschaft. In C. Deutschmann (Ed.), *Die gesellschaftliche Macht des Geldes* (Leviathan, Zeitschrift für Sozialwissenschaft, Special Issue) (Vol. 21, pp. 47–72).

Spahn, P. (2016). *Streit um die Makroökonomie—Theoriegeschichtliche Debatten von Wicksell bis Woodford*. Metropolis.

Spahn, P. (2024). Monetärer Keynesianismus—Versuch einer Rekonstruktion von Hajo Rieses "Theorie der Geldwirtschaft". In *Hohenheim Discussion Papers in Business, Economics and Social Sciences*, No. 02-2024. University of Hohenheim.

Sraffa, P. (1960). *Production of commodities by means of commodities*. Cambridge University Press.

Stadermann, H.-J. (2006). *Allgemeine Theorie der Wirtschaft. Vol. 2, Nominalökonomik*. Mohr Siebeck.

Stadermann, H.-J., & Steiger, O. (Eds.). (1993a). *Der Stand und die nächste Zukunft der Geldforschung*. Duncker & Humblot.

Stadermann, H.-J., & Steiger, O. (1993b). Hajo Riese als Geldtheoretiker und die Aufgaben der Geldforschung. In H.-J. Stadermann & O. Steiger (Eds.), *Der Stand und die nächste Zukunft der Geldforschung* (pp. 1–27). Duncker & Humblot.

Stadermann, H.-J., & Steiger, O. (2001). Nominalökonomik—Entwurf einer Theorie gegenseitiger Verpflichtungen. In H.-J. Stadermann & O. Steiger (Eds.), *Verpflichtungsökonomik—Eigentum, Freiheit und Haftung in der Geldwirtschaft* (pp. 81–104). Metropolis.

Tobin, J. (1958). Liquidity preference as a behaviour towards risk. *Review of Economic Studies, 25*(2), 65–86.

Townsend, H. (1938). Letter to Keynes. In *The collected writings of John Maynard Keynes, Vol. XXIX, The general theory and after—A supplement* (pp. 289–293). Macmillan. 1979

Walras, L. (1874). *Elements of pure economics – Or The theory of social wealth* (4th ed. 1926). Allen and Unwin. 1954.

Wicksell, K. (1901). *Lectures on political economy. Vol. I, General theory*. Routledge. 1934.

Woodford, M. (2003). *Interest and prices—Foundations of a theory of monetary policy*. Princeton University Press.

Chapter 8
Kurt W. Rothschild: An Innovative Eclectic Post-Keynesian Economist

Hagen M. Krämer

8.1 Introduction

This chapter explores the scholarly endeavors and lasting contributions of the Austrian economist Kurt Wilhelm Rothschild, born in 1914 in Vienna (Austria), to Keynesian and post-Keynesian thought, with particular emphasis on his engagement with income distribution theory. Rothschild was a prolific economist whose work spanned numerous areas of economic theory and policy. His contributions were characterized by an interdisciplinary approach to economic theory, incorporating insights from sociology, political science, and history. His work is characterized by a pragmatic, pluralistic, and eclectic methodology, reflecting his belief that no single economic theory can address the complexities of real-world phenomena. This perspective is vividly illustrated by his famous advocacy for a "box of tools"—a term borrowed from Joan Robinson—which underscores the necessity of employing multiple theoretical frameworks to understand different economic situations. Rothschild's academic journey and professional achievements have cemented his legacy as a pivotal figure in the field of economics, particularly in Austria and Germany. His numerous accolades include honorary doctorates from universities such as Aachen (1987), Augsburg (1990), Bremen (1995), and the Vienna University of Economics and Business (2004).[1] He was also the first honorary

[1] The award of an honorary doctorate from the University of Bremen was essentially an initiative of Peter Kalmbach, a professor at this university. As his doctoral student and research assistant, I was involved in the preparations for the award ceremony and had the opportunity to get to know

H. M. Krämer (✉)
Karlsruhe University of Applied Sciences, Karlsruhe, Germany
e-mail: hagen.kraemer@h-ka.de

J. G. Backhaus et al. (eds.), *Post-war Keynesianism in Germany and Western Europe*, The European Heritage in Economics and the Social Sciences 28,
https://doi.org/10.1007/978-3-032-00498-7_8

member of the German Keynes Society, founded in 2003.[2] Each year, the Kurt Rothschild Prize is presented in Austria to exceptional economists and social scientists who have demonstrated outstanding contributions in their research, in the spirit of its namesake.[3]

Rothschild's research interests were wide-ranging, and he published in many areas, advancing research in various fields. He consistently expressed his criticism of one-sided neoclassical theories. Rothschild favored a pluralistic approach, utilizing a range of tools and methods as required. However, he rejected being labelled as a "heterodox" economist,

> (...) because you can't have a theory that explains everything. Economics is so complex that you need several different theories to explain different situations. You need pluralism (...) You have many theories—neoclassical, Keynesian, institutionalist, and so on. They are all honourable theories, and all of them are important. (Rothschild & King, 2009, 151–152)

Nevertheless, Rothschild's work is best categorized as post-Keynesian (Springler, 2011). While his work is rooted in Keynesian principles, he goes well beyond the standard Keynesian framework by incorporating insights from sociology, political science, and history. His innovative approach emphasizes the role of social, institutional, and political factors in shaping economic outcomes—with a particular focus on income distribution—challenging the static equilibrium models that fail to account for dynamic social processes typical of traditional Keynesian theory. What further situates him within the post-Keynesian tradition is his view of unemployment as a major concern, his emphasis on the causal direction running from investment to aggregate savings, and his assignment of a central role in his distribution theory to the analysis of the evolving income shares of labor and capital. Rothschild's contributions, in essence, extended and enriched Keynesian thought, firmly anchoring him within the post-Keynesian tradition.

The primary areas of focus for Rothschild included employment, labor market issues, income distribution, and related topics, which he personally emphasized as his "special fields of interest" (Rothschild, 1991, 11). Since income distribution is a major theme in Rothschild's work, this chapter will focus on his contribution to the post-Keynesian theory of income distribution. Before addressing this topic, however, a brief overview of Rothschild's life, academic formation, and the historical context that influenced his thinking will be presented in Section 8.2. Section 8.3 explores his major contributions to post-Keynesian distribution theory, highlighting his interdisciplinary and eclectic approach. Section 8.4 concludes by synthesizing the key insights and reflecting on the relevance of Rothschild's ideas for contemporary economic research.

Kurt W. Rothschild better during his stay in Bremen. During this and later encounters, I found him to be an equally intelligent and educated, but above all absolutely likeable person.

[2] Peter Kalmbach was a founding member of the German Keynes Society with me and eleven other economists.

[3] https://renner-institut.at/angebote/kurt-rothschild-preis.

8.2 Biography

Rothschild's academic contributions encompassed price theory, labor market economics, bargaining power, growth and distribution, and economic policy. Throughout his life, he published 42 books, 183 essays, 174 contributions to edited volumes, and 146 book reviews.[4] Rothschild was an influential figure in Austria and Germany and is regarded, together with Josef Steindl (1912–1993), as a pioneer of Keynesianism in Austria (Chaloupek, 2014).[5] His modesty, upright character, and analytical tolerance were widely appreciated, making him an outstanding figure in the field of economics (Nowotny, 2014; King, 2014).

Rothschild's early scientific work included significant publications in prestigious journals such as the Economic Journal and the Review of Economic Studies. His research covered areas such as advertising, the degree of monopoly, and public expenditure. His work on price theory and market structures examined the role of monopolies and oligopolies, as well as power structures in markets. He criticized neoclassical assumptions about perfect markets and emphasized the need to consider real market structures and power asymmetries. His work on price formation and the dynamics in imperfect markets highlights the complexity and social implications of economic decisions.

8.2.1 Formative Years in "Red Vienna" (1914–1933)

Kurt W. Rothschild was born on October 21, 1914, in Vienna, Austria, into humble circumstances and a rather non-political family.[6] His upbringing was marked by the socio-political and economic dynamics of "Red Vienna,"a period during the 1920s and early 1930s when the city was known for its progressive social policies, extensive public housing projects, and a vibrant intellectual scene. This environment played a crucial role in shaping Rothschild's early worldview, particularly his awareness of social justice and economic inequality. Vienna was also a vibrant hub for discussions in the fields of sociology and psychology, with the young Kurt Rothschild playing an active role. These experiences left a significant mark on his personality and greatly contributed to his strong preference for an interdisciplinary approach in economic science (Altzinger, 2016, 3). Additionally, the Great Depression of 1929–1930 had a profound impact on him. The economic collapse

---

[4] Detailed biographical information about Kurt W. Rotschild can be found in Rothschild (1991, 1999, 2000, 2004, 2006); King (1994, 1995, 2010); Rothschild and King (2009); Altzinger et al. (2014) and on the website https://www.kurt-rothschild.at (Rothschild, n.d.).

[5] For an examination of the role of emigrant economists in post-war Keynesianism in Austria, see the chapter by Günther Chaloupek in this volume.

[6] He had no relation to the renowned Rothschild banking dynasty, a fact that was quite often inquired about during his lifetime (King, 2014, 22).

and the resulting widespread unemployment and poverty starkly illustrated the failures of the prevailing economic systems and policies. This period of economic turmoil solidified Rothschild's interest in economics and his desire to understand and address these issues.

8.2.2 Studying Law (1933–1938)

In 1933, Rothschild began his studies in law at the University of Vienna. He chose to study law, partly because he believed it would provide better career prospects, and partly due to his desire to fight injustice ("to defend innocent people against a reactionary judicial system" Rothschild, 1999, 3). During his time at university, he was introduced to the ideas of the Austrian School of Economics, including marginal utility theory. He studied the works of key figures, such as Carl Menger, Eugen von Böhm-Bawerk, and Friedrich von Wieser. These early influences provided Rothschild with a solid grounding in economic theory, although he would later diverge significantly from the Austrian School's methodological individualism and laissez-faire ideology, instead developing a problem-oriented approach to economics.

8.2.3 Exile in Scotland and Adopting Keynesian Theory (1938–1947)

Rothschild witnessed the political upheaval brought on by the rise of Austro-Fascism in 1934 and the "Anschluss"—Austria's annexation by Nazi Germany—in 1938. With the rise of the Nazi regime, the political situation in Austria deteriorated rapidly. As a Jew, Rothschild was forced to flee the country with his wife, escaping via Switzerland to Scotland (Rothschild, 1999, 4).

In Scotland, he received a scholarship to the University of Glasgow, where he studied political economy and philosophy under the guidance of his Professors Alec Macfie and Alec Cairncross. This period was intellectually formative for Rothschild, as he immersed himself in the works of John Maynard Keynes and other contemporary economists who were challenging the orthodox economic theories of the time. Reading Joan Robinson's (1937) book "Introduction to the Theory of Employment" was of significant importance to him, as it gave him intellectual access to the philosophy of John Maynard Keynes and enabled him "to enter a new world" (Rothschild, 1999, 5). After earning his degree, Rothschild served as an assistant lecturer at the University of Glasgow, where he taught price theory. This exposed him to theories of imperfect and monopolistic competition, sparking his interest in these areas.

Rothschild often recalled his early academic ventures with a touch of amusement, illustrating his youthful boldness with the anecdote,

> My first theoretical paper, which I did at the university, I immediately sent in youthful exuberance to the leading journal, the Economic Journal. He [referring to John Maynard Keynes] was the editor. After a few days, I received a letter where he wrote, "I like it, I will publish it."[7]

This early acceptance by Keynes himself served as a significant validation and encouragement for Rothschild's burgeoning career.[8]

During World War II, Rothschild was interned as an enemy alien, but he was soon released and allowed to continue his academic pursuits. He worked as a lecturer at the University of Glasgow and appreciated the open and unbiased academic atmosphere in Scotland. About Scotland, Rothschild admired that

> (…) a differentiated and differentiating view in political matters and tactics was accepted. This openness towards other opinions and the readiness to cooperate with "other" sides when the situation seems opportune impressed me and has not only left its marks on my views on politics and political action but probably also contributed to the *eclectic leanings in theoretical matters.* (Rothschild, 1999, 6; my emphasis)

His time in Scotland solidified his commitment to a pluralistic approach to economics, one that embraced diverse theories and methodologies to better understand and address economic issues. In his academic career, he pursued an interdisciplinary approach, viewing economic theories as tools for analyzing and solving concrete problems.

8.2.4 Return to Austria and Work at WIFO (1947–1966)

After World War II ended, Rothschild returned to Austria in 1947 where he faced resistance in obtaining academic positions due to the influence of former Nazis. He joined the Austrian Institute of Economic Research (WIFO), one of the leading economic research institutions in Austria. A recommendation from August Hayek was helpful in his application. His early years at WIFO were marked by challenges, including a skeptical attitude towards the quality of available economic data.

Rothschild made significant contributions to economic research at WIFO. He collaborated with prominent economists such as Josef Steindl (1979), with whom he developed a deep professional and personal relationship. Their work often focused on issues of economic development, income distribution, and the role of monopolies and oligopolies. In 1962, Rothschild completed his habilitation at the

[7] His first essay published in "The Economic Journal" is Rothschild (1942a), "A Note on Advertising". The original quote is in German and taken from the website "https://www.kurt-rothschild.at/leben/biographie/". All translations of German quotations into English are provided by the author of this chapter.

[8] It is remarkable that, early in his career, when Rothschild was only in his late twenties or early thirties, he already published in prestigious economic journals, such as Economic Journal, Review of Economic Studies, and Oxford Bulletin of Statistics (Rotschild, 1942b, 1942c, 1943a, 1943b, 1944, 1947).

University of Vienna, which allowed him to teach at the university level. His habilitation thesis, which dealt with issues of price theory and market structures, was well-received and further established his reputation as a leading economist in Austria.

During his time at WIFO, Rothschild also engaged in public policy discussions and contributed to the development of economic policies in post-war Austria. His work often emphasized the importance of addressing social and economic inequalities and the need for state intervention in the economy to promote stability and growth. His time at WIFO was marked by rigorous research and a series of important publications that solidified his position as a leading thinker in post-Keynesian economics.

8.2.5 Academic Career at the University of Linz (1966–1985)

In 1966, Rothschild was appointed to the newly founded University of Linz, where he served as rector in 1971/1972. His professorship provided him with an opportunity to shape the curriculum and academic direction of the economics department. He was known for his ability to facilitate lively and constructive discussions among faculty and students, and he often invited prominent economists to speak at the university. Rothschild's tenure at Linz was marked by his commitment to a problem-oriented approach to economics. He believed that economic theory should be grounded in the realities of economic life and that it should address pressing social issues. This perspective was reflected in his teaching, where he encouraged students to critically engage with economic theories and to consider their practical implications. During this period, Rothschild continued to publish extensively on a wide range of economic subjects, including price theory, labor market economics, and income distribution. His work was characterized by a deep skepticism of simplistic economic models and a commitment to understanding the complex realities of economic life.

8.2.6 Retirement and Further Publishing Activities (1985–2010)

After retiring from his professorship in 1985, Rothschild remained active in the academic community. He continued to work as a consultant at WIFO, participated in conferences, and published scholarly articles and books. His later works often reflected on the state of economic theory and the importance of maintaining a pluralistic and interdisciplinary approach to economics. Even in retirement, Rothschild's intellectual curiosity and commitment to social justice did not wane. He engaged in public debates on economic policy and continued to advocate for policies that addressed economic inequality and promoted social welfare. One of his final books, co-authored with Hans Bürger and published in 2009 (when he was already 95 years old), exemplified his enduring commitment to economic research and his belief in the importance of interdisciplinary perspectives (Bürger & Rothschild, 2009).

Rothschild passed away on November 15, 2010, in Vienna, leaving behind a legacy of intellectual rigor, social commitment, and a profound influence on the field of economics.

8.3 Kurt Rothschild's Contributions to Post-Keynesian Distribution Theory

8.3.1 Rothschild's Approach to Economic Theory

Rothschild's work was deeply aligned with the core principles of Keynesian economics. He was particularly drawn to its focus on macroeconomic phenomena, its openness to considering the role of the state and political action in shaping economic outcomes, and its emphasis on uncertainty in economic decision-making.

Rothschild made important contributions to the study of labor markets, focusing on issues such as unemployment, wage determination, and labor market institutions (Rothschild, 1954, 1961, 1968, 1988, 1993, 1994). His work on unemployment challenged the neoclassical view that unemployment is primarily voluntary or caused by rigidities in the labor market. He argued that unemployment often results from macroeconomic factors, such as insufficient aggregate demand, and that active government intervention is often necessary to achieve full employment.

Rothschild always insisted on the relevance of macroeconomic correlations and influences and took into account the overall economic situation, in particular the situation on the labor market (full or underemployment). His papers on inflation, stagflation, and the Phillips curve were highly influential and well-received within the academic community (Rothschild, 1971a, 1982). Rothschild (1999, 5) once stated that Keynesian economics had a significant influence and appeal for him because it provided a more effective and straightforward theoretical foundation for understanding socio-economic issues:

> The most important characteristics in this respect are the immediate access to macroeconomics, which points the way to considering state and political action; the stress on uncertainty and decisions under uncertainty (a bridge to psychology and away from the "mechanic" rationality of the homo oeconomicus); and the shift in emphasis towards the analysis of the socially most pressing economic problem, viz. unemployment, instead of starting with and concentrating on price formation and equilibrium conditions in more or less perfect markets. These characteristics appealed to me not only because of my special biases (or "philosophy"?), but also because they force one to pay more attention to realism and relevance than some other types of economic analysis. (Rothschild, 1999, 5)

This quote encapsulates Rothschild's perspective on the key strengths of Keynesian economics, highlighting its relevance to real-world economic problems and its departure from the more abstract and idealized assumptions of neoclassical economics. Rothschild's Keynesian orientation led him to prioritize the study of issues such as unemployment and income distribution, which he saw as central to understanding the functioning of modern economies. He believed that economists should actively address pressing social and economic challenges instead of concentrating solely on theoretical models of market equilibrium. He valued realism and relevance over the perfection of the analyses of market equilibria. In his labor market research, he analyzed how bargaining power shapes employment relations and wage outcomes. He demonstrated that labor markets are often characterized by power asymmetries and that wages and employment conditions are determined not only by market forces but also by negotiations and institutional and social frameworks.

Rothschild's contributions to post-Keynesian distribution theory were significant, particularly in the realm of macroeconomic income distribution. His influence on the wage and distribution debate is evident in his seminal book "Theory of Wages" (1954) and further expanded upon in his comprehensive article "*Der Lohnanteil am Gesamteinkommen* (*The Wage Share of Total Income*)" (1957). Rothschild generally accepted Kalecki's model, emphasizing the role of monopoly power in stabilizing the wage share. In the latter work, he critically examined the theoretically contentious stability hypothesis of the wage share, which had been considered a "stylized fact" in growth and distribution theories. By employing both theoretical and empirical evidence, Rothschild challenged this hypothesis, thereby advancing knowledge in the field.

In the following sections, I will first discuss Rothschild's engagement with Kaldor's post-Keynesian theory of income distribution. Then, I will present his perspective on the long-assumed constant wage share. Subsequently, I will examine Rothschild's critical engagement with Sydney Weintraub's theory of relative shares, as this reveals much about Rothschild's views on the appropriate approach on issues of income distribution.

8.3.2 Engagement with Kaldor's Growth and Distribution Theory

Kurt W. Rothschild critically examined Nicholas Kaldor's growth and distribution theory, thereby making significant contributions to the field. His involvement with Kaldor's distribution theory, beginning in the early 1960s (Rothschild, 1961, 1965), played a pivotal role in the advancement of distribution models grounded in circular flow analyzes, thereby enhancing their empirical relevance (Guger, 2011, 44). In Kaldor's original formulation, relative income shares were determined by investments and the predetermined savings behavior of profits and wage earners (Kaldor, 1955/1956). Rothschild (1959) argued that Kaldor's technical progress function rested on assumptions that were overly specific and lacked empirical support. He was skeptical of the constancy of class-specific saving propensities, suggesting that these propensities are influenced by historical and social contexts rather than being fixed independent variables. By relaxing these assumptions and integrating social dependencies into the behavior of economic actors, Rothschild (1961) introduced a more realistic framework and highlighted the potential role of unions in wage policy. In his 1959 paper, Rothschild (1959) criticized steady-state growth models for their limited variables and neglect of historical, social, and institutional details that are crucial for long-term analysis.

One of the problems Rothschild had with Kaldor's model was that income distribution is endogenously determined by purely economic factors. Attempts to increase real wages or profit margins either fail from the outset or lead to a distributive struggle resulting in inflation with a largely uncertain outcome. As such, there is no room for the influence of the social structure in Kaldor's model. However, the endogenous determination of distribution only holds within a specific range, the extent of which is determined by various influences, including exogenously given "social" factors (e.g., the minimum wage). If the level of relative shares compatible with a goods market equilibrium lies outside these ranges, a new equilibrium in the form described by Kaldor will not be achieved. Yet, regarding the influencing factors that operate within these margins, one might, along with Erich Preiser,[9] wonder that:

> ... neither the wage level nor the structural situation in the goods markets play a role.... It is clear that this cannot be, and since the formula is correct, the question arises as to where the error lies. (Preiser, 1964, 11)

Kaldor's model was subject to similar criticisms from both Preiser and Rothschild. Therefore, we will briefly examine Preiser's critiques at this point. Preiser identified the main shortcoming in Kaldor's model as the assumption that income recipients are willing to accept any income distribution that falls within the specified range, thus criticizing Kaldor's determined ranges as being too broad. Instead, he argues that it is more plausible to assume that income groups plan a specific distribution of income.[10] In the long term, they therefore realize a particular income distribution that corresponds to their relative power, thereby closing Kaldor's range of choice. The relative power of the parties competing for distribution, in Preiser's view, is expressed in the so-called "structural degree of monopoly," which functions as a datum for the distribution analysis. In this, Preiser (1964, 48) sees "the translation of historical power relations into economic categories. "In line with Kalecki's theory, the presence of a degree of monopoly is inherently linked to the existence of imperfect markets, where a markup pricing procedure is applied. Preiser understands his contribution as a complement to Kaldor's theory, insofar as the process depicted by Kaldor ensures a goods market equilibrium while simultaneously revealing the hypothetically possible income share distribution compatible with it. At the same time, the resulting share distribution is determined taking into account the social structure of society. Secondly, Preiser emphasized the impor-

[9] On Erich Preiser, an influential German Economist in the 1950s and 1960s, and his contributions to Keynesianism and distribution theory see Johannes Schmidt's essay in this volume.

[10] "... here a certain real wage, there a certain profit rate and, more recently, even sometimes a share in national income in collective bargaining" (Preiser, 1964, 49).

tance of Kaldor's mechanism in explaining income distribution over the economic cycle. He argued that this framework captures the oscillations around the structural degree of monopoly, which forms the core of long-term income distribution. However, Preiser's theory does not provide any further explanations regarding the emergence and development of the structural degree of monopoly over time. Preiser, therefore—much like Kalecki—often had to contend with accusations of tautology.

Rothschild (1965) modified the Kaldor model in a similar way to Preiser, but without resorting to a construct such as the degree of monopoly. In his approach, social power relations are evident in the fact that the parties strive for a certain income distribution or develop resistance if a limit is exceeded, which marks the distribution that is considered barely acceptable. If this tolerable limit is surpassed, the respective groups begin to take action: entrepreneurs respond to wage increases that appear too high to them with disproportionate price increases or with vigorous productivity-enhancing measures. On the other hand, employees counter price increases, which shift the distribution to their detriment to an unacceptable extent, with attempts to increase nominal wages. As in the Kaldor model, this can result in a wage-price spiral or price-wage spiral. However, Rothschild emphasizes that these lines of resistance are primarily short-term and thus have a business cycle-enhancing character, but that in the long term, investments would also create the necessary savings through income variation. In his 1961 work, Rothschild (1961) emphasized the importance of path dependence and historical experiences in determining economic growth and distribution variables. He referenced Erich Schneider[11] (1957) to illustrate the "Keynesian spirit" by incorporating a Kaldorian model without full employment. He also explored the concept of real wage resistance and class conflicts, developing a model that identifies the conditions for a maximum wage share (minimum profit share) based on the investment-income ratio.

These modifications of Kaldor's distribution theory demonstrate that it is feasible to incorporate circular flow relationships with approaches that consider the conflict between competing groups or classes. Consequently, they constitute significant contributions to the distribution analysis in a macroeconomic context. However, their immediate linkage to Kaldor's distribution theory remains unsatisfactory, since it is based on some untenable premises and implausible causal processes (Krämer, 1996). Power-theoretical influences must, therefore, be analyzed in a framework other than that proposed by Kaldor. In the section below, we will explore another variant of post-Keynesian distribution theory developed by Michał Kalecki, which gives a broader role to power elements. This discussion will focus on Rothschild's perspective on Bowley's law.

[11] For further insight into one of the most influential German Keynesian academic economists of the post-Second World War era, see Harald Hagemann's essay in this volume.

8.3.3 Bowley's Law: To Be, or Not to Be

In this section, we examine Rothschild's contribution to the debate on wage share stability. Early in his career, in his book "The Theory of Wages,"Rothschild (1954) discussed the relative shares of income, affirming *Bowley's Law*, which posits a constant wage share over time.[12] This law suggests that the proportion of national income allocated to wages remains more or less stable in the long run. Rothschild later criticized this alleged "law."

The hypothesis of a constant wage share has a long history as an ideological instrument of wage policy. Initially, wage-fund theorists regarded the wage bill as a fixed variable. This perspective implied that higher wages could only be achieved at the expense of employment or other workers' wages. In neoclassical theory, the marginal productivity framework—particularly in the form of the linear-homogeneous Cobb-Douglas production function—posited that the wage and profit shares were technologically predetermined by the fixed exponents on labor and capital inputs. Any attempt to enforce wage increases that exceed productivity growth, according to neoclassical theory, would make labor relatively more expensive, leading to its substitution by capital and potentially resulting in unemployment. The neoclassical theory of share distribution was shaped by a series of empirical studies conducted for Great Britain and the USA from the 1920s onwards. Similarly, the early post-Keynesian growth and distribution theory drew from these studies. Notably, the works of Bowley (1920), Bowley and Stamp (1927), and Bowley (1937) found a stable wage share of total income, establishing this as a stylized fact of macroeconomic growth and income distribution. Arthur Bowley (1937) concluded from this data that a stability in the proportion of earned income to total income persisted between 1880 and 1913, and between 1911/1913 and 1924. The studies apparently demonstrated the resilience of income distribution across various periods.[13] John Maynard Keynes (1936, 48), echoed this sentiment, describing the constancy of labor's share in the national dividend as "one of the most surprising yet best-established facts in the whole range of economic statistics."

Bowley's Law gained acceptance from numerous notable economists, including Paul Douglas, Michał Kalecki, John Maynard Keynes, Nicolas Kaldor, Paul A. Samuelson, Oskar Lange, Richard Goodwin, John Roemer, N. Gregory Mankiw, and Martin Feldstein. Keynes famously remarked on its miraculous nature, while

[12] The "law of the constant wage share" is named after the British economist and statistician Sir Arthur L. Bowley (1869–1957) (Darnell, 1981). It is considered to be a "great ratio of economics" (Klein & Kosobud, 1961).

[13] However, these results are highly dubious from today's perspective. For example, the wage bill did not include the salaries of white-collar workers. Furthermore, it represented an unadjusted wage share, meaning that changes in the proportion of self-employed persons to total employment were not considered. Additionally, the sources and methods of national accounting at that time were not as developed as they are today, raising legitimate doubts about the accuracy of the calculations for both the national product and the wage bill (Krämer, 2011).

Joseph Schumpeter labelled it a mystery, and Sidney Weintraub likened it to Newton's gravitational constant (Krämer, 1996).

The hypothesis of income-share constancy is a foundational assumption within various strands of distribution theories (Krämer, 2011). In neoclassical, post-Keynesian, and Kalecki's writings on distribution, arguments were presented as to why income shares are rather constant in the long run. It is a peculiar feature of distribution theories, following the era of classical political economy, that they have been constructed from the outset in such a way that they primarily reproduce and justify the constancy of relative income shares. As Rothschild rightly observed:

> … from the days of Douglas and Cobb via Keynes and Kalecki right up to Kaldor and later writers the "puzzle" of constant shares was a motivating force in distributional research. Behind the question why the wage share is what it is, there was the "deeper" and dominating question why the share is constant. (Rothschild, 1985, 777)

It is evident that, as a consequence of this limitation, distribution theory has been deprived of its original mission, which was to explain the laws that *change* the distribution of national income. Ricardo's belief that the exploration of these laws would one day become the subject of fruitful scientific research, expressed in a letter to Malthus (Ricardo, 1951/1959, vol. viii, 278–279), has therefore not been fulfilled.

What the various schools of thought have in common is that they model the constancy of relative income shares in such a way that either the factors determining income distribution themselves remain constant in the long run, or that there is a quasi-automatic compensation of the forces that influence income distribution (Krämer, 2011). However, if the fundamental assumption of share constancy is abandoned, such deterministic approaches and monocausal explanations are no longer suitable for explaining the level and changes in income shares.

In this context, the theory of Michał Kalecki, to which Rothschild referred in many of his writings, is an interesting case. Although Kalecki accepted Bowley's Law, his theory of income distribution is more open to variable income shares, as the distribution is determined by exogenous factors such as the degree of monopoly or the relative economic power of the socio-economic classes (ibid., 41). In his "The Determinants of the Distribution of the National Income," Kalecki (1938) established his theoretical framework. Unlike the neoclassical approach, his theory was grounded in imperfect competition and a pricing mechanism based on profit markups over variable unit costs. In Kalecki's economic theory, firms set prices based on their costs of production, Including wages and raw materials. They then add a markup to account for fixed costs such as machinery expenses, depreciation, and profits. This profit markup is influenced by structural factors such as the degree of monopoly power and the broader competitive conditions in the market. Kalecki explained Bowley's empirically observed constancy of the wage share, which he accepted as valid, by predicting a long-term increase in monopoly power due to tendencies toward industrial concentration (Kalecki, 1939). Simultaneously, he anticipated a counterbalance through stronger labor unions. However, regarding other determinants of income distribution in his model, such as raw material prices and the economic structure, Kalecki remained cautious about making long-term forecasts.

Kalecki's model was occasionally criticized as tautological. Rothschild (1957, 165) did not consider the accusation of tautology levelled against Kalecki to be without foundation. However, he did not regard this as a decisive issue, as Kalecki's theory on the impact of monopoly power provided valuable insights into price theory and the dynamics of competition. For example, he noted that the degree of monopoly was not only relevant for questions of income distribution but also influenced corporate pricing strategies as well as technical and sociological factors. Rothschild (1954) built upon Kalecki's model and analyzed it within the context of income distribution. He concurred with Kalecki's claim that offsetting alterations in the degree of monopoly and the price of raw materials had impeded any substantial alteration in labor's share (King, 1994, 438; Guger, 2011). More generally, he identified three primary factors influencing the share of wages in gross national income: the degree of monopoly, the ratio of raw material costs to total wages, and the economic structure characterized by varying sectoral weights. For instance, an increase in monopolization or a rise in raw material costs relative to labor expenses would lead to a decline in the wage share. With his detailed consideration of the most important theoretical and statistical aspects, Rothschild wanted:

> to prevent the assertion of a stable wage share (or a variant thereof) from becoming a generally accepted dogma - similar to Pareto's law of income distribution, for example - before a sufficiently sound statistical basis or a sufficiently profound theoretical explanation allows this assertion to be proven or refuted. (Rothschild, 1957, 184)

Although Rothschild did not explicitly question the constancy of relative shares in his 1957 essay, the statements in question demonstrated a certain skepticism about this stylized fact of growth and distribution theory, which was firmly established at the time.[14] In his later work, he abandoned the notion of constant relative shares and developed distribution models in which fluctuations in income shares were possible.

While the central determinants of distribution, such as relative power relations and technological progress, are not adequately addressed within either the neoclassical or Kaldorian models, Kalecki's theoretical framework provides the necessary analytical tools to consider these influential factors, as Rothschild already acknowledged. A methodological advantage of Kalecki's theory is that it does not rely on the steady-state methodology of neoclassical and the early post-Keynesian growth theory, which is often used in long-term distributional analysis. Kalecki's approach remains meaningfully applicable because it does not rely on Bowley's Law. Consequently, Kalecki's theory, along with extensions provided by authors like Sylos-Labini (1969, 1984), offers a potential point of departure for the development of a comprehensive distribution theory within the post-Keynesian paradigm.[15]

---

[14] In 1958, at the famous Corfu conference on capital theory, Nicholas Kaldor formulated a series of stylized facts that had a lasting influence on the discussion about growth and income distribution. The constancy of relative income shares was one of them. His article on capital accumulation and economic growth was published in 1961 (Kaldor, 1961).

[15] For a comprehensive overview of recent extensions and applications of post-Keynesian and Kaleckian models of growth and distribution, see Hein (2023).

Recent decades have validated Kurt Rothschild's cautious assessment regarding the long-term stability of the wage share. Contrary to the widespread thesis of its stability, the wage share has proven to be more volatile over the past 50 years than previously assumed (Krämer et al., 2023, 85). The loss of bargaining power of workers and trade unions, globalization, and the financialization sector are factors that have substantially changed income shares to the detriment of wage income in the last three decades (ibid., 86–91).

8.3.4 Sidney Weintraub's "Eclectic Theory of Relative Shares"

Based on the recognition that the three original versions of macroeconomic distribution theory (neoclassical, Kaldorian, Kaleckian) do not provide a comprehensive and satisfactory explanation of the factors that can change relative income shares in the long-run, Sidney Weintraub pleaded for eclecticism in distribution theory, because "… everything is a 'little right' in share theory" (Weintraub 1981, 23). In his widely discussed essay within the post-Keynesian spectrum, "Eclectic Theory of Relative Shares," Weintraub (1981) attempted to integrate various aspects of prevailing distribution theories. He believed that individual theories either placed unilateral emphasis on the demand side (Kaldor) or the supply side (neoclassical, Kalecki). Her argued, in the sense of Marshall's dictum, that "both sides of the scissors" are responsible for determining income distribution (Weintraub, 1981, 17).

Rothschild expressed reservations about Weintraub's (1981) essay. His concerns are not directed against Weintraub's plea for applied eclecticism in distribution theory. Rothschild himself has made it clear at various points that income distribution can only be adequately studied under the prevailing economic, institutional, and social conditions, and that monocausal explanations are therefore prohibited (see, for example, Rothschild, 1973; King, 1994). In his paper Rothschild, 1985), he addressed several additional points he believed warranted criticism. Firstly, he raised some technical issues with Weintraub's approach. One key point of contention was the significance of constancy in the "Wage-Cost Mark-Up" (k), a key variable in Weintraub's model. Rothschild demonstrated that even substantial changes in the distribution of income would have only minor effects on the value of k, casting doubt on its explanatory power. Secondly, Rothschild pointed out that Weintraub's theory lacked a clear and consistent analytical framework, which made it difficult to apply and test empirically. Thirdly, and most significantly, he raised methodological objections to Weintraub's equilibrium approach, which he shares with neoclassical and Kaldorian distribution theory. While it is appropriate to seek long-term stable relationships in markets, production, and consumption to determine a macroeconomic equilibrium solution for production and employment, this approach is not suitable for distribution theory, since:

> (…) there can be no such "peaceful" stability in the distribution field. Eclectic theory in particular must take into account that discontent over shares belongs to the essence of capitalist (if not any) societies. (Rothschild, 1985, 588)

Weintraub also acknowledged that power and conflict play an important role in distribution:

> Share theory lays bare the Ricardo-Marx-Sraffa judgement of conflict over income shares, despite the lulling marginal productivity harmonies by the many reincarnated J. B. Clarks. (Weintraub, 1981, 23)

However, at this point, Rothschild identified the limitations of Weintraub's equilibrium approach, noting its principal inability to address the ongoing struggle between socio-economic groups concerning income distribution. The ongoing conflict over income distribution suggests that what is often labelled as "disequilibrium" is not an anomaly but rather "an almost natural state in the distribution sphere" (Rothschild, 1985, 588), since the groups competing for a share of the product are continuously striving to increase their portion of national income. At best, a temporary balance of power emerges—one that can be reshaped at any time by shifts in the social and economic environment. Therefore, even when incorporating elements of power in a distribution theory—a concept strongly advocated in Rothschild's work—it cannot be assumed that a single specific income distribution exists that exactly reflects the relative strengths of competing groups. In reality, social groups have different ideas about what can be regarded as an adequate distribution. They therefore constantly try to realize their desired share of the pie with the tools at their disposal in the dispute over income distribution. In addition to the nominal wage level, firms' pricing also proves to be a strategic variable, as referred to in Kalecki's approach to distribution theory. In extreme cases where one of the parties does not accept the resulting distribution and fully asserts its means of power, distributional conflict inflation can occur. In such scenarios, it is evidently impossible to find an equilibrium solution.

However, even under less extreme circumstances, the determination of equilibrium values for distribution must be understood differently. The idea that exogenous parameters can be specified and that endogenous forces will work towards achieving a balanced distribution must be rejected. The never-ending interaction between endogenous factors of distribution and exogenous (especially non-economic) factors is characteristic of the distribution sphere. Rothschild's approach advocates for a distribution theory that avoids two extremes: the notion that every distribution resulting from a dispute is fundamentally feasible and the belief that economic mechanisms alone determine distribution. A realistic perspective shows that economic conditions establish the framework within which distribution disputes occur. The relationship between these two levels is not unidirectional but interdependent.

Rothschild attributes the relatively low fluctuations of relative shares around their "equilibrium values" observed most of the time in the real world to the significant resistance posed by the negatively affected group against more pronounced changes in distribution. Under normal circumstances, the balance of power does not undergo major changes. Following Rothschild's approach, the main task of an advanced distribution theory is to analyze the conditions that lead to changes in income distribution, thereby shifting the analysis into a dynamic context.

Following Rothschild's argument that income earners prioritize defending their relative income position, any given distribution can be partly explained by the income distribution prevailing in the past. This allows us, in the first step, to consider distribution as given and to analytically focus on the factors influencing changes in distribution. For Rothschild, it was essential that such an approach incorporates both economic and sociological influences. In line with his interdisciplinary vision, Rothschild (1973, 217) championed a "'Political Economy' of distribution, where economic and sociological influences are combined," incorporating changes in the supply of production factors due to legal and social institutions, as well as the exercise of economic power. He argued that what a synthetic theory of income distribution

> (...) *cannot* do is to give simple answers which will hold without respect to concrete situations and circumstances; but that is true of all disequilibrium theory. It is this what makes it so "sloppy" compared with pure equilibrium theory. (Rothschild, 1985, 592; emphasis in the original)

8.3.5 The Role of Bargaining Power

Rothschild's analysis of wage determination emphasized the role of bargaining power and institutional factors. He argued that wages are not solely determined by the marginal productivity of labor but are also influenced by the strength of labor unions, the level of unemployment, and government policies (Rothschild, 1988). This perspective aligned with the post-Keynesian view that wage determination is a complex process involving economic, social, and political factors.

The role of power not only in determining wages, but in income distribution in general was underscored by Rothschild (1971b, 1978, 2002). Already in 1957, he highlighted how elements of power influenced the distribution of incomes, including the political pressure exerted by unions to implement price controls to protect wage shares. He argued that institutional factors and the economic system itself must be incorporated into distribution analysis. Critiquing Kaldor's theory, which linked profit shares to investment rates and consumption propensities of workers and capitalists, Rothschild pointed out that reducing capital incomes might lower investment rather than consumption, thereby setting an upper limit for wages.

Rothschild identified several factors that could influence the wage share by affecting bargaining power, including:

- Macroeconomic Conditions: the overall state of the economy, including levels of unemployment and economic growth, which can affect the leverage of workers in wage negotiations.
- Labor Market Institutions and Bargaining Power of Labor Unions: the presence and strength of labor unions, the effectiveness of collective bargaining agreements, and labor laws that protect workers' rights enhance the bargaining power of labor unions.

- Economic Policies: government policies that influence the balance of power between workers and employers, such as minimum wage laws, social security systems, unemployment benefits, and tax policies.
- Degree of Monopoly: the extent of market power held by firms, which could allow them to set prices above competitive levels and capture a larger share of income.

These factors highlight the diverse influences on income distribution and underscore the importance of a comprehensive analysis to better understand labor market dynamics.

8.3.6 Rothschild's Contributions to Post-Keynesian Distribution Theory: A Summary

Summing up, Rothschild extended his analysis of income distribution beyond the immediate dynamics of the labor market to consider the wider institutional and political context. He argued that income distribution is deeply embedded in and influenced by a country's legal and regulatory framework, as well as by the prevailing political and ideological climate. Rothschild suggested that policies and institutions supporting collective bargaining, social welfare programs, and progressive taxation can help achieve a more equitable distribution of income. Conversely, deregulation, weakening of labor protections, and regressive tax policies tend to exacerbate income inequality. His work highlighted the need for a comprehensive political economy approach to understanding income distribution, one that integrates economic, social, and political dimensions.

A vocal critic of neoclassical distribution theory, particularly the marginal productivity theory of income distribution, Rothschild argued that this theory was overly simplistic and failed to account for the complexities of real-world economic relationships. He pointed out that marginal productivity theory assumes perfectly competitive markets, constant returns to scale, and the absence of power asymmetries—assumptions that rarely hold in practice. In contrast, Rothschild's approach acknowledged the importance of market imperfections, institutional factors, and power dynamics in shaping income distribution. His analysis of growth and distribution emphasized the complexity and context-dependent nature of economic progress. This perspective contrasts with the perceived precision of pure equilibrium theory and sets the stage for his multifaceted contributions. Recognizing the limitations of any single disciplinary perspective, Rothschild championed an interdisciplinary approach to understanding income distribution (Rothschild, 1973). He argued that a complete analysis must incorporate insights from sociology, political science, and psychology alongside traditional economic theory. In his view, economics should not be isolated from these other fields; rather, a comprehensive theory of income distribution requires an examination of the broader socio-economic environment, historical context, and institutional dynamics. He underscored this point by identifying "two fundamental problems" from Keynes (1936)—unemployment and the unequal distribution of income and wealth—as issues that remain central to economic policy and social well-being. His criticism of Kaldor's growth and distribution theory further exemplifies his insistence on grounding economic analysis in empirical reality and historical context.

A significant element of Rothschild's work was his strong advocacy for state intervention to redistribute income. He believed that reducing social inequalities and enhancing economic stability necessitated active policy measures designed to correct imbalances inherent in capitalist systems. Rooted in a Keynesian economic framework and enhanced by Kalecki's (1938, 1939, 1943, 1954) analysis—especially concerning the influence of firm pricing under monopolistic conditions on income shares—his proposals for redistribution focused on achieving social justice through corrective state action.

8.3.7 Rothschild's Themes in Contemporary Discussions

Kurt W. Rothschild's contributions have had a lasting impact on economic theory and policy. His work is recognized for integrating political and social dimensions into economic analysis, challenging the conventional neoclassical approaches, and advocating for state intervention to achieve social justice and economic stability. Rothschild's later works continued to reflect his eclectic and pluralistic approach (Kurz, 2014). He engaged in discussions about the nature of economics, emphasizing the importance of methodological diversity and the relevance of economic theories to real-world problems.

The relevance of Rothschild's insights remains strong in today's economic discourse, particularly in the areas of market power, mark-up pricing, and income distribution. For example, contemporary research presented at the Jackson Hole Conference in 2018, such as de Loecker and Eeckhout's (2017) study or van Reenen's (2018) paper on the rise of market power and its macroeconomic implications, resonates with Rothschild's emphasis on the role of monopolistic practices in shaping income distribution. Similarly, works like those of Autor et al. (2020) on the fall of the labor share and the rise of "superstar" firms further underline the importance of Rothschild's analysis of market dynamics and their impact on income shares.[16] These studies highlight the increasing market power of dominant firms and its adverse effects on labor's share of income, reflecting Rothschild's concerns about the concentration of economic power.

His theories also intersect with contemporary debates on distribution and economic growth (OECD, 2015; Ostry et al., 2014). The work of Piketty (2014) and others on the World Inequality Database (WID) and their analyses of unequal distribution and its effects on economic growth underscore the enduring relevance of

[16] However, it is noteworthy and unfortunate that those authors neither mention nor cite the works of Rothschild and Kalecki.

Rothschild's approach. Rothschild's emphasis on the need for a comprehensive and interdisciplinary analysis of income distribution is echoed in these modern discussions, highlighting the interconnectedness of economic, political, and social factors.

8.4 Concluding Remarks

Kurt W. Rothschild's academic legacy is characterized by an impressive breadth of inquiry, spanning price theory, labor market economics, income distribution, and the role of power and institutions in economic processes. His lack of association with a single major idea might explain why his work is not as widely recognized internationally, unlike the works of his contemporary colleague Josef Steindl (King, 1994, 431). His work consistently challenged the conventional neoclassical paradigm by exposing the limitations of overly simplistic models that assume a stable equilibrium dictated solely by impersonal market forces. Instead, Rothschild demonstrated that the distribution of income, growth, and the dynamics of economic power are shaped by a complex interplay of political, social, and institutional factors. His rigorous analysis of market structures and price formation questioned the conventional wisdom of perfect competition, arguing that real-world phenomena are better understood through a multifaceted framework that integrates insights from Marxian, Keynesian, and even neoclassical perspectives making him an innovative eclectic post-Keynesian economist.

He underscored that issues such as unemployment and income inequality—problems highlighted by Keynes in the 24th chapter of his General Theory—are central to economic policy-making and cannot be adequately addressed by static or monocausal models. Rothschild consistently emphasized that these issues should be at the forefront of economic analysis and policy-making. His work on income distribution, which is the focus of this essay, elucidated how shifting power relations and institutional dynamics continuously redefine the economic landscape, leading to a state of "natural disequilibrium" in income shares rather than fixed magnitudes. By rigorously integrating theoretical and empirical insights, he offered a more dynamic framework that acknowledges the inherent conflicts and constant evolution of economic structures, influencing the distribution of national income. His contributions to post-Keynesian distribution theory remain profoundly influential and relevant to contemporary economic discourse.

Advocating for methodological openness and multi-paradigmatic approaches, Rothschild argued that realistic insights and practical relevance in economics could only be achieved by embracing a diverse set of theoretical approaches. This methodological openness was crucial in his addressing of the dynamic and complex nature of real-world economic events. In his words:

> In all these cases the reliance on "one eye" only and blindness on all other eyes (of which there should be many) leads to a very uneven distribution of weights and interests regarding various theoretical approaches which is not independent of the ruling "Zeitgeist". (Rothschild, 1999, 7)

Central to his methodology was the advocacy for Robinson's "box of tools" approach—an invitation to embrace multi-paradigmatic analysis.[17] Rothschild argued that no single theoretical lens is sufficient to explain the intricacies of economic reality. He advocated for a set of theoretical frameworks, emphasizing that

> a multitude of theoretical approaches (the "box of tools") combined with situational and interdisciplinary supplementary considerations (...) is at least helpful if not essential to interpret real events. (Rothschild, 1999, 7)

Ultimately, Rothschild expressed a firm commitment to:

> (...) a methodological understanding that multiparadigmism and openness are unavoidable if realistic insights and relevance for practical affairs are to be achieved. (Rothschild, 1999, 6)

He believed that "the whole post-war development can be explained by such combinations (...)" (ibid.) drawing from Marxian, Keynesian, and neoclassical perspectives. He recognized that each of these theoretical traditions offer valuable insights, even if they were sometimes contradictory. The Marxian perspective highlighted "(...) the influence of changes in productive relations and group conflicts on the shifts in market and political power (...)" (ibid.). Keynesian and post-Keynesian theories provided a framework for understanding the possibilities of government intervention in the economy. Neoclassical theory, despite its limitations, could elucidate "(...) the intricacies of various new market mechanisms." However, he cautioned against the misuse of theories, noting that

> (...) vulgar Marxism was misused as a legitimation for the Soviet economic system, vulgar Keynesianism supported the idea of the welfare state, and a vulgar neoclassical theory is supposed to justify free markets and deregulation (*ibid.*).

Rothschild's work was also characterized by a strong ethical and social commitment to using economics as a tool for promoting social justice and human well-being. He maintained that economics should not merely be an academic pursuit but a means for social transformation. He once stated that he had

> (...) an ethical and social "bias" that economics should contribute to a "better" world with less unemployment, less poverty, or – to formulate it more pathetically – to a world that is guided by the Utopian battle cry of the French Revolution: Liberté, Egalité, Fraternité. (Rothschild, 1999, 6)

In conclusion, Kurt Rothschild's legacy is one of intellectual rigor, interdisciplinary inquiry, and a steadfast commitment to addressing societal challenges and enhancing human welfare through economics. His multi-paradigmatic approach, ethical orientation, and persistent critique of conventional models offer enduring insights into the complexities of modern economies. He provided valuable contributions to post-Keynesian economics, significantly advancing the field with his comprehensive and nuanced perspectives. His work on labor markets and income distribution

---

[17] While this metaphor is widely attributed to Joan Robinson, Harcourt and Kerr (2009, p. 18) note that Robinson adopted the "box of tools" metaphor from A.C. Pigou.

remains a vital point of reference for those seeking to understand and address the evolving challenges of economic inequality and the interplay of power in shaping our economic world.

References

Altzinger, W. (2016). *Kurt W. Rothschild—Was he a heterodox or an orthodox economist?* FMM Conference Paper, Conference "Towards Pluralism in Macroeconomics?", 20 October–22 October 2016. Berlin. https://www.boeckler.de/pdf/v_2016_10_21_altzinger.pdf

Altzinger, W., Guger, A., Mooslechner, P., & Nowotny, E. (2014). *Economics as a multi-paradigmatic science. In honour of Kurt W. Rothschild (1914–2010)*. Österreichische Nationalbank. https://doi.org/10.57938/b.2014.001

Autor, D., Dorn, D., Katz, L. F., Patterson, C., & Van Reenen, J. (2020). The fall of the labor share and the rise of superstar firms. *Quarterly Journal of Economics, 135*(2), 645–709.

Bowley, A.L. (1920). *The Change in the Distribution of the National Income, 1880-1913*. Oxford University Press.

Bowley, A.L. & Stamp, J.C. (1927). *The National Income: 1924*. Oxford University Press.

Bowley, A.L. (1937). *Wages and Income in the United Kingdom since 1860*, Cambridge University Press.

Bürger, H., & Rothschild, K. W. (2009). *Wie Wirtschaft die Welt bewegt. Die großen ökonomischen Modelle auf dem Prüfstand*. Braumüller-Verlag.

Chaloupek, G. (2014). Kurt Rothschild's impact on Austria's economic policy. In W. Altzinger, A. Guger, P. Mooslechner, & E. Nowotny (Eds.), op. cit (pp. 169–172).

Darnell, A. C. (1981). A.L. Bowley, 1869–1957. In D. P. O'Brien & J. R. Presley (Eds.), *Pioneers of modern economics in Britain* (pp. 140–174). Macmillan.

de Loecker, J., & Eeckhout, J. (2017). T*he rise of market power and the macroeconomic implications*, NBER Working Paper, Nr. 23687, Cambridge MA 2017.

Guger, A. (2011). Kurt W. Rothschild - der Lehrer, Preis- und Verteilungstheoretiker. *Kurswechsel, 2*, 41–52.

Harcourt, G.C. & Kerr, P. (2009). *Joan Robinson*. Palgrave Macmillan.

Hein, E. (2023). *Macroeconomics after Kalecki and Keynes: Post-Keynesian foundations*. Edward Elgar Publishing.

Kaldor, N. (1955/1956). Alternative theories of distribution. *Review of Economic Studies, 23*, 209–230, quoted after N. Kaldor (1980). *Essays on value and distribution* (2. ed.). G. Duckworth.

Kaldor, N. (1961). Capital accumulation and economic growth. In F. A. Lutz & D. C. Hague (Eds.), *The theory of capital* (pp. 177–222). Martin's Press.

Kalecki, M. (1938). The determinants of the distribution of the national income. *Econometrica, 6*(2), 97–112.

Kalecki, M. (1939). The distribution of the national income. In *Essays in the theory of economic fluctuations, London, quoted after: W. Fellner & B.F. Haley (1946) (eds. for the American Economic Association), Readings in the theory of income distribution* (pp. 197–217).

Kalecki, M. (1943). Political aspects of full employment. *The Political Quarterly, 14*(4), 322–331.

Kalecki, M. (1954). *Theory of economic dynamics*. Routledge.

Keynes, J. M. (1936). *The general theory of employment, interest and money*. Macmillan.

King, J. E. (1994). Kurt Rothschild and the alternative Austrian economics. In E. Matzner & E. Nowotny (Eds.), *Was ist relevante Ökonomie heute? Festschrift für Kurt W* (pp. 13–35). Metropolis-Verlag.

King, J. E. (1995). *Conversations with post Keynesians*. Interview with Kurt W Rothschild (pp. 217–233). Macmillan.

King, J. E. (2010). An inspiration to generations of economists. *Entelequia. Revista Interdisciplinar, 12*, 309–312. https://revistaentelequia.wordpress.com/2010/10/30/nota-biografica-sobre-kurt-w-rothschild/
King, J. E. (2014). Remembering Kurt Rothschild. In W. Altzinger, A. Guger, P. Mooslechner, & E. Nowotny (Eds.), op. cit. (pp. 20–37).
Klein, L. R., & Kosobud, R. F. (1961). Some econometrics of growth: Great ratios of economics. *Quarterly Journal of Economics, 75*(2), 173–198.
Krämer, H. M. (1996). *Bowley's Law, technischer Fortschritt und Einkommensverteilung*. Metropolis-Verlag.
Krämer, H. M. (2011). Bowley's Law: The diffusion of an empirical supposition into economic theory. *Cahiers d'économie Politique / Papers in Political Economy, 61*, 19–49.
Krämer, H. M., Proaño, C. R., & Setterfield, M. (2023). *Capitalism, inclusive growth, and social protection. Inherent contradiction or achievable vision?* Edward Elgar.
Kurz, H. D. (2014). Heterodox economics in Austria: The case of Kurt W. Rothschild. In W. Altzinger, A. Guger, P. Mooslechner, & E. Nowotny (Eds.), op. cit. (pp. 87–111).
Nowotny, E. (2014). Kurt Rothschild—Some personal remarks and memories. In W. Altzinger, A. Guger, P. Mooslechner, & E. Nowotny (Eds.), op. cit (pp. 15–19).
OECD. (2015). *In it together. Why less inequality benefits all.* OECD Publishing.
Ostry, J. D., Berg, A., & Tsangarides, C. G. (2014). *Redistribution, inequality, and growth.* IMF staff discussion note 14/02. International Monetary Fund.
Piketty, T. (2014). *Capital in the twenty-first century.* Belknap Press, Harvard University Press.
Preiser, E. (1964). *Wachstum und Einkommensverteilung* (2nd ed.). Carl Winter-Universitätsverlag.
Ricardo, D. (1951/1959). *The works and correspondence of David Ricardo.* In P. Sraffa (Ed.), with the collaboration of MH Dobb (Vol. I–XI). Cambridge University Press.
Robinson, J. (1937). *Introduction to the theory of employment.* Macmillan.
Rothschild, K. W. (1942a). A note on advertising. *Economic Journal, 52*(205), 112–121.
Rothschild, K. W. (1942b). Monopsony, buying costs and welfare expenditure. *Review of Economic Studies, 10*(1), 62–67.
Rothschild, K. W. (1942c). The degree of monopoly. *Economica, 9*(33), 24–39.
Rothschild, K. W. (1943a). A further note on the degree of monopoly. *Economica, 10*(37), 69–70.
Rothschild, K. W. (1943b). Advertising in war-time. *Oxford Bulletin of Statistics, 4*(8), 169–175.
Rothschild, K. W. (1944). Public expenditure in the national income: A note. *Economica, 11*(41), 19–22.
Rothschild, K. W. (1947). Price theory and oligopoly. *Economic Journal, 57*(227), 299–320.
Rothschild, K. W. (1954). *The theory of wages.* Blackwell.
Rothschild, K. W. (1957). Der Lohnanteil am Gesamteinkommen. *Weltwirtschaftliches Archiv, 78*, 157–202.
Rothschild, K. W. (1959). The limitations of economic growth models. Critical remarks on some aspects of Mr. Kaldor's model. *Kyklos, 12*(4), 567–588.
Rothschild, K. W. (1961). Some recent contributions to a macroeconomic theory of income distribution. *Scottish Journal of Political Economy, 8*(3), 173–199.
Rothschild, K. W. (1965). Theme and variations—Remarks on the Kaldorian distribution formula. *Kyklos, 18*(4), 652–669.
Rothschild, K. W. (1968). Zur Arithmetik und Interpretation von Lohnquoten. *Hamburger Jahrbuch für Wirtschafts- und Gesellschaftspolitik, 13*, 143–158.
Rothschild, K. W. (1971a). The Phillips curve and all that. *Scottish Journal of Political Economy, 18*(3), 245–280.
Rothschild, K. W. (Ed.). (1971b). *Power in economics.* Penguin.
Rothschild, K. W. (1973). Distributive aspects of the Austrian theory. In J. R. Hicks & W. Weber (Eds.), *Carl Menger and the Austrian school of economics* (pp. 207–225). Clarendon.
Rothschild, K. W. (1978). Arbeitslose, gibt's die? *Kyklos, 31*, 21–35.
Rothschild, K. W. (1982). Stagflation: Was bleibt von der Phillipskurve? *Wirtschaft und Gesellschaft, 8*(2), 183–194.

Rothschild, K. W. (1985). Some notes on Weintraub's eclectic theory of income shares. *Journal of Post Keynesian Economics, 7*(4), 575–593.

Rothschild, K. W. (1988). *Theorien der Arbeitslosigkeit*. Oldenbourg.

Rothschild, K. W. (1991). Glimpses of a non-linear biography. *Banca Nazionale del Lavoro Quarterly Review, 176*(March), 3–13.

Rothschild, K. W. (1993). *Employment, wages and income distribution: Critical essays in economics*. Routledge.

Rothschild, K. W. (1994). The theory of wages revisited. In H. Hagemann & O. F. Hamouda (Eds.), *The legacy of Hicks* (pp. 60–74). Routledge.

Rothschild, K. W. (1999). To push and to be pushed. *The American Economist, 43*(1), 1–8.

Rothschild, K. W. (2000). Kurt W. Rothschild (born 1914). In P. Arestis & M. Sawyer (Eds.), *A biographical dictionary of dissenting economists*. Edward Elgar.

Rothschild, K. W. (2002). The absence of power in contemporary economic theory. *The Journal of Socio-Economics, 31*, 433–442.

Rothschild, K. W. (2004). "Der Heiligenschein ist angekratzt, aber der Neoliberalismus ist noch immer sehr stark". Interview with Kurt W. Rothschild by C. Sauer and M. Schratzenstaller. *Intervention, 1*(2), 5–12.

Rothschild, K. W. (2006). "Die Gefahr ist die Gewöhnung", Interview with Kurt W. Rothschild by W. Altzinger and M. Schürz. *Kurswechsel, 4*, 37–48. http://www.beigewum.at/wordpress/wpcontent/uploads/037_interview_mit_kurt_rothschild.pdf

Rothschild, K. W. (n.d.). *Kurt W. Rothschild*. Leben und Werk. https://www.kurt-rothschild.at/

Rothschild, K. W., & King, J. E. (2009). A conversation with Kurt Rothschild. *Review of Political Economy, 21*(1), 145–155.

Schneider, E. (1957). Einkommen und Einkommensverteilung in der makroökonomischen Theorie. *L' Industria. Rivista di economia e politica industriale / Review of Industrial Economics and Policy, 2*, 256–268.

Springler, E. (2011). Kurt Rothschilds postkeynesianische Methodologie. *Kurswechsel, 2*, 18–26.

Steindl, J. (1979). Stagnation theory and stagnation policy. *Cambridge Journal of Economics, 3*(1), 1–14.

Sylos-Labini, P. (1969). *Oligopoly and technical progress* (2nd ed.). The MIT Press.

Sylos-Labini, P. (1984). *The forces of economic growth and decline*. The MIT Press.

van Reenen, J. (2018). I*ncreasing differences between firms: Market power and the macro-economy*. Paper presented at the Jackson Hole Conference 2018. CEP Discussion Papers dp1576. Centre for Economic Performance LSE, London.

Weintraub, S. (1981). An eclectic theory of income shares. *Journal of Post Keynesian Economics, 4*(1), 10–24.

Chapter 9
Post-War Keynesianism in Austria: The Role of Emigrant Economists

Günther Chaloupek

9.1 Economic Thinking in Austria Before German Occupation ("Anschluss") 1938

Until the mid-1960s, there were only three universities in Austria: Vienna, Graz, and Innsbruck. The main economic chairs at the University of Vienna in the 1930s were held by Hans Mayer, "the last knight of the Austrian School" (Klausinger, 2015a), and Othmar Spann, whose anti-liberal and anti-socialist "universalism" ("*Ganzheitslehre*") influenced the ideology of the clerico-fascist regime (*Ständestaat*—corporate state, "Austrofascism") that ruled Austria from 1934 to 1938. At the other universities, economics was taught by rather obscure scholars, with the exception of Josef Dobretsberger, an economist with Catholic background, who briefly also served as minister of social affairs in the authoritarian government.

Economic chairs were located in the law faculties. There was no economics degree in the true sense. Economics was only a minor part of the law curriculum, and occupied a larger part in the curriculum of the state sciences (*Staatswissenschaften*) which were also located at the law faculty. The curricula originated from the nineteenth century, remaining essentially unchanged until the 1960s.

The main task of the Vienna *Hochschule für Welthandel* (since 1975 *Wirtschaftsuniversität*), a kind of business school, has traditionally been the teaching of practical knowledge in international economics and management sciences. It

For comments on earlier versions of this contribution the author is indebted to the participants of the Heilbronn Symposion 2024, and to Felix Butschek and Hansjörg Klausinger.

G. Chaloupek (✉)
Austrian Chamber of Labour (retired), Wien, Austria
e-mail: guenther@chaloupek.eu

J. G. Backhaus et al. (eds.), *Post-war Keynesianism in Germany and Western Europe*, The European Heritage in Economics and the Social Sciences 28,
https://doi.org/10.1007/978-3-032-00498-7_9

was granted the right to award doctoral degrees only in 1930. Economics was represented by the Spann follower, Walter Heinrich and Richard Kerschagl, Richard Strigl of the Austrian School had an honorary professorship. (Klausinger, 2015b).

The hotspot of economics with respect to empirical research was the Austrian Institute of Business Cycle Research (*Österreichisches Institut für Komjunkturforschung*), which was—after Friedrich Hayek's move to the London School of Economics—headed by Oskar Morgenstern. With respect to its principal task of observation and analysis of the current development of the economy, the institute abided by its mandate to present facts and abstain from comments on issues of economic policy. The institute's series of theoretical publications which started with Hayek's book *Geldtheorie und Konjunkturtheorie* indicates that, with respect to theory, the institute remained under the strong imprint of the Austrian School which emphasized the priority of theory even with regard to analysis of practical problems. Under Morgenstern's directorate, the institute became more tolerant towards other currents of thinking when non-liberal economists joined the professional staff (Josef Steindl, Adolf Kozlik, Ernst John). The prominence which several members of the institute obtained after their emigration should not obscure the fact that, due to its aversion towards methods of empirical research based on macroeconomic aggregates, the institute was lagging behind in international comparison. The first estimate of national income was published only in 1936. The publication of a draft of an expansionist policy program of 1937 was suppressed by Morgenstern (Steindl, 2004).[1]

Marxist economics played a central role in the tradition of Austro-Marxism, established in the last decades of the Habsburg Monarchy by Rudolf Hilferding, Otto Bauer, and Karl Renner. At the law faculty of the University of Vienna, Marxism was no more represented after the departure of Carl Grünberg to the Frankfurt Institute of Social Research in 1924.[2] Due to the lack of professional job opportunities, Marxist economists sought work in journalism and in institutions for adult education.

Der Österreichische Volkswirt, a by-weekly economic journal whose circulation extended beyond the borders of the country, especially to the succession states of the Habsburg monarchy, provided the basis for a high level of economic journalism in Austria. In this context, the by-weekly journal *Arbeit und Wirtschaft*, edited by the Austrian Chamber of Labour and the central trade union organization, with its wide spectrum of contributions to theoretical and practical-political issues deserves to be mentioned.

---

[1] For a more extensive account of early reception of Keynes at the Institute of Business Cycle Research see Guger (2016).

[2] The Austro-Marxist philosopher and sociologist Max Adler held a chair at the philosophical faculty.

Discussion circles, of which the Mises-seminar became the most famous, were the hotbed of high theory which flourished in Austria between the world wars. A forum for economic debate was also provided by the *Nationalökonomische Gesellschaft*, chaired by Hans Mayer and Ludwig Mises as deputy. The flagship for publications in economic theory was undoubtedly the *Zeitschrift für Nationalökonomie*, which had succeeded the *Zeitschrift für Volkswirtschaft, Sozialpolitik und Verwaltung* in 1930.

If, at the level of economic theory, the Austrian School occupied a dominant position, at least seen from a Viennese perspective, this does not at all imply that the country's policy stance was liberal. There were elements of economic liberalism—maintenance of the gold parity of the Austrian *Schilling* and balanced budget—which were embedded in the Austrofascist policy of anti-liberal corporatism (anti-competition, protectionist).

9.2 Emigration of Austrian Economists in 1938 and Before[3]

According to Hagemann and Krohn (1999) and other sources[4] some 100 economists of Austrian origin emigrated to the United States, to England, and other countries in the 1930s. Emigration started before German occupation in 1938, to escape consequences of political repression under Austrofascism, and out of fear of Nazi-Germany,[5] but most economists left after March 1938. Most of the emigrant economists were Jews who were forced to leave Austria. In a few cases, economists who were not Jews left Austria to avoid degradation or prosecution because of their political orientations (e.g., Oskar Morgenstern, Josef Steindl). Some 70 percent of the total emigrated to the USA, leaving some 20 percent for England and 10 percent for other countries.

Of the almost 70 Austrian economists who emigrated to the USA, a large part lacks a distinct theoretical and/or political profile. They worked in more or less narrowly specialized fields of economics or in business economics, and can therefore not easily be assigned to a distinct school of thought. As economics had been taught as part of the law curriculum, some of the emigrants had earned their living as lawyers and only turned into economists abroad. For the majority, orientation towards a certain school of thought determines their thinking and writing—among those, the Austrian School of Economics is the most important.

---

[3] This section draws on my previous publications on emigration and remigration of economists from Austria (Chaloupek, 2016, 2017a).

[4] Mainly the sources of Chaloupek (2011). Information on biographical details given in this contribution are from Hagemann/Krohn, unless otherwise stated.

[5] The prominent cases of Hayek, who received a call to the London School of Economics in 1931, and Mises, who moved to the *Institute des Hautes Etudes* in Genva after his retirement in 1934, represent a different type of emigration.

9.2.1 Emigration to the US

After the occupation of Austria by Nazi-Germany, most of the participants in the previous Mises seminar emigrated to the U.S. The Austrian School was well connected internationally, and there had also been intensive contacts with the USA since the 1920s. The Austrian Institute for Business Cycle Research received funding from the Rockefeller Foundation. However, the climate of opinion for the economic policy doctrines of "Austro-liberalism" had become increasingly unfavorable under the presidency of Franklin D. Roosevelt (since 1933). At American universities, the influence of Keynes rose rapidly after the publication of his "General Theory of Employment, Interest and Money" in 1936. From viewpoint of the Austrian School, a dubious "heterodoxy" dominated politics and increasingly also the academic economic scene in the USA.[6] With respect to politics, "the Austrians found themselves in the wilderness" (Klausinger, 2006, 627).

At least, the "Austrians" were able to continue to publish their work—now in English—in academic journals. Several rose to prominence and obtained positions at prestigious universities, while keeping distance to core elements of the school's orthodoxy. For example, Oskar Morgenstern had turned away not only from Mises' theoretical apriorism, but also from the latter's "rigid system of economic policy." Gottfried Haberler followed a synthetic approach in his book "Prosperity and Depression" (1937), a survey of existing theories of the business cycle.

Of the other Austrian economist emigrants to the USA who did not belong to the Austrian School, as non-socialists I mention Karl Pribram, who had briefly served in the ministry of social affairs of the Austrian republic, where he was responsible for preparing social policy legislation, before moving to the International Labour Office in Geneva, and later to the University of Frankfurt (Chaloupek, 2019). His magnum opus "*A History of Economic Reasoning*" was published posthumously in 1983; Walther Federn, the editor of the *Österreichische Volkswirt* between 1924 and 1934; and Peter F. Drucker, who branched off into management science where he acquired high reputation after the war.

Most of the socialist emigrants were attached to Marxism and Marxian economics. Unlike the economists of the Austrian School, the socialists hardly had any contacts to academic institutions in the USA. Scholarly tracts in Marxian economics,[7] such as those published by Alfred Braunthal (1927) and Otto Leichter (1923), were unsuited to serve as a basis for continuing a career of a professional economist. Leichter went into journalism, Braunthal became a staff member of the American and later of the international trade union movement. Eduard März (1908–1987), who had worked at the Austrian branch of IBM, was able to continue this activity in

---

[6] In his 1934 book Limits of Economic Policy, Morgenstern arrogantly dismissed the policies of the New Deal as "senseless and contradictory" (p. 131), and to top it off, called Keynes a "quack" (p. 110; if not mentioned by name, then at least unmistakably).

[7] Most important, contributions to the debate about calculation in the socialist economy—see Chaloupek (1990).

the USA and also complete a PhD program at Harvard University under the supervision of Joseph Schumpeter.[8] Committed to Marxian economics, März also familiarized himself with Keynesian economics and developed a synthesis of these two approaches. He taught as a volunteer in the context of educational programs of the US Navy and, until his return to Austria, at various colleges on the east coast.

Maria Szésci's (1914–1984) family came to Vienna from Budapest in 1919 after the Hungarian revolution failed shortly afterwards. After the occupation of Austria by Nazi Germany, Maria Szécsi was forced to emigrate to the USA in 1938. There she was finally able to complete her university studies in economics, history, and political science, which she had been prevented from doing at the University of Vienna due to the repressive measures of the Austrofascist regime. She had teaching positions at the University of Chicago and at Roosevelt College there. (Chaloupek, 2013).

Non-Marxist socialists Albert Lauterbach and Adolf Kozlik accepted teaching positions at US colleges. Bert F. Hoselitz continued with his studies of economics at the University of Chicago where he was appointed to full professor in 1953. Karl Polanyi, who was a member of the Austrian Social-democratic party and a staff member of the *Österreichische Volkswirt*, emigrated to the USA, finally settled in Canada.

It is worth noting that the Austrian socialist economists in the USA did not have an institution like the New School for Social Research which provided opportunities for left-wing Jewish economists from Germany (Emil Lederer, Adolph Lowe, Alfred Kähler, Hans Neisser, Gerhard Colm) to continue their professional careers.[9]

9.2.2 *Emigration to Great Britain*

Only a few of the 22 economists who emigrated to England belong to the Austrian School. The politically left-leaning economists are clearly in the majority, but there are hardly any prominent Marxists among them. Almost half of the emigrants from England returned to Austria after the war.

Of the economists of the Austrian School who emigrated to England, Friedrich A. Hayek is a special case. He was appointed to a professorship at the London School of Economics in 1931. He would undoubtedly have had to expect political persecution by the Nazis after the occupation of Austria. Hayek therefore did not take German citizenship, but became a British citizen in 1938. Paul Rosenstein-Rodan (1902–1985) started his career as assistant to Hans Mayer at the University

[8] For more details on März's biography, see Matis (2017).

[9] At the New School for Social Research, a "graduate faculty had been founded by Alvin Johnson, the president of the New School, where in 1933 he created the 'University in Exile' to provide a safe haven for scholars who were endangered by totalitarian regimes." (Hagemann, 2014)

of Vienna before becoming a lecturer at University College in 1931 and later a professor at the University of London. In Vienna he attended the Mises-seminar and was joint editor of the *Zeitschrift für Nationalökonomie* with Oskar Morgenstern until 1934. Rosenstein-Rodan later became one of the founders and most prominent representatives of development economics.

Friedrich Hertz (1878–1964), who worked as secretary of the Austrian Industrial Association (the predecessor of today's Federation of Austrian Industries) and in the civil service, was one of the few economists who opposed the theory that the Republic of Austria was not a viable economic entity, basing his argumentation on his own estimates of aggregate national income. (Hertz, 1925). In his book "*The Economic Problem of the Danubian States*" (1947), Hertz provided national income calculations for the monarchy and the succession states.

The left-wing Austrian emigration to England was politically organized in the "Free Austrian Movement" ("FAM"), which was dominated by the Communist Party,[10] and in the "London Office" ("*Londoner Büro*"), a branch of the Austrian social democrats' foreign representation. Josef Steindl and Kurt Rothschild became internationally known as economic scholars after the Second World War.

After studying at the Vienna *Hochschule für Welthandel*, Steindl (1912–1993) worked at the Institute for Business Cycle Research. He had to leave the institute after German occupation and emigrated to England. With the support of Hayek and Haberler, Steindl received a research scholarship at Balliol College at the University of Oxford. Later he was at the Oxford Institute of Statistics, where he worked with Michal Kalecki, whose theories had a significant influence on Steindl. In England, Steindl wrote his main work, "Maturity and Stagnation in American Capitalism", (Steindl, 1952) which was only published 2 years after his return to Austria to the Institute of Economic Research.

Kurt Rothschild (1914–2005) was one of the last Jewish students to receive a doctorate in law from the University of Vienna in 1938. With a scholarship, he studied economics at the University of Glasgow from 1938 to 1940, where he then worked as a lecturer until 1947.

Hans (John) Mars (1898–1985) had already emigrated to England in 1934 when he lost his job in the Vienna Chamber of Labor after the February Uprising. His three-volume *Gewerkschaftliches Handbuch des Akkordwesens* (Handbook of Piecework) was published by the Chamber of Labour in 1931. In England, too, where Mars taught at various colleges and universities, most recently at the University of Manchester, he dealt with questions of labor and household economics.

Karl Forchheimer (1880–1959) came from Prague and received his doctorate in law from Prague's German university. In 1913 he joined the Central Statistical

[10] According to Prager (1975), 63ff.

Commission in Vienna as a civil servant, and at the end of the war he was working in the State Office for Social Welfare (later the Ministry of Social Affairs). As adjunct to Karl Pribram, who also came from Prague, Forchheimer was involved in drafting the numerous social laws passed after the war, and soon after Pribram's departure he became head of the legislative department. Forchheimer had studied economics in Prague and published a paper on the theory of incomplete monopoly, which anticipated key elements of the theory of monopolistic competition (Forchheimer, 1908). In 1938 he was dismissed because of his Jewish descent. In 1939 Forchheimer emigrated to England,[11] where he worked for the Oxford Institute of Statistics and published a number of statistical studies. In England, Forchheimer became acquainted with the teachings Keynes and their impact in the Anglo-Saxon countries.

Like Kurt Rothschild, several other younger emigrants in England devoted themselves to studying economics. Theodor Prager (1917–1986) had already gone to London in 1935 after being expelled from all higher schools for political reasons. Prager studied at the London School of Economics under Hayek, Lionel Robbins, and Nicholas Kaldor, among others, and received his doctorate in 1943 with a thesis on "German Banking in Depression and Recovery." He was heavily involved in student and intellectual organizations and in political organizations associated with the Communist Party, as well as in the FAM. Prager worked as an economist at the London Institute for Political and Economic Planning (PEP) from 1943 onwards.

Philipp Rieger (1916–2007) also studied economics after his release from the concentration camp and his escape to England, but initially worked as a metal worker to earn a living. He studied at the University of London and later at the LSE and worked as an education officer at the Pakistan High Commission from 1952 to 1957.

Stefan Wirlandner (1905–1981) was originally a milliner and worked in the Vienna Chamber of Labour after graduating from the workers' college. Dismissed after the Austrofascists seized power, he became involved with the illegal Revolutionary Socialists. He trained as an auditor at the Vienna *Hochschule für Welthandel*. After the occupation of Austria, he emigrated to Great Britain, where he joined the army and worked for the British wartime intelligence service (Pirker, 2015).

Karl Ausch (1893–1976) was editor of the social-democratic tabloid *Das kleine Blatt* until democracy was abolished by the authoritarian corporate state. In 1937 he emigrated to England, where he worked for the social democrats' London office.

Emigrants of the younger generation account for a major part of emigration to Great Britain, universities provided opportunities for emigrants from Austria with sympathies for socialist ideas and/or Keynes to further pursue their studies, and to become acquainted with Keynes' theory.

[11] Forchheimer was a distant cousin of Hayek's close friend Herbert Fürth, and got a letter of recommendation from Hayek (personal information from Hansjörg Klausinger).

9.3 Economy and Economic Policy in Austria After World War II

During the first years that followed the war, highest priority was given to the reconstruction of the production system in order to bring national income back to pre-war levels as soon as possible (1945–1952). A return to a market economy with free price and wage formation was not seen as a real possibility in the first years after the war. It was more or less self-evident that the system of rationing and control of food, raw materials, and energy inherited from the war economy would be retained, as would be the administrative controls over imports and exports and foreign exchange. The swift nationalization of large industrial companies, banks, and electricity producers created the conditions for making massive investments in the basic industries and in infrastructure. Another challenge for economic policy was the danger of hyperinflation due to the surplus of savings accumulated during the war. In this field, Austria did not apply a shock-therapy, as Germany had done with its currency reform of 1948, but relied on a gradual approach through five wage-price agreements between 1947 and 1951. Final stabilization of prices was achieved only in 1953. After the recession of 1952 rapid economic growth continued until the 1960s. From 1953 to 1962 Austria's GDP increased at an average annual rate of 6.3 percent, which was significantly above OECD average (Butschek, 1985, 65ff).

During the period of reconstruction, Keynesianism was of little practical relevance.[12] The moment for economic policies for full employment and economic stability came some 10 years after the war, when Austria's GDP had surpassed pre-war levels. This involved orienting economic policy towards the goals of growth, full employment, and overall economic stability. At least as important in this context was a fundamental change in economic thinking. The economic process was viewed through Keynesian macroeconomics, which became fundamental to economic policy. The comprehensive view of the economy in terms of aggregates (consumption, investment, national income, etc.) was based on the newly introduced national accounts, through which statistics on these aggregates and the gross national product (GNP, later GDP) were provided, and changes recorded from year to year. Short-term forecasts have also been drawn up on this basis since the 1950s.

The Marshall Plan provided strong impetus for the introduction of the new economic policy techniques. In order to meet the criteria for obtaining this financial assistance, economic plans with overall aggregates and disaggregated projections had to be drawn up. Since there were only a few experts who mastered such techniques, the Institute for Economic Research was entrusted with the task of the ERP office ("European Recovery Programme").

On the fundamental question of the economic order under the conditions of a restored normality, as it arose in the early 1950s, there were not only different

[12] In its outlook on future developments, Rothschild's study of the Austrian economy in the inter-war period (Rothschild, 1947) focuses on economic planning, without referring to Keynesian macro-policy.

positions between the governing parties ÖVP (the conservative Austrian People's Party) and the Socialist Party SPÖ, but also within the SPÖ and the trade union movement (see Sect. 9.5).

In the mid-1950s, a permanent form of social partnership institutions for price and wage policy was formed. The social partnership was born as a regulatory concept accepted by all interest groups and both parties of the coalition government.

9.4 The Role of Returnees in Austria's Economic Policy and Their Influence on Economic Thinking

Whereas almost half of the economists who had emigrated to England permanently returned to Austria, only five out of 60 came back from the USA. To a considerable extent, reasons for this striking difference originate from the private sphere. If most emigrants had worked hard to adjust to the new social environment and to establish a stable basis for their living in the USA, by the end of the war their standards of living were far above the income an academic economist could expect in Austria after the war and in the foreseeable future. Many of the emigrants had already become US citizens, or would soon be entitled to it. Moreover, as a country part of which was under Soviet occupation and surrounded by countries with communist regimes, Austria did not appear to be a safe place to live, looked at from the other side of the Atlantic.

But apart from that, for the economists of the pre-war Austrian School, post-war Austria did not appear as a country that was hungry for their political and theoretical messages. If the USA had turned into a wilderness for Austro-liberalism, laissez-faire policies were even less in place in an impoverished country suffering from heavy war-time destructions.

For returnees from Great Britain the situation was different. If, originally, the purpose of the emigrant organizations was to provide financial and other support to compatriots who had found a shelter in Britain, towards the end of the war the associations prepared for organizing the return of their members to support reconstruction of the political system in Austria after its reconstitution as an independent state, of its economy and society. With their knowledge of Keynesian macroeconomics, and with their political affiliations to left wing parties (social-democrats or Communist) the returnees were eager to contribute actively to the economic reconstruction of their country.

However, the returnees were by no means welcome at the universities. Hans Mayer still held the main chair for economics at the law faculty of the University of Vienna. He emphasized his distance towards Austro-liberalism in an address written at the occasion of Ludwig Mises' 70th birthday. After having paid respect to Mises' achievements in economic theory, Mayer rejected Mises' claim that "the Austrian School" would postulate free competition as an "ideal model of an economy," whereas the alternative between "extreme liberalism" and "totalitarian planning" had already been left behind (Mayer, 1951/1952, 516).[13] After Mayer's retirement the teaching of economics "reached its lowest point" (Steindl, 2004, 401) at the University of Vienna (for some 10 years to come). For more than a decade, knowledge of modern economics and of new techniques of economic analysis could not be acquired from universities in Austria. This deplorable situation was even surpassed by the economics department at the Vienna *Hochschule für Welthandel*, where Spann's "universalism" dominated until the 1970s (Klausinger, 2015b).

For a long time, the universities were not prepared to adequately recognize the academic achievements of the emigrants. The efforts of Steindl and März to obtain habilitation were rejected, and Morgenstern was denied an honorary professorship by the University of Vienna. This attitude only changed with new appointments at the end of the 1960s (Erich Streissler at the University of Vienna). Steindl (Vienna) and März (Salzburg) were belatedly appointed honorary professors. Rothschild was appointed to a full professor's chair at the newly founded Linz University in 1966.

Given the rejection by universities, the returnees turned to other institutions: the Institute of Economic Research and the Chamber of Labour. Thanks to the knowledge of new economic theories and modern methods of empirical economic research that they had acquired during their emigration, they were able to exert an increasing influence on the economic policy discourse in Austria through these institutions and through their publications and lectures since the 1950s. Last but not least, the transfer of knowledge brought about a significant increase in the general level of the state of economic science.

The Austrian Institute of Economic Research (*Österreichisches Institut für Wirtschaftsforschung*—"WIFO") was re-established in 1945, as successor of the previous Institute of Business Cycle Research, which had lost its independence after German occupation. In its theoretical and methodical orientation, the WIFO differed from its predecessor in important respects. Under its directors Franz Nemschak (member of the staff since 1941) and Ernst John (member of the staff since 1935) the WIFO became predominantly empirical in its orientation. At the same time, the institute turned away from the theoretical approach of the Austrian School to a theoretical pluralism, which was open for Keynesian economics. Most importantly, this change in theoretical orientation opened the door for the application of modern macroeconomics in theory and empirical research. In practice, considerable obstacles had to be overcome, since most of the WIFO's economists were graduates from the law faculties and had to acquire knowledge of modern economics through self-study (Butschek et al., 2022, 32). Given the failure of Austrian universities in this field, it was the returnees who helped to ease this bottleneck.

Kurt Rothschild returned to Austria in 1947. He was hired by the WIFO upon recommendation of Friedrich Hayek. As staff member and senior economist, he worked there until his appointment to the University of Linz in 1966, retaining close ties to the institute as consultant until the end of his life. Labor markets and external

[13] Hayek's cautious inquiry for a chair at the University of Vienna in 1961 was welcomed by the ministry of education, but the way the faculty of law and state sciences proceeded in this matter suggests that it was not enthusiastic about his application (Klausinger, 2024).

trade were Rothschild's main areas of research.[14] Seidel (1985) refers to several of Rothschild's essays, which give indications of his approach to issues of economic policy, e.g., that the problem of post-war inflation and price stabilization could not be solved in an economic and socially acceptable way by monetary restriction (Rothschild, 1948); or when he cautioned against unconditional liberalization of external trade (Rothschild, 1954).

Unlike the Institute of Business Cycle Research, the WIFO did not have a series for theoretical works. Rothschild's numerous theoretical books and articles appeared outside of the institute. Rothschild's version of Keynesianism is characterized by an eclectic, "multi-theoretical" approach," which combined a variety of schools of thought in the analysis of multi-dimensional problems.[15]

Josef Steindl returned to Austria and joined the WIFO in 1950. Of his work for the institute, the study on the effects of an additional billion Schilling on the economy is perhaps his most important contribution to the popularization of Keynesianism in Austria (Steindl, 1956). Therein he combined the multiplier concept with input-output-analysis to trace primary and secondary effects on income and employment, and to show the differences in effectiveness resulting from different categories of expenditure (investment in construction, in machinery, in consumption). Theoretically, Steindl's Keynesianism integrates elements of Kalecki's approach (Guger, 2016).

Unlike the emigrant members of the WIFO, Hans Seidel's political background was not socialist. Having joined the institute in 1946, he soon acquired a key role both in the WIFO's empirical work and its theoretical orientation. Seidel's understanding of Keynesianism "was tailored to the corporatist system, which is based on the cooperation of capital and labor. In the early 1950s, the view prevailed in the labor movement that a planned economy was not feasible under the given circumstances, but that full employment would also be possible under capitalism. Bourgeois finance ministers ran budget deficits during the recession in order to support effective demand. This 'consensus Keynesianism' largely corresponded with the textbooks by Paul Samuelson and Erich Schneider (neoclassical Keynesian synthesis) that were widely used in German-speaking countries" (Seidel, 2012, 466). Seidel had little interest in left-wing Keynesianism of the Kalecki-type. From the 1960s, Seidel played an important role as advisor to governments of varying political orientations. He was appointed to deputy director in 1962, succeeding Franz Nemschak at the head of the institute in 1970. From 1981 to 1983 he served as state secretary in the ministry of finance, from 1984 to 1991 He was director of the Institute of Advanced Studies (IHS).

As one of the first emigrants to Great Britain, Stefan Wirlandner returned to Austria in May 1945. As head of the economic policy department and later deputy

[14] Seidel (1985), with his knowledge as staff member of the institute since 1946, was able to identify Rothschild's authorship of several of his contributions which appeared in the monthly periodical *Monatsberichte*. Until 1965 all articles were published anonymously.

[15] On Rothschild's theoretical work see King (1994), and the contribution by Krämer in the present volume.

director of the Vienna Chamber of Labour he negotiated the currency reform and the five price and wage agreements. From 1960 he was a member of the board of directors, from 1961 to 1969 he was deputy general director of the Austrian National Bank, and from 1969 he was a board director of the Investment Credit Bank. Wirlandner had no ambitions with respect to economic theory, seeing his role as economic policy expert. Having familiarized himself with Keynes' theory and Joan Robinson's publications during emigration, thanks to his knowledge of modern macroeconomics he soon emerged as one of the key players on the side of labor and the SPÖ in Austria's economic policy. Alongside his job Wirlandner studied at the University of Vienna and received his doctorate in 1950 with his dissertation "The Theory of Utility Value and Employees." Wirlandner was one of the first political functionaries who understood the advanced role of economic expertise in policy, taking the initiative for establishing a research unit in his organization.

The economic research department (*Wirtschaftswissenschaftliche Abteilung*) of the Vienna Chamber of Labour was the first modern think tank in an Austrian interest association. A first attempt to establish a special unit of this type was made in 1950[16] upon the initiative of Wirlandner. (Chaloupek, 2017b) Most of the 11 publications of the Chamber's first research unit were empirical, but the series also included a translation (by Wirlandner, with his own comments) of Joan Robinson's Essay on Marxian Economics (Robinson, 1951), and Karl Forchheimer's brochure *Keynes' neue Wirtschaftslehre. Eine Einführung* (1952).

Forchheimer's brochure was the first attempt in Austria to make Keynes' new economic theory known to a wider public. Although its circulation was probably quite limited, it still deserves high appreciation for its compact exposition of the Keynesian view of the economic process, the differences between traditional (neo) classical theory which had advocated laissez faire, and the Keynesian approach with its emphasis on active economic policies to reach a state of full employment in a market economy. What makes Forchheimer's tract most original is the emphasis on a theoretical innovation of which Keynes himself had not been explicitly aware of. The main difference is that "he does not study the behavior of individuals in the economy, but the processes in the economy as a whole. He practices 'macro-economics' instead of 'micro-economics.'" If estimates of national income had been available for some time, "it was not clear what to do much with the meaning of this concept. It was only Keynes who assigned it a central place and established its relationship to other variables in the economy as a whole and the relationships between these variables" (Forchheimer, 1952, 29). After elaborating on the policy prescriptions deduced from Keynes' "General Theory" Forchheimer discusses the question in what sense the new theory represents a "new worldview" (p. 65). "Obviously, his teachings have provoked the neoclassical orthodoxy," but, on the other hand, "demands of total control of the economy have been voiced from the Marxist doctrine with much more revolutionary consequences. Keynes's merit is

[16] When the Chamber of Labor was founded in 1921, a "statistical office" was set up with Benedikt Kautsky as director. The office's official publications were statistical in content (statistical yearbook, wage statistics based on its own surveys).

that he sought, and, as it seems, found, a way that does not require a complete break with tradition" (p. 69).

The first research department did not have the personal resources for a successful application of the new theoretical approach in empirical studies. The Chamber's economic research department that exists today was established in 1956, again upon Wirlandner's initiative, when Eduard März was appointed to head the new unit. März had decided to return to Austria from the US under the impression of the ideological terror of the McCarthy era. His intensive publication activity only began after his return, first in the field of economic history, then equally in the areas of economic theory and economic policy. From 1956, März built up the first modern think tank in an Austrian interest association with an economics department in the Chamber of Labour. The studies in this department contributed significantly to the development of modern economic policy in Austria (Chaloupek, 2017b). März was involved in economic policy committees and in the programmatic discussions of the SPÖ. Although he was denied a teaching position at the University of Vienna, with his widely read publications[17] and his lecturing activities he became the teacher of the following generations of young economists oriented towards the SPÖ and the trade union organization.

In 1948 Maria Szécsi returned to Austria, where she initially worked in the communist-controlled "World Federation of Trade Unions." With her critical attitude, she increasingly distanced herself from the Communist Party, which she left after the Hungarian uprising in 1956. From 1960 Szécsi worked in the economic research department of the Chamber, which nominated her as member of the Economic and Social Advisory Board, a body of economic experts within the framework of Austrian social partnership, established in 1963, which played a key role in the development of the conceptual basis of Austria's economic policy. Of Szécsi's publications, her study on the long-run tendency of the wage share in national income is the most important (Szécsi, 1970).

Philipp Rieger returned to Austria in 1957, where he joined the department at the invitation of Stefan Wirlandner, whom he had met during the Canadian internment as an enemy alien. In 1965, he became a member of the Board of Directors of the Austrian National Bank. In his functions and publications, Rieger was always a committed advocate of Keynesian economic policy (Expansion, Stagnation und Demokratie, 1982).

Theodor Prager was brought to Austria by the Communist Party of Austria in November 1945, where he worked as an economist in the party's Central Committee. In 1963 Prager joined the economic research department of the Chamber of Labour. Prager's intellectual self-image was that of a Marxist who was open to other theories, especially Keynes'—see his 1963 collection of essays *Wirtschaftswunder oder*

---

[17] Most important, his book *Die Marxsche Wirtschaftslehre im Widerstreit der Meinungen* (1959), and numerous articles in monthly journals *Arbeit & Wirtschaft* and *Die Zukunft;* also his book *Österreichs Wirtschaft zwischen Ost und West* (1965). Also, März published key studies on Austrian banking history and on Joseph Schumpeter (März, 1983).

keines? (Economic Miracle or None?) In a review essay, Erwin Weissel,[18] one of the young members of the Chamber's economic research department, gave Prager credit for having abandoned the Marxist dogma of the inevitability of crises in the capitalist economy. Weissel (1965) argued that prosperity in Western European countries in the post-war period could be attributed to two principal causes: Keynesian economic policies, and competition between economic systems. Prager left the Communist Party of Austria after the Warsaw Pact invaded Czechoslovakia in 1969.

Adolf Kozlik returned to Vienna in 1959, but he was dissatisfied with his position as director of a community college (*Volkshochschule*). In 1963 Kozlik was appointed associate director of the newly founded *Institut für Höhere Studien* (Institute of Advanced Studies, IHS). Once more dissatisfied, he accepted a call from a Canadian University, but he died at the age of only 52 on his way to Canada. In his writings, Kozlik combined mainstream neoclassical and Keynesian theory with Marxist political economy. His most ambitious books were published posthumously (*Der Vergeudungskapitalismus,* 1966). In his critique of the capitalist system, which in many ways resembles that of J.K. Galbraith, Kozlik casts doubt on the sustainability of economic growth and rising standards of living which characterized the Golden Age of post-war economic development. He identifies the system's tendency to produce affluence and scarcity simultaneously as likely causes of future crises of capitalism (Rothschild, 2004).

Eduard März never ceased to feel as a Marxist economist. Compared with Forchheimer's tract, März's account of the Keynesian theory (März, 1954) was more critical with respect to several elements. In view of existing relationships of political power, he was an advocate of Keynesian economic ideas and policies. At the same time, he doubted that full employment could be achieved permanently in a capitalist economy, which in the long run was prone to stagnation. Referring to Keynes' remark in the last chapter of his General Theory, "that a somewhat comprehensive socialisation of investment will prove the only means of securing an approximation to full employment" (1954, 378), März concludes that "a systematic application of the Keynesian therapy would have a fundamental reconstruction of the existing economic order as precondition" (1959, 212). He accepted Keynesianism as a preliminary stage of socialism. In this sense, he propagated a system of overall economic planning according to the model of the French *planification* which had attracted considerable attention not only from left wing parties in Western Europe during the 1960s (März, 1965). Together with his colleagues in the Chamber, and in co-operation with economists from the business organizations Economic Chamber and Federation of Austrian Industry, he worked on recommendations on a variety of specific economic policy issues. März was a member of the *Beirat für Wirtschafts- und Sozialfragen* (Economic and Social Advisory Board) of the Austrian Parity

[18] In the 1960s, Erwin Weissel, 1930–2005, published several articles on fiscal policy and studies on the structure of wages. He is the translator of Joan Robinson's Accumulation of Capital, and of a collection of her essays.

Commission which is a joint institution of Austrian social partners and the government.

In Austria, Keynesianism was practiced mostly in institutions outside of the universities. Until the late 1960s, the universities ignored, or even rejected Keynes' new economics. In an article of 1952, Hans Mayer expressed his fundamental opposition to Keynes' "new foundation" of economic theory. He gives Keynes credit for the application of the multiplier concept in dynamic analysis. Keynes' treatment of the role of long-term and short-term expectations, which "belongs to the best parts of the 'General Theory', … provide deep insights into the psychology of investment markets and mass psychology of the capitalist economy" (Mayer, 1952, 47). But on the whole, he considers the Keynesian system "a network of confusions and errors" (p. 40), in particular the idea of an equilibrium position of the economy below full employment, the tendency of declining scarcity of capital, and the need for a "nationalization of investment." What is most striking in Mayer's reluctance against Keynesianism is his rejection of macroeconomic thinking, of the use of "global concepts" (*Globalbegriffe,* p. 41). For Mayer, this is "a setback" in the development of economic theory, a step backwards behind the Austrian School, for which "macroeconomic magnitudes and their relationships are deduced ex post from microeconomic processes" (p. 50f).[19]

In Western Germany, the situation after 1945 was different. While declared Keynesians like Erich Schneider and Andreas Paulsen held economic chairs at important universities, economic policy after the currency reform was officially anti-Keynesian under Minister Ludwig Erhard and the dominance of the concept of Social Market Economy. Somewhat paradoxically, the strong impact of Keynesian economics on economic thinking in Austria can, to a considerable extent, be attributed to the fact that returned emigrants, due to their rejection, worked in institutions outside the universities, and thus became involved, directly or indirectly, in decision processes of economic policy.

9.5 Keynesianism in Austria's Economic Policy in the Period of Prosperity

During the phase of administrative control of distribution of foodstuffs and other essentials, of raw material supplies and resource allocation for investment and of foreign exchange, the Ministry of Finance and the so-called *Ministerium für Vermögenssicherung und Wirtschaftsplanung* (Ministry of Asset Protection and Economic Planning), which existed until 1949, were occupied by ÖVP politicians. When the situation normalized in the 1950s, the ÖVP switched to a market

[19] Wilhelm Weber (1953), who held the economic chair at the University of Vienna after Mayer's successor Alexander Mahr, gives a more thorough account of Keynes' theory, but his evaluation is largely negative.

economy program (so-called "Raab-Kamitz course") and advocated privatization, a revival of the private capital market and a reduction of income taxation (Butschek, 2008, p. 304f). At the same time, a pronounced anti-cyclical budget policy was pursued, especially in the recession of 1951/1952, under ÖVP finance ministers. There were massive tax incentives for investment through accelerated depreciation. The high volume of investment in the nationalized steel industry and in the electricity generating industry was maintained. In 1955, the General Social Insurance Act finally established old-age pensions for all employees, which had already been provisionally introduced by the application of German social security law after the occupation. An institutional framework for the system of social partnership was established in the early 1960s under the tripartite Parity Commission with professional sub-committees for control of prices and wages and the Economic and the Social Advisory Board.

The ÖVP sympathized with the social market economy program that had been so successful in Germany, but without adopting essential elements of its content, as the party gave priority to the protection of small businesses through anti-liberal, for a long time still highly restrictive trade regulations, a protectionist tariff policy, and protection of traditional monopolies and oligopolies in the private sector. These priorities stood in stark contrast to Eucken's concept of "free competition" as a regulatory postulate of the social market economy.

On the threshold of the transition from the reconstruction phase to economic normality, the SPÖ and the trade unions campaigned for a further development of the war and post-war control system into a system of institutionalized economic planning, and for further nationalization. The planned economy was a core component of the "Third Way" pursued by the social democrats, which differed from "socialism" of the Soviet-communist type by its consistent adherence to parliamentary democracy and by maintaining a mixed ownership system. In terms of its program, it took many years for the SPÖ to gradually dissociate itself from its Marxist heritage (Chaloupek, 2006).

In practice, however, the question had been decided since the early 1950s, when the market-economy system was restored in its basic features and the Austrian economy's 20-year period of prosperity had begun. Since the ministries responsible for economic policy, with the exception of the Ministry of Transport and Nationalized Industries, were in the hands of the ÖVP, the SPÖ's economic policy course was primarily shaped by experts from the ÖGB and the Chamber of Labour. Keynesianism thus became the de facto dominant orientation. For pragmatic reasons, at first Keynesianism was provisionally accepted as the conceptual basis of a labor-oriented economic policy that is supposed to be capable of overcoming capitalism in the long term.

Representative of this view is the editorial foreword to Forchheimer's introductory brochure on Keynes' New Economic Theory, almost certainly written by Wirlandner. Labor's interest organizations can only achieve an increase in the standard of living of workers and employees under conditions of economic prosperity and full employment, while their power wanes in a crisis. At the same time, the question is raised as to whether eliminating capitalism's vulnerability to crises "strengthens the forces that aim to reorganize society." When "Keynes shows the causes of the disturbances and believes he has found suitable remedies ... his theses also arouse the interest of the working class, which welcomes all efforts aimed at alleviating or eliminating the pressure of the crisis." On the other hand, it is emphasized that Keynes, as a representative of "bourgeois science," does not, like Marx, "investigate the laws of motion of capitalist society in order to overcome the existing order; he wants to preserve it" (Forchheimer, 1952, 9f).

When the question of the future economic order arose and became more urgent after the end of the reconstruction phase, it was Stefan Wirlandner who firmly and explicitly advocated a market economy system within which the goals of full employment, economic growth, and real wage increases were to be achieved through Keynesian macro-policy (Feichtinger, 2016, 83ff; Butschek, 2015, 44f). He must have had the benign tolerance or tacit support of important functionaries of the ÖGB and SPÖ, who no more adhered to the traditional orientation of a democratic Marxist socialism, but did not want to expose to the charge of becoming "a traitor of socialism."

Economic policy in Austria was—and still is—characterized by a high degree of pragmatism. Unlike other countries, Austria did not have a clearly defined official or semi-official guiding concept until the era of Austro-Keynesianism (1970–1995) (Rothschild, 1989, 116). Nevertheless, Austria's economic policy in the 1950s and 1960s was based on conceptual ideas that were explicitly or implicitly recognized by the parties and interest associations. Such a common understanding was explicitly present to a high degree with regard to the objectives of the so-called "magic triangle," and implicitly in the form of a Keynesian macro policy tailored to the requirements of a small state. Due to the central role of the social partnership's wage and price policy, Keynesian policy in Austria was not limited to a mechanistic "hydraulic Keynesianism." At least equally important was the reduction of uncertainty in the expectations of economic agents by stabilizing the framework conditions for business calculation and investment decisions.

The policy of Austro-Keynesianism was able to build on this foundation, which became the explicit guiding principle of economic policy for more than two decades after the end of the Bretton Woods system of fixed exchange rates.[20] With its core-elements anti-cyclical fiscal policy, social partnership system to control increases of prices and wages to maintain international competitiveness under the condition of a fixed exchange rate (no devaluation of Schilling in relation to the DM), Austro-Keynesianism was Austria's declared economic policy concept between 1970 and 1995, when the country finally joined the European Union.

[20] With regard to the theoretical foundations see Seidel (1982), Tichy (1984); for an ex-post evaluation see Chaloupek and Marterbauer (2008). For a comprehensive history of Austro-Keynesianism see Dirninger (2017).

References

Braunthal, A. (1927). *Die Entwicklungsgesetze der kapitalistischen Weltwirtschaft*. Jungsozialistische Schriftenreihe.
Butschek, F. (1985). *Die österreichische Wirtschaft im 20.* Jahrhundert: WIFO/Gustav Fischer Verlag.
Butschek, F. (2008). *Österreichische Wirtschaftsgeschichte*. Verlag Böhlau.
Butschek, F. (2015). Im Wandel der Zeit. In G. Chaloupek (Ed.), *Eduard März als Wirtschaftshistoriker und Wirtschaftspolitiker* (pp. 39–52). ÖGB-Verlag.
Butschek, F., Tichy, G., & Walterskirchen, E. (2022). *Von der Konjunkturforschung zum Kompetenzzentrum. 95 Jahre Österreichisches Institut für Wirtschaftsforschung*. Böhlau Verlag.
Chaloupek, G. (1990). The Austrian debate on economic calculation in a socialist economy. *History of Political Economy, 22*(4), 659–675.
Chaloupek, G. (2006). Plan versus Markt: wirtschaftspolitische Grundsatzpositionen in den ersten Jahrzehnten der Zweiten Republik. In H. Androsch, A. Pelinka, & M. Zollinger (Eds.), *Karl Waldbrunner Pragmatischer Visionär für das neue Österreich* (pp. 199–210). Verlag Carl Gerolds Sohn.
Chaloupek, G. (2011). From stabilization to depression. Comments in the Österreichische Volkswirt on economic policy in Austria between 1923 and 1929. In J. G. Backhaus (Ed.), *The beginnings of scholarly economic journalism the Austrian economist and the German economist* (pp. 73–91). Springer-Verlag.
Chaloupek, G. (2013). Maria Szécsi-März (1914–1984). *Arbeit & Wirtschaft, LXVII*, 10. 22f.
Chaloupek, G. (2016). Die Emigration von Ökonomen aus Österreich in die USA und nach Großbritannien und der Einfluss der Rückwanderer auf Wirtschaftspolitik und Wirtschaftsdenken. In M. Mesch (Ed.), *Wie kam der Keynesianismus nach Österreich? Band 2 der Reihe Die Ökonomik der Arbeiterbewegung in der Nachkriegszeit* (pp. 13–44). ÖGB Verlag.
Chaloupek, G. (2017a). The influence of emigrated economists on economic thinking and economic policy in post-war Austria. In W. Zacharasiewicz & M. Prisching (Eds.), *Return from Exile—Rückkehr aus dem Exil* (pp. 393–411). Verlag der Österreichischen Akademie der Wissenschaften.
Chaloupek, G. (2017b). Ein think tank für die Arbeiterbewegung - die AK-Wirtschaftswissenschaft in ihren ersten zwei Jahrzehnten. *Wirtschaft und Gesellschaft, 43*, 403–419.
Chaloupek, G. (2019). Karl Pribram. Ökonom und Pionier der österreichischen Sozialgesetzgebung. *Wirtschaft und Gesellschaft, 45*, 403–418.
Chaloupek, G., & Marterbauer, M. (2008). Was bleibt vom Austro-Keynesianismus? Dauerhafte Wirkungen der postkeynesianischen Wirtschaftspolitik in Österreich 1970–1995. In H. Hagemann, G. Horn, & H.-J. Krupp (Eds.), *Aus gesamtwirtschaftlicher Sicht. Festschrift für Jürgen Kromphardt* (pp. 45–67). Metropolis-Verlag.
Dirninger, C. (2017). *Austro-Keynesianismus*. Böhlau Verlag.
Expansion, Stagnation und Demokratie. (1982). Festschrift für Theodor Prager und Philipp Rieger. *Wirtschaft und Gesellschaft, 8*(2).
Feichtinger, J. (2016). Keynes-Rezeption vor dem "Austro-Keynesianismus" der Ära Kreisky. In M. Mesch (Ed.), *Wie kam der Keynesianismus nach Österreich? Band 2 der Reihe Die Ökonomik der Arbeiterbewegung in der Nachkriegszeit* (pp. 73–112). ÖGB Verlag.
Forchheimer, K. (1908). Theoretisches zum unvollständigen Monopole. *Jahrbuch für Gesetzgebung, Verwaltung und Volkswirtschaft im Deutschen Reich, 32*, 1–12.
Forchheimer, K. (1952). Keynes' neue Wirtschaftslehre. Eine Einführung. Schriftenreihe der Arbeiterkammer Wien, Verlag des Österreichischen Gewerkschaftsbundes, Wien.
Guger, A. (2016). Frühe Keynes-Rezeption am Institut für Konjunkturforschung bzw. WIFO. In M. Mesch (Ed.), *Wie kam der Keynesianismus nach Österreich? Band 2 der Reihe Die Ökonomik der Arbeiterbewegung in der Nachkriegszeit* (pp. 45–72). ÖGB Verlag.
Haberler, G. (1937). *Prosperity and depression*. League of Nations.

Hagemann, H. (2014). Introduction. German perspectives on the social sciences. *Special Issue Social Research, 81*(3), 503–517.
Hagemann, H., & Krohn, C.-D. (Eds.). (1999). *Biographisches Handbuch der deutschsprachigen wirtschaftswissenschaftlichen Emigration nach 1933*. K.G. Saur-Verlag.
Hertz, F. (1925). Zahlungsbilanz und Lebensfähigkeit Österreichs. In *Schriften des Vereins für Sozialpolitik 167 "Probleme der deutschen Zahlungsbilanz, Zweiter Teil"* (pp. 1–62). Duncker & Humblot.
Hertz, F. (1947). *The economic problem of the Danubian states*. Victor Gollancz.
Keynes, J. M. (1936). *The general theory of employment, interest, and money*. Macmillan.
King, J. E. (1994). Kurt Rothschild and the alternative Austrian economics. In E. Matzner & E. Nowotny (Eds.), *Was ist relevante Ökonomie heute? Festschrift für Kurt W. Rothschild.* Metropolis Verlag.
Klausinger, H. (2006). 'In the wilderness': Emigration and the decline of the Austrian school. *History of Political Economy, 38*(4), 617–664.
Klausinger, H. (2015a). Hans Mayer, last knight of the Austrian school, Vienna branch. *History of Political Economy, 47*(2), 271–305.
Klausinger, H. (2015b). Die Volkswirtschaftslehre an der Hochschule für Welthandel 1918–1973. Department of Economics Working Paper Series, 202. WU Vienna University of Economics and Business, Wien.
Klausinger, H. (2024). Kleines Zwischenspiel in Wien: Friedrich A. von Hayeks gescheiterte Berufung 1961/62, forthcoming in Zyklos 8.
Kozlik, A. (1966). *Der Vergeudungskapitalismus*. Europa Verlag.
Leichter, O. (1923). *Die Wirtschaftsrechnung in der sozialistischen Gesellschaft*. Verlag der Wiener Volksbuchhandlung.
Mars, H. (1931). *Gewerkschaftliches Handbuch des Akkordwesens, 3 Bände*. Bund d. freien Gewerkschaften Österreichs.
März, E. (1954). Die Hauptpunkte der Keynes'schen Theorie, Versuch einer kritischen Würdigung. *Schmollers Jahrbuch, 74*, 35–47.
März, E. (1959). *Die Marxsche Wirtschaftslehre im Widerstreit der Meinungen*. ÖGB-Verlag.
März, E. (1965). *Österreichs Wirtschaft zwischen Ost und West*. Europaverlag.
März, E. (1983). *Joseph Schumpeter - Forscher Lehrer und Politiker*. Verlag für Geschichte und Poltik.
Matis, H. (2017). Exil—Rückkehr—Innovationstransfer Am Beispiel der österreichischen Wirtschaftsgeschichte. In W. Zacharasiewicz & M. Prisching (Eds.), *Return from Exile—Rückkehr aus dem Exil* (pp. 379–392). Verlag der Österreichischen Akademie der Wissenschaften.
Mayer, H. (1951/1952). Zu Professor Mises' 70. Geburtstag. *Zeitschrift für Nationalökonomie, 13*, 513–516.
Mayer, H. (1952). John Maynard Keynes' "Neubegründung" der Wirtschaftstheorie. In E. Lagler & J. Messner (Eds.), *Wirtschaftliche Entwicklung und soziale Ordnung* (pp. 39–55). Verlag Herold.
Pirker, P. (2015). Rückkehr aus dem Exil. *In: Arbeit & Wirtschaft, LXIX*(3), 18f.
Prager, T. (1963). *Wirtschaftswunder oder keines?* Europaverlag.
Prager, T. (1975). *Zwischen London und Moskau. Bekenntnisse eines Revisionisten*. Europaverlag.
Robinson, J. (1951). *Grundprobleme der Marxschen Ökonomie, kommentierte Übersetzung ins Deutsche von Stefan Wirlandner*. Verlag des Österreichischen Gewerkschaftsbundes.
Rothschild, K. W. (1947). *Austria's economic development between the two wars*. Frederick Muller.
Rothschild, K. W. (1948). Die internationale Wirtschaft zwischen Inflation und Deflation. *Monatsberichte des Instituts für Wirtschaftsforschung, 21*, 13–17.
Rothschild, K. W. (1954). Zur Reform des österreichischen Zolltarifs, in: Monatsberichte des Instituts für Wirtschaftsforschung 27, Beilage 24.

Rothschild, K. W. (1989). Ziele, Ereignisse und Reaktionen: Reflexionen über die österreichische Wirtschaftspolitik. In H. Abele, E. Nowotny, S. Schleicher, & G. Winckler (Eds.), *Handbuch der österreichischen Wirtschaftspolitik, 3. Auflage*. Manz-Verlag.
Rothschild, K. W. (2004). Adolf Kozlik 1912–1964 - eine Erinnerung. *Wirtschaft und Gesellschaft, 30*, 273–281.
Seidel, H. (1982). Austro-Keynesianismus. *Wirtschaftspolitische Blätter, 29*(3), 11–15.
Seidel, H. (1985). Rothschild als Wirtschaftsforscher. In *"Es ist besser, eine wichtige Frage zu stellen, als eine unwichtige zu beantworten" Über die Persönlichkeit und das Wirken von Kurt W. Rothschild* (pp. 17–28). Institut für Sozial- und Wirtschaftswissenschften.
Seidel, H. (2012). Wirtschaftsforschung zwischen Empirie. *Theorie und Politik, in: WIFO Monatsberichte, 85*(6), 461–470.
Steindl, J. (1952). *Maturity and stagnation in American capitalism, Blackwell, Oxford, reprinted with a new introduction 1976*. Monthly Review Press.
Steindl, J. (1956). Wie wirkt die Ausgabe einer zusätzlichen Milliarde Schilling? In WIFO Monatsberichte 29 Sonderheft 9.
Steindl, J. (2004). Zeitzeuge. In F. Stadler (Ed.), Vertriebene Vernunft, Bd. II/1 (pp. 399–407). Verlag für Jugend und Volk 1987, Neudruck LIT-Verlag.
Szécsi, M. (1970). *Der Lohnanteil am österreichischen Volkseinkommen 1913 bis 1967 (= Heft III der Beiträge zu Wirtschaftspolitik und Wirtschaftswissenschaft)*. Kammer für Arbeiter und Angestellte für Wien.
Tichy, G. (1984). Hauptkonflikte der Makropolitik in Österreich: Austrokeynesianismus als Versuch eines wirtschaftspolitischen Brückenschlages zwischen den makrotheoretischen Extremen. In G. Bombach, B. Gahlen, & A. Ott (Eds.), *Makroökonomik heute: Gemeinsamkeiten und Gegensätze. Schriftenreihe des wirtschaftswissenschaftlichen Seminars Ottobeuren Band 12*. Verlag Mohr Siebeck.
Weber, W. (1953). *Wirtschaftswissenschaft von heute*. Springer Verlag.
Weissel, E. (1965). Wirtschaftswunder oder Keynes? *FORVM, XII*, 133–135.
Wirlandner, S. (1950). *Die Nutzwertlehre und die Arbeitnehmer, maschinschriftl*. Dissertation, Universität Wien.

Chapter 10
John Maynard Keynes' Influence in Norway

Arild Sæther

10.1 The Norwegian Post-World-War-I Economy

10.1.1 The Pre-War Picture

In the Treaty of Kiel in 1814 the King of Denmark-Norway ceded Norway to Sweden. The Norwegians revolted, established their own constitution and parliament, but were compelled to enter a union with Sweden under a shared monarchy. Gaining full independence in 1905, the country sought to avoid involvement in any international conflicts. However, the global landscape was fraught with tension, and in 1914 it erupted.

Since 1905 Norway had been through a period of economic expansion, but it relied heavily on international trade. Its merchant marine, the fourth largest in the world, was crucial for its welfare. However, this fleet also represented a potentially invaluable resource for Great Britain. Conversely, Germany would try to restrict its possibility to benefit from its use. When the war broke out the Norwegian government declared neutrality.

10.1.2 The Cost of Neutrality

At the same time, it took control of the economy, introduced a wide range of economic measures, and mobilized its military capability. The country was squeezed between the belligerent nations. When it was not capable of upholding an impartial

A. Sæther (✉)
Agder Academy of Sciences and Letters, Kristianstad, Norway
e-mail: arild@saether.no

J. G. Backhaus et al. (eds.), *Post-war Keynesianism in Germany and Western Europe*, The European Heritage in Economics and the Social Sciences 28,
https://doi.org/10.1007/978-3-032-00498-7_10

neutrality, Germany used its submarines against its merchant marine. Consequently, Norway became a neutral ally of Britain. Due to submarine warfare half its fleet was lost. More than 2000 sailors lost their lives.

The entire economy declined during the war years. Social costs were considerable. The war created a society with an uneven distribution of income and wealth. A small minority became wealthy. Low-income families experienced a sharp decline in their standard of living.

10.1.3 The Collapse and the Auri Sacra Fames

When the war ended Norway first experienced a boom. However, when it ended in 1920, the collapse was exceptionally strong. Prices in many commodity markets dropped dramatically. In many factories production was no longer profitable. The results were production cuts and in many cases bankruptcies and closures. Unemployment increased sharply and became a nightmare that weighed heavily on the Norwegian economy during the interwar period.

This crisis was amplified by the policy of Nicolai Rygg,[1] the newly appointed director of the Bank of Norway. It was the duty of the bank and the government to bring the gold standard back. At the start in 1920, he had wide support from the economists at the University of Oslo, but this support soon turned into a heavy resistance. The economists had probably followed the British debate and the views of John Maynard Keynes. Keynes fought against the *auri sacra fames* (the accursed lust for gold) (Hession, 1984, 219). However, Rygg could not be turned around, and the gold standard was again adopted in 1928. Most Norwegian economists hold that this had a disastrous effect on the economy. The varying governments during the second part of the 1920s and the first half of the 1930s did not have the ability to fight the crisis.

10.2 John Maynard Keynes a Nobel Peace Prize Candidate

10.2.1 The Economic Consequences of the Peace

The Paris Peace Conference, aimed at regulating the settlements between the victors and the vanquished of WWI, commenced in January 1919. In the 2 months leading up to the Conference, Keynes worked diligently to prepare the British Treasury's position. In an early memorandum, he asserted that reparation demanded of Germany, for the damage caused, must consider its capacity to pay. It must not be

[1] Nicolai Rygg (1872–1957), Cand. jur 1894, econ. studies in Göttingen, Geneva and the US, director Statistical Bureau of Senses 1913–1920, director of the Bank of Norway1920–1946.

so severe as to crush Germany's productive power, for, in the end, apart from movable properties, it could pay only by exporting goods to earn foreign currency. Two questions were crucial: what damage had Germany inflicted, and what capacity did it have to compensate for this damage? It should have been evident to most involved that these amounts did not align. However, the American, British, and French politicians were reluctant to confront reality.

At the conference, as a member of the British delegation, Keynes fought vigorously for a treaty grounded on reality, and for a plan that would restore Europe to its former stability. He strongly opposed imposing harsh terms. He advocated cancellation of inter-allied debts and the implementation of more lenient provisions in the treaty. However, he failed. When he was presented with an overview of the final proposal in early May 1919, he was horrified. The reparation clauses were 'unworkable' and demonstrated a high degree of unwisdom in almost every direction. He wrote to the Treasury requesting "to be relieved of his duties by 1 June if possible, and no later than 15 June in any event" (Skidelsky, 1983, 370–371).

The Treaty of Versailles was signed on June 28, 1919. By that time, John Maynard Keynes had already begun writing a book about the economic conditions in Europe following the war. In December of that year, his book, *The Economic Consequences of the Peace*, was published. It is widely regarded as one of his most significant works. In this book, he examines the treaty's impact on the economic stability of Europe, emphasizing that Germany's position in global markets was severely compromised. He argues that this deterioration would inevitably lead to an economic crisis and political turmoil. Furthermore, he contends that the punitive terms of the Treaty were unsustainable and would exacerbate the crisis. Skidelsky (1983, 374) asserts that the book deserves recognition as Keynes's finest work, stating, "the writing is angry, scornful, and, rarely for Keynes, passionate: never again were his denunciations of bungling and lying, or his moral indignation, to ring so loud and clear."

Quickly translated into several foreign languages, the book became an international bestseller. Prior to its publication, Keynes had been known primarily among academic elites; afterwards, he became an international celebrity.

10.2.2 Keynes Nominated for the Peace Prize

When the Swedish inventor, entrepreneur, scientist, and successful businessman Alfred Nobel[2] in 1895 bequeathed much of his fortune to establish prizes for significant achievements, he decided, for unknown reasons, that the Norwegian Parliament should award the Peace Prize.[3] From the outset, the selection of winners has been

---

[2] Alfred Nobel (1836–1896), a Swedish engineer, scientist, author, pacifist and inventor of dynamite, who had earned a fortune and founded the Nobel prizes.

[3] In 1895, Norway was still in a union with Sweden.

based on a list of nominees submitted to the Nobel Prize Committee, appointed by Parliament.

Lars Jonung (2022, 399) claims that it is evident that Keynes' book about the disastrous economic consequence of the Versailles Treaty and the debates that it initiated, prompted two professors of economics at the University of Munich, Georg von Mayr and Walther Lotz, to nominate him for the 1922 Nobel Peace Prize. They did this because of "the courageous and unbiased account in Keynes's writings about the living conditions created by the Peace Treaty."

According to standard procedure, a short list of nominees was created, and each nominee was evaluated by an advisor. The appraisal of Keynes was assigned to the committee's consultant, Wilhelm Keilhau,[4] who was also a Docent of economics at the University of Oslo. He provided a detailed analysis of several pages, in which he also offered favorable comments on Keynes' follow up book, *A Revision of the Treaty* published in 1922.[5] His judgment of Keynes candidature is positive: "He agreed with Keynes' analysis, recommendations, and critique of the Treaty of Versailles. He heaped praise on Keynes for contributing to a peaceful Europe" (ibid., 402f).

Keynes did not receive the prize for that year, and the Nobel Committee decided not to award any prize. It must have been disappointing for Keynes not to receive the prize, especially since Keilhau, in a clear violation of the code of conduct regarding consultants, had informed him that he was a strong candidate. (ibid., 406) However, a new letter was sent nominating him for the year 1923. This time, it was signed by four professors, the two previously mentioned and in addition Adolf Weber and Otto von Zwiedineck-Südenhorst, also from the University of Munich. "This letter amounts to a commendation of Keynes's ongoing efforts for peace in the world" (ibid., 399). Keilhau's evaluation from the previous year was utilized, but no prize was awarded for this year either.

10.2.3 The Keilhau and Worm-Müller Debate

The year after 1924, Keynes was again nominated by the same professors and Keilhau was again asked to produce a new assessment. This appraisal concentrated on Keynes' recent works, and Keilhau pointed to his book *A Tract on Monetary Reform* published in 1923. Keilhau argued that the book is "a clear, panoramic and deep treatment of the economic problems of the postwar period that no other author would be capable of preparing" (ibid., 407). However, the 1924 nomination was also marred by a debate that took place in the Oslo daily newspaper *Dagbladet*

[4]Wilhelm Keilhau (1888–1954), Cand. jur. 1912, Dr. phil. 1917, Docent 1921, Professor 1934. Chaired the Norwegian delegation to Bretton Woods.

[5]In this book Keynes analyzed the problems he saw as the Versailles Treaty was implemented.

between Keilhau and Professor Jacob Worm-Müller.[6] In this debate, Worm-Müller, who had followed the recent debate in English newspapers, accuses Keynes of having unjustly criticized the American president Woodrow Wilson, and for having given a false testimony about his participation in some important meetings during the negotiations in Paris. This was, according to Jonung, strongly refuted by Keilhau but reiterated by Worm-Müller. The dispute between them turned rancorous. (ibid., 409) The Nobel Committee decided not to award a Peace Prize for the year 1924 either. The reasons were not given.

10.2.4 Why Was Keynes Not Awarded the Peace Prize?

The reasons why Keynes did not receive the Nobel Peace Prize are not known. Jonung (2022, 413–417) discusses several possibilities, and a few should be mentioned. In the 1920s, only people who worked in international organizations or were high ranking government officials received the prize. Keynes was not a political actor, nor did he, at this time, hold an official position. It was also clear that Keynes did not fit in. He was a voice not only outside the establishment, but a strong critic of it. The composition of the Nobel committee could also be a reason as it consisted of members of the political parties in the Norwegian parliament. These politicians could also have feared that a prize for Keynes would be seen as Norwegian support for Germany. The fact that it was only professors from Germany who had nominated Keynes may also have played a role. In addition, Worm-Müller's violent attack on Keynes in a major newspaper might have had a negative influence.

10.2.5 The Positive Impact of the Nominations

However, the nominations of Keynes for the Nobel Peace Prize, the positive appraisals by Keilhau and even the debate in the newspaper, must have had a positive impact. It is important to note that the Nobel Committee invited Keynes for three successive years 1924, 1925, and 1926 to come to Oslo to give a series of lectures. The first time Keynes answered positively but was prevented because of lectures at Cambridge. The second and third times the reasons are not known. The nominations of Keynes for the Nobel Peace Prize and particularly the newspaper debate had made Keynes a well-known name in Norway.

[6] Jacob Worm-Müller (1884–1963), Dr. phil. 1919, Docent in history1919, Professor 1929. Delegate to the Leage of Nations, delegate to the founding of United Nations, and a delegate for some years.

10.2.6 What Could Have Been the Effect of a Peace Prize?

Today the Nobel Peace Prize award is reported worldwide as an important event. This was not the case in the 1920s. However, if the already famous John Maynard Keynes, with his harsh critique of the Versailles Peace Treaty and his pessimistic outline of the consequences it would have for peace in Europe, had been awarded the Prize, it could have opened the eyes of at least some important European politicians. This could have led to changes in the policies that were pursued. But, as is well known, this did not happen, and the consequences were catastrophic.

10.3 How Keynes Was Brought Into Norwegian Politics

10.3.1 Keynes in Post-War England

The world economic crisis at the end of the 1920s and beginning of the 1930s hit most European countries hard. The crisis confronted economists with great challenges. Many believed that the economies would by themselves find solutions and that governments should not intervene, regardless of how many years the crisis would last.

After leaving the treasury and after the publication of his two books about the Versailles Treaty Keynes concentrated on his work at Cambridge University. His main task was to find new theories that would solve the problems caused by the economic crisis. As such he also took part in the economic political debate. His view was that governments had responsibilities towards their population and to find solutions to the miseries of its people. A few events and publications should be mentioned.

In November 1924 Keynes was invited to give a memorial lecture at Oxford University. The lecture called *The End of* Laissez-Faire has been considered a decisive step in his efforts to expand the state's role in the economy. Keynes argued that the belief in an economy based on pursuit of individual self-interest, free markets and limited government, as outlined by Adam Smith, could not cope with the post-war economic problems. In 1926 he repeated the lecture at the University of Berlin, when it was also published as a pamphlet in English and German that was widely read by academics.

In May 1928 Keynes, together with Hubert Henderson,[7] wrote a pamphlet for the English Liberal Party entitled *Can Lloyd George Do It? - The Pledge Examined.*[8] Keynes, who was a strong supporter, answered with a decisive yes. By using a hundred million pounds a year, half a million unemployed could be given work. They

[7] Sir Hubert Douglas Henderson (1890–1952), important English economist and a close associate of Keynes. Both members of a think tank established by prime minister David Loyed George.

[8] He had been very critical to Lloyd George's role in the Treaty of Versailles.

could build houses, roads, railways, telephones, and telegraph lines, and they could drain marshland to extend the agricultural area. Furthermore, he claimed that the increased incomes would give the government higher taxes and that these together with a reduction in the defense budget would be sufficient to make the works self-financing. Government debt would therefore not increase. The *"multiplier"* can be seen in the background of these computations (Munthe, 1999, 26).

In the election campaign of 1929, the Liberal Party came up with the slogans like "We can conquer unemployment" and "Let us mobilize for prosperity." Keynes supported its proposals against the bureaucrats in the treasury, who thought these proposals were extravagance and would cause inflation and bankruptcy. They also claimed that public investments would not reduce unemployment because it would oust private investments. Increased public investments would increase the demand for savings and since savings were limited this would increase the interest rate, which in turn would make private investments unprofitable. The basic view of the ministry was that savings were scarce, and Keynes had to go into extensive discussion to show that this was not the case (ibid., 27).

10.3.2 Who Brought Keynes to Norway?

The world economic crisis at the end of the 1920s and beginning of the 1930s hit Norway more severely than most other European countries. GDP per capita fell by more than 8% in 1931, unemployment among members of the labor unions was almost 19%, and during the winter of 1931–1932 unemployment among union members rose sharply. In the winter of 1932–1933 it rose to more than 40% and across the entire labor force it was more than 15%. Although people at that time had more respect for the authorities than today, this situation caused serious social unrest.

In 1932 the Oslo daily newspaper *Arbeiderbladet*, which was the main media outlet for the labor party, hired a new financial journalist Ole Colbjørnsen (1897–1973). Eriksen and Sæther (2010, 5f) claim that it was him who brought Keynes' new economic ideas to Norway.

Who was Colbjørnsen? He grew up, in poor conditions, on a small tenant farm in southern Norway. He was talented and became a brilliant student in mathematics and physics at the University of Oslo. However, he experienced a political awakening, and he saw Soviet as the proper "land of dawn." He wanted to take active part in this historical project. He learned Russian and went into Soviet service. From 1921 he worked for different Soviet enterprises, and he participated in the preparation of the first Soviet five-year plan. At the end of the 1920s he worked as a consultant in the development of Soviet foreign trade policy, making several visits to its trade delegation in London. From 1929 to 1931 he worked as director of a Soviet shipping company in London.

However, during the 1920s Colbjørnsen became increasingly skeptical towards Stalin's dictatorship, and in 1931 he defected from Soviet service and moved back to Norway, to become a financial journalist. During his years in London, Colbjørnsen had closely followed the economic debate in the newspapers, and also the new developments in British economic policy. He was impressed by the views of Keynes, who dominated the debate. Keynes wanted the government to play an active role in fighting unemployment and improving the conditions for millions of poor people. He also wanted to discover and develop new economic theories that could be used to solve present economic problems.

Although Colbjørnsen still believed that a democratic socialist planned economy was the best, he was impressed by Keynes' views that it was possible with an active government to secure full employment in a society based on a market economy. He accepted Keynes' views and brought his proposals with him when he returned to Norway. As a financial journalist he wrote numerous articles advocating these proposals and solutions to the economic problems. These articles were again, "more influenced by the liberal English economists than by Lenin and his disciples" (Munthe, 1999, 143f). His main points were that the crisis with its massive unemployment was unnecessary and could, even in a non-socialist society, be avoided with effective intervention by the state. Munthe writes that "Ole Colbjørnsen was the first Keynesian in the Labour Party. He rejected the party's dogma that socialization of capital would solve all problems, and designed a practical, down-to-earth crisis policy" (ibid., 141).

At that time the economic policy of Norway was not much different from that of the UK. The non-socialist parties had a clear majority in the parliament but could not agree to form a strong government. The Socialist Labor Party had not yet recovered from the internal feud between the socialist factions in the 1920s. Until 1933 the political slogan for the ruling non-socialist governments was *"Vente på bedre bør"* (let us wait for fair wind), and the economic policy was built on the principle that the government and local municipalities should save before they could spend. Consequently, they claimed that the burdens on private business life would be less, activity would increase, and employment would grow. Unfortunately, this did not work. Until 1933 the Labor Party had no alternative to this short-term policy.

This changed when Colbjørnsen arrived. In addition to his work as a journalist he took an active part in the creation of the Labor Party program before this year's election. He also played an important role in the work with its **Norwegian three-year plan**, which presented a comprehensive expansive anti-crisis policy in the spirit of Keynes. Before this election the party had advocated revolution, now Colbjørnsen showed an alternative way based on Keynesian economics. He stated that it was ridiculous in a relatively poor country to have tens of thousands out of work. "We cannot be poorer by working" was his central message. With his slogan "The whole people at work," and a comprehensive economic program to bring the country out of the crisis the Labor Party got more than 40% of the vote. Under its chairman Johan Nygaardsvold[9] it formed a government in 1935, after it had entered the so-called crisis settlement with the Farmers' party.

---

[9] Johan Nygaardsvold (1879–1952), Prime Minister 1935–1940, and in exile London1940–1945.

10.3.3 Ragnar Frisch and the Economic Crisis

Two professors at the University of Oslo, Oskar Jæger[10] and Ingar Wedervang,[11] felt that in the country's difficult economic situation, both teaching and research in economics at the university had to be strengthened. They succeeded to convince the Norwegian parliament, to create a professorship in economics and statistics for Ragnar Frisch,[12] who then declined an attractive offer of a tenured professorship from Yale University and returned to Oslo in 1931 (Bjerkholt, 2018, 17). In his early career, Frisch had not concerned himself with the current actual economic problems. During this stay at Yale University 1930–1931, as guest of Irving Fisher, he began to show a growing interest in economic policy. Munthe (1999, 25) claims that Frisch became strongly influenced by his host and other American economists. When he returned to Oslo, he advocated tax relief and monetary policies as the economic instruments to move the Norwegian economy out of the crisis.

10.3.4 Colbjørnsen's Attack on Frisch

In spring 1932 Frisch gave three radio lectures on business cycles. Here he strongly attacked what he called the saving mania in both the private and public sector of the economy. The following year he wrote three articles in the daily newspaper *Dagbladet,* published in a little brochure *Sparing og circulasjons-regulering* (savings and circulation regulation), where he presented his thoughts about the causes of the present economic crisis and his ideas of how it would be possible to get out of it. The crisis was not a production or poverty crisis, but a sales crisis and an organizational crisis. Therefore, he saw no need for fundamental changes in the economic system. What was needed was a public system, which did not directly interfere with production, but influence it indirectly by removing the special sales and organizational obstacles. The government's objective should be to utilize all available resources, both labor and capital. The state should not only redistribute purchasing power, it should also increase supply through tax relief. Here it was essential that the deficit was not financed with loans in the market, which were in competition with private loans, but with an increase in credit. Public works were not a part of his plan. Rather, economic activity should be stimulated in the

[10] Oskar Jæger (1863–1933), Cand. mag. 1888, Dr. phil. 1894, Cand. jur. 1897. Professor of statistics and economics 1902–1930.

[11] Ingar Wedervang (1891–1961), Cand. oecon. 1913. Dosent 1925, Professor 1927, Funded, together with Ragnar Frisch, Institute of Economics, University of Oslo 1935, Rector Norwegian School of Economics Bergen 1937–1942 and 1945–1956.

[12] Ragnar Frisch (1895–1973), Cand. oecon. 1919. Dr. phil. 1926, Rockefeller Scholarship 1926–1929, Docent 1929, Professor 1931, Funded, together with Ingar Wedervang, Institute of Economics, University of Oslo 1935. Introduced new terms into economics such as micro and macroeconomics and econometrics. Nobels honorary prize in economics 1969.

consumption sphere. When the economy had reached its equilibrium with full employment, the government should "withdraw from the play" (Eriksen & Sæther, 2010, 4).

The analysis and recommendations in these articles were harshly reviewed by Colbjørnsen. He attacked the professor for giving benefits to people that already earned so much that they had no problems in paying tax. Why not give support to the unemployed? Or even better: Why not use the money to put people to work? He claimed that Frisch was just scratching the surface of the crisis and that he should have been discussing the problems of private capitalism and its basic weaknesses. Frisch's proposals were just another example of a reflation initiated by the government. He was surprised that Frisch did not embrace the program of the Labor Party, and that he did not see that private capitalism had failed and that the road forward was a socialist planned economy.

Frisch counterattacked and claimed that the main weakness of Colbjørnsen's planned economy was that he did not put enough emphasis on private initiative. According to Frisch a planned economy had to be organized in such a rational way "that one can utilize the tremendous energy source which is implied in the will and initiative of each individual."[13]

10.3.5 The Colbjørnsen and Frisch Collaboration

Surprisingly the discussion between the two had, in a short time, the consequence that they started to cooperate. How this came about is not clear but it is known that Frisch in the autumn of 1933 had a private meeting with the top parliamentarians of the Labor Party and that this meeting changed his opinion (Munthe, 1995, 281).

Eventually, Frisch and Colbjørnsen started a fruitful collaboration and joined in the work of developing the Labor Party's crisis plan of 1934. Frisch gave up his proposal about tax relief and accepted the proposal for a strong increase in public spending and its financing by an increase in taxes. Colbjørnsen on the other hand accepted that increased public spending should be partly financed by loans. His major concern was the effect on the real economy. In 1933 together with Axel Sømme (1899–1991),[14] Colbjørnsen had published *En norsk 3-års plan* (a Norwegian 3-year plan), which provided that the state should heavily invest in the economy, as a first step to a fully socialist economy.[15] He strongly believed that private investment was not capable of curing unemployment.

[13] Arbeiderbladet 15.05.33.

[14] Axel Christian Zetlitz Sømme (1899–1991), Dr. phil. 1931, professor in economic geography at the Norwegian School of Economics 1948–1969.

[15] Stortingstidende 20.03. 1934. 407–417.

10.4 Keynes and the Parliament's Finance Debate in 1934

10.4.1 Keynes and the Norwegian Parliament Debate

The above-mentioned Labor Party's crisis plan had an aftereffect that also made Keynes' name known among the members of the Norwegian parliament. This plan, together with plans from the other political parties, had been submitted to *Den pengetekniske komite* (The Monetary Technical Committee). This committee was a professional committee that had been appointed in the spring of 1932 with the director of the Central Bureau of Statistics Gunnar Jahn[16] as chairman. Professor Wilhelm Keilhau was also a member. Its purpose was to subject proposals submitted to parliament to a purely professional assessment before any political consideration.

The Technical Committee pointed out that the Labor Party's crisis plan was so large that it could create inflation. However, it did not distance itself in principle from loan financing of emergency work. The committee referred to Keynes' book *A Treatise on Money* from 1930.

10.4.2 Keynes Misinformed by Frisch

Colbjørnsen and Frisch believed that the committee had misinterpreted Keynes. They claimed that the committee had interpreted him to mean that savings had to occur first before investment could be made. Frisch, who happened to be in Cambridge at that time, translated the committee's statement into English and presented it to Keynes, who wrote a clarifying letter. This letter was presented to Parliament by the Labor Party's leader Johan Nygaardsvold, as a proof that the *Technical Committee* members were not experts and that the world-famous economist John Maynard Keynes showed that there was no professional basis for the criticism of the Labor Party's crisis plan. (Munthe, 1999, 149) If there were any members of parliament who beforehand did not know the English economist Keynes, they now had no doubt that he was a significant economist who should be listened to.

But the debate in Parliament had an aftermath. Director Gunnar Jahn took up the matter and demonstrated that the translation Frisch had presented to Keynes was incorrect. The committee had not claimed that savings had to come before investment. According to Munthe (1999, 149), Frisch expressed his pleasure at Jahn's explanation and correction and stated that there was no disagreement between them!

[16] Gunnar Jahn (1883–1971), Cand. jur. 1907, Cand. oecon. 1909, Director Central Bureau of Statistics 1920–1945, Director of the Bank of Norway 1945–1954.

10.4.3 An Aftermath That Created More Aftermaths

But this aftermath did not end here. Two years later, in 1936, the Labor Party newspaper *Arbeiderbladet* had forgotten Frisch's incorrect translation and claimed that Messrs. Gunnar Jahn and Wilhelm Keilhau in the Parliaments Technical committee had been sharply reprimanded by more modern and authoritative academic economists Ragnar Frisch and Keynes, and that they deserved reprimands both from Nygaardsvold in parliament and in our newspaper. Professor Keilhau refuted this presentation, to no avail.

Later repercussions came in the years 1961, 1965, and 1983. In 1961, in a preface to a memorandum by Hans Jacob Kreyberg's *Overview of the Keynes Models*, Ragnar Frisch wrote that "in connection with Keynes' theory and its application in Norway, the 1934 parliament debate on the Labour Party's crisis program has a certain historical interest." An appendix includes an excerpt from the debate in Parliament, including the letter Frisch wrote to Keynes and Keynes' response. However, it did not include Gunnar Jahn's demonstration that Frisch had misinformed Keynes.

Four years later in 1965, the same happened again when Frisch published a booklet *Politkk i pakt med fremtiden* (Politics in Accordance with the Future). Here again he reproduced excerpts from the finance debate in the 1934 Parliament, including the letter Frisch wrote to Keynes and his response. The impression given by Frisch is that he and Keynes had shown parliament the right path. In this booklet Frisch again refers to the meeting in Parliament where "it fell to my lot to fight by Johan Nygaardsvold's side." He reproduces from the debate the section with his letter to Keynes and Keynes' reply, but he does not include Gunnar Jahn's and Wilhelm Keilhau's corrections. "Thus, readers were not informed that his account of the committee's attitude towards Keynes was a misinterpretation. The episode speaks volumes about Frisch's desire to appear 'progressive'" (Munthe, 1999, 150). It should be mentioned that Kreyberg's presentation of the *Keynes models* was studied thoroughly by economic students in the 1960s and 1970s. Furthermore, the booklet published by Frisch was read by politically interested people.

Almost 50 years later it became clear that Ragnar Frisch's representation of what happened in the Parliaments 1934 finance debate had taken hold. In the journal *Sosialøkonomen* from 1983 a small article called *Keynes og norsk økonomisk politikk* (Keynes and Norwegian economic policy) appeared. This article, which is not signed, appeared at the occasion of the centenary of Keynes' birth. Here the debate in the parliament and the exchange of letters between Frisch and Keynes are reproduced, but not the corrections![17] It can honestly be said that a falsehood has been made into truth!

---

[17] Sosialøkonomen 1983/07, 32–36.

10.5 Honorary Doctor at University of Oslo 1938

10.5.1 The General Theory of Employment Interest and Money

When Keynes published *The General Theory of Employment Interest and Money* in 1936, it had been known for some time that he had a book in preparation, and there were high expectations about what this book would contain. The book was also based on his participation in the economic and political debate. Many early reviews of the book were highly critical. From the outset there has been controversy over what Keynes really meant. And yet, in posterity Keynes' *General Theory* has been seen as a turning point in the history of economic science. From the very beginning it won an enthusiastic audience, particularly among young economists, who had been waiting for a remedy against economic depression. Paul Samuelson expressed it in this way: "Bliss was in dawn to be alive, but to be young was very heaven" (quoted from Eriksen & Saether, 2010, 9). Furthermore he claimed that the those below age 35 years were "contaminated", but that those above age 50 never got it, while those in between came gradually to accept the new theory, sometimes without knowing it themselves. England and the US were soon won for the new theory.

10.5.2 The Norwegian Reception of the Book

However, the reaction in Scandinavia was rather cool. The Swedes said straight out that what was important in the book was old news for the Stockholm School. In addition, they had many critical comments.

In Oslo, at first there was a remarkable silence. With Keynes' early emphasis on consumption rather than investment, Frisch and most of his colleagues, at the University of Oslo, had a different approach to what could bring economies out of the crisis.

However, there is no evidence that Frisch's policies to fight the crisis had even indirectly been influenced by Keynes. Keynes was, according to Frisch, only one of many in "this group of modern money theoreticians who had worked their way to an active view" (Nordvik, 1977, 315). This implied that Frisch believed that Keynes, when his *General Theory* was published, was not such an inventive scholar as he liked to present himself. His stroke of genius was not his ideas or theories but in his way of presentation, that is how his "thoughts are combined and described." The book was "powerful, pointed and convincing," but Frisch (1947, 56) added that "by no means it was everywhere clear and precise."

Frisch expressed an irritation that Keynes had not caught up with the latest developments in science to understand that there was relatively little news in the content of the book. Frisch was undoubtedly right when he claimed that an expansive policy was not a new thing. Norwegian university economists had favored the idea about budget deficits, even with no antecedent saving, a few years before the *General Theory*. What separated Keynes from Frisch was primarily that Keynes developed a macroeconomic theory that supported an expansive policy. This had not been a concern for Frisch. And when the so-called Keynesian revolution was more a theoretical than a political turning point, Keynes can be said to be more original than what Frisch thought.

Frisch's skepticism toward Keynes was also connected with their different views on the methodology of economics. Keynes did not think much of econometrics. In addition, he undoubtedly sinned against the rules that Frisch had listed for correct model building. In Frisch's opinion Keynes was not explicit enough in his assumptions or sufficiently precise in his logical conclusions. Keynes also did not see the same need as Frisch for empirical investigations.

10.5.3 Keynes Doctor Honoris Causa

When the reviews of *The General Theory* in foreign journals mounted to a whole literature, and the impact also hit the public, the silence of the Oslo economists became unsustainable. The situation demanded a reaction. When it finally came it was positive. Keynes was awarded *Doctor Honoris Causa* at the University of Oslo 20 on March 1938.[18] His distance towards Keynes did not prevent that Frisch, on this occasion, cooperated with his colleagues, but it was professor Keilhau and the later professor Erling Petersen, who oversaw the ceremony.

The justification for the creation of Keynes as an honorary doctor can be found in an article Keilhau wrote for the occasion in *Statsøkonomisk Tidsskrift*. Here he first discusses Keynes' works: "When placed alongside each other, they do not fit into any systematic whole. They represent stages on the strange and contentious path of life. At critical junctures, critics can cite Keynes against Keynes, and today it is nearly impossible to form a definitive opinion on the final positions he seeks to achieve" (Keilhau). He concludes: "So we may think that it is bold to grant this man the degree of honorary doctor. But we must remember that science itself is constantly marching forward into the unknown. Scientific progress consists precisely in an incessant revision of the doctrines that previous scientists considered to be certain and final results. A scientist who, in each new work, personally ensures the revision of his previous positions, is therefore, from a purely human perspective, particularly deserving of such an honour" (1938, 82). Hence, there was no doubt that Keynes deserved to be appointed as an honorary doctor at the university.

For unknown reasons, Keynes did not come to Oslo for the award, so that the British ambassador Sir Cecil Dormer received the prize on behalf of Keynes.

---

[18] The Doctor Honoris Causa is awarded for significant scientific contributions or outstanding work for the benefit of science.

10.5.4 Continued Skepticism

Both Frisch and Keilhau stayed skeptical toward the writings of Keynes. At the end of his article, Keilhau wrote: "In one way, however, the reception of The General Theory raises a rather interesting psychological problem: Why is it that this book, which is so exaggerated in its critique and which in many of its ways of thinking stops halfway, is created with excitement from a huge audience, and even in certain circles has won the reputation of being an epoch-making pioneering work?" (ibid., 97).

As late as 1940 they published a collection *Sosialøkonomiske Utsnitt* (Economics segment) of "original texts" from great works in economics. This collection has not a single sentence from the *General Theory.* However, it contains a section from *A Treatise on Probability* which Keynes had published in 1921. They were perhaps of the opinion that this work was his most valuable contribution to economics. It was therefore other economists than Frisch that introduced Keynes to the students at the University of Oslo. To some degree it was the students themselves who had started to read the *General Theory.*

10.6 The Teaching of Keynes

10.6.1 A New Study Program in Economics

The most decisive period in the development of economics as a science in Norway was marked by the foundation of the University Institute of Economics in 1932. During its first years it was financed with money from the Rockefeller Foundation. In 1934 a new five-year study program in economics with a modern curriculum was introduced. Ragnar Frisch's research on microeconomic theory and econometrics had a strong imprint on the institute's orientation e.g., he eliminated the entrepreneur from the theory of production, Sæther and Eriksen (2014).

10.6.2 The First to Lecture on Keynes

The first to lecture on Keynes' *General Theory* at the University of Oslo was Erling Petersen.[19] As scholarship recipient he had participated in the team that created Keynes honorary doctor at the university. On this occasion he wrote an article in *Statsøkonomisk Tidsskrift*, in which he brought up the discussion that had taken

[19] Erling Petersen (1906–1992), Cand. oecon 1937. Dr. Phil. 1939. Professor Norwegian School of Economics (NHH) 1941–1952, Professor University of Oslo 1953–1976. Member of Parliament from the Conservative party 1950–1973.

place about the book. He concludes: "Many are those who have read Keynes' book *The General Theory* and disagree. Fewer are those who can read it and say that they haven't learned anything new. But I don't believe there is anyone who can read it and claim that it hasn't provided impulses for new thoughts on this or that" (Petersen, 1938, 114).

The year after, in 1939, Petersen started to lecture on Keynes' book to his students. The same year he defended his doctoral dissertation, and in 1940 he was appointed professor at the newly founded Norwegian School of Business Economics in Bergen, where he continued his teaching on Keynes. In 1948 he published a long article *Diskusjonen om Keynes General Theory* (The discussion about Keynes' General Theory). It presents the main features of the *General Theory* without the use of any mathematics. Within a short time this article was sold out, and the first part called *Hovedtrekkene i Keynes´ «General Theory»* (The Main Features in Keynes' «General Theory") was published as a compendium, which was used as textbook for more than 25 years. In his lectures Petersen stressed that "Keynes theory was primarily a theory of employment. Therefore, it has also been a theory of no employment or unemployment" (Petersen, 1948b, 12). In this context, however, it is important to emphasize that in Petersen's presentation of Keynes' theory the entrepreneur does have a role, contrary to Frisch's version of the theory of production. Petersen also raises the question of why state control of all investment activity had become associated with Keynes. He concludes that Keynes' theory cannot be taken as a defense of a 'planned economy' that involves detailed central direction (Petersen, 1948b, 82).

10.6.3 The Mathematization of the General Theory

In his lectures on economic policy at the University of Oslo in 1957 and 1958, Bjørn Thalberg[20] discussed parts of Keynes' *General Theory.* He found that his students had a need for, and demanded, an exact analytical description of the main points in the book. He therefore recapitulated Keynes' main theory in a mathematical model. His lectures were published as a compendium *En analytisk presisering av Keynes 'General Theory'* (An analytical precision of Keynes 'General Theory') in 1959. Thalberg makes it clear to his students that Keynes *General Theory* is, like any other theory, not general in the sense that it is relevant regardless of the questions asked or regardless of institutional conditions and market forms. Keynes is concerned with analyzing the extent to which existing production possibilities are utilized. The background is largely the free competition system. His model is therefore not very suitable if, for example, prices are largely set by a price directorate, if most goods

[20] Bjørn Thalberg (1924–2013). Cand. oecon 1954, Dr. Phil1966, Lund university 1962, Professor in Economics from 1968, Emeritus 1990.

are rationed, if business is dominated by monopoly companies, or, for example, if most investment decisions are made by public bodies.

In 1961 Hans Jacob Kreyberg[21] published his compendium *Oversikt over Keynes—modellene* (A Survey of the Keynes Models).[22] It is a short presentation of Keynes' *General Theory* in four mathematical models. Thalberg's and Kreyberg's compendia became an important part of the curriculum in macroeconomics for the students at the University of Oslo in the first three decades after the war. Students of economics with a good understanding of mathematical language could familiarize themselves with what they thought to be Keynes' theories, without being distracted by philosophical considerations. However, whether Keynes, as the moral philosopher he also was, would have approved of this presentation of his economic theories is another question.

During the first half of the 1960s Leif Johansen[23] lectured on public finance. These lectures were published, in two volumes 1962 and 1963, and as one volume in 1965, *Offentlig økonomikk* (Public Economics).[24] In the next decades, this book became a standard textbook in public finance for Norwegian students of economics. Strangely enough, given Johansen's communist views, and his emphasis on central economic planning, he decided to write the book "within the framework of simple macroeconomic models of the Keynesian type" (Johansen, 1962, 23).

With these books Keynes, and what was believed to be his economic theories, had won a secure place in the teaching of economics for Norwegian students, who, according to Berg and Hanisch (1984, 218), viewed macroeconomics and Keynes' models as the same.

It should also be mentioned that, when Trygve Haavelmo[25]was promoted to professor in 1948, he started to lecture on a wide range of economic theory, until he retired as emeritus in 1979. Before, he had become known for his article in 1944: *Multiplier Effects of a Balanced Budget* (Haavelmo, 1944). The findings of this

[21] Hans Jacob Kreyberg (1924–1983), Cand. oecon. 1951, The Kings Gold Medal 1956, Lecturer at The Norwegian Institute of Technology (NTH), Trondheim in 1959, Dr. phil. 1970, Docent 1970 and Professor 1973.

[22] In a preface to the compendium Ragnar Frisch, who did not teach Keynes theories, explains how it came about. "In the spring of 1957 I should give a series of lectures on economic planning in Holland, it occurred to me that it could be useful to bring with me some notes on Keynes theory in case it, beside the more thorough technical oriented lectures on planning, could be requests for some popular lectures on his theory. I had very little time and was happy when Kreyberg on the spot made some excellent pencil notes, which I could have in my pocket if needed. As it turned out there was no need for the notes, however they accompanied me on several trips to Cairo where I should give advice on economic planning." So, at last he concluded that a presentation of Keynes' theory could be valuable for the students in economics.

[23] Leif Johansen (1930–1982), Cand. oecon. 1954, Dr. Phil. 1956. Prof. 1958–1982. He was a clear candidate for the Nobel Memorial Prize in Economics.

[24] A couple of years later these volumes was translated to English and published in one volume as *Public Economics*, North Holland. It was also translated to other languages and has been used as a textbook at many universities.

[25] Trygve Haavelmo (1911–1999), Cand. oecon. 1933, Dr. Phil. 1946, Professor 1948–1979, Nobels Memorial Prize in Economics 1989.

article were incorporated into many textbooks of macroeconomics and public finance. Haavelmo's lectures were attended not only by his students, but also by several graduate candidates, who were granted leave by their employers to attend his lectures, and by the staff of the institute. Several of his lectures were prepared and published based on notes taken by some of his students. Here we draw attention to two of these. Based on notes from his lectures in the autumn semester 1953 and spring semester 1954 Bjørn Thalberg, published the memorandum *Investeringsteori* (Investment Theory) in 1955. Haavelmo lectured on many subjects, in which Keynes' theories were discussed, e.g., the series of lectures of 1977 which his student Jens Chr. Andvig took notes and published as *Den Keynesianske Revolutionen* (The Keynesian Revolution) in 1979.

10.7 The Planned Economy and Keynesian Economics 1945–1980

10.7.1 Was Keynes Forgotten?

When the Labor Party, with John Nygaardsvold as prime minister, formed the government after the 1935 Parliament election, they could have put the crisis plan with Keynesian policies into effect (Eriksen & Sæther, 2010, 7). However, this did not happen. Colbjørnsen was seen as a theorist, and maybe some even questioned his loyalty because of his years in Soviet service, he therefore did not get an appointment in the government. Frisch was also seen as a theorist and an unpractical politician. His proposals were unrealistic, and he tended to 'shoot pigeons with cannons,' as it was said. The new government pursued a contractive fiscal policy in those "years of neglected possibilities" (Vogt, 1961, 29). However, the business cycle turned in 1935, partly because of the rearmament in Germany, and the economic situation gradually improved towards the outbreak of World War II.

10.7.2 The Oslo School and Keynesianism

Both Colbjørnsen and Frisch were disappointed. Colbjørnsen moved away from Keynesian policies and advocated "industrial socialism." Frisch concentrated on his research and the new study program at the University of Oslo, whose first graduates completed their studies in 1939. He became increasingly skeptical of a market economy and advocated more and more a centrally planned economy. World War II, with the Norwegian government in exile in London, gave the proponents of such a planned economy breathing space to develop the institutional, judicial, and economic system necessary for such an economy.

In the first post-war election in 1945 the Labor Party won a majority. Its politicians wanted to change the economic system into a planned economy. Frisch, together with Trygve Haavelmo and Leif Johansen and the candidates that had graduated from the new study program, participated in the development of what has been called the Oslo School, emphasizing the use of econometrics and mathematical models, development of national accounts, the use of macroeconomic planning models, and detailed state governance. For the next three decades this school dominated economic policy in Norway, where market forces to a large extant had been substituted with administrative decisions (Eriksen & Sæther, 2010, 7).

Some economists have called the policies pursued in Norway until the end of the 1970s "Keynesian." This is true in the sense that mathematical models called Keynesian were used as curriculum for the students of economics. However, it is an open question if these models and the policies that were carried out using these models were really Keynesian. It is enough to recall that Thalberg (1959/1969, 1) had emphasized that Keynes theory built on perfect competition, and the policies of the Oslo School largely had eliminated competition in many markets.

10.7.3 The Downfall of the Oslo School and the Collapse of the Planned Economy

In the first three decades after the war there was no challenge to the Oslo School and its strong emphasis on economic planning and detailed state governance of economic life. This changed in the second half of the 1970s when it was challenged because of the poor performance of the economy. Most Norwegian historians and economic historians have claimed that the growth in the Norwegian economy in the first 30 years after the war was average compared with the other OECD countries. This is correct. However, to achieve this result the investment ratio in Norway was substantially higher. Consequently, growth in private[26] and public consumption[27] was substantially lower.

In the second half of the 1970s it became clear that the Oslo School's economic planning policies was not able to ensure competitiveness and growth of the Norwegian economy (ibid., 9). A government-appointed committee concluded in its report of 1979 that a decentralized market economic system would be better able to tackle the challenges than a centralized economic planning system.[28] According to the historian Harald Espeli (1992, 191), the proposals from this committee were "the official Norwegian version of the ideological reorientation to the market." The

[26] I have an example myself. As a first-year student in 1963, a friend and I drove to Hamburg where we bought two used Volkswagen cars. We drove these back to Oslo and sold them at a profit. Today Norway sells used cars to the poorest countries in Europe.

[27] Several hundred Norwegians went abroad to study because there were no study places for them at home.

[28] NOU 1979:35 Structural Problems and Growth Potential in Norwegian Manufacturing Industries.

proposals were controversial, and it took more than a year before the government responded that there was "broad agreement that our country should essentially be based on a decentralized market economy as a system. At the same time, there was agreement that the market economy must be regulated through framework conditions, i.e., laws, regulations, taxes and fees, etc."[29] In its response, the government broke with the strategies that had been the basis for the work in the ministries for more than 30 years. Thus, during the 1980s the elaborate system of detailed economic planning and control policies developed by the Oslo School came to an end. Today only the use of mathematical models, econometrics, and national accounts is left.

If Norwegian economists and politicians often refer to the period of the planned economy as Keynesian, this can be questioned. It is an open question, how Keynes would have reacted to the work carried out at the so-called "Iron Triangle," i.e., the Economic Institute, Statistics Norway, and the Ministry of Finance, which tried to construct a model for the entire Norwegian economy.

10.7.4 The Teaching of Economics After the Oslo School's Downfall

When the Norwegian planned economy was dismantled in the eighties, and an economy based on free markets was gradually introduced, the nature of teaching in economic theory, and especially macroeconomic theory, also changed. The one-sided emphasis on mathematical models was gradually discontinued.

In the 1980s, there was a general trend in the teaching of macroeconomics to reduce the use of mathematics. This was partly due to the fact that knowledge of mathematics was not emphasized to the same degree as earlier at some of the new business schools. Another reason was the common use of textbooks in English and a substantial increase in available textbooks in economics in this language. However, important and pedagogically eminent textbooks in economics have been published in Norwegian, to mention the most relevant: Dedekam jr. A (2004/1993), Steigum E (2018/2004), Steigum E and H-M Straume (2022), Holden S (2021/2016). All these books present Keynes and Keynesian theories, together with Neo-Keynesian economic models.

There can be no doubt that the teaching of economics at Norwegian universities and business schools after World War II had Keynes and Keynesian models as cornerstones of macroeconomics. The extent to which this has been reflected in the policies that have been pursued is another matter.

[29] St.meld. nr. 54, 1980–1981 *Industripolitiske retningslinjer for de nærmeste årene framover* (Industrial policy guidelines for the coming years).

10.8 The Long Way Back to the Market

10.8.1 A Reintroduced Market Caused a Crisis

The expiration of governmental control of the economy and the formal termination of the control system for the financial markets was called the "freedom release" in the Norwegian economy. As a consequence of financial deregulation, there was a significant expansion of the banking system, which led to a rapid increase in loan growth. Parallel with increasing production and export of oil and gas Norwegian banks became engaged in international financial centers and risky credit operations. However, bankers had no experience with competitive credit markets, and as both public and private institutions began to consolidate their books, a recession began.

Between 1988 and 1990, the crisis intensified as smaller banks succumbed to failure. This created a credit freeze between the banks and an increase in lending rates. At first smaller banks went bankrupt. Credit began to freeze between banks as the lending rate began to rise. There was a shortage of capital, and several banks were threatened with bankruptcy. The government intervened and most banks in danger were saved through mergers with solvent banks. By 1992 Norway made its currency floating and allowed for interest rates to fall. In the next few years production and employment began to rise. Loan defaults abated, banks were able to consolidate, but eventually the country's largest banks could not survive without the support of the guarantee funds.

10.8.2 Were the Economic Policies of Norway Keynesian?

In the summer of 1997, there was a debate in the Oslo newspaper *Dagens Næringsliv*. The question was whether the economic policy that Norway had followed since World War II was Keynesian or not. The debate was sparked by an interview with the then Minister of Finance Jens Stoltenberg[30] of the Labor Party. It was not just a debate among scholars about economic history. It had general relevance because history was also used by politicians to justify their policy.

In the interview,[31] Stoltenberg proclaimed that "We believe in Keynes." The good times don't come by themselves, but the Labor Party has made an important contribution. The interviewer asked whether Keynes wasn't a bit old and out of date now. "No, Keynes has written and said a lot, and not everything is as precise, which is why professing to be a Keynesian can mean a lot of different things. But the main message often associated with Keynes is that government budgets should be used to smooth out fluctuations in the economy. Keynes was often rightly and wrongly

[30] Later Stoltenberg became Secretary General of NATO.

[31] Dagens Nyheter 26.061997.

perceived as the one who formulated cyclical and counter-cyclical policies – and I believe that Norway has practiced that the last years."

In the debate that followed,[32] the economic historian Einar Lie maintained that the Labor Party had pursued a Keynesian pro-cyclical policy throughout the post-war period, but that it was not particularly successful. Tore Jørgen Hanisch and Espen Søilen believed that post-war policy was based on a regulatory mindset, while monetary policy did not work because of the politically controlled low interest rate. It was only after the planned economy had been abolished that in the 1990s a Keynesian counter-cyclical policy was successful.

10.8.3 The Financial Crisis, Corona and Keynes' Comeback

After the bankruptcy of Lehman Brothers on 15 September 2008, much of the trust between banks disappeared and the international financial market collapsed.

International stock markets, including the Norwegian one, also fell sharply. With strong government finances due to high oil revenues, Norway was nevertheless less affected by the crisis than other countries. The Bank of Norway was quick to provide liquidity in the money market and other measures of relief. The financial crisis revealed significant shortcomings in the system that was supposed to regulate and supervise the financial system.

In Norway, as in many other countries Keynes' teachings were once again put on the agenda, often formulated as "Keynes' comeback" by economists and the daily press. In 2009, Finance Minister Kristin Halvorsen[33] referred to Keynes when she was explaining how the government was trying to clean up after the financial crisis. It is not known whether this was what led to Keynes' *The General Theory* being translated into Norwegian in 2011. However, it is the first time that this major economic work has been translated.

The outbreak of the contagious disease COVID-19 and the pandemic that took off in the winter of 2019 and 2020 led to economic closedown in many countries, bringing with it a severe setback for the Norwegian economy. A partial shutdown of society and reduced demand from both home and abroad led to a significant downturn in economic activity and historically high unemployment in the spring of that year. The decline was exacerbated by a drop in oil prices. Numerous policies were introduced by the government and the Bank of Norway in order to support businesses and workers and mitigate at least some of the negative economic impacts from the pandemic and lockdowns.

---

[32] Tore Jørgen Hanisch (1945–2006) was Professor of Economic History at University of Agder Einar Lie (1965-) is Professor of Economic History at University of Oslo. Espen Søilen (1963-) was Associate Professor of Economics at the Norwegian School of Economics in Bergen.

[33] Kristin Halvorsen (1960-) was a politician and member of parliament. Minister of Finance 2005–2009. Minister of Education 2009–2013. She is today Director at Cicero Center for Climate Research.

Marie Berg Reinertsen[34] (2021) writes in her book *John Maynard Keynes De politiske konsekvensene* (John Maynard Keynes—the political consequences), that the Corona crisis and the economic crisis packages that followed have once again brought to the fore the ideas of John Maynard Keynes. He is attributed enormous influence, while there is almost always something crippled about the actual solutions that are designed in his name.

During the banking crisis 1987–1992, the financial crisis 2008–2011, and the Corona crisis 2019–2022 Keynesian economics played a significant role. Many Norwegian economists believe that John Maynard Keynes will continue to play an important role in economic theory and policy.

References

Andvig, J. C. (1979). *Den Keynesianske Revolusjonen (The Keynesian Revolution)*. Memorandum Institute of Economics, University of Oslo.

Berg, T., & Hanisch, T. J. (1984). *Vitenskap og Politikk. Linjer i norsk sosialøkonomi gjennom 150 år (Science and Politics. Trends in Norwegian political economics through 150 years)*. Aschehoug Co.

Bjerkholt, O. (2018). *Ragnar Frisch (1895–1973), Memorandum, No. 08/2018*. Institute of Economics, University of Oslo.

Dedekam, J. A. (2004/1993). *Makroøkonomi i Samfunnsøkonomi og økonomisk politikk (Macroeconomics in economics and economic policy)*. Fagbokforlaget Vigmostad og Bjørke.

Eriksen, I. E., & Sæther, A. (2010). Keynesian economics and the Oslo school. *Nordic Journal of Political Economy, 36*, 2–17.

Espeli, H. (1992). *Industripolitikk på avveie. Motkonjunkturpolitikken og Norges Industriforbunds Rolle 1975–1980 (The counter-cyclical policy and the role of the Norwegian Confederation of Industry 1975–1980)*. Ad Notum, Gyldendal.

Frisch, R. (1932). *Sparing og Circulasjon regulering (Savings and circulation regulations)*. Fabritius.

Frisch, R. (1947). *Noen trekk av konjunkturlæren (Some elements of the business cycle theory)*. Aschehoug & Co.

Frisch, R. (1965). *Politikk i pakt med fremtiden (Politics in agreement with the future)*. A/L Orientering.

Haavelmo, T. (1944). Multiplier effects of a balanced budget. *Econometrica, 13*(4), 311–318. Reprinted in *Readings in fiscal policy*, published by the American Economic Association 1955.

Hession, C. H. (1984). *John Maynard Keynes. A personal biography of the man who revolutionized capitalism and the way we live*. Macmillan Publishing Company.

Holden, S. (2021/2016). *Makroøkonomi (Macroeconomics)*. Cappelen Damm Akademiske.

Johansen, L. (1962). *Offentlig økonomikk Del 1 (Public economics part 1)*. University Press.

Jonung, L. (2022). Why was Keynes not awarded the Nobel peace prize after writing the economic consequences of the peace? *The Scandinavian Journal of Economics, 124*(2), 396–419.

Keilhau, W. (1938). John Maynard Keynes. In *Statsøkonomisk Tidsskrift. Årgang 52* (pp. 81–98).

Keynes, J. M. (1922). *A revision of the treaty*. Macmillan and Co., Limited.

Keynes, J. M. (1930). *A treatise on money. Two volumes. I. The pure theory of money. II. The applied theory of money*. Macmillan and Co., Limited.

[34] Marie Berg Reinertsen (1980-) is an economist in Oslo newspaper *Morgenbladet*.

Keynes, J. M. (1936). *The general theory of employment interest and money*. Harcourt, Brace and Company.

Munthe, P. (1995). Ragnar Frisch, Ole Colbjørnsen og Arbeiderpartiets kriseplaner (Frisch, Colbjørnsenat the labour partys crises plans). *Norsk økonomisk tidsskrift, 109*, 275–302.

Munthe, P. (1999). *Populister og originale økonomer. (Populists and original economists)*. Tano-Aschehoug.

Nordvik, H. W. (1977). *Krisepolitikken og den teoretiske nyorienteringen av den økonomiske politikken i1930 årene (Crisis politics and the theoretical reorientation of economic policy in the 1930s)*. Historisk Tidsskrift.

Petersen, E. (1938). Diskusjonen om Keynes' "the general theory of employment interest and money" (The discussion about Keynes' the general theory). In *Statsøkonomisk Tidsskrift. Årgang 52* (pp. 99–115).

Petersen, E. (1948b). *Hovedtrekkene i Keynes´ «general theory» (the Main features in Keynes' «general theory»). Part 1*. Næringsøkonomisk Forskningsinstitutt.

Reinertsen, M. B. (2021). *John Maynard Keynes De politiske konsekvensene (John Maynard Keynes the political consequences)*. Cappelen Damm.

Sæther, A., & Eriksen, I. (2014). The entrepreneur—A lost actor that should resurrect. Proceedings of the 3rd international conference on management and economics, ICME. University of Ruhuna, Sri Lanka, pp. 11–32.

Skidelsky, R. (1983). *John Maynard Keynes. Hopes betrayed 1883–1920*. Macmillan.

Steigum, E. (2018/2004). *Moderne Makroøkonomi (Modern macroeconomics)*. Gyldendal Forlag.

Steigum, E., & Straume, H.-M. (2022). *Innføring i moderne makroøkonomi (introduction to modern macroeconomics)*. Gyldendal Forlag.

Thalberg, B. (1955). *Investeringsteori (Investment theory), based on notes from professor Haavelmo's lectures in the fall semester of 1953 and the spring semester of 1954*. Institute of Economics, University of Oslo.

Thalberg, B. (1959/1969). *En analytisk presisering av Keynes' general theory. (An analytical precision of Keynes' general theory)*. Memorandum Institute of Economics, University of Oslo. Reprinted by the University Press.

Vogt, J. (1961). *Kristiania Hypothek- og Realkreditbank 1886–1961*. Nasjonaltrykkeriet.

Chapter 11
Hans Wolfgang Singer: Thoughts on a Keynesian World Economist During the Period of German Post-War Reconstruction

Hans A. Frambach

11.1 Introduction

Born in Elberfeld, Hans Wolfgang Singer studied economics under Joseph Schumpeter and Arthur Spiethoff in Bonn, among others, and took up a position as a research assistant with the latter after graduating in 1931. After the Nazis seized power in 1933, Singer emigrated to England via Turkey, where Schumpeter helped him to obtain a two-year postgraduate scholarship at King's College, Cambridge University in England. This enabled him to complete his dissertation on *Materials for the Study of Urban Ground Rent* in John Maynard Keynes' environment, which he had begun in Germany, in November 1936. Singer is the fourth doctoral student in the Faculty of Economics at Cambridge University. Singer's time at Cambridge, where Keynes worked on the *General Theory*, was just as formative for him as Keynes' basic attitude of protecting people from hardship and misery. On Keynes' recommendation, Singer was involved in a pioneering study on unemployment in Great Britain commissioned by the Pilgrim Trust, which was largely supervised by William Beveridge. The report on the study, written by Hans Singer, Walter Oakesthott, and David Owen, was published in 1938 under the title *Men without Work. A Report made to the Pilgrim Trust* (Cambridge University Press). From material not used in the report, Singer published the book *Unemployment and the Unemployed* in 1940. During the war, Singer worked as a lecturer at the University of Manchester, after the end of the war also briefly at the Ministry of Town and Country Planning and then at the University of Glasgow.

Hans Singer was a great admirer of William Beveridge, who, like Keynes, was interested in people living on the edge of subsistence. Singer closely followed the

H. A. Frambach (✉)
Faculty of Economics, University of Wuppertal, Wuppertal, Nordrhein-Westfalen, Germany
e-mail: frambach@wiwi.uni-wuppertal.de

J. G. Backhaus et al. (eds.), *Post-war Keynesianism in Germany and Western Europe*, The European Heritage in Economics and the Social Sciences 28,
https://doi.org/10.1007/978-3-032-00498-7_11

development of Beveridge's *Social Insurance and Allied Services* (New York: Macmillan 1942) and in 1943 wrote his famous essay on the necessity and financial viability of this new social system, the "Beveridge Plan," *Can We Afford 'Beveridge'*? By focusing on the problems of the unemployed and socially disadvantaged, Singer turns his attention to the economically less developed countries, to which, he criticizes, economic theory has paid little attention. He begins to trace the causes of the increasingly unequal distribution of world income. In 1947, Singer accepted the offer to support David Owen in setting up the Department of Economic and Social Affairs of the newly founded United Nations. Here in New York, he began an unprecedented career in which he would play a leading role in representing the UN in many of its organizations. During most of his time in New York, Singer continues to teach as a visiting professor at the New York School for Social Research on the problems of international trade. In 1969, Hans Singer left the UN and moved to England to the Institute of Development Studies (IDS) at the University of Sussex in Brighton. Even after his retirement in 1985, Singer would remain associated with the IDS throughout his life.

During the war, Hans Singer observed economic events in Germany in particular. He publishes 12 articles on the German war economy solely in the Economic Journal edited by Keynes and further articles in other scientific journals on the topics of German war financing and rationing practices. After the war, he will no longer be concerned with Germany. However, in the spirit of Singer, this contribution examines the attempt made in post-war Germany to establish the Beveridge Plan as an alternative system of social security to the existing Bismarckian system. Even if the attempt ultimately failed, the approach is remarkable, as it can be described as Keynesian in that it is based on Keynesian values and Keynesian economic policy and clearly differentiates itself from a classic or neoclassical full employment policy. Thus, an economic policy that actively intervenes in the economic process, distributive justice, and public debt are called for as a means of increasing welfare, whereby ideas such as those developed in Singer's early work on unemployment and later in the Beveridge Report come into play as a deeper foundation.

However, it was not only in England itself that the implementation of the Beveridge Plan proved to be difficult. In Germany, particular difficulties arose, which can be explained not only by the persistence and survival will of the institutions and organizations of the existing social insurance system, but also by the vehement resistance of professions representing particular interests, which succeeded not least in mobilizing political forces. Ultimately, it was not possible to replace the traditional German social insurance system in Germany with the Beveridge system. Nevertheless, elements of the Beveridge system found their way into the German insurance system via concepts such as the "social plan" (Sozialplan), just as Keynesian economic policy was to accompany the golden years of the social market economy. Keywords are the guarantee and expansion of social security on the basis of an efficient economy, the ideal of full employment policy, to be achieved through active state demand and credit policy.

Hans Singer was not involved in German reconstruction, his focus was on the developing countries. However, the path taken in Germany to introduce the

Beveridge system in particular and a Keynesian economic policy in general is in line with Singer's findings and convictions.

11.2 Biographical and Stages of Scientific Orientation

Sir Hans Wolfgang Singer was born on 29 November 1910 in Elberfeld and died on 26 February 2006 in Brighton. The family, whose father Heinrich was a doctor and pharmacist, lived at what was then Bahnstraße 15 (today: Hoeftstraße 15). Hans Singer graduated from the Humanist Grammar School in Elberfeld (now Wilhelm-Dörpfeld-Gymnasium) in 1929 and, at his father's insistence, began studying medicine at the University of Bonn. He becomes a member of the Socialist Student Association. As early as the second semester, inspired by advice from fellow students about Joseph A. Schumpeter's lectures in particular, he switches to studying economics, which he completes in 1931 with a diploma. He then took up a position as an assistant to Arthur Spiethoff (1873–1957) with the intention of writing his doctoral thesis on urban housing construction and land prices (Shaw, 2002, pp. 6–8; Röder & Strauss, 1999, p. 704).

The climate changed when the Nazis came to power in 1933. Singer's father Heinrich, who had been wounded in World War I, was denounced by a Hitler youth who claimed that he had touched children indecently during a school medical examination. In a dubious court case that took place in Elberfeld from 18–20 July, the father, who had a heart disease, was sentenced to 18 months in prison and died in Münster prison on 17 December 1933 (Gedenkbuch für die NS-Opfer aus Wuppertal). The mother Antonia, born in 1889, survived the Nazi era and died in New York in 1949 (she had lived there in the household of Hans, his wife Ilse Lina and their two sons Ernest and Stephen in the district of Queens) (Prauss, 2011, p. 22; Röder & Strauss, 1999, p. 704).

In the summer of 1933, Hans Singer emigrated to Turkey via Switzerland. He wanted to complete his doctoral thesis at the University of Istanbul as a research assistant to Wilhelm Röpke (Hagemann, 2016, p. 143f.). On 24 October 1933, Singer wrote to Schumpeter from Elberfeld, Weststraße 6, asking him to support his emigration to the USA. Schumpeter arranges a two-year postgraduate scholarship at King's College, Cambridge University, which enables him to continue the dissertation he had begun in Germany. Singer leaves Turkey in March 1934. The journey to Cambridge takes him via Germany. He married his fiancée Ilse Lina Praut in Hildesheim on 24 March 1934. The marriage lasted a lifetime, 67 years, until Ilse Lina's death on 13 March 2001.

Hans Singer received his doctorate on 13 November 1936 with the topic: "Materials for the Study of Urban Ground Rent"; he was the fourth doctoral candidate in the Faculty of Economics at Cambridge University. The thesis was largely supervised by Colin Clark (Singer, 1992, p. 6), for whom Keynes had obtained a position as a lecturer in statistics at the University of Cambridge. In Cambridge, Singer is introduced to the Keynesian way of thinking, as it is the time when the

General Theory and the accompanying discussions and seminars are being developed. When he later asked himself what he, Singer, had actually learnt from Keynes, he replied: "Everything!" (Singer, 1992, p. 6). However, he explains more precisely that, in addition to the central Keynesian terms and concepts, it was the "Keynesian values" that impressed him, namely human resources as the true resources of a country and that the task of economic analysis is precisely to protect these from waste and dissipation, which automatically focuses attention on poverty and unemployment. Singer's interest in the problems of "depressed areas," which has always been there anyway, is reinforced by Keynesian values (Singer, 1992, p. 6f.).

In line with this interest, Singer, immediately following his dissertation, was included in the pioneering study on unemployment in Britain commissioned by the Pilgrim Trust on the recommendation of Keynes. This was a study of unemployment in Britain, initiated by William Temple, Archbishop of York and later Archbishop of Canterbury, and supervised by William Beveridge as principal adviser. The study was undertaken from 1936–1938. It primarily analyses the social effects of unemployment and the consequences of long-term unemployment in particular on those affected. The aims of the study are to analyze 1. the effects of unemployment on the ordinary men and 2. to gain insight into the minds and feelings of those affected, in addition to collecting statistical information (Singer et al., 1938, p. 3). The members of the team live temporarily with poor families in the regions studied in order to get a first-hand feel for the problems (Jolly, 2006a, b, p. 148).

The experience gained from this study had a strong influence on Hans Singer's further scientific career (Shaw, 2002, p. 20f.). In the introduction to the report on the project, which appeared under the title *Men without Work* in 1938 and was written by Hans Singer, Walter Oakeshott, and David Owen, William Temple mentions the involvement of the psychologist Dr. Wagner in the study (Temple, 1938, ix f.). Ludwig Wagner (1900–1963) was one of the initiators of the study *Die Arbeitslosen von Marienthal* (The Unemployed of Marienthal), which was carried out by Marie Jahoda, Paul Felix Lazarsfeld, and Hans Zeisel. Wagner, a close friend and political campaigner of the Austrian social democrat Lazarsfeld (1901–1976), was the husband of Gertrude Wagner (1907–1992), who was a full-time employee of the "Austrian Economic Psychology Research Centre" from the very beginning and was thus part of the research team around Jahoda, Lazarsfeld, and Zeisel (Müller, 2012). Oakeshott was a master at Winchester College, and Owen secretary of the Civics Section of Political and Economic Planning, both of whom were released from their duties for the project.

Singer was interned at the beginning of the war, but was released after just six weeks following personal intervention by Keynes and Archbishop Temple. He worked as a lecturer at the University of Manchester, after the end of the war also briefly in the Ministry of Town and Country Planning and then at the University of Glasgow (Jolly, 2006a, b, p. 148). Following the Pilgrim Trust Unemployment Enquiry of 1938 and material collected there but not used in the report, Singer wrote the book *Unemployment and the Unemployed* in 1940. He contradicts, among other things, the then widespread idea of a fixed number of jobs that people simply had to take and instead emphasizes the importance of matching people and jobs and the need for technological change (Singer, 1940, pp. 3–13). There is also no such thing as *the* "unemployed man," rather only "unemployed men" (Singer, 1940, p. 59).

> (…) it is better to think of unemployment as an indication that the jobs available for the people, and the people available for the jobs, do not fit in with each other. It is not sufficient that the jobs should be there and that the people should be there, but a certain machinery is necessary to bring the jobs and the people together. That machinery is not doing satisfactory work. (Singer, 1940, cit. 13)

Singer speaks of five barriers to matching people and jobs: 1. The distance between job seekers and available jobs, 2. The lack of qualifications, 3. The age of those affected (there are fewer job vacancies for older unemployed people than for younger ones), 4. Gender (low-paid jobs for women and younger jobseekers), and 5. structural change (with a very negative impact on trade in the UK, particularly between the two world wars) (Singer, 1940, pp. 13–19). This perspective represents a clear departure from classical full employment economics and in particular the idea of economic processes always following the same general laws. Although not explicitly mentioned by Singer, the consistency of his view with at least the Keynesian view of the employment problem is almost obvious.

Singer classifies four types of "unemployments" (Singer, 1940, pp. 59–68): the first is a form of temporary unemployment that occurs, for example, when supply chains are interrupted, i.e. a company or industry has to temporarily cease production due to the delayed or non-delivery of raw materials. The second form is more or less a seasonal process, such as the non-employment of ice cream sellers in winter. The third form of unemployment would today be described as the result of structural change. Jobs are lost due to technological progress, since fewer employees are needed or those with different qualifications to those previously employed are wanted. The fourth form of unemployment is of an administrative nature and can be found in the unemployment administration system itself. The problem is more "statistical" than real. For example, the questions are whether recipients of social assistance or benefits should be included in the unemployment figures, from and up to what age those capable of working should be recorded as unemployed and how to proceed in cases where labor market employment (Erwerbsarbeit) is not sufficient to support the family. Singer cites the example of the low-income earner with many children who, regardless of the number of children, receives an individual wage that is below the amount he would receive through the social welfare and unemployment benefit system. Special attention must be paid to this type of unemployment among low-income earners with large families or low-skilled workers who have no prospect of earning enough to support their families.

Through his intensive preoccupation with the problems of poverty and unemployment, Singer also finds direct access to the work on the development of the welfare state. Through the Pilgrim Trust's unemployment project, he became acquainted with Sir William Beveridge, whom he admired and whose work on social insurance, in particular the "Beveridge Plan," i.e. *Social Insurance and Allied Services* (New York: Macmillan 1942) and the 1944 publication *Full Employment in a Free Society* (London: Macmillan). As with Singer, Beveridge's interest is also focused on people who live on the edge of subsistence: The unemployed, the sick, widows, pensioners, large families. Singer studies the Beveridge Plan thoroughly and with the view of economic policy learnt from Keynes. In his 1943 essay on the necessity and financial viability of the new social system presented by Beveridge, *Can We Afford 'Beveridge'?* Singer answers this question with the words "that not only could we afford it, but we could not afford not to afford it" (Singer, 1984a, p. 276; Singer, 1992, p. 7). In the article, Singer analyses the fundamental question with both intellectual rigor and thoughtfulness, "of *how much* improvement we can afford, and at what point does the price of any further improvement begin to be excessive?" (Singer, 1943, p. 237).

With regard to the importance of the financial dimension of government spending, he puts forward four arguments on what he calls the meaninglessness of currency symbols, positions he illustrates using the "cut the money cackle" and "let-us-count-the-cost" schools. Firstly, it is stated that "money is in itself meaningless except as a ticket for goods" (Singer, 1943, p. 238). Money or goods are just as meaningless as a ticket for a concert that has been cancelled. However, the expenditure to be made under the Beveridge Plan is about real goods, not a cancelled event (Singer, 1943, p. 238). Secondly, Singer cites the idea of opportunity costs in the form of the consideration of whether the means for the Beveridge Plan would be better invested elsewhere. It should be borne in mind that "The real costs of what we are enjoying is in the sacrifice of other opportunities for enjoyment" (Singer, 1943, p. 238).

In the context of unemployment and one of the primary objectives of the Beveridge Plan, to mitigate the effects of unemployment and create employment opportunities, it is considered justified to end the cackle about costs (Singer, 1943, p. 239). In other words, when it comes to avoiding mass unemployment in particular, spending doubts should be abandoned in favor of additional employment opportunities. Now, thirdly, on the issue of adherence to the state budget, Singer makes it clear that the state budget is a distributive and not an absorptive body, through which taxes are not imposed on the consumer without the provision of a service in return. In this respect, taxes to finance social expenditure should not be seen as a burden. Singer also considers it absurd to interpret rising national debt as a sign of national bankruptcy. On the contrary, additional debt would make it possible to reduce genuine costs in the form of later social expenditure—a clear plea in favor of implementing the Beveridge reforms, including through higher levels of debt (Singer, 1943, p. 240f.). Finally, fourthly, Singer gives the additional costs of £318 million estimated by Beveridge himself in the report for its implementation. Overall, the total expenditure is calculated at £858 million, whereby the difference includes the actual social expenditure at the 1938 level as well as the price increases and increased pension burdens that have occurred in the meantime (Singer, 1943, p. 243). The relative and not the absolute order of magnitude is decisive for the justification of the financing of the Beveridge Plan:

> To say that the Beveridge Plan will cost £300 millions may be meaningless; but to say that the combined provision for the Beveridge beneficiaries might take 10% of the National Output means that if average working hours per week are 45, each producer works 4½ hours a week in order to provide those benefits. (...) It can be seen that while absolute money amounts matter very little, the relations of money amounts matter a good deal, and it is in such terms that we shall conduct our actual enquiry as to whether the Beveridge Plan can be afforded. (Singer, 1943, p. 241)

As already mentioned, Beveridge had estimated the total expenditure of his plan, if fully realized, at £885 million. This included expenditure on what was conceivable in the social field at the time: "from family allowances to funeral grants and touching the life of almost everyone 'from the cradle to the grave,'" whereby family allowances were a novelty that Beveridge was required to integrate; the projections were based on an unemployment rate of 10% (Singer, 1943, pp. 242, 244). Based on figures from the pre-war year 1938 and a national income of £5000 million, Beveridge assumed a 25% increase by the time the war was over and thus around £6250 million. Singer put the £318 million in additional expenditure in relation to the estimated national product. He compared the resulting 5% with, among other things, the approximate increase in national product of 4%, which was achieved by reducing the average unemployment rate in the years 1919–1939 from 14 to 10% (10% is assumed in the Beveridge Plan) (Singer, 1943, p. 246f).

Men without work and *Unemployment and the Unemployed* are Singer's central contributions on the topics of depressed areas and unemployment and, like his contribution on the Beveridge Plan, they reflect the "typical Keynesian" approach. In general, Singer, like Keynes and Beveridge, recognizes the social problems and in particular unemployment with its negative effects on people as the main challenges facing societies and therefore also the central subject area with which economic theory and politics should be concerned. For Hans Singer, at any rate, these major social challenges were the reason for his intensive study of the problems of development planning, and can be seen as the basis for his later work on developing countries (Singer, 1984a, p. 277; Singer, 1992, p. 7).

Concretely, Singer criticizes the prevailing economic research and theory for hardly having addressed what he sees as the world's biggest economic problems, those of the developing countries, as the economic theories are too national in their approaches and, moreover, mostly argue from the perspective of large industrialized countries and a short-term view. The short-term view in particular would be expressed in Keynes' frequently quoted statement "In the long run we are all dead," and would have a special significance in regard to underdeveloped countries and peoples, as the short-term problems of industrialized countries, mostly economic stability, would not have the highest urgency for developing countries (Singer, 1949, p. 1). Due to the economists' preoccupation with mostly national data and problems, which tend to treat the (for developing countries so important) problems of foreign trade and foreign trade relations as secondary, a general trend towards rising per capita incomes and a more even distribution of income, as Hans Singer already noted at the end of the 1940s, had been established, but the argumentation was not very convincing. While a shrinking proportion of the world's population has rapidly increased its standard of living, the standard of living of a growing majority of the world's population has risen much more slowly or even remained constant (Singer, 1949, p. 2).

Singer observes that the increasing inequality of global income is at least partly due to an important structural change in international economic relations, namely the change in the price ratios between primary materials and manufactured goods. He highlights the development of massively falling commodity prices over long periods of time (before the Second World War) as particularly remarkable, while in industrialized countries the prices of industrial goods have remained the same and increased wages and the monetary prices of production factors have been well compensated for by increases in efficiency. In addition, in developing countries the efficiency gains in the production of primary materials were not expressed either by rising standards or higher prices, but by a larger quantity required in exchange for a certain amount of goods produced (Singer, 1949, p. 3). In other words, the conditions for the underdeveloped countries exporting primary materials are deteriorating, while those of the rich industrialized countries are improving. As is well known, this was to become a key issue for Singer and would culminate in the famous Prebisch-Singer thesis.

At the time, when Keynesians were primarily concerned with the short-term fluctuations in commodity prices, Singer's work was controversial. Terms of trade had not developed in favor of manufactured goods as a result of scarcities and rising marginal costs and diminishing marginal returns from technological progress, according to the conventional wisdom (Singer, 1992, p. 11). Singer shows that the exchange ratios between the exports of developing countries (agricultural goods) and those of developed countries (industrial goods) have systematically changed over time to the disadvantage of the former (while prices for agricultural goods remain constant, developing countries have to pay relatively more and more for industrial goods from developed countries) (Singer, 1950, pp. 269–274; Singer, 2018, p. 13565):

> The industrialized countries have had the best of both worlds, both as consumers of primary commodities and as producers of manufactured articles, whereas the underdeveloped countries had the worst of both worlds, as consumers of manufactures and as producers of raw materials. (Singer, 1950, p. 272)

Independently of Singer, the Latin American economist Raúl Prebisch (1901–1986) had made similar discoveries. The Singer-Prebisch thesis emerged, which established a structural tendency towards a decline in the terms of trade for developing countries (Singer, 2018, p. 13562). From this, a policy was derived (at least for data up to the beginning of the Second World War) to support developing countries in building up their own industry and to prevent the import of industrial goods from developed countries with the help of protective tariffs ("import-substituting industrialization"—ISI) (Schiller, 2004; Singer, 2018, p. 13565). Among other things, Singer warns against handling the development of poorer countries through a policy of increasing effective demand, as this was developed for industrialized countries and not for underdeveloped countries. Accepting inflation if production increases are achieved through a shift from consumption to investment would place a far greater burden on poorer countries than on rich ones (Singer, 1949, p. 9f.). Later, Singer also criticized governments in developing countries, which often promise increased consumption and economic development at the same time. In contrast to industrialized countries, an economic recovery would only be possible after an increased production capacity had been achieved, i.e. consumption must be restricted at the beginning of development so that investments can be made. In addition, national economists working for government agencies in the national or international arena often overestimate the importance of public programs and measures and tend to underestimate private sector factors and forces (Jöhr & Singer, 1969, pp. 53, 56).

11.3 Embedding the Footprint and Scientific Career

In 1947, Hans Singer accepted an invitation from David Owen, his former colleague in the Pilgrim Trust's investigation into unemployment, who was now head of the Department of Economic and Social Affairs at the newly founded United Nations. In New York, Singer is to support him in setting up the new department. An initial two-year agreement turns into 22 years, during which he represents the UN in many of its organizations such as the UN Department of Economic and Social Affairs, the UN Industrial Development Organization, the UN International Children's Emergency Fund, the UN World Food Programme, the UN Economic Commission for Africa, the International Labor Organization, and the Asian Development Bank (Jolly, 2006a, b, p. 149). In addition to this main activity, Singer also taught for years as a visiting professor at the New York School for Social Research at the invitation of Alvin S. Johnson, its president and co-founder. His activities and teaching in New York centered on international trade problems.

In 1969 Hans Singer left the UN to become a Professorial Fellow at the Institute of Development Studies (IDS) at the University of Sussex in Brighton, founded in 1966, and was appointed full professor in 1975 (Hagemann, 2016, p. 145). At the University of Sussex, Marie Jahoda held the Chair of Social Psychology from 1962, until 1958 she was Professor of Social Psychology at the New School for Social Research. Even after his retirement in 1985, Singer would remain associated with the IDS throughout his life, as is impressively demonstrated by the 97 books and reports as well as 61 further reports for the UN and 176 articles he published there (Jolly, 2006b, p. 150). In many of these works, and especially those he carried out for the ILO in the 1960s and 70s, his early findings from the studies on unemployment and its consequences are applied (Singer, 1992, p. 10). The Prebisch-Singer thesis is also adapted several times to the changing circumstances and differentiated more strongly between types of countries than types of goods, and greater importance is attached to technological developments (Jolly, 2006b, p. 151; Singer, 1984a, pp. 283–288). Singer later repeatedly emphasizes that his original economic policy recommendation for import-substituting industrialization was linked to the

Keynesian conviction of constructive government intervention and social welfare planning, which was related to England's economic policy during the war and Beveridge's social plan (Hagemann, 2016, p. 158f.; Singer, 1998, p. 654).

Singer's creative achievements and merits at IDS can hardly be overestimated. Together with Richard Jolly, Singer led the ILO Mission to Kenya in the early 1970s. They published key findings of the mission in 1973 in an essay entitled "Unemployment in an African setting: lessons of the employment strategy mission to Kenya" in the *International Labour Review* 107 (2). In this report, the authors present the main features of the so-called "redistribution from growth" approach. In order to combat the economic problems, the informal sector must be taken into account (Singer & Jolly, 2012, p. 126) and, above all, wages below the subsistence level must be eliminated.

> The report of the mission recommends a major shift in government policies concerning the informal sector – a shift towards active encouragement and support. This would require a new look at health standards, housing standards, licensing policy, access of the sector to loans and technology, policies relating to industrial estates and rural industrialization, government contract policy and specifications, technological research decisions on products appropriate to the Kenyan economy, the development of subcontracting by larger-scale enterprises (specifically including foreign investors) and so on – all of these being relevant to any fundamental re-orientation of existing policies. (Singer & Jolly, 2012, p. 127)

This ILO report outlines the basic framework of a development policy strategy of the alliance of the Sussex IDS, the ILO, and the World Bank and shows how it will develop into the ILO's later "basic needs" approach (Eßlinger, 1999, p. 653).

In his 1998 article "How relevant is Keynesianism today for understanding problems of development," Singer specifies the fundamental ideas of Keynesianism to which he feels committed. He identifies the end of the golden age of Keynesianism with the beginning of rising inflation rates and stagnant growth in the early 1970s (Singer, 1998, p. 104). Singer emphasizes Keynes' own rough and frequently used categorization of labor supply into the "fully employed" and the "fully unemployed" (Singer, 1998, p. 111), and points out that this division is of little use for developing countries, as the lack of social security systems there means that "fully unemployed" is simply synonymous with the deprivation of a livelihood (Singer, 1998, p. 111). Fundamental to Keynes, however, was the concept of disguised unemployment and the idea of self-sustaining dynamic economic growth over time, i.e. development, as expressed in the equilibrium formula of the Harrod Domar model, which is based on Keynes' multiplier concept and the importance of physical investment (capital accumulation), which is the best way to influence a growth rate leading to full employment (Singer, 1998, p. 111).

Singer also agrees with many of Keynes' other views and basic ideas. For example, Keynes' primary concern was not so much how to maintain a state of full employment once it had been achieved, but rather how to reduce unemployment (Singer, 1998, p. 111). The Keynesian principle of effective full employment is paramount, to be achieved through high effective demand and the promotion of public investment. Whatever the cause of economic fluctuations, in the event of economic contractions, savings are higher than investments, so that the state can lead out of these depressive constellations if it finances expenditure with bonds and thus keeps the savings not required by the economy in circulation. And apart from this effect, bond-financed government spending would also have a positive impact on the expectations of entrepreneurs (Jöhr & Singer, 1969, p. 38f.). Much of the neoclassical doctrine cannot be dismissed entirely, but only once full employment has been achieved, because the idea of the market as a welfare-maximizing allocative force would only work under full employment (Singer, 1998, p. 114): "The Keynesian dog should be wagging the neoclassical tail." Under conditions of trade liberalization, privatization, deregulation, and observance of the fiscal and monetary 'fundamentals' "the tail is wagging the dog, with unhappy results for development economics and, more important, for the developing countries" (Singer, 1998, p. 114).

The liberalist view is criticized for its fundamental rejection of any combination of measures that seek to unite the principles of competition and planning. For example, v. Hayek is criticized for his basic attitude that neither of the two principles can really work in a mixed form and that the result achieved must be worse than if one had consistently relied on only one of the two principles. The liberalist view would simply lack the logical reasons to explain the existence of only two coordination systems (market economy and socialism) and the rejection of the possibility of a third system (Jöhr & Singer, 1969, pp. 74f., 177).

11.4 Post-War Keynesianism in Germany?

While Hans Singer published a total of 12 articles on relevant problems and areas of the German war economy during the Second World War only in the Economic Journal and further articles in other journals on the topics of German war financing and rationing practices in the face of goods shortages and inflationary risks in wartime (Hagemann, 2016, p. 150), he would hardly deal with Germany academically after the end of the war. At least there are no more relevant publications. It can also be assumed that the Singer family's personal experiences during the Nazi era have extinguished any interest in Germany. This is how Odile Stamberger, the daughter-in-law of Hans and Ilse Singer, put it to the historian and journalist Christina Prauss (2011, p. 1) in 2009: "Because we completely cut ourselves off from Germany after the war and didn't speak German either."[1]

Hans Singer only returned to his home town of Wuppertal-Elberfeld once in the course of his life. Bernd Biervert, an economist at the University of Wuppertal who died in 1996, had met Singer at a conference in the 1980s and invited him to give a talk at the Faculty of Economics (Schiller, 2004). Bernd Biervert told the author of this contribution about the meeting several times in the early 1990s, about Singer's

[1] "Denn wir haben uns ja von Deutschland nach dem Krieg ganz abgesperrt und auch nicht Deutsch gesprochen." (Prauss, 2011, p. 1)

emotional lecture to students and about visiting the places of his childhood and youth. However, Hans Singer's relationship with the city of Wuppertal always remained a critical one, as various attempts by Singer to rehabilitate his father Heinrich from the accusations made in 1933 failed. Singer expressed his disappointment in several letters from the 1980s to Ulrich Flöhse (1944–2012), a longstanding city councilor, school director and historian who was strongly committed to Singer's project.

> Of course, I still think back a lot to my memorable visit to Wuppertal, which brought me back to my youth and my childhood home. Some of the memories were very painful, especially those of my father's fate, and that is also an area of great disappointment for me.[2] (Singer, 1984b)

> I am very disappointed that not even the slightest gesture was made to liquidate the 'judgement' - after my visit to Wuppertal I would have expected something different.[3] (Singer, 1987a)

> in my opinion, my father's case should not be seen so much as a legal matter (although it is), but as a moral and political issue. I simply cannot imagine that a simple declaration of rehabilitation or declaration of the 'judgement' as 'null and void' could cause any difficulties. It would be a simple distancing from the crimes of the Nazi era.[4] (Singer, 1987b, p. 252)

A political rehabilitation of Heinrich Singer was carried out by the city of Wuppertal in connection with a ceremony to name a street "Hans-Singer-Weg" on 21 August 2024, at which Hans Singer's granddaughters Lucia and Jo Singer also attended.

What can be said about Hans Wolfgang Singer, a student of Schumpeter and Keynes, and postwar Keynesianism in Germany? Well, basically not much in the first instance. However, it becomes interesting to consider that the Beveridge Plan, which is based on Keynesian principles and in whose genesis Singer is also involved, played a decisive role as an option for a new social security system in the context of German reconstruction. First and foremost, the common interest of the three great economists Beveridge, Keynes and Singer should be mentioned, which consists of advocating human capital and the need for social security, especially for the socially disadvantaged. All three are ardent supporters of the idea of the welfare state.

Beveridge, who, as head of a commission of experts, presented his report on the reform of the social security system to the British Parliament in November 1942 and

---

[2] "Ich denke natürlich noch viel an meinen erinnerungsreichen Besuch in Wuppertal zurück, der mir meine Jugend und mein Elternhaus wieder nahegebracht hat. Manche der Erinnerungen waren sehr schmerzlich, vor allem die an das Schicksal meines Vaters und das ist auch der Bereich einer schweren Enttäuschung für mich." (Singer, 1984b)

[3] Ich bin sehr enttäuscht, dass nicht die kleinste Geste auch nur gemacht wurde, das 'Urteil' zu liquidieren – nach meinem Besuch in Wuppertal hätte ich etwas anderes erwartet." (Singer, 1987a)

[4] nach meiner Meinung sollte der Fall meines Vaters nicht so sehr als eine legale Angelegenheit (obwohl es das auch ist), sondern als eine moralische und politische Frage betrachtet werden. Ich kann mir einfach nicht denken, dass eine einfache Rehabilitierungserklärung oder Erklärung des 'Urteils' als 'null und nichtig' irgendwelche Schwierigkeiten bereiten könnte. Er wäre eine einfache Distanzierung von den Verbrechen der Nazi-Zeit." (Singer, 1987b, p. 252)

favored tax-financed basic provision for all, to be supplemented by personal contributions. In Europe, this needs-orientated type of social security system was primarily implemented in the Scandinavian countries alongside the UK. In addition to his well-known theoretical contributions, Keynes had undertaken various initiatives on the international stage after the war, quite independently of the Beveridge Plan, to improve states in social and economic distress, for which he considered the regulation and control of capital movements to be just as necessary as the regulation of foreign investment. He was deeply suspicious of the free play of the financial markets and, according to Singer's testimony, even spoke of the prevalence of a casino mentality there: "He was deeply suspicious of financial markets and the 'casino economies' which dominated them. 'The proper job of finance is to see that nothing is done on purely financial grounds'" (Singer, 1998, p. 107). Keynes' attempts to add to the World Bank and the International Monetary Funds as two UN organizations created as a result of the Bretton Woods Agreement, a third institution, an International Trade Organization (ITO), whose main task would be to stabilize primary commodity prices, failed. In fact, the ITO was duly negotiated and established in Havana in 1947, but never materialized because it was not ratified by the US Congress, and neither the General Agreement on Tariffs and Trade (GATT), concluded in 1947, nor the World Trade Organization (WTO), newly established in 1994, have functions such as Keynes had envisaged for the commodities sector (Singer, 1984a, pp. 279–282; Singer, 1998, p. 107).

Against the background of his in-depth knowledge of Keynesian economic analysis and all the details of the Beveridge Plan, Singer increasingly turned to the practical side of economic policy and in particular to questions of distribution, whereby he also endeavored to counter mainstream economics and its concentration on the problem of allocative efficiency with a stronger orientation towards distributive justice and distributive efficiency, as demonstrated by Alfred Marshall, Richard Henry Tawney and William Beveridge. With Keynes and Beveridge—both of whom were "proponents of active state intervention"—Singer (1984a, p. 277; 1992, p. 8) argues in favor of an active state economic policy as a necessary prerequisite for solving social problems, explicitly including government debt. For Singer, this was nothing other than the logical continuation of his earlier work on unemployment and the welfare state, as well as the reason for a more intensive examination of topics such as securing the basic needs of children and the fate of people in the so-called underdeveloped countries (Singer, 1984a, p. 280f.).

In the 300-page Report on Social Insurance and Allied Services, the aim is to create a comprehensive social security system in which the focus of social legislation is no longer just on workers, but on the population as a whole. The system proposes centralizing all existing social insurance schemes and extending them to all British residents, employed and unemployed, workers and commoners, salaried employees and freelancers, etc. All adults except housewives and pensioners should pay compulsory contributions and receive state social benefits in return—in old age, in the event of unemployment, illness, disability, and also for women in the event of widowhood and maternity (Studer, 2023, p. 8). In Germany, the existing system was based on the contribution-financed system established in the Bismarck era in the last decades of the nineteenth century and linked to (dependent) gainful employment, whose benefits were based on the number and amount of contributions paid in. In addition to Germany, France, and Italy in particular had orientated themselves on this system in Europe. As the Beveridge Plan was being implemented in England itself and ratified in 1948, there were also endeavors to introduce the system in France, Germany had the opportunity to literally join the bandwagon of modern development.

A major criticism of the Beveridge system from the very beginning was its financing. Even in England, the demands for a free healthcare system, the assumption of all child allowances and the adoption of measures to ensure full employment entirely from tax revenues had caused fierce resistance. However, the main reasons that led to the implementation of the Beveridge Plan, at least in England, were the experience of mass unemployment in the wake of the Great Depression at the beginning of the 1930s, which was still fresh in the minds of the population, and the fear of a strengthening of the Soviet-style planned economy and its actual implementation, all the more so as organizations such as the League of Nations (the forerunner of the UN) and the International Labor Organization had also dealt with concepts of central planning in the 1930s. After the years of war economy and shortages, people were looking for ways to lift the spirits of the civilian population through the prospect of a higher standard of living (Studer, 2023, p. 8). And the post-war period was generally expected to be a period of recession and unemployment, just as had been the case after the First World War (Singer, 1984a, p. 281).

In Germany at the time of the Allied occupation (1945–1949), attempts to reorganize the social security system that had been destroyed on the ground proved to be extremely complex. In order to be able to transfer the principles of the Beveridge system, the concept of social security in particular had to be considered anew and comprehensively, as the various forms of previous income security were very heterogeneous. Social security was now differentiated according to the principles of "insurance" (Versicherung), "provision" (Versorgung), and "welfare" (Fürsorge). The "insurance principle" includes compulsory insurance for certain sectors of the economy, a classification of insurance providers according to risk, contribution financing by employees and employers without state subsidies, the independent organization of insurance companies in the form of public corporations with self-administration rights of employers and employees in accordance with their participation in the financing, excluding alternatives under private law, and the legal entitlement to the benefits defined by law in terms of their amount, with the granting of legal recourse. The principle of equivalence of contribution and benefit applies. Under the "provision principle," there is an entitlement to maintenance from public funds, analogous to the principle of civil servants' pensions. Finally, the "welfare principle," as a kind of residual category, covers the facts of the old poor relief, but strips them of their discriminatory character as a matter of official discretion (Kaufmann, 2016, p. 286f.).

The first joint draft of the Control Council (Kontrollrat) of the four occupying powers on the subject of the social insurance system to be established also provided for health, pension, and accident insurance to be combined organizationally and transferred to newly established social insurance institutions at the level of the federal states. There was considerable resistance to this from the German side, as the previous independence of the three branches of insurance would have had to be abolished and at the same time the variety of independent insurance organizations that previously existed within individual branches of insurance would have had to be eliminated, with the consequence, e.g. for the health insurance funds, of the liquidation of all existing different health insurance funds (Betriebs-, Land-, Innungs- und Ersatzkrankenkassen) and their practical transfer to the general local health insurance funds (Allgemeine Ortskrankenkassen) (Hockerts, 1980, p. 26). And this is just one of many aspects of an imminent paradigm shift in the social insurance system. The Social Policy Committee of the Council of the Federal States strictly rejected the abrupt change to a "standardized state insurance system without self-governing bodies."

Even for the trade unions and the Social Democratic Party of Germany (SPD), a potential dismantling of the proven German social security bodies was not readily conceivable. Not to mention the numerous special interests that made themselves heard, from private insurance companies fearing for their existence, to doctors interested in maintaining a private patient base, to organizations representing the self-employed in professional insurance schemes. Even Lord Beveridge had been able to gain an impression of the situation here during a visit to Germany in August 1946 and, in the interests of the German Trade Union Confederation (DGB), had argued in favor of submitting the draft of the Control Council to the Social Policy Committee of the Zonal Advisory Council, on which the various representatives of the German institutions were also represented. In articles in The Times at the end of August 1946, Beveridge expressed his annoyance that there had been no consultation with political leaders or the trade unions during the complete reorganization of the German social security system, parts of which had already been reversed (Hockerts, 1980, p. 35, n. 52).

It was not until the 1950s that the ideas of a social security system modelled on the Beveridge Plan were reintroduced (Babendreyer, 2007, p. 251). An economic and social policy along the lines of the Beveridge model seemed to open up certain prospects for an improved situation, which now used the idea of full employment as a central link. On the one hand, an economic policy aimed at full employment was intended to reduce the number and extent of social emergencies caused by unemployment and, on the other, to increase the contribution and tax revenue available for social security. The view of the nature of social benefits also changed as a result. The fundamental view shifted from seeing social benefits as a burden on the economy to perceiving them as a productive investment in labor potential and an element of consumption that stabilizes the economy. It almost seems as if the lesson learnt in the Weimar Republic about the absurdity of a social policy detached from economic policy has now been incorporated into the program in line with the Beveridge Plan (Hockerts, 1980, p. 224).

With the Beveridge Plan in Germany focusing on health, occupational, and economic security, including a "humane minimum security" for dependent workers in old age, a basic pension for the self-employed and a supplementary old-age pension for farmers (Auerbach et al., 1957, p. 89, see also 25f.), an aim emerged that met with cross-party agreement. In particular, the proposal for a tax-financed minimum pension for all citizens was also very well received by the trade unions and communists. The SPD attempted to launch a major reform program under the headings of "social plan" (Sozialplan) and "social reform" (Sozialreform) on a non-partisan basis. The project was modelled on the Beveridge Plan with the idea of integrating the changes as far as possible into the existing institutions and traditions in Germany, particularly in a state healthcare system and a "flat rate pension" for the entire population. However, after this attempt failed, the focus in the early 1950s was on developing an independent concept, which was called a "social plan" (Sozialplan) (Hockerts, 1980, p. 220f.).

The chief planner of the social plan was Walter Auerbach (1905–1975), the "grey eminence of social democratic social policy" (Hockerts, 1980, p. 222, n. 21), who was involved in the preparation of the Beveridge Plan during his exile in London as an adviser to the British Transport Workers' Union, but was not a member of the Beveridge Commission, although he continued to correspond with Lord Beveridge until 1952 (Babendreyer, 2007, p. 250). Auerbach was one of the pioneers of the modern Social Law Code (Sozialgesetzbuch).[5] He was convinced of the Keynesian economic policy and emphasized in particular the need for a credit policy in order to achieve a consistent economic upturn with the goal of full employment (Babendreyer, 2007, S. 174, p. 255f.). For him, the idea, based on Keynes, was that even different financing from contributions or taxes does not allow for different social-ethical judgements and that the expenditure for the various social benefits should be covered by the national income of the current period (Auerbach et al., 1957, pp. 16, 179).

Even the Christian Democratic Union (CDU), although it had very different ideas about the extent and form of state economic regulation, established a close link between economic and social policy. Its 1953 Hamburg Programme even called for the "expansion of social security" on the "foundation" of an efficient economy, an "active employment policy," and "job creation policy" including retraining measures and the effective expansion of "health care and preventive healthcare" (Babendreyer, 2007, p. 271; Hamburger Programm, 1953, pp. 34f., 40; Hockerts, 1980, p. 224f.). There was agreement between the parties on the establishment of a comprehensive health and rehabilitation service and the maintenance of employment, i.e. the avoidance of mass unemployment, as necessary conditions for the success of social insurance, whereby the SPD had renounced earlier demands for a

[5] After his return from England, Dr Walter Auerbach held the office of Vice President of the Central Labour Office of the British Occupation Zone in Lemgo from 1946 to 1948 and was State Secretary in the Lower Saxony Ministry of Labour and Social Affairs from autumn 1948. From October 1969 until his retirement in April 1971, he worked as State Secretary in the Federal Ministry of Labour and Social Affairs (Independent Historical Commission) and, until his death in 1975, headed the "Expert Commission for the Social Code", which had been set up in the Federal Ministry of Social Affairs to incorporate social law into the new Social Code to be created at the time (Löffler, 1975, p. 247; Röder & Strauss, 1999, S. 24).

connection between social planning and economic planning (Hockerts, 1980, p. 224f., n. 30). The SPD's social plan was now "Keynesianism with a social democratic flavor" (Pirker, 2006, p. 164).

Ultimately, the Bismarckian system was implemented in Germany against the original intention of the Allied occupying powers to install the Beveridge system. The Allies were to refrain from making their own decision and leave this to the first German Bundestag. The CDU/CSU, FDP and DP (German Party) parties formed a governing coalition that was unanimously determined to restore the foundations of traditional German social insurance.

Hans Wolfgang Singer himself no longer played any role at all. His academic training with Keynes and his environment, his early projects on the topics of unemployment and social welfare and finally his involvement with the Beveridge system pushed him in the same academic direction as the development of the social security system in Germany after the war. Although the Beveridge system was not able to establish itself in Germany and other Central European countries, it became the basic model in the Northern European countries. In the meantime, neither system exists in its pure form; instead, a convergence in the country comparison is evident over time. The reasons for this can be seen in the common objectives of both systems in terms of increasing individual security and minimizing social risks, but also in the similarity of the problems faced by the various countries, such as poverty and income inequality (Rohwer, 2008, p. 26f.). However, the ever-increasing discrepancy between rich and poor, the growing numbers of people in need, even beyond the consideration of social security systems, was a lifelong concern of Hans Singer, who would go on to become one of the world's best-known development economists. His life's work has been honored with many awards. He was awarded honorary doctorates by seven universities alone: in 1989 by the University of Santa Fe (Argentina), in 1990 by the University of Sussex, in 1994 by the Technical University of Lisbon and the University of Glasgow, in 1998 by the University of Innsbruck, in 1999 by the University of Kent, and, on the occasion of the 60th anniversary of the assassination of Adolf Hitler on 20 July 2024, by the University of Freiburg, together with Albert O. Hirschmann. On 22 November 1994, he was knighted by Queen Elizabeth II. Hans Wolfgang Singer died in Brighton on 26 February 2006 (Eßlinger, 1999, p. 654; Hagemann, 2016, p. 145f.; Schiller, 2004).

The Faculty of Economics, the Schumpeter School of Business and Economics at the University of Wuppertal, whose invitation Singer accepted in 1983 for his one-time visit to his native city of Wuppertal after his emigration, will remember him as one of the great pioneers of an economic theory and policy for developing countries.

References

Auerbach, W., Bruch, E., Ebert, H., u.a. (1957). *Sozialplan für Deutschland*. J.H.W. Dietz, Berlin, Hannover.

Babendreyer, E. (2007) *Walter Auerbach*. Sozialpolitik aus dem Exil, Univ.-Diss., Duisburg, Essen.
Eßlinger, H. U. (1999). Singer, Hans Wolfgang. In H. Hagemann & C.-D. Krohn (Eds.), *Zur deutschsprachigen wirtschaftswissenschaftlichen Emigration nach 1933* (pp. 650–656). K. G. Saur.
Gedenkbuch für die NS-Opfer aus Wuppertal: In: https://www.gedenkbuch-wuppertal.de/de/person/singer [access 24.03.2024]
Hagemann, H. (2016). Hans Singers two heroes: Der Einfluss von Schumpeter Keynes auf einen Pionier der Entwicklungsökonomik. In H. Hagemann & J. Kromphardt (Eds.), *Keynes, Schumpeter und die Zukunft der entwickelten kapitalistischen Volkswirtschaften* (pp. 139–167). Metropolis.
Hamburger Programm der CDU. (1953). Hamburger Programm 4. Bundesparteitag, 18.-22. April 1953, Hamburg. In: https://www.kas.de/documents/252038/253252/Hamburger+Programm+%28Quelle%29.pdf/f72d77e5-7581-4e80-80cd-652518392fdb?version=1.1&t=1685619797572, pp. 31–44.
Hockerts, H. G. (1980). *Sozialpolitische Entscheidungen im Nachkriegsdeutschland. Alliierte und deutsche Sozialversicherungspolitik 1945 bis 1957*. Klett-Cotta.
Jöhr, W. A., & Singer, H. W. (1969). *Die Nationalökonomie im Dienste der Wirtschaftspolitik*. 3. exp. (German) ed., 1. (Engl.) ed. 1955. Vandenhoeck & Ruprecht, Göttingen.
Jolly, R. (2006a). Obituary. Sir Hans Singer. Economist who saw how terms of trade marginalised the world's poorest people. In: The Guardian, 01.03.2006.
Jolly, R. (2006b). Hans Singer – the gentle giant. *Development, 49*(3), 148–152. [palgrave.development.1100280.pdf (springer.com)]
Kaufmann, F.-X. (2016). *Varianten des Wohlfahrtstaats. Der deutsche Sozialstaat im internationalen Vergleich* (6th ed, 1st ed.). Suhrkamp.
Löffler, S. (1975). Sozialgesetzbuch als "Ei des Columbus"? *Sozialer Fortschritt, 24*(11), 246–247.
Müller, R. (2012). *Die Marienthal-Studie*. https://agso.uni-graz.at/archive/marienthal/studie/00.htm
Pirker, D.-D. (2006). *Die SPD - Eine Partei mit Zukunftschancen? Studienarbeit*. Grin-Verlag.
Prauss, C. (2011). Lady Ilse Singer geborene Plaut aus Hildesheim zu ihrem 100. Geburtstag Ein Blick in ihr Familienalbum. In: https://www.goethegymnasium-hildesheim.de/images/dokumente-PDF/Ilse_Plaut_HiJaBu_2011.pdf
Röder, W., & Strauss, H. A. (Eds.). (1999). Biographisches Handbuch der deutschsprachigen Emigration nach 1933, Bd. 1: Politik, Wirtschaft, Öffentliches Leben, 1. ed. 1980, K. G. Saur München
Rohwer, A. (2008). Bismarck versus Beveridge: Ein Vergleich von Sozialversicherungssystemen in Europa. In *ifo Schnelldienst*. Vol. 21/2008 – 61. Jg., pp. 26–29
Schiller, G. (2004). Weltökonom aus Elberfeld. In *Wuppertaler Unimagazin*, Vol. 29 (Nov/Dec). University of Wuppertal, Wuppertal [https://web.archive.org/web/20080108015410/http:/www.presse.uni-wuppertal.de/html/module/publikationen/magazin_29/singer.htm]
Shaw, D. J. (2002). *Sir Hans Singer. The life and work of a development economist*. Palgrave MacMillan.
Singer, H. W. (1940). *Unemployment and the unemployed*. P. S. King & Son.
Singer, H. W. (1943). Can we afford beveridge?. In *Fabian Research Series*, Vol. 6, Nos. 64–68 (1942-43), 1. and 2. repr. 1972 and 1979 by Kraus-Thomson Organization Ltd., Nendeln/Liechtenstein, pp. 235–256.
Singer, H. W. (1949). Economic progress in underdeveloped countries. *Social Research, 16*(1), 1–11.
Singer, H. W. (1950). The distribution of gains between investing and borrowing countries. In R. Jolly (Ed.), (2012) *Milestones and turning points in development thinking*. Palgrave Macmillan, Houndmills, Basingstoke, Hampshire, pp. 265–277. Orig. in: *The American Economic Review*, 40(2), 473–485.

Singer, H. W. (1984a). The terms of trade controversy and the evolution of soft financing: early years in the U.N. In G. M. Meier & D. Seers (Eds.), *Pioneers in development* (pp. 275–303). Oxford University Press.

Singer, H. W. (1984b) Letter from Hans Singer to Ulrich Föhse, 25. Nov. 1984. Begegnungsstätte Alte Synagoge, Sammlung Föhse, Wuppertal.

Singer, H. W. (1987a). Letter from Hans Singer to Ulrich Föhse, 08. Nov. 1987. Begegnungsstätte Alte Synagoge, Sammlung Föhse, Wuppertal.

Singer, H. W. (1987b). Letter from Hans Singer to Ulrich Föhse, n.d., Dec. 1987. In U. Schrader (Ed.), *Antworten aus der Emigration: Briefe und andere Quellen jüdischer Flüchtlinge aus Wuppertal in der Sammlung Ulrich Föhse* (pp. 250–253). Begegnungsstätte Alte Synagoge.

Singer, H. W. (1992). *The influence of Schumpeter and Keynes: On the development of a development economist. Diskussionsbeiträge aus dem Institut für Volkswirtschaftslehre der Universität Hohenheim Vol. 68/1992*. University of Hohenheim.

Singer, H. W. (1998). How relevant is keynesianism today for understanding problems of development? In S. Sharma (Ed.), *John Maynard Keynes. Keynesianism into the twenty-first century* (pp. 104–115). Edward Elgar.

Singer, H. W. (2018). Terms of trade and economic development. In J. Eatwell, M. Milgate, & P. Newman (Eds.), *The New Palgrave Dictionary of Economics, 1. ed. 1st edition, 1987* (pp. 13562–13566). Palgrave Macmillan. https://doi.org/10.1057/978-1-349-95189-5_1612

Singer, H. W., & Jolly, R. (2012). Employment, incomes and equality: Lessons of the ILO Employment Strategy Mission to Kenya. In R. Jolly (Ed.), *Milestones and turning points in development thinking* (pp. 121–134). Palgrave Macmillan. (Orig. in: International Labour Review 107 (2), pp. 103–116) under the title Unemployment in an African setting: lessons of the employment strategy mission to Kenya).

Singer, H. W., Oakesthott, W., & Owen, D. (1938). *Men without work. A report made to the pilgrim trust*. Cambridge University Press. https://babel.hathitrust.org/cgi/pt?id=uc1.$b93765&seq=6&q1=singer (access: 08.03.2024)

Studer, B. (2023). Schlüsselmomente der Weltgeschichte: Der Beveridge-Plan. In https://www.researchgate.net/publication/372478280_Schlusselmomente_der_Weltgeschichte_IV_Beveridge_Plan, pp. 6–11

Temple, W. (1938). Introduction to Hans Singer. In W. Oakesthott & D. Owen (Eds.), *Men without work. A report made to the pilgrim trust* (pp. ix–xii). Cambridge University Press.

Unabhängige Historikerkommission zur Aufarbeitung der Geschichte des Reichsarbeitsministeriums in der Zeit des Nationalsozialismus, https://www.historikerkommission-reichsarbeitsministerium.de/Biografien/Walter-Auerbach (access 08.03.2024)

MIX
Papier aus verantwortungsvollen Quellen
Paper from responsible sources
FSC® C105338

If you have any concerns about our products,
you can contact us on
ProductSafety@springernature.com

In case Publisher is established outside the EU,
the EU authorized representative is:
Springer Nature Customer Service Center GmbH
Europaplatz 3, 69115 Heidelberg, Germany

Printed by Libri Plureos GmbH
in Hamburg, Germany